RELATIONSHIP OF MANUAL AND PEDAL PITCHES

Pitch on Stop Key	Note that Speaks When *Any Key* Is Depressed	
	Manual	Pedal
1/2′	4 octaves above	5 octaves above
1′	3 octaves above	4 octaves above
2′	2 octaves above	3 octaves above
4′	1 octave above	2 octaves above
8′	UNISON	1 octave above
16′	1 octave below	UNISON
32′	2 octaves below	1 octave below
64′	3 octaves below	2 octaves below

FORMS OF REED PIPES

FORMS OF REED PIPES

A Rack of twelve Reed pipes photographed in the reed voicing room of the Moller Organ Company. No. 1 on the left is an Orchestral English Horn showing conical cap and wide slot for the emission of the sound. No. 2 is a Fagotto of open structure and spotted metal top. No. 3 is a Trompette, hooded to direct the sound towards a certain area and to keep dust from falling into the pipe. No. 4 is a Rohrschalmei with an open top. No. 5 is a Krummhorn of very slender scale. No. 6 is a Holzregal with a wooden resonator. No. 7 is an Hautbois with an open, inverted-conical structure. No. 8 is an English Horn with cap and large opening for the emission of the sound. No. 9 is a Musette with a conical section on top of an inverted-conical section, the top being open. No. 10 is an Oboe Schalmei with a widely flaring bell on the top of its narrow cylindrical section. No. 11 is a Knopfregal with a hood to subdue its tone. No. 12 is a Singendregal with some Vox Humana quality. These are middle C pipes, except the left two, which speak at tenor C. Some of these pipes were designed by Adolph Zajic, Moller's Reed voicer.

Courtesy: Moller Organ Company.

Dictionary of
PIPE ORGAN STOPS

Detailed descriptions of more than 600
stops, together with definitions of many
other terms connected with the organ, and
an examination of the acoustical properties
of many types of pipes and the various
divisions of the organ.

by

STEVENS IRWIN

G. SCHIRMER, INC.
New York, N. Y.

Contents

Introduction

This Dictionary is intended to serve as an introduction to the stops of the pipe organ. It contains material on the tone qualities, names, and the system of indicating pitches of organ stops, as well as some suggestions for the use of the stops. Some scientific background, harmonic structures, and the acoustics of organ pipes are also discussed. It is hoped that the student of the King of Instruments may obtain some knowledge here that will aid him in his study. This book is organized to give the organist basic facts about the stops with as little effort as possible. The stop-names that one sees on consoles or reads about are almost all here.

The subject matter is intended to be orthodox in treatment, and presented with respect for the natural laws of physics. It does not vary from the viewpoint of the traditional literature on the organ. It is not slanted towards any particular school of thought in the organ world. The Classical, Baroque, and Romantic philosophies are all included in the discussions of the stops. Most of the book is taken up with an alphabetical arrangement of the stop-names, with several charts and illustrations to help the reader to visualize the almost unlimited dimensions of sound in the organ.

This book includes much material not available from other sources, and also many of the basic facts in new arrangement. For the beginner, it presents descriptions of how the stops sound to the ear, and suggestions for their combination. For the more advanced reader, there is much intimacy of detail on the elusive problem of why certain shapes of pipes make certain tone qualities. For the busy church organist there are suggestions on how to make more effective accompaniments. For the arm-chair listener to high fidelity organ records, great numbers of which constantly come from both Europe and America, there are tonal descriptions of the stops listed on the record jackets, perhaps spelled a little differently, since German, French, and Italian stop-names vary somewhat.

The pipe organ is a subject of universal breadth, sounding a variety of beauty for its listeners. Its mechanism is thoroughly modern, but its pipe-structures are not new. The 200 or more truly different forms of pipes have practically all been known for centuries. The *flue organ pipe*, one of the very few mechanisms that have no moving parts, is one of the most ancient and venerable of all musical instruments. The organ is essentially ecclesiastical in its traditions. From the high galleries over the choirs of Europe it has evolved into forms suitable for concert halls, civic auditoriums, schools, residences, and broadcasting studios.

The glory of the organ is heard in its pealing choruses of Diapasons, its variety of tone colors, the immense range of its eleven-octave spectrum of pitch, and the profound bass. Variety is one of the chief trade marks of the organ. Every organ is a new adventure for the listener as well as the organist, and yet very few of the world's organs have ever sounded even one quarter of their tonal combinations. Organs are designed for the musical functions they are to perform, and they must also sound well in the particular acoustical environment they are intended to fill with music, as well as fit into the space available for their structures. Their success depends upon the skill and knowledge of the builder, and the ability of the organist to draw from their stops tones appropriate to the music. The listener has but to sit back and enjoy the weaving of the many colors, dynamic levels, stop-pitches, and sustained notes that only the organ can create.

It is hoped that the reader will find this book useful for reference. It may also be read straight through; its short alphabetized articles contain many facts on the subject of acoustics.

All criticisms and opinions are welcomed by the writer.

STEVENS IRWIN

To the Beginner

INTRODUCTION

The unique contribution of the pipe organ to the world of music is its Chorus of Diapasons. These neutrally timbered stops are given the same pitches as the natural harmonics of any vibrating air column. A well-developed Chorus spreads the sound of the organ all the way from the bottom threshold of hearing up to the brilliant top, where sound passes into that zone in which the ear is relieved of too strict a comparison between the very high frequencies, sounding not only as notes, but also as the commonest range of partials. The ear hears the pitches of all stops most precisely in the ranges between C^2 and G^5. This represents the upper middle ranges, and the lower part of the high range. Composers write music, of course, in all the audible ranges. The organ, more completely than any other instrument, extends its notes both up and down the spectrum of pitch, making fifth-sounding and third-sounding as well as octave-sounding pitches for all of the notes of the harmony. Thus the Diapason Chorus gives the listener the experience of hearing the whole range of musical pitch without being confused by other aspects of the music, such as a pointed tone color following the notes of a melody or the building up of great masses of tone that may be pleasant but do not reveal the harmony. The Diapasons are very successful in causing the listener to concentrate on the form of the music and on the beauty inherent in the weaving together of two or three countermelodies. Diapasons permit the whole musical *structure* to reveal itself in all of its beauty, standing alone as pure sound.

The organ also sounds with a great number of tone qualities. There are dozens of varieties of each of the 200 or so truly distinct species of timbre, such as the Gamba, Diapason, Rohrflöte, and Trumpet. One organ could not contain them all, and, indeed, the different tones that just one stop can make in different parts of an auditorium can vary more than two different stops, such as, for example, the Rohrflöte and Harmonic Flute. New tone colors are not being discovered to any great extent in the present era of organ building, but some of those that charmed the listener between 1600 and 1800 are being reproduced in modern organs with present-day technical skill. And it is being realized that some of the older organ builders knew a great deal about blending several ranks of Diapasons into one luminous and well-unified ensemble that was at the same time dignified and animated in tone. The early Classical Diapason and its Octave may be heard in some recent installations very much as they were heard in the days of Bach and even earlier. The early builders also created many varieties of Reed stops, some imitations of the Schalmei, Musette, and the many little shepherds' pipes heard at the time. Koppel-flöte and Quintaten, as well as several other useful ensemble flues and solo Reeds, have come to us from this early period. All of these stops, as well as the metallic and brilliant Regals, are being built into some present-day organs, especially those designed to play the music of that period.

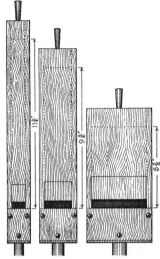

A classic picture from Audsley's works, showing three pipes of different lengths, but all speaking the same note at 256 cycles per second. Different scales make this possible, in apparent violation of the often-stated laws of physics.

The Pedal division also marks the organ as being unique among musical instruments. It adds a third band of notes to any music being played, and gives support to the manuals' tones, balancing them with the proper loudness, timbre, and with an even greater pitch range. It is in the pedals that some of the richest timbres of the organ can be heard, for the overtones of the pedal stops fall quite well into the middle and lower high ranges of pitches, where the ear is very sensitive to changes in both pitch and loudness.

THE STUDENT

Many beginners at the organ are attracted by the *sustained* and sedate sound, the endless variety of tonal combinations and great power of the ensembles, and the fact that just *one* person can operate the organ's controls as he brings forth the music from the keys. However, the organ demands from the player a few techniques that other musical instruments do not. He must be able to follow three staves of music at the same time. He must learn how to adapt the music to an entirely different set of stops and a different number of manuals in each organ. Stop-pitches as well as tone qualities must be expertly combined in order to make a balanced and intelligent effect. The mechanical controls of the organ must be operated at the same time that the music is being played. This is for some students the most difficult point to learn; for others it is the most interesting challenge that could be made. A few young organists become so interested in the instrument itself that they fail to maintain interest in the music to be played. These may be so impressed by the great volume of sound that they can produce and the pleasure derived from making endless stop combinations that they fail to learn to play well. It is necessary to approach the organ with all of these points of view in proper balance. This instrument does require more attention to the mechanical aspects of music-making than any other, but the listener must not be made aware of this by even the slightest pause. And then there is the student who falls in love with the visual forms of the console or chambers. That tall row of slender spotted metal Serpent pipes standing up against the back wall of the organ chamber is a sufficient joy for him!

THE PEDALS

The biggest problem that the beginner has to face in coming to the organ from the piano is the pedalboard. He may be surprised to find it is a keyboard with naturals, flats, and sharps just like a manual. He may be further surprised to find that it is not simply a droning support to the manuals' tone, but a source of melody and even solo tones. It is standardized at 32 keys, from CCC to G (the G just below middle C). The feet must eventually be brought under the control of the subconscious mind if the music to be played is to receive proper concentration. It is also necessary to strike any key on the keyboard without feeling the toe-spaces, simply because there is usually not time to look or feel the way. This is not so difficult a job as one who has never done it might be tempted to assume. It is only necessary to remember that the beginner at the piano once faced the problem of learning to think of the bass clef as being different from the treble clef. The pedals are no more difficult to master than this was, and they are another bass clef.

PROBLEMS

The choosing of appropriate stops for the manuals and pedals seems to be a major concern for many organists. To select stops with some confidence it is necessary to sense the meaning of the music and the intent of the composer in its interpretation. Some players do this instinctively without the slightest concern; others can never depend upon themselves. It is not wrong to play a phrase on the Gemshorn 8' and Open Flute 4' when the writer calls for a selection of Diapasons, but it probably is not a wise thing to do, because the writer undoubtedly is experienced in such matters. However, there is always the possibility that the player may be able to improve upon the suggestions printed in the music. After all, each organ has different stops on it, and some are always available that the writer would not dare to call for. Some choices of stops, as playing a Nocturne on the 'Cello instead of the Oboe, are certainly within the organist's province to decide. Too free an interpretation of the registration, however, can but lead to poor rendition of the music.

Another problem that faces many organists is the selection of stops when the music gives no suggestions. Every player from time to time must use hymn books, song books, piano music, and even manuscript transcriptions. Even some organ music with three staves contains no suggestions for the registration. In such a case it is necessary for the player to sense the message that the music has to tell. He must at the same time consider that each stop in the organ has a personality of its own. Some stops are neutral-colored and just build up ensembles. Others are added to obtain brilliance or to complete the harmonic structure of the combination. Some are serene and quiet, while others are useful as accompaniments to more colorful tones. There are military Trumpets, shimmering Strings, stops that suggest the sylvan, the grotesque, or the joyful aspect of music, and stops that are velvety and smooth. Some are emotionally moving; some are merely adjuncts to other stops. It is frequently not a matter of right or wrong to choose certain stops for certain pieces. The famous organists vary a great deal in their registration for the same pieces, although certain classics are always given a standard registration to maintain their most beautiful effects.

Which manual to play a particular piece of music on is also a great problem to some organists. It is not always necessary to look for directions in the music. It is merely required that a suitable tonal combination be on any available manual. The solo stop or the accompaniment stop may be on any manual. Who is to object to a solo played on the Choir's English Horn or Philomela and the accompaniment on the Solo's French Horn?

The selection of notes to be played on the pedals when no regular pedal staff is in the music can also be a problem. The bass notes of the manuals may be duplicated on the pedals, or the tenor line may be accented, or the organist may make up his own line of notes in any way appropriate to the spirit and form of the music.

Many miscellaneous problems also confront the student. In colder climates it is difficult to find a church in which to practice. Practice organs in homes, theater organs, lodge organs, and organs in colleges and schools may be available. The pedalboard is necessary for any real progress, and some may be attached to the piano, but these do not provide the student with the opportunity to learn the art of depressing and releasing the organ's keys, commonly known as the *organ's touch*.

CONSOLE PROBLEMS

Although famous organists sometimes have to play an entire recital on a strange organ because of the late arrival of a train or plane, there is no substitute for a good rehearsal. Rarely does an organ have all of its mechanical controls in perfect order. Also important is the fact that no two organs in the world are alike, not even two small church organs in the same town. Before the organist plays a church service or a recital it is wise to test every control that is on the console. Many surprises may turn up, and there is not time enough between phrases of the music to make a substitution of stops, release a sticking piston that may attach the Positiv to the Great, or hold up a tremolo stop key that may have a broken spring under it. In some of the world's largest organs it is not too unusual to see a cardboard "Out of Order" sign strung over the stop controls of a whole division. It is also necessary to know whether or not the intermanual couplers carry through to the intramanual couplers, which they do on only a few organs. Whether the order of the manuals from bottom to top is Great-Swell-Choir-Solo or Choir-Great-Swell-Solo is usually apparent at a glance, but not in every case. Whether the combination pistons affect the pedal stops on the first touch, second touch, or not at all is also important. Oh for a General Cancel piston!

It is a well-known fact that all divisions do not have their own swell pedals. Does the Choir pedal also operate the Great swell box, or are only some of the Choir's pipes in the Great? Which pedal stops are extensions from the manuals? Did you know that it is impossible to keep the Solo Organ in tune at any time because of the air currents in the building? How is a substitute to know that the regular organist had a rank of Trumpets put into the holes of the old Schalmei that was shipped back to the builder? How is a substitute to know that the choir will not march until a signal button is pressed? Did that Tuba refuse to play because its blower has a special switch? How is the visiting player to know that the 32' Contra Bombarde was only "provided for"? What, no Great to Pedal 4' coupler!

VARIETY IN ORGANS

The variety of organs met with is one of the chief points of charm for the organ student. After he has learned to play several pieces of the standard organ repertory and to correlate the motions of his feet and hands well enough not to be too conscious of his efforts, he will be interested in playing organs other than the one on which he practices. Variety among organs as well as variety in the musical literature he learns to play is a necessity in maintaining interest. Most organs are in churches because the organ has peculiarly been the property of the church through the centuries, but many have also been placed in this century in residences, theaters, radio studios, schools, and many other buildings. The music played on them includes every type of composition from the popular to the classical and religious. Organs are designed for the type of music that they are to play. There is such a thing as a versatile organ that can play all types of music, but it is necessarily on the large and expensive side because of the variety of stops it requires. The larger church organs are designed for recital and concert use as well as the service. Residence organs reflect the interests of their owners. They range all the way from fully equipped unit organs of the orchestral type to American Classic with many mixture stops. Large cities may have organs in their high schools; those in the New York City system are justly famous. Colleges have both concert organs in their auditoriums and practice organs for their students. The United States has its share of the biggest and best-designed organs in the world. The two biggest are in this country as well as at least fifteen exceptionally large ones. However, the student should not get the idea that the bigger organs are necessarily better in tone or design, though many of them are, because of the expense and care expended upon them. Maintenance is a problem to the owners. Its cost ranges from one hundred to one hundred thousand dollars a year.

There is enough standardization among the organs in this country to allow an organist to play one organ if he can play another. The concave and radiating pedalboard is seen almost everywhere. Different types of stop controls do not present a serious problem. Sometimes when a new church is being built, and the local theater manager is aware of the temporary need, the organist may suddenly be confronted by a four-manual giant with every variety of Flute, String, and Reed that he ever heard of. He may be very much surprised to hear the well-developed Diapasons and the magnificent bass in the pedals; many theater organs are quite well designed, but they are not heard at their best on many occasions. Or the organist may be asked to play a small church organ in a neighboring city. Perhaps it has but four ranks of pipes, almost no pedal stops, and no mutations or mixtures. It may have but one combination available for the hymns, and that so muddy and opaque that the tenor and alto parts cannot be heard moving through the chords of the music. The organist is still expected to perform well.

It might even be within the organist's experience to play one of the recently built Baroque organs in this country. He will look in vain for the familiar indications of a Great and Swell. Instead he will probably find a Hauptwerk, Brustwerk, and Rückpositiv. Much of the organ will be unenclosed, and swell pedals will be at a minimum. However, the Diapasons will sound transparently beautiful and bright, as will also the Octaves and mutations, and will permit him, even at full ensemble, to hear every note in each chord clearly. The Reeds will surprise him the most, because they will be both brilliant and distinctive in timbre, yet able to blend with any fraction of the Diapason Chorus without seeming intrusive. There will be a scarcity of 8' unisons; instead, the 4', 2-2/3', 2', 1-1/3', and 1' pitch-positions will be occupied by a Nachthorn, Principal, Koppelflöte, Block-flöte, or Sifflöte, in any sequence that pleases the designer of the organ. The mixtures will be designed to fill in the missing pitches, and the whole organ will seem "loud," but will merely be bright-toned and easy to listen to. The pedals will be built up in a vertical line of pitches like the manuals, and will be topped by a bright Reed or two to hold up the manual ensembles. String stops will be absent from the scheme, and the familiar Viole Céleste will be nowhere to be seen. The truly "Classic" organ in the Busch-Reisinger Museum, in Harvard University, made by Flentrop of Zaandam, Holland, is built after the best procedures of 250 years ago. Very low wind pressures, direct-tracker action, and unnicked pipes are featured. However, to the ear the outstanding thing is the amazing *articulation* heard from *each pipe* in this instrument. It is, of course, most interesting to hear the music of this early period played on it, and it has been well recorded. Its percussive and fully alive tonality comes from pipes unenclosed, and is indeed a revelation to many lovers of the organ who had grown used to hearing only over-nicked pipes.

Foreign organs will interest many of the more serious students. Many feel that they must eventually go to see them and play them to complete their round of experiences. The organs in the southern regions of Germany and in England seem to interest most travelers from this country. Each section of Europe has its own organ-building traditions, and there are many beautiful instruments still in existence and working well after very long periods of service. Tracker actions, now coming into this country to a certain extent, can be played abroad in many countries. Since the link between the pipe-valves and the keys in these organs is *mechanical* rather than electrical (like pressing a door-bell button), it is possible for an organist to vary *acceleration, weight of touch,* and perhaps other factors in order to bring forth a variety of initial harmonics in the tone. Each tracker organ can be designed a little differently from any other one to change even this effect. Many historical organs exist in Europe that are famous for some particular point of tonal development. Some out-of-the-way places have organs that are tonally the equal of many of the more famous instruments.

RECITALS

The organ student should attend recitals, and find a seat, if possible, where he can observe the technique of the player. His own problems may be more quickly solved by watching someone else operate the organ, and perhaps playing a piece of music that is difficult for him. Probably the most revealing thing about a recitalist is the way in which he correlates rhythm and meter. The phrasing of the music will show his intelligence in interpreting the music's message. These basic points do not differ from the orchestra's or vocalist's work. The organ, however, has many individual characteristics in its structure and tone, and the music of the other instruments is rarely held suitable for its finest effects. The most conspicuous is the Diapason Chorus. It may consist of a single rank of 8′ pipes, hardly a Chorus, to be sure, but that is all many smaller organs have to offer. Bigger instruments frequently have from twenty to seventy Principals and Diapasons in their Choruses, and inexhaustible combinations that can approach the music from every tonal direction imaginable.

The listener should try to hear each pitch and note played as well as the general effect of the music. The more he observes the details of the music, the more will he gain pleasure from it. In the Foundation family of stops the organist builds up combinations of *pitches* rather than just tone colors. It is interesting to distinguish between overtones and notes played from the musical score. It is not always possible to do this, but necessary to some extent in order to appreciate the form of the composition. Good acoustics, proper tuning, and a well-designed specification all aid in doing this. Polyphonic music not only shows off the tones of an organ better than mere chords of massed stops and the solo-and-accompaniment techniques, it is also more substantial fare for the listener. The weaving of two or more melodies together creates opportunities to contrast different timbres at various pitch levels and at different dynamic levels. Countermelodies on Diapasons and Gemshorns and mutations may make up most of certain pieces, but the Flutes and Reeds, as well as certain Strings, will be heard from time to time. The professional organist knows how to exhibit the stops of an organ in such a way as to make the listener sense their dispositions and degrees of entertainment value. Tone colors as such are needed by all of the different types of organs: concert, church, residence, and school. However, they will have to give way in importance to the even more basic factor of combining stop-pitches for the attainment of a certain harmonic structure. The organ must retain this strong point of its individuality in order to remain alive in the interests of those who follow it.

The velvety Schöngedeckt and the Salicional relieve the ear from too steady a diet of the Foundation stops. The Trumpet and Rankett, and even percussions like the Cymbalstern and Glockenspiel, sound in the most classical of music. The best recitalists use these and other stops to establish a variety of effect, and to make the music as vivid as possible. The way that each stop or combination travels over the line of notes and imparts its own personality to it is of the greatest interest to most listeners. The union of the music and the organ's tones creates a different esthetic pattern on each instrument, and it is the newness and variety of these patterns of hearing that fascinate most organists. The choice of a certain Flute for a certain melody determines the substance of its effect on the ear. The listener hears both music and organ as one.

Few recitalists bring out the full power of the organ because that would dampen the audience's interest in the details of the timbres and the notes played, such as breaks in the mixtures' ranks, the way a Gemshorn changes color as it ascends the scale, and the exact loudness of a Principal. Also of interest may be the relative loudness of the ranks in a combination, the way particular stops either lose their identities in combination or mutate the tones of other stops, and the interplay of the basic factors of *pitch, loudness,* and *timbre* on each other. As the organist must join together the mechanical controls of his instrument and the esthetic factors in the music, so the listener will have to "hear" the structure and design of the organ. True, all stops cannot stand out in perfect dimension, but identification of the notes played and a clean statement of timbre, rather than meaningless groups of stops drawn together, are necessary for intelligent listening. Many players use stops singly much of the time, and it seems that they are hesitant to combine them at all for fear they will erase their best tones and cleanest effects. While this is an excellent philosophy to follow some of the time, the combining of stops offers new tone qualities that otherwise are not available. An organ of ten stops does not have only ten tone qualities; it has millions, many of which are acceptable in some type of music.

The organ and its music are for everyone. Few fields of interest have so many "buffs." There are wide appeals, both esthetic and mechanical. Many types of players exist also. A few are dedicated recitalists and *live* their instrument day and night, making all kinds of personal sacrifices for it and its music. There are, as well, some whose work takes them elsewhere, but who play on Sundays in a church, contributing their time and ability to the congregation. There are also teachers, builders, maintenance personnel, and an increasing number of electronic engineers connected with the field of the organ.

Some Definitions

Acoustics. The whole science of sound waves, including musical tone and architectural acoustics. Acoustics is a division of *Physics*.

Action. The element that connects the valve under the pipes with the manual and pedal keys. Trackers of wood and metal, pneumatic tubes, many combinations of electropneumatic elements, and the direct operation of each valve by merely a magnet and its circuit (the key closing the circuit) represent the evolution of the organ's action. All are in use today.

Acute tone. Timbre that is rich in the third-sounding partials, or in the third-sounding ranks of a combination.

Ancillary division. A "floating" division that can be coupled to any manual, i.e. that is without its own manual, such as the String, Bombarde, Echo, or Processional. It has its own swell box if enclosed and its own tremulant. Its highly specialized ranks may be isolated to keep them from disturbing blend in a regular division.

Audibility range. In its widest sense, this is as high as 22,000 vibrations (cycles) per second, and as low as 6 per second, as in a large bass drum. Below 16 per second the individual vibrations seem to come as individual "explosions" of energy, and are percussive in effect. Between 8,000 and 16,000 per second is but *one* octave. Overtones extend upward far beyond the limit given here. Listeners may have a "dead spot," as between 11,000 and 13,000 per second. Middle C is 261.6 cycles per second.

Baroque stops. Organs built in Europe between 1600 and 1750 contained both flue and reed stops of amazing vitality of tone and great clarity. These are being reproduced today in some organs because they have individuality of color yet blend excellently in ensemble tones. Mostly heard are the *Principals*.

Beating reed. Practically all reeds made today "strike" the flat side of the shallot instead of penetrating into it. Such a reed is said to be a beating reed. This system ensures better tuning and adjustment of timbre.

Belled pipes. Both reed and flue pipes have bells in certain stops. These release certain higher-pitched partials absorbed by cylindrical pipes of the same general dimension. Belled Clarinets are among the most successful.

Beveled lip. When a pipe has the angular portion, or bevel, visible on the outside, right above the mouth, it is a beveled pipe. The tone resulting is rounder, as in the Clarabella and Gedeckt, than in the *inverted* stop.

Block. The "languid" of a wood flue pipe, acting to direct the wind across the outside of the upper lip. This horizontal structure is located at the bottom of the air column, or body of the pipe, between the foot and the upper lip. In a reed pipe it is the solid circular metal piece connecting the air chamber of the boot with the air chamber of the resonator. It is pierced by the socket and top of the hollow shallot.

Blower. A circular fan in all modern organs which compresses the air into *wind* for the pipes. It is usually electrical in operation. Several fans on one axle permit "taps" of different pressures, such as 3 inches for the Great, 6 inches for the Solo, etc. Centrifugal blowers deliver 40 inches or more.

Body of pipe. The pipe-structure itself, above the supporting foot. It vibrates to sound in conjunction with the air column. Success in tone, and usually resonance, comes from cooperation between the two.

Boot. A cone-shaped enclosure of a reed pipe containing the shallot and its reed. It permits pressure to be built up around the reed.

Brass. An alloy of much usefulness in organs. Reed tongues, shallots, some short resonators (Krummhorn, Regal, Oboe Schalmei), and other parts are always made from it, although substitutes (aluminum, steel) have at times been tried. Its resilience gives a brilliant tonality to all pipes.

Breaks in pitch. As the scale ascends in Mixtures and other very high-pitched ranks, it is designed to fall back to a lower point to keep it and its overtones audible, to keep the smaller pipes in tune, and to keep up *volume* of sound (impossible in the smallest air columns).

Cap. The wooden section on the front of a pipe below the mouth, usually of a hardwood (walnut, maple). This is also a generalized name for the closures of the circular metal pipes (Quintaten, Pommer).

Céleste. Two or more ranks of pipes, usually *above* tenor C, undulating together in a definite pattern of beats, from one to seven in a second. Softer, brighter timbres are usually employed for célestes, like *Vox Céleste*.

Chorus. A combination made from the stops of one family of tone, such as all Diapasons and Principals, all Reeds, etc. They can be set on universal pistons and played from one manual by 8′ couplers.

Chorus reeds The louder, heavier-toned reed stops, like Bombardes, Tubas, Trumpets, Trombas, and Cornopeans. They supplement the main flue Chorus. They are at 16′, 8′, and 4′ as a chorus-unit on most manuals.

Clang. An inharmonic, but pleasant, fringe of partials which sounds along with the strictly on-pitch harmonics. The ear receives much pleasure in contrasting the effect of harmonics and these inharmonics in all stops. The Diapasons, Flutes, and some basses are practically without clang, but it is theoretically never absent from a pipe's tone. Off-pitch stops make a secondary "clang." Mixtures clash with loud Reeds' clang in all cases. Lighter-toned forms come from beating between overtones.

Clarion. A standardized name for an 8′ pedal Chorus Reed, and one of 4′ on the manuals. Just *Trompette 4′* may be seen, however, on the manuals, since some organists prefer this light-toned octave Reed.

Classification of stops. The traditional classification of the organ's many stops into:

1. Foundation ⎫
2. Flute   ⎬ "flue"
3. String   ⎭
4. Reed

permits less misunderstanding than other systems. Exceptions are the valvular *Diaphones* (Foundation tones usually), and the *Magnaton,* which is a valvular reed mechanism (also Foundation). Subdivisions below this taxonomical set-up are mostly as a "group," such as the String *diminutives.*

Combination. The particular stops drawn together, perhaps by couplers.

Conical pipe. A flue pipe, such as the Erzähler, having a body that tapers upward to a narrow diameter. It places greater strength in the lower-pitched part of the train, and generally weakens even-numbered harmonics.

Console. The "key desk" of an organ, containing manuals, pedals, stops, couplers, music rack, and other devices used in playing.

Contra. A term used to denote the sub-unison pitch, at 16′ on the manuals, and 32′ on the pedals.

Cornet. A solo *compound* stop whose ranks do not break back in pitch.

Coupler. A device to group together stops from different divisions or manuals, as the Cornet from the *Solo* with the Dolce from the *Great*. Within one division octave, sub-octave, and unison-off couplers also exist.

Crescendo pedal. A balanced, pre-set pedal, to the right of the swell shoes, and slightly elevated, which brings on all of the stops of a division gradually, sometimes also the intermanual 8' couplers. It must be remembered that the sequence of stops really sets up a combination.

Curve of reed. The exact design of curvature of a reed-tongue is one of the major factors controlling which harmonics sound and at what strength.

Cut-up. The *height* of a flue mouth in relation to its width.

D'Amore (D'Amour). A term to signify *solo*, soft, delicate quality.

Dissonant tone. Any musical pitch, either a fundamental or an overtone, that is not compatible with the tone as a whole.

Division. A group of ranks of pipes, being *regular* when it has its own keyboard, or *ancillary* when it is played from another. Separate swell shoes, tremulants, pistons, and intramanual couplers are usually provided for each.

Doppel. A term to indicate a double-mouthed flue stop, open or stoppered.

Double. A term used to denote the sub-unison pitch, at 16' on the manuals, and 32' on the pedals.

Ears. Projections on each side of a flue pipe's mouth, designed to keep regular the pitch and loudness, by eliminating cross winds.

Echo. This term denotes a soft form of an otherwise *mf*, *f*, or *mff* stop. Some specimens, such as *Echo Diapason*, are merely less intense than the average.

Edge-tones. When a flue tone is generated by wind, tiny vortices from on the upper-lip, and even along the sides of the wind-reed. Some of these are supported by the air-column, others lost by friction. A few survive to give a cymbal-like fringe to the timbre. Edge-tones are the origin of all flue pipe sounds.

En Chamade. Expressed as *Cromorne en Chamade* or *Trompette en Chamade*, this term signifies a horizontal mounting of loud Reeds out in the air-mass of a church, away from the confines of the organ chambers.

Enclosed pipes. Pipes in a swell chamber can be regulated in loudness by the swell pedal's operating the Venetian shutters, but this also blanks out many of the higher overtones, deindividualizing the stops.

Ensemble. A combination made from the stops of one division, or the whole instrument. Percussions and short-resonatored Reeds may be excluded.

Ensemble tone. The composite sound of a division, such as the Great, Choir, or Positiv, along with the proper pedal tone, or the sound of the entire instrument, perhaps with a judicious selection of couplers, swell box positions, or ancillaries. There are also ensembles of Diapasons and their mixtures, Chorus Reeds, and Strings, although the Flutes are mostly looked upon as specialized tone for counter melodies or combination or solo work. See Bonavia-Hunt, *The Modern British Organ*, Chapter IX: "Tonal Architecture."

Equal-tempered scale. The modern scale in which each semi-tone is derived as 1.059463 x the frequency of the semitone below it, based on A^1 as 440.

Flue. The "wind-way" between the languid (or block) and the lower lip (or cap) of a flue pipe. The flue's design is of great importance to timbre.

Flue pipes. Organ pipes that sound their notes from edge-tones supported by the air columns within the bodies of the pipes. This air-mechanism is so efficient that the whole *eleven octaves* of the organ can be so produced.

Flue stops. Non-reed stops, namely Foundation, Flute, and String families.

Flute family of stops. Stopped, open, and half-open (i.e. half-stoppered) ranks, with generally rounder timbres and larger scales than Foundation or String ranks. Extremes in pitch exist in this family.

Fluty tonality. A timbre that is simple in harmonic structure, called *pure*. The Clarabella (open) and the Gedeckt (stoppered) are examples.

Foot-hole. The round opening cut in a pipe's foot, to admit wind to the flue or boot of a reed.

Foot of pipe. The conical portion at the bottom of a pipe, supporting the pipe, and conveying wind to the flue. It forms a valuable resonance cavity.

Formant. The total effect of a pipe's physical structure on its tone.

Every pipe vibrates itself to add additional partials, and to subtract a few partials from the air column by its inertia. Material, form, and mass control formants.

Foundation family of stops. Open ranks, usually metal, which sound a strong fundamental, accompanied by fewer overtones in stops of greater scale.

Free reed. A reed that enters the confines of the shallot when it swings in its vibrating motion. Such a bright-toned stop is hard to keep in adjustment. Famous are the Krummhorn, many woodwind stops, the Trompette, and brilliant short-resonatored forms.

Fundamental. The lowest member in a train of harmonics, excepting an occasional sub-harmonic. Prime tone, ground tone, and *first* harmonic are synonymous.

Grand. A term to signify large scale and powerful intonation.

Gross. This term indicates sub-unison pitch *or* large scale at unison.

Harmonic. One of the series of frequencies that *each* pipe creates as its whole tone quality, restricted to even multiples of the fundamental's frequency in the science of acoustics. *Overtone* is synonymous above the fundamental, or first harmonic. Thus, the third harmonic is the second overtone. *Harmonic partial* is synonymous with harmonic, *upper partial* with overtone.

Harmonic analysis. The listing of the various harmonics and their strengths of any musical tone. This becomes more difficult above the thirty-second. Many transients come and go in the tone continually, especially the very faint ones. Bass and high treble notes have fewer harmonics than the middle and high bass ranges.

Harmonic bridge. A horizontal bar, circular, parabolic, or semi-circular in form, fixed across the front of a flue's mouth. It steadies harmonic content and causes the pipe to speak more quickly.

Harmonic pipe. A double-length (sometimes triple-length) flue or reed pipe, designed to increase power in the lower train of harmonics, *not brilliance in the higher harmonics.* The flues have a hole, or row of holes, near their middles (rarely at some other harmonic position), but the reeds have no need for holes in their pipes. Stopped, chimnied, and open flues can all be provided with additional harmonic lengths.

Headpiece. A variety of tops for the reed resonators exists, some creating unusual timbres, others lowering the pitch by extending the resonance column. Still others can eliminate certain unwanted harmonics from the tone.

Hohl. A term to signify that a pipe is *hollow* in timbre, which means that the even-numbered harmonics are weak and the odd-numbered stronger.

Holz. This prefix tells the organist the pipes are made from *wood*.

Hood. A horizontal headpiece (really a mitre) set on the top of Chorus Reed pipes, usually quite powerful. It projects the tone and keeps dust from the reeds. Short hoods absorb practically no valuable components in the tone.

Horn (Cor, Corno). A term to signify that all or most of the lower six to eight partials are of about equal strength, although perhaps as a soft stop.

Imitative stops. Orchestral tones have long been simulated in the pipe organ. Practically all have now achieved an individuality of their own, quite distinct from the orchestral, mostly because of inability to reproduce acceleration of human wind, muscular movements, and cane reed edge-tones.

Inharmonic. An individual pitch in the tonal complex of any pipe or percussion, not a true harmonic because its frequency (cycles per second) is not a multiple of that of the fundamental, or first harmonic. The Reeds, louder flues, and all percussions are characterized in color by sounding variable inharmonics. However, most inharmonics are higher in pitch in the train than the true harmonics, perhaps above the eighth to sixteenth, depending on loudness, pipe-design, and family of stop. Inharmonics are forced to be *transient* because they are more easily dissipated by the unusual forms of beating they cause than the stronger true harmonics, which somewhat support each other. Mixture ranks are less inharmonic in effect than a unison Chorus Reed's components. In any scale (*Equal-tempered*, Major Diatonic, Modal) any pipe or instrument at any pitch sounds inharmonics from perfectly in-tune notes. Many are inaudible. Initial, steady, and dying-away periods each create their own. Formants also create some soft ones. See TRAIN OF HARMONICS.

Initial tones. Faint harmonic or inharmonic tones heard in the very short acceleration period of any pipe, particularly in the larger ones. These finally flow into the steady tone timbre, but not before they have considerably affected the mind's estimation of the quality and dynamic sounding. The "chiff" of a Flauto Traverso is thus explained, and a Diapason's purr. *Articulation* is influenced by initial tones.

Intermanual couplers. Couplers that draw stops of *different* divisions or manuals together, at 16', 8' (unison), or 4' pitch, as Swell to Great.

Intramanual couplers. Couplers that add a 16' or 4' tone to the (unison) keys sounding, as the Swell to Swell 4', or the Pedal to Pedal 8'.

Inverted-conical pipe. A flue or reed pipe flared from a narrow section at the bottom to a wider section at the top. In flues, like the Dolcan, this releases more and higher-pitched partials, particularly the even-numbered. In reeds, for example all Chorus Reeds, this creates an "open," strong timbre.

Inverted lip. As in the Hohlflöte, Melodia, and Waldflöte, the wooden, rarely metal, upper lip is flat on the outside, beveled on the inside. This form gives more brilliance to both initial and steady-tone partials. It is most helpful to a wooden 4' open Flute, sometimes as a *Clear Flute*.

Klein. This prefix denotes a gentle, perhaps soft tonality, as in the Kleingedeckt.

Labial. This is a term for flue pipes.

Languid. The "block" of a metal pipe, acting to direct the wind-reed against the upper lip's surface. It is a horizontal structure in most cases located in the bottom of the body of the pipe. Depressed and curved forms are, of course, not strictly horizontal. See BLOCK.

Lead. A soft and tone-absorbent metal, rarely used pure, but mixed in almost all metal pipes with tin, a tone-resilient metal. Pure lead makes a very dull tone, and is rarely used even for a 16' metal Flute.

Leathered lip. Wrapping the upper lip of a big-scale flue stop with leather or even a thick layer of pipe metal, which is much more permanent, creates an intense, commanding, round tone, usually heavy with fundamental. This may obviate the stop's use in ensembles, but not as an interesting solo voice, most usable on the Solo Organ. Well-designed bass pipes need no wrapping of the upper lips if made sufficiently thick not to absorb tone.

Lieblich. A prefix to denote a smooth, solo-like, sometimes warm flue tone.

Lingual. This is a term for reed pipes.

Lip. Used without adjectives, it means the upper lip of a flue pipe. It is the edge struck first by the wind-reed. It does not appear to vibrate back and forth, but, of course, all parts of a flue pipe (and a reed pipe) really vibrate with the air column's motions. See FORMANT.

Magna. A term to indicate a loud, commanding tone in a flue or reed stop.

Main organ. The body of the instrument, usually containing the Choir, Great, Swell, Solo, and Pedal divisions, perhaps just a Great, Swell, and Pedal. Ancillary or Echo divisions are built elsewhere in the auditorium. In rare cases there are two main organs, as in St. Bartholomew's New York.

Major. This prefix denotes *contrast* between two stops of the same species, like the *Major Vox Humana* and the *Minor Vox Humana* in a large theater organ. The term may be used for just one stop, such as *Major Flute*. See MINOR.

Manuals. Keyboards for the hands. From one to seven exist in organs. Four is the desired standard, three are often seen, and the small organs have but two. Names vary from continent to continent. Above about 15,000 pipes seems to require at least a fifth manual. One manual may control several divisions.

Minor. This prefix denotes *contrast* between two stops of the same species, like the *Major Violoncello* and the *Minor Violoncello* of any organ. It does not exist alone. A *Mezzo* Saxophone indicates one of moderate loudness. Three stops of the same species may make it necessary to use this term. See MAJOR.

Mitred pipe. It is frequently necessary to bend the longer pipes in order to fit them into the architectural scheme. In some cases they can be laid horizontally, like the 32′ Contra Ophicleide in the West Point Cadet Chapel Organ. Of course *any* physical change in a pipe's structure affects its total tonality, but the bass waves are so strong that practically no harm is done to them by the bending.

Mouth. The opening at the bottom of the front of a flue pipe. Its textures and dimensions do much to control timbre. High mouths make duller tones.

Mixture. A compound stop whose ranks are designed to break back in pitch as the scale (on the keys) ascends. The 16′, 8′, and 4′ series are all supplemented by their own Mixtures. The pedal's 32′ can be too. As much variety exists in these stops as in others, and all are custom-designed.

Musical scale. A series of vibrations regulated according to some definite pattern of interval-succession. Many different scales have been used throughout history. See EQUAL-TEMPERED SCALE.

Musical tone. A regular number of vibrations per time period (as per second) will immediately attract the attention of the mind, and be distinguishable from "noise." Pitch, dynamic, and timbre are all noticed in musical tones.

Mutation. A single rank (or pitch on a unit organ) of neutral-toned flue stop, which is *not octave-sounding,* used to color or augment in pitch any other stop or combination. Pedal mutations are important. The Gedeckt, Open Flute, Quintade, Principal, Gemshorn, Dulciana, and Dolce are used for mutations.

Muted. A term used to indicate an abridged harmonic content, as *Muted 'Cello.*

Nicks. Small, wedge-shaped incisions cut by the voicer on the front of a languid (or block) or on the back of a lower lip (or cap), or both. These lessen harmonic content in both initial acceleration tone and steady tone. Unnicked pipes in Classical organs have a pronounced articulation. Romantic specimens lack this display of initials. See INITIAL TONES.

Open flue pipe. An unstoppered pipe sounding an octave above a stoppered pipe of about the same dimension (length).

Orchestral. This term, as in *Orchestral Saxophone* or *Viole d'Orchestre,* signifies an imitative tone color. Practically, it means a full train of overtones and a plentiful supply of pronounced initial partials.

Overtone. One of the series of frequencies that *each* pipe sounds above its fundamental ground tone, contributing, with the fundamental, most of the essence of tone quality. A Gedeckt sounds above five, a loud Tuba about sixty; overtones vary in number even between pipes of one stop. See HARMONIC.

Pallet. The vibrating device in the boot of a Diaphone.

Partial. One of the series of frequencies in the complex tone made by any organ pipe. Although generally synonymous with overtone, *upper partial* is more strictly correct for overtone. A purer definition, used by physicists, includes *all* inharmonics, harmonics, and even edge-tones and transient tones. See HARMONIC.

Pedals. The keys for the feet, 32 in number on most modern organs, ranging from CCC to G (below middle C), about two and one-half octaves. The concave, radiating pedalboard permits greatest accuracy in depressing and releasing keys. The pedal unison pitch is 16', octave pitch is 8', and sub-unison is 32'.

Percussions. Musical instruments in the organ operated by being struck by pneumatic or electromagnetic hammers, either *chromatic,* like the Xylophone, or *non-chromatic,* like the Cymbal. Muscular control is lacking in the action, so exact expression is impossible. Chimes and Harp are the most commonly heard.

Percussive quality. The *suddenness* of the vibration of any flue or reed pipe, or of the actuation of any particular harmonic, indicated by the steepness of a curve (on a graph). High wind pressures, like 10 inches, make this sort of timbre, valued in the (slower) bass pipes and the louder Chorus Reeds. All short treble pipes speak suddenly without exception. The ear is incredibly acute in sensing each harmonic's entrance into the tone, and this factor determines, as much as the harmonics' pitches, color and quality. Mixtures are thus dazzling and brilliant in many cases because of the suddenness of their speech from pipes often below four inches in speaking length.

Phonon. A term to indicate a loud, round-toned sound, not brightness.

Piston. A push-button between the manuals, above the manuals, in the keyjambs, or for the feet, used to draw quickly another combination, and at the same time to release the old combination. Mechanical actions, like *All Couplers Off Choir Organ* or *Grand Cancel,* depend on pistons, chiefly because these are small in size, and simple and accurate to use.

Pitch. Musical frequency of a fundamental or overtone is perceived by the mind as so many vibrations (impacts of the air on the eardrum) in a time-period. Musicians are chiefly interested in pitch as expressed in musical *notes.* Since there is a great range of notes possible from the pipe organ, it is necessary to have a system of naming each note in an octave, particularly since combinations (and Mixtures) generally sound several notes from each key depressed. This multiple-note pattern is one of the characteristics of the organ. Capital letters are used here throughout the compass so that only one variable is needed. Lower case letters are used for middle C and upwards in some references. The reader may, therefore, find either c^1 or C^1 for the note of middle C, and c^2 or C^2 for the C above. The octave below middle C is simply a capital *C* without a superscript. Going down into the bass we find CC, CCC, and CCCC. The complete range of the pipe organ, *eleven octaves,* is from the profound Resultant's low pedal CCCCC up to the very high C^7 heard in quite a few Mixtures. Middle C, the anchor of most organists' thinking, is near the middle of this vast range of 133 notes.

Notes other than C must also be symbolized. Notes within *any* octave are expressed in a manner similar to the C lower than they. Thus, the BB is immediately below *C* (and this is "tenor C") ; $A\sharp^4$ and B^4 are just below C^5 and above their *base* of C^4. This system refers to the *pitches* of the scale; it names also the keys of the pedals and manuals when *unison pitch* is referred to. Refer to the chart entitled THE ELEVEN-OCTAVE

COMPASS OF THE PIPE ORGAN in order to see the octaves all laid out in sequence. Also see AUDIBILITY RANGE, EQUAL-TEMPERED SCALE, HARMONIC.

Plain metal. A pipe alloy consisting of less than 35% tin, the rest being lead, and used for the dull-toned stops, but never higher pitches. See TIN.

Polyphonic bass. A bass flue rank sounding two tonalities, one soft (and dull) from limited wind, and the other louder from greater wind supply.

Profunda. A term to indicate 16′ manual pitch, or 32′ pedal pitch.

Quinty tone. A timbre from a stop that is voiced to sound an obvious third harmonic, or from a combination dominated by a *Twelfth* rank.

Rank of pipes. A single row of pipes, manual or pedal, controlled by a "stop." The large bass pipes may be given a special windchest of their own.

Reed family of stops. As opposed to "flue" stops, which have no moving mechanical parts in their interiors, the reed stops have vibrating tongues of soft brass, each one held up against its shallot by a wooden wedge. Timbre can be varied in the extreme because just *neighboring* harmonics can be greatly different in volume, unlike a flue's.

Reedless "Reeds." The Estey Organ Company has produced several orchestral woodwinds from *flue* pipes that successfully imitate the prototype. They are solo and ensemble tones of distinction.

Reed pipes. The vibrating reed in the boot is tuned to approximate in pitch the inner sympathy of the air-mass in its resonator. If not far apart, one can "pull" the other's pitch into mutual agreement, making a resonant sound. If too far apart in pitch, the tone "flies off" and the tuner must start again. Small flue pipes are used to "top" reed stops, with no break in the tone usually being obvious between them. See REED FAMILY OF STOPS.

Reed stops. Non-flue stops, including Chorus Reeds, imitative Reeds, and short-resonatored Reeds.

Reed tongue. The moving element in a reed pipe. It must be designed to roll downward across the face of the shallot according to a definite pattern of motion in order to produce the desired harmonics at the correct strengths. Inharmonics are quickly formed in the lower part of the train if this curvature is not according to the idealized formula.

Registration. The selection of stops, sometimes printed on the music, that is appropriate for a piece of music.

Resonator. The "pipe" of a reed stop, designed to keep under control the reed's motions, and at the same time give strength by resonance to the important harmonics created by the reed. The resonator cannot create any musical tones itself; it merely resonates by sympathy those created by the reed.

Resultant. The beating tone produced by sounding together any note and its fifth in a 64′ or 32′ Acoustic Bass stop. Above about GGG, depending upon the acoustics of the building, this tone sounds like two tones.

Reversible piston. A piston that turns "on" and "off" upon alternate motions of finger or toe. The Great to Pedal piston is usually of this type.

Rohr. A small-diametered brass pipe (chimney) inserted in the stopper of an otherwise stopped Flute (such as *Rohrflöte, Rohrbordun*) for the purpose of sounding a few traces of the even-numbered harmonics of the pipe. The compound tone that results can be easily heard in resonant buildings. The length and diameter of the rohr are important, as are the dimensions of the main body, in controlling the rohr's harmonics.

Romantic stops. As opposed to the "Classical" stops, the theater organ of the early part of the present century contained several stops that had very obvious developments along some particular harmonic structure. The Tibia Clausa had a very intense fundamental, as did the Diapason Phonon. The cutting Viole d'Orchestre, and even some 'Cellos, sounded a complete gamut of higher-pitched harmonics from their narrow bodies. The tinsel-toned Kinura, although making the pitch-line, frequently stood out above all other Reed stops. Of course there is a moderate overtone development possible in all of these Romantic stops, at least when they are placed in certain concert organs. Exaggerated timbres are really not necessary, but are used to give pleasure to the audience.

Scale of pipe. The relationship between the cross-sectional area of a pipe to its speaking length. Large scales generally give less bright tones, and vice versa.

Second touch. When a manual or pedal key is depressed a little farther down, this touch brings on the stops drawn in a special "second touch" section. It is valuable for accenting certain parts of the music, sounding Chimes, the 32′ pedal octave on certain notes, or by a Tuba Magna. It is not peculiar to the theater organ. It is valuable in all large instruments, including the church organ. The second touch stops can be made up of solo stops from all divisions, couplers, melody octave couplers, or percussions. Usually not all manuals have this touch.

Sforzando piston. A toe or finger piston, sometimes both, which brings on every stop and coupler in the entire organ, except, perhaps, the short-

resonator Reeds and the percussions. Since most couplers point towards
the Great, this is usually the manual to play for full effect. On some organs
the Swell is made a Master Pedal also by this piston.

Shade. A pipe-metal flap mounted on the top of wood pipes, like the
Clarabella, for tuning and regulating the brightness of the timbre. Depressing it makes the tone flatter and also a little less developed harmonically.

Shallot. A hollow, conically shaped brass tube mounted on the bottom
of the block of a reed pipe. Its larger diameter is towards the bottom of
the boot, in which it is enclosed, and is sealed by a cap. The smaller, open
end is inserted in the block and serves as the bottom of the air column
of the resonator. On one flattened side is mounted the reed-tongue, whose
vibrations the shallot carries to the resonator, for expulsion to the atmosphere. The French Horn has a "closed" shallot, meaning one with a smaller
opening. The Trompette has a very "open" shallot, meaning one that is
entirely open to receive every possible harmonic for the resonator's amplification. Builders have their favorite shape of opening for each stop.

Short-resonator Reeds. When a reed vibrates, the particular harmonics
that the resonator does not amplify are mostly lost a few feet from the
organ. If a resonator is too short to support the lowest *seven* harmonics,
these will not carry very far to the ear, but the *eighth* harmonic and those
above it will be well amplified, and can carry quite a distance. Since many
of the higher harmonics are "off-pitch" to the equal-tempered scale, much
of the tone of the Dulzian, Regal, Schalmei, Vox Humana, or Rankett will
sound brilliantly dissonant — in other words, strangely penetrating and
protruding from other tones, as in a polyphonic line with a Diapason and
Flute. Odd-shaped resonators exaggerate this effect along many lines of
development. Brass is most acceptable for these stops, because it creates
brightness.

Slot. An opening, usually rectangular, near the top of a flue or reed
pipe, spaced according to many complex formulas. It emphasizes certain
partials in the flues, and increases brightness in the Reeds.

Socket. The cylindrical piece of metal sitting in the top of a reed block,
designed to hold the resonator upward, and connect it with the shallot.

Sonora. A term intended to denote a loud and assertive stop, either
reed or flue, not necessarily brilliant.

Sordo. A term to indicate a soft or muted stop.

Speaking length. In a flue pipe, this term indicates the active portion
of the air column, generally considered as from the upper lip line to the

first opening reached in going up the pipe, such as, perhaps, a slot in a Keraulophone. Adhesion of the air to the walls controls vibration as do the mass and shape of the air-column.

Specification. The stop-list of an organ, also containing the true number of "pipes" for each stop, mechanical adjuncts, and all pipe materials, wind pressures, etc.

Spitz. All stops having this prefix are conical in shape. See CONICAL PIPE.

Spotted metal. Pipe metal that is between 35% and around 70% tin, the rest being lead. It is used for most Strings, because it creates a great number of overtones, particularly if thick enough for the air-mass. Some builders make all metal pipes spotted, even down to the CCC pipes. The 32′ octave to CCCC may have spotted upper lips, or perhaps mouth-sections, the rest being some sort of plain metal or zinc. In reeds, whole resonators are frequently spotted, perhaps only the top sections of the 16′ and 32′ octaves.

Steady tone. The tone that comes from a pipe after the acceleration of the initial tones has died away. This tone, too, has transients, a whole series of its own harmonics and inharmonics, and quite a few cymbal-like edge-tones to make the brighter effects noted in some Mixtures and smaller-scaled pipes.

Stentor. A term to indicate a very loud pedal or manual stop.

Stop. In "straight" organs *a stop is a row of pipes*, one for each key, and desirably also an added treble octave to supply the Octave Coupler with proper power in the top octave of the keyboard. In unit organs the *stop* may not have its own pipes, but "borrowed" pipes from another stop or division. However, to make both an 8′ and a 4′ Dulciana, as on a Choir Organ, from one rank of pipes is considered expedient. Softer stops are more easily adapted to unification than louder stops. Special scales have been worked out to minimize the imbalance of tone resulting from unification of louder stops.

Stopped flue pipe. Closing the end of a flue pipe lowers the pitch of the fundamental and overtones one octave below the pitch that would be heard from the same pipe if it were left open. Traces of the even-numbered harmonics enter the tone, but otherwise the odd-numbered are the only harmonics heard.

String family of stops. The incisive, bright-toned family of flues is characterized by narrower than average scales, plentiful harmonics, low cut-up of the mouths, and sometimes high wind pressure to create that really brilliant timbre never forgotten once it has been heard.

Stringy tonality. The String's harmonics are more plentiful than most stops'. Lessening the scale of any pipe, the other dimensions remaining the same, makes a stringy tone because it creates more friction between the walls of the pipe and the air-motion. The *Violin Diapason* is a hybrid between the fundamental purr of the Diapason and the Violin's brightness.

Sub. This prefix indicates a pitch one octave below unison, such as 16' on the manuals, and 32' on the pedals.

Super. This prefix indicates a pitch one octave above the *Octave* pitch, such as 2' on the manuals, and 4' on the pedals.

Sustainer. A device, usually a piston of some sort, to hold the notes depressed until the player can make an adjustment of the stops or play additional notes on another keyboard. It is found mostly in European organs.

Swell box. An enclosure of wood, concrete, or metal for the purpose of permitting the organist to control loudness by means of a swell pedal (shoe) that opens and closes a set of Venetian shutters in front of the pipes. The Swell and Solo Organs are most commonly found in swell boxes. Any other division, including the pedal, may also be enclosed.

Swell pedal. A balanced pedal, movable in from four to sixteen stages, that closes the swell shutters when drawn backward, and opens them when depressed. Many large organs have the swell shutters of two or more divisions under the control of one swell pedal. Pistons can be provided to indicate electrically to a swell pedal mechanism which sets of swell shutters are to be operated. The Swell Organ's pedal is often used as a *Master Pedal* because it is usually next to the Crescendo, permitting the organist to operate all swell pedals as well as the Crescendo by the same motion. See SWELL BOX.

Synthetic stops. Two or more stops compounded together to make up a stop-tone are not generally a satisfactory combination. However, it is a necessity in some small organs to make an *Oboe* from an 8' and a 2 2/3', or a *Clarinet* from an 8', 2 2/3', and a 1 3/5'. Synthetic pedal basses are more likely to sound like the stop intended. A complete set of mutations on an organ is good background for this type of experiment. The 3 1/5' and 1 1/7' are also useful in synthetics.

Timbre. This is *tone quality* in its widest sense. It depends upon the pitch, *number*, relative loudness, and design of harmonics present in a stop. Initial and steady-tone transients also are important in the timbre, especially in the brighter stops and Mixtures. Some overtones, unbelievably high-pitched, sound from the orchestral Reeds, and aid greatly in identifying tone quality. Percussiveness, exact loudness, steadiness of the pitch, and even the dying away characteristic identify a stop's tone color. A note of CCC on a Trombone can give as many as 5,000 partials, beats, secondary beats, and other effects from just one pipe. The wavering in pitch of any *harmonic* is important to the ear, and the higher-pitched ones constantly waver according to varying patterns. A dull Gedeckt is a contrast indeed after some brighter tones! The terms *timbre-creator* and *source of timbre* imply the strengthening of the regular series of harmonics (or overtones), which, in all organ stops except covered ranks, like the Bourdon, are practically the same. See TRAIN OF HARMONICS, TRANSIENTS.

Tin. One of the most useful metals in pipe alloys. *Pure tin* — an alloy of about 90% to 96% tin and the rest lead — has been used in some beautiful Mixtures, Salicionals, Viols, etc. Spotted metal is at least 35% tin, the rest being lead. See LEAD, SPOTTED METAL.

Tracker action. A purely mechanical action between keys and pipe-valves, controlled to a remarkable extent by the *acceleration* (velocity) and the *mass* (weight) of the hand and fingers of the player. Different series of partials may be heard from the pipes when a different design of muscular motions of the player is used. This requires great skill and these subtle variations must be distinctly heard.

Train of harmonics. Each organ pipe or instrument sounds a complex of frequencies, never just the fundamental "note." Excepting for an occasional sub-harmonic, this train consists, *in order,* of:

1. the first harmonic, i.e. the *fundamental,* which is on the pitch of the printed note only in manual *unison* stops;
2. a series of true harmonics that rise in pitch, and that vary in their loudness relationship; they number from a mere two or three in the very dull Gedeckts to more than forty in a Tuba or Tibia Plena; they are mostly consonant with their fundamental but dissonant to the scale's notes;
3. a fringe of super-harmonics that vary in and out of existence many times in a second because of inner beating; they are practically all dissonant to both their fundamental and the scale's pitches;
4. some inharmonics generated by all pipes, even the Diapason; they form some elements of the timbre; the ear obtains pleasure in contrasting them with the true harmonics; they are dissonant with all components; they are usually few in number, perhaps just initial;
5. a narrow zone of *gaussian* edge frequencies, usually very soft, perhaps inaudible, and which are dissonant even with each other.

This description applies to pipes that are perfectly in tune, that is, having fundamentals on the equal-tempered scale positions. To the above must be added the tonal effect of the *formant* of each pipe, as well as acoustical factors operating in the room. Raising the wind pressure extends the

The Big Wanamaker Console

THE BIG WANAMAKER CONSOLE

Six-manual console of the Grand Organ in the John Wanamaker Store, Philadelphia, Pa. The manuals, upward, are called: Great, Swell, Choir, Solo, Ethereal, and Stentor. Additional to these divisions are the ancillaries: String, Echo, Orchestral, and Percussion, which can all be coupled to any of the first six manuals by stop tablets. A magnificent Pedal with many stops for ancillaries as well as main divisions, including eight 32' ranks, supports the manuals. Swell pedals, not visible, are, from left: Percussion, Echo, Orchestral, String, Choir, CRESCENDO, Great, Swell, Solo, Ethereal, and Stentor. Meters for these ten pedals are above music rack, and operate as rows of lights, the Crescendo Indicator is line below these. Tremulant controls for fast, slow, etc. are either side of music rack. Visible toe pistons, bottom, operate reversibly the 32' ranks. The white one in center reads, "Tutti FFF." Tablets above top manual are mechanicals, as Pedal Divider, Crescendo off Choir, Couplers Silent, etc. Sliding expression levers for the fingers can be seen under each manual. These operate swell shutters. Notice mirror at top left for following conductor. Two hundred horsepower blow this organ, in three widely separated locations in the court.

Courtesy: John Wanamaker, Philadelphia.

train in both number and loudness of components. Distance from the pipes "cancels" some frequencies. See in this chapter CELESTE, FORMANT, HARMONIC, INHARMONIC.

Transients. Tones of a myriad of pitches that come and go with the steady tone of a pipe, mostly extremely high, perhaps inaudible. The initial harmonics (some are really inharmonics) can be referred to as *transients*. All make some contribution to the timbre of a pipe or ensemble. Their pitches vary constantly with temperature, humidity, etc. They constantly beat each other in and out of existence, forming a tonal pattern too complex for even the best analyzer.

Tremulant (Tremolo). A mechanical device that changes the wind pressure according to a regular pulsation, usually from two to seven times in a second. Each pulsation reduces both the pitch of all pipes and the strength and number of partials of all pipes every time the wind pressure lowers. If intense, and in a church service, this can be hard on the singers, because it fluctuates the pitch of all notes, especially the higher partials that corroborate the pitches. Every division, except perhaps the Positiv, can use a Tremulant. The pedal basses are too slow in cycling their vibrations to be much affected by the Tremulant. Fan devices can serve as Tremulants, and do not waver the pitches, but they may be hard to hear.

Tuning a pipe. All organ pipes must be tuned because different materials — hardwoods, plain metal, spotted metal, zinc (basses), and plain lead — expand and contract differently within the same temperature change. Unfortunately tuning devices, such as flue collars, reed springs, and stoppers, do not *fully* return to original "in-tune" position once they have been moved out by letting the church grow cold. After several weeks of change, perhaps ranging over fifty degrees Fahrenheit, they remain badly out of tune.

Tuning spring (wire). Reed pipes are tuned in two ways: the reed-tongue and the resonator "pipe" both vary in length. The spring that moves up and down over the vibrating reed controls its pitch, moving downward to sharpen and upward to flatten the frequency. Various forms of slides and collars tune the resonator, moving upward to flatten and downward to sharpen the frequency. There is never complete sympathy between these two sounding devices, but the resonator can "pull" the reed's pitch into agreement with it, as a Diaphone's "pipe" can control its pallet, if there is not too much difference between their pitches. If there is, the tone "flies off," and the tuner must start all over again.

Undulating stop. The Resultant of the pedals beats its proper "pitch" by means of the beats between fifths. The Viole Céleste beats in a myriad of patterns, even changing according to different combination of notes. All stops "beat" simply because harmony between notes is based on additive and subtractive tones. The mind sorts out differences between the pure harmonics and the inharmonics by means of their beats. In the broad sense, every stop produces undulations in order to establish its identity. See CÉLESTE.

Unenclosed pipes. Pipes that are unenclosed are able to project their tones more efficiently over the whole air-mass of an auditorium better than those that are enclosed. The enclosed pipes, even when the shutters are open, lose a great deal of individuality because the higher partials must be absorbed upon impact with all structures. The Mixtures, Diapasons of the major Chorus, and some Chorus Reeds sound more interesting when in the open, and certainly perform their functions more adequately. A balance must be worked out for every organ between the enclosed and unenclosed portions. Sometimes *part* of a Great or Choir is enclosed.

Unison-length pipes. A unison-length flue or reed pipe naturally adjusted to the frequency of its *fundamental*. Pipes longer than unison amplify the lower part of the train at the expense of the higher. Reeds shorter than unison-length amplify higher components, and let the lower-pitched go unstrengthened. The unison-length pipe amplifies the fundamental more than any other component.

Ventil system. On some European organs a special drawstop or lever, called a ventil, must be moved to admit wind to either the stop mechanism or the windchest in order that stops of that division can sound. Sometimes just the Reeds and mixtures are placed under a ventil's control. This is done to give the organist more flexibility in combinations, since the other stops of the *same* division can be under a different ventil.

Voicing a stop. The pipe designer determines the salient dimensions of a rank of pipes. After the pipe-maker produces the mute pipes the voicer opens up the flue to the proper dimension and tunes the pipe. If it is necessary he cuts up the mouth or arches it properly to control the number of harmonics in the tone, a higher mouth giving fewer. The ears may have to be bent into another position, but this is unusual. The bridge, if any, is attached in the optimum position, bringing into proper relationship the fundamental and its overtones. The foot-hole may have to be pared out to admit more wind. The Reeds, too, require a lot of adjustment, especially in regard to the curvature required and the adjustment of the wedge. The finisher may have to make further changes in either the tuning or voicing after the organ is installed.

Vowel cavities. Certain short-resonator Reeds, like the Vox Humana and the Euphone, have been given cavities in their resonators which amplify overtones that together can produce a vowel's sound. Although not of too much import musically, such pipes have been useful as a development along the line of making timbres of great individuality. The Vox Humana usually makes an *ee* sound, but it can be made to sound *oo* or *uu* as well.

Wedge. A triangular piece of wood that is pressed up between the metal block of a reed pipe and its reed-tongue in order to hold both tightly together. The reed is thus pressed against the shallot at its top.

Weighted reed. The longer 16' and 32' reed-tongues can be controlled in tone and pitch much more efficiently if a (brass) weight is screwed tightly against them near their bottoms, or points of greatest motion. This is particularly true in reeds under higher pressure. Such a device naturally absorbs some of the overtones formed, but this is not a handicap in timbres in this pitch-range. The weight really eliminates some of the unwanted inharmonics that are common to all reeds.

Windchest. The box of compressed wind that the pipes sit upon. Under each pipe is some sort of valve that is opened by the key (and stop) action.

Wind pressure. The wind that the pipes are given must be raised in pressure above that of the surrounding atmosphere. In smaller buildings that are easier to fill with sound this pressure can be from one to four inches (of water in a U-tube gauge). The Solo and Bombarde Organs in large churches may need as much as six to eight inches. Unusual Chorus Reed and String divisions are sometimes given from ten to twenty-five inches. Extremely loud Ophicleides and Bombardes have been given even fifty inches in a few organs. The one-hundred inch pressure in the Midmer Losh organ in the Convention Hall, Atlantic City, N. J., is now famous because the Chorus Reeds voiced for this extreme pressure have been tonally successful and most penetrating and brilliant even with the entire ensemble. Eight inches is top pressure in most big organs.

Wood pipes. The material that a pipe, reed or flue, is made from adds to and subtracts from the overtone structure that is heard. Flexibility, modes of vibration, and absorptive power in the cells all control this tone. Although wood is more absorptive than spotted metal, it is also more resonant in some ways and lends a most beautiful formant of its own structure to many stops. A wooden Gedeckt is generally considered more beautiful than a metal Gedeckt, although the latter can serve well, particularly on the manuals.

Zauber. This prefix indicates a pipe both harmonic and stoppered.

The Dictionary

ACOUSTIC BASS. See RESULTANT.

ACUTA. A manual mixture stop containing a *third-sounding rank* of some prominence of tone. Because of the sharp effect on the ear of this rank, which sounds, for example, at some higher E every time a C is played, it should be used only in combinations that can assimilate its tone. Chords, and also couplers, will intensify this sharp effect, and also *every overtone* heard from its small-scale open metal pipes. It is a specialized source of brilliance and incisive tone for use with louder flues and Reeds. It can add some brass-like quality to the Trumpets, and a close-toned, pointed effect to all combinations, including the Diapason Chorus or a special solo combination. It need not be a loud stop, but it is usually quite high-pitched, perhaps containing a 1 1/7', 4/5', or 1/2' rank. A few examples are unbroken in pitch; these should be called compound stops, since *mixtures* always have ranks broken in pitch. Other mixtures may contain this stop's pitches, but not its stronger third-sounding rank, which is pitched at 1 3/5' (8' series), 3 1/5' (16' series), or 4/5' (4' series). This stop is not so useful a general source of brilliance as the Cymbal or Grand Mixture. It is considered an ensemble tone, and can make a marked contrast with Diapasons and other flue stops. Spotted metal Diapasons make its tone, but at high pitches the timbre is hardly apparent, and the listener is mostly aware of pitch. Three examples follow, with notes sounded by the middle C key. Roman numerals denote the number of ranks of pipes in each example:

Example No. 1		Example No. 2		Example No. 3	
III		IV		IV	
C^4	1'	C^4	1'	E^4	4/5'
G^3	1 1/3'	G^3	1 1/3'	C^4	1'
E^3	1 3/5'	E^3	1 3/5'	G^3	1 1/3'
		C^3	2'	E^3	1 3/5'

Sharp Mixture indicates this same mixture. Synonyms: SCHARF, VOX ACUTA.

AEOLINA. A single rank of very soft String or Foundation pipes of 8', tuned slightly *sharp* or *flat,* and intended to be added to any other soft stop, such as the Aeoline, Dulciana, Dolcan, or Spitzflöte. This rank may be an Aeoline, Echo Dolce, or Dolcan, and is useful on the Choir or Echo Organ, where a slight wavering of the pitch often proves valuable in both

30

voice and organ accompaniments. Most Aeolina ranks can easily be returned to the normal pitch, and another rank substituted as a new Aeolina stop. By making different combinations, the organist can create a great variety of soft célestes of his own choosing. See AEOLINE, CÉLESTE, UNDA MARIS.

AEOLINE. One of the softest Strings in the organ, at 8' on the manuals, and sometimes at 16' on the pedals, perhaps on the Echo Pedal. It is delicate and refined in tone, not at all keen or thin. It is light, bright-toned, and its overtones are in great quantity. It is not orchestral in sound and never reaches the volume of the Ethereal Violin. It is more brilliant and sedate in tone than the Gamba or Salicional, but much softer than both. Like the Echo Salicional and Viola d'Amore, it is classified as a diminutive String. It provides timbre for the Choir Organ, but by itself is not a good accompaniment to the voice, as the Erzähler, Dolce, and Gemshorn are. It lacks their pointed definition of the pitches of the music. Its usefulness in combination and its soft dynamic make it a frequent member of the Great's ranks, where it can contrast with the Swell's Flutes and louder Strings. It is not so noticeable as the Voix Céleste, even when played in chords, and it makes an *Echo Céleste* from its own ranks. It creates a background of silvery tone against a running Flute melody, as from the Harmonic Flute or Koppelflöte. Its very small open metal pipes have a high tin content to ensure the flood of overtones necessary to create this timbre. Large ears support the harmonic bridge in front of each mouth. Low cut-up and sharp upper lip make this String tone brilliant. See VIOL.

AEOLINE CÉLESTE. An undulating stop of 8' on the manuals, formed from two ranks of Aeoline pipes, *normal-sharp* in many examples. It is almost too soft to be in the String Organ, except in a building where it can be heard. Its shimmering, delicate sound may be heard from the Choir, the off-pitch rank being removable. It is background and accompaniment tone, not making an effective sound unless chorded, perhaps with the intramanual 4' coupler. The well-known Voix Céleste is not made from the Aeoline but from two ranks of Salicionals. See AEOLINE, CÉLESTE.

AEQUALPRINZIPAL. A stop-name that indicates the major 8' Diapason or Principal (or Diapason-Flute hybrid) on any manual. See DIAPASON.

AMOROSA. A hybrid Flute stop of 8' on the manuals, having a tone color somewhere between a soft String and an open Flute of small scale. It is a useful soft accompanimental or combinational stop, or a source of timbre to other soft *flues*. Synonym: FLAUTO AMABILE.

APFELREGAL. One of the oldest forms of Regals, at 8' on the manuals, and also 8' on the pedals. As in the human voice apparatus, the short resonators amplify only the *high-pitched* overtones, rather than the reed's fundamental and octave components, which lends much individuality to the tone color. This Regal has a thin, whining, nasal voice useful in carrying the exact pitches of the notes a considerable distance, as down the long nave of a cathedral. The weaker overtones may be subdued, even made fairly soft by the pipe, but this is not one of the guttural Regals. The Regals are valuable because they alert the ear, and thereby emphasize certain tones of the music. They are the product of small organs in large buildings. This, like most other Regals, can sound remarkably metallic in certain specimens; occasionally it is simply a thin, nasal, humming sound, blending with other stops without giving more than a fringe of color. It is most useful with flues, not other Reeds, not as a solo stop, but in contrasting simultaneously sounding melodies Beautiful Regals can be heard on recordings, mostly from European organs. Such a stop as this sounds strange to organists trained in the Romantic school. Emphasis on the higher and more dissonant partials presents a new tone color in the spectrum of the pipe organ to many players, and yet one heard over ten centuries ago, when the Regal was a small Portativ organ *consisting entirely of reed pipes.* In that period, long before the Regal was associated with an open Principal and perhaps a stoppered rank, some churchmen would take delight in carrying it from church to church for their services.

The resonators of the modern Apfelregal are very short: from one-sixteenth to one-quarter the unison length, as compared to the unison length of a Trumpet rank. They consist in the traditional examples of narrow (brass) cylindrical pipes surmounted by spherical forms that have many round tone-openings all over their surfaces. This kind of pipe chokes most of the lower harmonics and emphasizes some of the higher-pitched. In other words, the lower, more *on-pitch* harmonics are choked, and the higher, more *dissonant* harmonics are let out of the pipe. The voicing of this Reed is as much a matter of the shape of the shallot and its reed as the shape of the pipe. Builders frequently interchange the names of the Regals. See KNOPFREGAL, REGAL.

BALLAD HORN. An 8′ manual Reed stop whose timbre is quite like that of the Waldhorn. On theater and concert organs this name is used to designate a whole series of mellow, somewhat brassy, pleasant-toned horns voiced for the Solo manual. The Ballad Horn's smooth and pungent effect combines the best elements of the brass-like timbre and the warm quality of the Orchestral Horn. It is a very effective tone for playing the melody line, especially as heard in the popular and sentimental songs of the day. Most examples are harmonically full and a little on the big side in loudness. This is not a French or Orchestral Horn, and cannot be used for the same type of effects. Neither does it have any of the Baryton's thin tone. The resonators are of full length and may be flared in their top halves in addition to the normal flare in Horn stops. See FRENCH HORN, WALDHORN.

BARPFEIFE. A Reed stop of the Regal group, at 8′ or 4′ on the manuals, and 16′ or 8′ on the pedals. This smothered, very reedy, hollow,

THE ELEVEN-OCTAVE COMPASS OF THE PIPE ORGAN

Name of Note (Also name of manual and pedal key as based on unison pitches)	Length of Open Pipe Needed to Make This Pitch (Also length of unison-length reed resonator)	Length of Stopped Pipe Needed to Make This Pitch	Pitch (Number of vibrations or cycles per second)
C⁷	⅜ inch	3/16 inch	16,744.03
C⁶	¾ inch	⅜ inch	8,372.02
C⁵	1½ inches	¾ inch	4,186.01
C⁴ (top manual key)	3 inches	1½ inches	2,093.00
C³ (high C)	6 inches	3 inches	1,046.50
C² (treble C)	1 foot	6 inches	523.25
C¹ (middle C)	2 feet	1 foot	261.63
C (tenor C)	4 feet	2 feet	130.81
CC (bottom manual key)	8 feet (8′)	4 feet (8′)	65.41
CCC (bottom pedal key)*	16 feet	8 feet	32.70
CCCC	32 feet	16 feet	16.35
CCCCC	64 feet	32 feet	8.17

*The top pedal key is G (below middle C).
Equal-tempered scale interval is 1.059463. A¹ is 440 vibrations per second.

Chart Explanation: The Eleven-Octave Compass of the Pipe Organ

This chart shows the great range of pitch (i.e. frequency) that can be heard in the pipe organ — not all organs, of course, but a few of the largest. Only two organs actually have pipes that go as low as 64′ in pitch, but many have 64′ Resultants. The very high mixture pitches are much more common. Most organs do not go above C⁵ or C⁶ in the treble. The overtones of the small open pipes go far above the top of this chart, and influence the timbre even though they cannot be consciously heard. The pitches given are derived from A¹ as 440 cycles per second. The reader can obtain any *octave* of this note by multiplication or division. The equal-tempered scale interval can be used to obtain any *note*. For example, AAA# can be found by multiplying AAA at 55 cycles per second by 1.059463. The BBB above can be found by multiplying this frequency at AAA# by the same figure.

cavernous tone is one of the oldest types of organ stops. It is useful in adding timbre to the pedals, but encounters competition from the Rankett and Schalmei there. It has been effectively used as a 16′ Positiv Reed. The 32′ manual or pedal *Barpfeife*, Sordunregal, and Rankett are to be heard in Continental Europe. Their *short* resonators fit easily into the chambers, and their unique and sometimes guttural timbres lend distinct effects in contrast to other lines of notes, mostly in Classical literature. The Barpfeife at any pitch can sound with a certain degree of sympathetic or near-Vox Humana quality, but most of the longer resonator types (including the deep basses of even the shorter quarter to eighth lengths) will assume a soft "rattle" or percussive reedy tone that is very pleasant. On the manuals it is not so useful as a solo voice by itself, but combines well with the softer flue stops, giving good pitch definition and a timbre that is distinctive and unlike any other in the organ. It is less brilliant than the Regals, louder than the Dulcian, and not so dull as the Euphone. The resonators are short, of very wide flare, and fully capped in the American types. The sound emerges from a slot near the top of each pipe. Resonators vary considerably in shape. See REGAL.

BARYTON. A soft Reed stop of 8′ manual pitch and 8′ pedal pitch, sounding in the more modern examples somewhat like a hybrid between a Vox Humana and a soft horn, with emphasis on the horn's overtones. The older forms inclined more towards just a soft, sympathetic, humming sound. Both solo and ensemble effects are possible with this stop. It is heard more in the pedals in Europe and the manuals in America. The theater organ contains some examples, often of the louder, more pungent variety.

BASSET HORN. An imitative Reed stop of 8′ manual tone, always voiced for solo playing, suggesting the color of the Clarinet, but lighter and more open in tone than this instrument. Rather than having a woody, hollow timbre, the Basset Horn has a peculiar broadness and a "sweetness" in tone, both of which characterize this stop. It is a fourth-manual stop, rarely on a two-manual instrument. Its pipes are larger in scale than the Clarinet's, and it is not so useful at the 16′ pitch because its overtones are harder to identify in the bass range. Synonyms: COR DE BASSET, CORNO DI BASSETTO.

Corno di Bassetto
or *Basset Horn* pipe

BASS FLUTE. An *open* wood (occasionally metal) Flute of 16′ or 8′ on the pedals, rarely on the manuals. It is neutral rather than "dull" in quality, and voiced to supplement the other pedal stops, such as the Double Diapason, Diapason, Gemshorn, or Violone. It may be synonymous with the *Flute Ouverte*. It fills up all of the lower harmonic positions in the pedals, adding volume, firmness, and pitch definition. It may be a soft bass line by itself. To the

Bourdon it adds the open pipe's partials. It is usually an inconspicuous tone, having less individuality than most other stops. It is useful in binding the Strings to the Diapasons or Flutes. It is valuable in all organs of any size, and may be obtained by extending an open manual Flute downward, but it is preferable to make it "straight." Both the 16′ and 8′ pitches can come from one rank in the pedals, since most organists play but one note at a time. Synonyms: FLÖTENBASS, FLÛTE BASS.

BASS HORN. A 16′ pedal Reed voiced like the instrument of the same name. The *Tuba Horn* stop has been substituted for this name. It is also a Tromba of soft voice in some cases. This stop-name is peculiar to the orchestral type of organ, in either a residence or a theater.

BASSOON. See ORCHESTRAL BASSOON.

BASSOON REGAL. A 16′ manual and pedal Reed sounding like a very reedy, brilliant, and thin form of the Fagotto or Bassoon. See REGAL.

BASS VIOLIN. See CONTRABASS, CONTRA VIOLONE.

BAUERFLöTE. A stoppered wooden Flute of 4′, 2′, or 1′ on the manuals, yielding a clear, bright, whistle-like tone that is not at all shrill. It is moderately loud and can be a solo stop upon occasion, or a source of brilliance for flue combinations. The upper octaves are open, because no builder makes stopped pipes for the higher treble notes. It is rarely a high pedal stop.

BEARDED GAMBA. A String stop of keen and cutting quality, at 8′ on the manuals, and rarely at 16′ on the pedals. This stop is essentially a Gamba in tone, but has a flat strip of pipe-metal, the "beard," soldered across the lower area of the mouth of each pipe and up against the bottoms of the ears. Sometimes it touches the front of each pipe below the mouth and sometimes it does not. In either case it slows the speech by causing additional friction to the air entering and leaving the mouth. This gives the pipe time to build up additional initial tones that seem to "spit" in the manner of the bowing sounds of the old instrument. These initial partials are not so true in pitch as those of the steady tone that comes later, and they rarely merit the name *harmonics*, since they may not be exact multiples of the frequency (pitch) of the fundamental. See GAMBA.

BELL CLARINET. An imitative 8′ manual solo Reed which produces a brighter-than-average orchestral Clarinet tone. The widely flaring bells at the tops of the half-length or unison-length cylindrical metal pipes permit an added parcel of very high but soft overtones to escape the pipes. This Clarinet speaks with a new variety of brightness rather than with more of the quinty effect heard from most organ Clarinets. See BELL FLUTE, CLARINET.

BELL DIAPASON. A Flute stop of 8′ manual tone formed from Diapasons of large scale with wide bells on their tops. The tone is loud and also very fluty because of the higher mouth cut-up. The bells do impart some brightness, but that of the full-length taper is more noticeable. This is a solo or ensemble Flute around *f* or *mf*, quite like the Principal Flute in tone. The additional soundboard space and added expense generally do not warrant specifying this stop, except as a form of variety in very large organs. The large ears are used for tuning. See BELL FLUTE. Synonym: FLÛTE À PAVILLON.

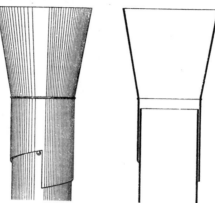

Belled top as on a Flûte à Pavillon

BELL FLUTE. An open metal Flute of 8′ or 4′ manual pitch, with a bell-shaped top of from one-half to one-eighth speaking length on each medium-scale cylindrical pipe. Some additional high overtones do escape these pipes and make the tone brighter, an opposite effect from that of the conically topped Koppelflöte. This may be a solo or ensemble Flute. Synonym: GLOCKENFLÖTE.

BELL GAMBA. A *conical,* not cylindrical, Gamba with very long slender bells on its pipes' tops, sounding at 8′ on the manuals, occasionally at 16′ on the pedals. Its tone is delicate, bright, and stringy, but not pungent or especially keen. It is a superior type of solo or ensemble Gamba tone in some organists' opinion. Bending the large ears inward flattens the pitch, and outward sharpens the pitch. See GAMBA. Synonym: GLOCKENGAMBA.

Bell Gamba, of more slender scale than the Bell Flute of the same note.

BLOCKFLÖTE. An open metal Flute of 4′, 2′, or 1′ manual pitch, and 4′ or 2′ pedal pitch, with a full-toned, penetrating, but clean timbre that is *round,* not sharp. This modern Flûte à Bec is most effective and very valuable as a tonal "top" for manual or pedal combinations. Its clear, telling tone is almost equally usable with the Strings, Reeds, other Flutes, or Diapasons. It is preferred in the Chorus of the Positiv or Great by some organists. It is sometimes placed in the Great Organ as a second 2′ stop, softer, of course, than the Diapason Fifteenth 2′. It is not so useful in the Solo as the more colorful Piccolo Harmonique

or Sifflöte 2'. It is ideal as a pedal rank of high pitch, giving some point
to the pedal's line of notes without lending enough tone color to rival the
manual's. It is not unknown in some mixtures, and can form mutation
pitches on pedals or manuals. There is some variation in the structure of
this Flute, but it is usually of medium to large scale, sometimes slightly
conical in shape to eliminate those rough partials that may appear in a
cylindrical pipe of short length. A few specimens are huge in scale and
have a prominent tone without much timbre. Most ranks have wide mouths
of moderately high cut-up. This name has been used for a large-scale
stopped metal Flute. See SIFFLÖTE.

BOMBARDE. A powerful, heavy, penetrating Chorus Reed of 16' or 8'
on the manuals, and 32', 16', or 8' on the pedals. The modern Bombarde
is voiced to support a whole ensemble, but the older form of this stop was
little louder than a big Fagotto in tone. The degree of brilliance voiced
into this stop at any of its pitches varies with the other Reeds present
in the same organ. If only a Bassoon or Fagotto is present, it is likely
to be quite bright; if an Ophicleide or a Tuba Magna is present, even in
another division from this stop, it is likely to be much less bright than
it usually is. It is never so brilliant as the Tubas or Trombone, nor so
free in tone as the Posaune or the Trumpets. Neither does it have that
firm, sometimes hard, tone heard in the deeper Tubas. It is equally at
home as a manual or pedal stop, but most organists remember it as a 16'
pedal rank. It can make a manual 4' Clarion tone in large Reed Choruses.

When a 32' pedal Bombarde sounds it is difficult to tell whether it is
heard individually because it is too loud, too strong in its fundamental
ground tone, or simply deeper than any other rank. Any opinion would
have to be based on an analysis of its overtone structure. Those stops
that blend better sound with a certain degree of sameness with other
stops. The big Bombarde pipes sit in a midway position between the dull
Contra Diaphone and the brilliant Contra Trumpet. The Bombarde is
versatile for this reason; it can be adapted to either bright or dull stops,
if its dynamic value is right. Its tone does not disturb the big flues, like
the Double Diapason, the Swell ensemble, or the louder solo stops. Rather,
it blends with them, heightening their carrying power and making their
tones more vigorous. It does not take the place of the Double Diapason on
either manuals or pedals, because its overtones are *slightly* off the same
pitches as those of the flue Chorus. Reed overtones vary in dynamic from
time to time.

The Bombarde's percussive attack on the ear is very sudden. This
makes it sound in contrast to the flues, which generate their sound waves
in more thousandths of a second, if we compare like pitches. Starter
pneumatics swing the very long brass reeds into motion the instant the
organist puts his foot on a pedal key, and dampen them when released.
Nevertheless, these long reeds can be heard decelerating after the other
pipes have ceased to vibrate. In some cases this sound may be reverberation, since the bass notes usually last longer than the middle and high
notes when reflected.

The manual 8′ Bombarde is a very useful Chorus Reed that can build
up the tones of the rest of the organ, sound with an assertive, bright *solo
brass* tone, and even combine with the Diapason Chorus upon occasion
in order to give it additional firmness and pitch definition. It may be more
useful on a large Great than a Tromba or Trumpet, especially in a large
building. It has also found use in the Altar or Sanctuary Organ as a
firm support to the flues in hymn singing. It lacks the éclat needed for
the fanfare quality, although at 8′ it can support a loud Reed Chorus.
The Solo Organ may contain a Bombarde Chorus. The Stentor and
Bombarde Organs usually include a Bombarde, often at 16′ pitch. Three
examples of Reed Choruses that include this stop follow. They are typical
of a loud manual division:

Bombarde Clarion	4′		Harmonic Clarion	4′		Harmonic Clarion	4′
Bombarde	8′	or	Bombarde	8′	or	Bombarde Quinte	5⅓′
Contra Bombarde	16′		Contra Bombarde	16′		Ophicleide	8′
						Contra Bombarde	16′

The addition of a Stentor Mixture III or VI of loud Diapason pipes would
make these Choruses more usable in ensembles. They require a heavy 32′
pedal Reed for balance of tone. The 2′ Chorus Reed is almost unknown.

Bombarde pipes have the appearance of most Chorus Reed pipes. They
are inverted-conical in form, with trebles of double length for sufficient loudness. Thick walls, sometimes of laminated metal, prevent the
dissipation of the lower harmonics by the walls of the pipes themselves.
The degree of flare is greater in the less brilliant forms, and more
slender in examples of less fundamental. Spotted metal in all but the 32′
octave may be seen, although this octave, and also the 16′ octave, may
have this metal in just the upper halves or thirds of their pipes. The 8′
and 4′ ranks are not sufficiently brilliant without it. To withstand the
intense vibration, the shallots and reeds are of thick stock. If the wind
pressure is high, they are even thicker. The top diameter of the CCCC
pipe is around 22 to 9 inches, and the CCC pipe around 10 to 6 inches.
Lower octaves should be unenclosed to permit the long sound waves to
extend themselves without obstruction into the air spaces. See CONTRA
BOMBARDE, TUBA.

BOMBARDE QUINTE. A Chorus Reed of 5-1/3′ on the manuals, and
10-2/3′ on the pedals, formed from Bombarde pipes of less than average
loudness and brilliance. Since this stop forms the *third harmonic* of the
sub-unison series, it is found in only the largest organs, and should be
drawn only with a loud Chorus Reed, of 16′ manual and 32′ pedal pitch.
With the lighter-toned ensembles it creates tonal imbalance. Reeds at
these "quint" pitches have a limited use, which is mostly to complete the
louder choruses in the pedals and manuals. The manual's 5-1/3′ stands
in the same pitch relationship to the 16′ sub-unison stops as the 2-2/3′
Twelfth does to the 8′ series. The 10-2/3′ is the "Twelfth" of the 32′
pedal series. The forty to sixty overtones that each pipe of these two
ranks would add to any ensemble are all completely off the pitches of both
the *notes* of the scale and the *overtones* of all other ranks (except other

stops of these same unusual pitches). This unusually full sound would have an effect on the ear somewhat like that of a soft but penetrating cymbal, except that the cymbal's harmonics are even more irregular in mathematical proportion to the fundamental's pitch. Couplers, if used, would further complicate the matter for the ear's analysis. Reverberant acoustics, perhaps a high ceiling, and judicious treatment by the organist all help to make this stop assimilable to the ear. This is a stop not always placed on the Crescendo Pedal circuits. See BOMBARDE, QUINT.

BOMBARDON. A Chorus Reed of 16′ or 8′ on the manuals, and 32′ or 16′ on the pedals. It imitates to a limited degree the old brass instrument of the same name. The tone is harmonically full and rich, but not so loud or intense as that of the Bombarde, but it is always louder and somewhat more developed harmonically than the Fagotto. It is never brass-like, like the Buccina or Trombone, nor is it light in weight like the Oboe. It can support on both manuals and pedals an ensemble of moderate power. It is sometimes placed in a large organ to form a contrast with the louder Reeds. It is similar in construction to the Bombarde, but is of smaller scale.

BORDUNALFLÖTE. An open wood Flute of 8′ or 4′ on the manuals, distinctly different from other open Flutes in tonality and construction. Its slender walls are inverted-pyramidal in shape, that is, flaring outward towards their tops, and either square or rectangular in cross-section. This form of air column gives the tone a "warmer" and also brighter tone quality, because the taper permits additional harmonics to escape, as in the Oboe's resonator. Like the Dolce, also of tapered form, this stop is a soft tone which can lose its characteristic tone color if its overtones are absorbed by organ chamber walls or auditorium. It is a solo stop in need of a very soft accompaniment, like the Dolcan, and an accompaniment or soft ensemble stop. It is rarely seen in any organ. Synonym: PORTUNAL-FLÖTE.

BOURDON. One of the commonest stopped Flutes in the organ, at 16′ or 8′ on the manuals, and 32′, 16′, or 8′ on the pedals. It is usually wooden, but may be metal in the 8′ rank or the upper octaves of any rank. The sub-unison of the Swell or an occasional mutation may be a Bourdon rank, since it gives a firm fundamental pitch and blends moderately well. Very few organs in the world exist without some sort of stopped Flute, and this Flute is usually a Bourdon, or at least takes its name. The owners of one very large organ have suggested that they may build a 64′ octave for their pedal division. Such a stop would descend to only 8.17 vibrations per second at the low CCCCC. The longest pipe would be about thirty-two feet long, and could be mitered or laid horizontally against a wall if the necessary height were not available, without impairing the tone.

The Bourdon always gives a dull tone, frequently from walls of great thickness. The height of the mouth's *cut-up* and the air-tight tuning *stopper* do the most to characterize its tone. Air entering the windway, or flue, between the cap at the bottom of the front of the pipe and the block, impinges on the outside of the upper lip. The mouth permits this air-reed to vibrate back and forth in order to make the musical tone, and an especially high mouth, like this one, the Tibia Clausa, and most Gedeckts, makes very little overtone-forming friction with this air-reed. *The stopper excludes the even-numbered harmonics*, except those that creep around the high, square corners of the mouth. Nicking the windway, rounding the upper lip and smoothing it, lowering the wind quantity, and

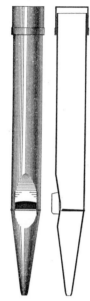

Bourdon tenor C pipe with metal tuning collar and large ears.

increasing the scale are all ways that the builder can use to obtain a Bourdon of deeper and duller tone. Also to be considered is the basic fact that a big mass of air in any pipe is a heavier sounding body that will make a louder tone just because there is more of it to vibrate, although with slower acceleration of its steady tone than a smaller pipe gives. Generally, greater *loudness* comes from larger pipes of lower pitch, but greater *intensity* of tone comes from pipes that are able to accelerate the air in an auditorium more quickly, such as pipes with greater resonance, high treble pitch, and two or more ranks of the same pitch (like a II-rank Kleinerzähler). Intensity of tone is not related to loudness, timbre, scale, or to any family of stops. It is, therefore, not a marked property of big Bourdon pipes, because it takes the biggest (lowest in pitch) an eighth-second or a quarter-second to accelerate into full steady tone. This is one reason why the deeper Bourdons can be used with both loud and soft combinations of stops. Ignoring the effect of distance, a small-scale Bourdon in a small church can have the same timbre and loudness as a large-scale Bourdon in a large church, but the intensity is greater in the smaller scales, since they accelerate in fewer hundredths of a second. The ear is very much aware of *quickness* of speech, and interprets this factor as *quality*.

Bourdon pipes should be placed as close to a smooth, thick wall* as possible to reflect their sound waves outward. Long *bass* sound waves have a way of shaking nearby structures instead of traveling outward to the ear. This insures that the profound fundamentals will not be lost. Bass tones are quite non-directional, and seem to come from everywhere. Tone openings of from three-quarters to nine-tenths of the sound chamber space will not block the tone.

Bourdon pipes of all pitches are usually rectangular, with their mouths on the shorter sides for increased depth of tone. Mouth cut-up varies a great deal, but one-half the width of the mouth is fairly common. The dimensions of the low CCC (16′ pedal) pipe vary all the way from 6 x 4

*Robert Hope-Jones, who was an idealist in such matters, constructed one of his organs, still playing and in good repair, in front of a heavy masonry wall fifteen feet thick. Both high and low pitches are well transported in this auditorium clear to the back row of seats.

to 17 x 14 inches, the larger scales being a little more resonant and perhaps slower in speech. The low CCCC (32′ pedal) pipe varies between 9 x 7 and 29 x 20 inches, all inside measurements. Huge scales are not uncommon and are necessary to bring this stop's volume up to the point of filling a very large building with sound. Manual varieties are inclined towards a more square cross-sectional shape to increase their blend with the 8′ and 4′ stops. The Bourdon's *harmonics* are the same as those of other stopped Flutes. In the 8′ rank (pedal or manual) the 8′, 2 2/3′, 1 3/5′, 1 1/7′, and 8/9′ sound, with only the first two (or one) obvious to the ear. The 4′, 2′, 1 1/3′, and 1′ are heard only from the open flue and Reed (8′) ranks, except that *traces* of these components enter the tone through the square corners of many stopped pipes, especially when of high cut-up. The fundamental (first harmonic) is the prominent tone heard from the Bourdon. It may be called both the *unison* and *fundamental* when the stop is pitched at 8′ on the manuals or 16′ on the pedals. Otherwise the fundamental coincides with the pitch on the stop key, but the word *unison* would not be correct. Moving the huge stoppers upward flattens the pipes, and vice versa.

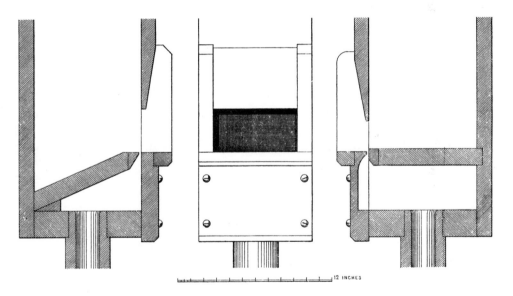

Bourdon of moderate scale with 12-inch marker at bottom. High mouth generates very few harmonics, and these of the odd-numbered series.

The Bourdon supports the fundamental in combination with other stops of the same pitch. It may be a Great stop of 8′ or a Swell stop of 16′, but some organists prefer the lighter-toned Rohrbordun, Gedeckt, or Quintade at 16′. The Bourdon does blend quite well, but soft ranks need an Echo Gedeckt or its equivalent. Its pronounced "Twelfth" and perhaps "Tierce" mesh with the components of the other stops. It does not stand apart as a 16′ or 8′ Tibia Clausa. On a large Solo it is useful at 8′ as a device to steady tone and make certain stops more colorful. In past centuries in Europe some great churches had a profound pipe or two to rumble during the singing of hymns. This satisfied the congregation emotionally and deepened all stops. Being of indistinct pitch, one or two big pipes were all that was needed. The 32′ pedal specimen in the Church of the Heavenly Rest, New York City, speaks without barking a higher harmonic, and is of great intensity on each note, not on only the bottom notes. It is usable with the Dulciana or Vox Humana alone, or as a substantial support to the full ensemble. This organ was built by the Austin Company. Sugar pine with birch or maple fronts, perhaps cherry caps, constitute many Bourdon pipes. Oak or mahogany may make some mouth or lip portions. See MAJOR BASS.

BOURDON DOUX. A soft 16′ manual Bourdon designed to combine with other stops in order to deepen and delineate their tones. See BOURDON, GEDECKT.

BOURDONECHO. A very soft small-scaled stopped Flute of 16′ or 8′ on the manuals, and 16′ on the pedals. It is a source of soft ground tone for combinations with other flue stops. If skillfully combined, it can put their timbres in clearer contrast and emphasize their pitches. See BOURDON, LIEBLICHBORDUN. Synonym: ECHO BOURDON.

BRASS TRUMPET. A very brilliant and penetrating Chorus Reed stop of fiery and free-toned brass color and 8′ manual pitch. It has almost twice the number of partials as its orchestral counterpart, and a louder sound. It may be heard from the Solo, Fanfare, or perhaps another ancillary division. Some examples are of only moderate power and quite light in tone, depending upon the other stops in the organ. This Trumpet has the maximum of clang-tone and number of upper partials, as well as the exponentially shaped resonators of solid brass to project them into space. These resonators are also well polished and do not absorb the great number of very soft, high-pitched components the inverted-conical pipes of the Trompette do. Therefore, these high but soft partials are allowed to escape the pipes and are more likely to reach the ears of the listener. Such a brilliant stop makes an interesting contrast with the full organ or Diapason Chorus, whether it is installed in the main organ or by itself in another location. Processional marches, recessionals, or such pieces of music as Purcell's *Fanfare in C major* display this stop well. It is the most brilliant but not the loudest Reed in the organ. Many examples are still playing throughout the country, and most are known as *Gottfried Trumpets* in honor of Anton Gottfried, who built many of these stops. Synonym: ORCHESTRAL TRUMPET.

BUCCINA. A Chorus Reed of 16′ or 8′ on the manuals, and 32′ or 16′ on the pedals. Its light, loud voice is Trombone-like in color. It is very valuable in both Reed and flue combinations, adding a moderate amount of clang and just enough pungency to alert the ear. It does not come through the pedal line like the bigger Reeds, but rather adds a harmonic fringe to the other stops. The 8′ Buccina is not a common stop, but very useful on both Swell and Solo organs. The recently installed Aeolian Skinner organ in St. Thomas's Church, New York City, has a 16' specimen in the pedal division. Its inverted-conical pipes are half unison length, and the top diameter of the CCC resonator measures 4 inches. *Buccine* is sometimes used instead of *Buccina*. See TROMBONE.

BUZAIN. A Chorus Reed of 16' or 8' on the manuals, and 32' or 16' on the pedals, resembling the Posaune in tone and construction. Some of the older examples are coarse and too penetrating in tone, but new methods of reed manufacture have eliminated secondary noises. See POSAUNE.

CAMPANA. A brilliantly high Flute (or Foundation) rank on the manuals at 1' or ½'. This is not a mixture component but an independent octave-sounding stop. The pipes are so short and the pitch is so high that the stop has no apparent color, and might be called by almost any name. When skillfully used by the organist it resembles the tinkling of small bells in the distance. It may be added to an 8' or 4' flue of soft value, like the Gedeckt or Dolcan. Since the pipes are almost impractically small, the pitch must break often. Synonym: ZIMBELFLÖTE.

CARILLON. A manual mixture composed of from two to six ranks of open metal Foundation pipes, sounding at octave, fifth, and third positions above the keys depressed. Although not always brilliant in timbre, it suggests the sounding of small bells. In smaller organs this mixture stands out less in tone and is likely to have fewer ranks. It is a refined and beautiful adjunct to the tones of any chorus of flue stops, especially when heard at some distance from the organ. It frequently contains a 1' component to maintain pitch impression and hold the *Quint* ranks. It may contain a Seventeenth or Twenty-fourth, as some examples do, for mixtures and cornets cannot be standardized completely; they must be custom-designed for each particular organ. The Carillon's very small pipes go out of tune easily, sometimes just before a recital. They also should be turned with their small mouths pointed directly to the tone opening. Otherwise they might not be heard, because high-pitched (i. e. short) sound waves project themselves only directly forward, unlike the bass (i. e. long) waves which can overcome all obstacles from any angle. Unenclosure is to be preferred, particularly for this stop, since swell shades always baffle many of its *high* partials. The pipes are spotted metal or pure tin. Notes from middle C:

Example No. 1 II		Example No. 2 III		Example No. 3 VI		Example No. 4 VI	
G^3	1 1/3'	G^4	2/3'	*C^6	1/4'	C^5	1/2'
C^3	2'	E^4	4/5'	G^5	1/3'	G^4	2/3'
		C^4	1'	C^5	1/2'	E^4	4/5'
				G^4	2/3'	C^4	1'
				C^4	1'	G^3	1 1/3'
				G^3	1 1/3'	E^3	1 3/5'

*These very small pipes break in pitch every half octave, but at least at every octave. Ranks are arranged according to ascending pitch, moving upward.

Two examples of unusual timbre follow. Their pitches may be seen to be spread quite far apart — and on alternate positions, since No. 5 skips the 2′ and 1 1/3′ pitches, No. 6 the 1 3/5′ and 1′ pitches:

Example No. 5		Example No. 6	
III		III	
C^4	1′	E^4	4/5′
E^3	1 3/5′	G^3	1 1/3′
G^2	2 2/3′	C^3	2′

Synonym: GLOCKENSPIEL.

CÉLESTE. An undulating, beating stop composed of at least one rank of purposely mistuned pipes. Two ranks are usually found, and are most successful if of similar loudness, timbre, and position in the organ. The organ's célestes create the soft, orchestral timbre, simulating the effect of many viols or, perhaps, woodwinds. Most examples are at 8′, but large String ancillaries have célestes at higher pitches. The famous John Wanamaker organ in Philadelphia has a String division with 88 ranks, including a 32′ Gamba and mixtures. Its célestes are at 8′, 5 1/3′, 4′, 3 1/5′, 2 2/3′, and 2′. The pipes are Viols, Muted Viols, Gambas, many Dulcianas, and a Nasard Gamba of 8′. All families except Reeds have formed célestes. Practically every small organ has a céleste, usually from Salicionals (or Violins). Some organs have several. Theater organs have had huge célestes of complex beats, from even six or more ranks of Viole d'Orchestre pipes. Such stops are more imitative when on the soft side. The most classical of organs have had none, but these almost seem to be an experiment, so universal is the céleste principle. Célestes are not wanted in the purer-toned flue ensembles. like a Positiv or some Choirs. Some stops that have made célestes follow:

Foundation stops	String stops	Flute stops
Dolcan	Aeoline	Celestina
Dolce	'Cello	Dolce Flute
Dolcissimo	Ethereal Violin	Dulciana Flute
Dulciana	Gamba	Flauto Dolcissimo
Echo Dulciana	Muted Violin	Flûte d'Amour
Erzähler	Salicional	Harmonika
Gemshorn	Viola	Spitzflöte
Ludwigtone	Viole d'Orchestre	Zartflöte

Out-of-tune stops of all families will céleste together to a small extent, because different materials expand and contract at different rates with changes in temperature. Thus an organ is always célesting to some small extent even when just tuned, as does every orchestral instrument and voice. Even the harmonics of a *single* pipe céleste, since they are not created by nature precisely in proportion to their fundamental. The overtones of all pipes create extensive beats with the notes of the even-tempered scale (as sounded by the fundamentals of other pipes). Mixture pipes céleste with the overtones of. the Strings, bright Flutes, and Reeds. Spurious *inharmonics* (which have no relationship with their fundamentals) also account for some of the célesting, because they cannot be fully voiced out of a rank, particularly Reeds. These effects all add up to the impression that music is variable in pitch and somewhat warm in color. Truly on-pitch overtones would sound very unpleasant to all listeners. The Diapason is voiced to cut off its harmonic series just before a large parcel of dissonant harmonics make their appearance in the tone, around the twelfth to the twenty-second. A Chorus of in-tune Diapasons thrills because it sounds as such a novelty to ears that are trained by nature to listen to an infinite variety of célesting from trees, wind, etc., and also because of the mathematical proportions between its notes, ranks, and harmonics. The ear will create célesting effects, by habit, in all sounds.

The number of beats between two middle C notes of 262 and 264 is found by subtraction, or 2 per second. Twice in a second these two pipes will grow stronger then weaker, as well as *brighter then duller*. Since célestes are chorded usually, the complexities of beating between harmonics are much too great for practical consideration, especially since the *tremulant changes the pitch of each harmonic* every time it beats. A three-rank String céleste with the middle C pipes sounding at 262, 264, and 265 vibrations per second would produce three different undulations per second: two, three, and one. These would also affect each other, because a beat undulates with a beat. Such a céleste is referred to as a *normal-sharp-very sharp* céleste, and is orchestral in effect, mostly being used for the brighter Strings.

The célestes of less than brilliant tone, the Foundation and Flute célestes, are tuned to beat more slowly, even so slow as one-half to one undulation in a second, since a faster beating wipes out too many of their overtones, making the sound extremely dull. The String célestes range from three or four to as high as seven undulations in a second. At between seven and about fifty undulations per second the ear interprets the sound as being disagreeable. Above fifty, the beating is so fast that the ear accepts it as a complicated mass of tone that it cannot possibly analyze.

The pattern of pitches that the organ builders use most frequently is the *normal-sharp* pattern. It has the advantage of a little psychological lift just because it is sharp rather than flat, because raising the pitch always makes an appeal to the listener. The *normal-flat* pattern is used for the Dulciana Céleste and the Spitzflöte Céleste in many cases, creating a sedate and quiet impression. The *sharp-flat* pattern of pitches is perhaps the most useful for accompanimental célestes, since each rank is less off the normal pitch than in the other patterns. But it has the disadvantage of denying the organist the independent use of a normally pitched rank for other combinations. The *normal-flat-very flat* pattern is useful only in contrast to the *normal-sharp-very sharp* céleste. Both may be used to heighten the orchestral effect in a String Organ. The *flat-normal-sharp* pattern of pitches wastes one rank of pipes, and is rarely used, unless unequally proportioned. A large organ may have a special type of céleste, perhaps in a String ancillary, made from a 4' *normal* Viole and a *sharp* 8' Viole. Higher-pitched célestes are useful in large String ensembles, including the basic pitches of 4', 2 2/3', and 2'. It must be remembered the basic purpose of a céleste is to build up some degree of opaqueness as well as create warmness of pitch, no doubt using chords.

The beautiful Ludwigtone, which can be designed according to many rhythms of undulation, vibrates according to a *sharp-flat* pattern. This stop makes it easier for the singer to sound well with the organ accompaniment. It also has a more pervasive and intimate sound with a solo stop, such as the Viola d'Amore or Corno d'Amore. In any céleste the off-pitch rank can be made softer to relieve the throbbing effect. Reducing the overtone development of either rank achieves another sort of softening of the timbre, because each overtone sets up a complex system of undulation with all other *pipes* sounding with it. Many célestes go down to just middle C, while others go to tenor C or G. The upper bass frequencies are low enough to sound confusing to the ear, which is trained to identify notes as distinguished from overtones. Fewer beats in the bass and more in the treble can prevent a feeling of confusion.

Specifically, the name *Céleste* refers to some sort of Voix Céleste in most cases, although a Viole Céleste may be so indicated. Such a term, like "Tuba," is hardly specific as to species of tone. The Voix Céleste is frequently on the Swell of a small organ. Some large instruments have a series of célestes. In the First Church of Christ, Scientist, Boston, the specifications give: *Swell Organ:* Viole Céleste, Dolce Flute Céleste, Echo Viole Céleste; *Choir Organ:* Viola Céleste, Unda Maris (tenor C); *Solo Organ:* Dolcan Céleste, Viole Céleste. The Hauptwerk, Great, and Positiv are without célestes, as is also the Bombarde. Automatic devices, such as a special piston, or the *first* contact on the Crescendo Pedal, are sometimes provided to silence all célestes. Some large organs have II-rank stops, not as célestes. Organ magazines provide the student with an opportunity to study current trends in the matter of celestes by their stop-lists. See VIOLE CÉLESTE, VOIX CÉLESTE. Synonyms: VOIX CÉLESTE, VOX CÉLESTE.

CELESTINA. A very small-scaled open wood Flute of 8' or 4' on the manuals, with a tone color that is a hybrid between a bright but soft String and an open Flute. Pipe-forms differ, as do also dynamics, but *pp* is one of the softer indications made. This Flute is a timbre creator for other soft stops and an accompaniment stop for soft solo voices, such as the Dolce.

'CELLO. See VIOLONCELLO.

'CELLO CÉLESTE. An undulating String stop of 8' on the manuals, composed of two ranks of 'Cello pipes, sometimes of heavy walls and large scale. It may be of wood construction, one of the special laminated metals, plain pipe-metal, spotted metal, or even pure tin, or any combination of two of these materials; they are arranged in order of increasing ability to form a bright tone that is rich in overtones. This is a favorite Solo Organ céleste of many organists, although the Gamba Céleste gives some competition. It is moderately loud, stringy, and some examples are a little pungent. It can sound warm, resonant, and even cutting in tone, depending upon the organist's taste. It is always full-toned and rich in partials. It is frequently a String Organ stop. See CÉLESTE, VIOLONCELLO.

'CELLO VIOLIN. A String stop of 8′ on the manuals, and sometimes at 16′ on the pedals. Its timbre resembles the keen, brilliant Viol as well as the big-toned, pervading timbre of the 'Cello. It forms, like other String stops, a céleste. It is a solo as well as an ensemble tone, most useful on the String or Swell Organ. If extended into the bass, it makes a keen, penetrating pedal stop brighter than the Violone. See VIOL, VIOLONCELLO.

CHALUMEAU. See SCHALMEI.

CHAMADE. See TROMPETTE EN CHAMADE.

CHIMNEY FLUTE. See ROHRFLÖTE.

CHORALBASSET. A Diapason of 4′ or 2′ on the pedals, specially voiced to make clear and prominent the melody of a hymn tune or plain-song, or any other part of the music assigned to the Pedal Organ. See DIAPASON.

CLAIRON. See CLARION.

CLAIRON HARMONIQUE. See CLARION HARMONIC.

CLARABELLA. An open wood Flute of 8′ or 4′ on the manuals, frequently on the Great Organ. It sounds with a smooth, strong, neutral-timbered open Flute quality that is moderately soft, although some examples are inclined towards the *mf* dynamic. It is midway between dull and bright, which is one of the reasons for its value as a stop. It is not assertive like the Major Open Flute or a large-scale Hohlflöte, but its effect is telling in any but a very loud combination. Its functions are to *fill up* in an inconspicuous manner the lower parts of the trains of harmonics in the other flue stops, to *smooth* any other stop that may be a little rough in tone, and to *firm* the fundamental pitch of any combination. The Hohlflöte and Waldflöte can do the same things, but their tones are produced by open wooden pipes with inverted (smooth on the outside) lips. The Clarabella, which has its bevel on the outside of each pipe's lip, lacks the added "chiff" of bright initial harmonics in these other Flutes, and it might seem "less bright" for this reason. It does not destroy the tone qualities or dynamic values heard in other stops by either its 8′ or 4′ rank, unless the stop is really soft. It projects the exact loudness and tone qualities of other stops more efficiently to the far ends of an auditorium because it provides a strong wave form on which their tones may be transported. It therefore amplifies the effect of the tone colors, the inner harmonies of the notes played, and also the pitch impression. Although not vivid in color itself, it makes other stops, chiefly flues, more colorful and graphic to the ear. Since it has from fourteen to twenty of its own harmonics, it is not a conspicuous stop, but, like all Flutes, it can be a solo stop at certain times.

The higher harmonics of the Clarabella are weak, and the lower part of its train is evenly and gradually tapered off in loudness as the upper pitches are reached. Thus it can mask roughness in another stop, like a Gamba or bright String. To the Diapasons it can add firmness and a little brightness. To the solo Reeds it can add some roundness of tone and a firmer pitch. Many shapes and scales of the original Bishop Clarabella exist; like the Hohlflöte, it is amazingly adaptable. Its low cut-up, moderate scale, and smoothed and beveled mouths build up its tone.

CLARIBEL FLUTE. An open wooden Flute of 4′ on the manuals, similar in tone and function to the Clarabella. It may be lighter in tone than a Clarabella. Although smaller in scale and less resonant than the Clarabella, it is an ideal open 4′ Flute for addition to solo flues, like the Philomela, Viola, Gamba, or Harmonic Flute. It can brighten their tone qualities, firm their pitches, and smooth their peaked harmonics without damaging their individual characteristics. It is clear and bright, but hardly to be described as "liquid" in tone by itself. See CLARABELLA.

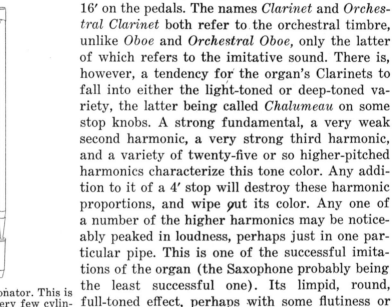

CLARINET. An imitative Reed of 8′, rarely 16′, on the manuals, and 16′ on the pedals. The names *Clarinet* and *Orchestral Clarinet* both refer to the orchestral timbre, unlike *Oboe* and *Orchestral Oboe*, only the latter of which refers to the imitative sound. There is, however, a tendency for the organ's Clarinets to fall into either the light-toned or deep-toned variety, the latter being called *Chalumeau* on some stop knobs. A strong fundamental, a very weak second harmonic, a very strong third harmonic, and a variety of twenty-five or so higher-pitched harmonics characterize this tone color. Any addition to it of a 4′ stop will destroy these harmonic proportions, and wipe out its color. Any one of a number of the higher harmonics may be noticeably peaked in loudness, perhaps just in one particular pipe. This is one of the successful imitations of the organ (the Saxophone probably being

Clarinet resonator. This is one of the very few cylindrical reed pipes.

the least successful one). Its limpid, round, full-toned effect, perhaps with some flutiness or pungency, makes a beautiful solo stop, most likely on a Swell or Solo Organ. It is not so versatile a source of timbre as the Fagotto or Krummhorn. Its medium-scale cylindrical resonators are one-half unison length. The Clarinet at 16′ on the manuals is very useful and can be obtained by itself with an intramanual 16′ coupler and the Unison Off coupler, since it is usually only at 8′. *Major Clarinet* is a louder form. Synonym: ORCHESTRAL CLARINET.

CLARINET FLUTE. An open or half-covered Flute of wooden construction, at 8′ or 4′ on the manuals. Although it is not a reed mechanism, voicers can give this Flute any desired degree of third harmonic, sibilant reediness, or brightness, by mouth and scale adjustments. This stop has no standard pipe-form.

CLARION. A Trumpet (sometimes a Tuba) of 4′ manual pitch and 8′ pedal pitch. These *octave* Chorus Reeds supplement the unison Trumpets and Trompettes. The fiery "top" this stop gives to Reed ensembles is balanced on the bass side by the sub-octave Reeds (16' on the manuals, 32' on the pedals). The complete form of the Chorus Reed ensembles would appear:

Manual		Pedal	
Clarion (octave)	4'	Clarion (octave)	8'
Trumpet (unison)	8'	Trumpet (unison)	16'
Contra Trumpet (sub-octave)	16'	Contra Trumpet (sub-octave)	32'

Manual octave and sub-octave couplers would raise to *nine* the number of pipes sounding in this chorus from just one key. Chording the notes would increase the *brilliance* of the tone as well as the dissonance of some of the upper partials. However, this dissonance when heard from well-voiced pipes is one of the pleasant contrasts of the organ. The ideal Clarion tone must refer to that of the unison Reeds, since its chief function is to extend the range of the partials, as well as augment those of the unison. This Octave, although free in tone and very brilliant, should not obscure the unison Trumpet. When heard together, without the 16' rank, they should sound as a *unity of tone,* and make one of the most useful solo stops of the organ. The addition of the 16' must necessarily bring in more weight because bass pitches chord less easily than those of the middle and high registers. *Clarin Real* indicates a loud form.

The effect of the Clarion should not be overwhelming, although it is often used as a climax stop for ensembles. Many organists prefer a Trompette of 4' because it sounds lighter and blends with the unison Trumpet a little more easily. There is also the advantage of having a Trompette 8' for solo use when it is played an octave lower. Also, it should be remembered that the octave coupler makes the Clarion 4' sound at the 2' pitch, as the sub-octave coupler makes a 32' manual voice of the 16' Trumpet. The complete chorus with couplers sounds one 32', two 16', three 8', two 4', and one 2' notes *for each key.* The organist must use such power judiciously, and balance it with the proper bass. It should also be kept in tune to prevent the multitude of dissonances that quickly creep into Reeds.

The Clarion's pipes resemble those of the other Chorus Reeds. They are sometimes double or triple length to ensure the proper power in the treble notes, because small reed pipes of any sort cannot sound loud enough for the heavier bass pipes if they are of only unison length. In the smaller organs the specifications may call for only an 8' Trumpet. The organist can then have recourse to the octave and sub-octave couplers when an increase in power or brilliance is needed, but chords that extend beyond an octave will lose a little power, since the *same* pipe may receive duplicate orders from two or more keys. The solo power of such a combination remains unimpaired, however. Sometimes the Clarion or Clarion Harmonic needs a Mixture for added brilliance. See CLARION HARMONIC, TRUMPET. Synonyms: CLAIRON, TRUMPET CLARION.

CLARION HARMONIC. An octave Chorus Reed of 4' on the manuals, and 8' on the pedals, voiced to yield an unusually powerful and assertive treble Trumpet tone of the free type rather than the firmer Tuba type.

Making the resonators of all the pipes of this Trumpet double (or triple) length does not make the tone more brilliant in so far as the *number* of partials is concerned, although it may sound more brilliant because there are stronger partials nearer the fundamental's pitch. Harmonic-length reed pipes wipe out the very high-pitched (perhaps dissonant) partials, which helps to make a better Chorus Reed ensemble. They also increase the total power of the pipe. Both of these factors are advantages in the loud treble Reed, and *harmonic* pipes are usually included at the high pitches even though the name does not appear on the drawknob. Weight of tone and better blend with the big flue stops is also achieved. However, the type of tone in the harmonic reed pipe is at least theoretically straying away from the *fanfare* sound now and going towards the Tuba sound, which is an ensemble as well as a solo sound. See CLARION. Synonyms: CLAIRON HARMONIQUE, HARMONIC CLARION.

CLARION MIXTURE. A manual Mixture stop of brilliant and assertive tone, composed of open metal flue pipes resembling a loud Diapason or Stentorphone in timbre. They may also be on very high wind pressure, larger in scale, or more brilliant in voicing than most mixture pipes. In modern times when a good Clarion is available from any builder, this Mixture is not so frequently seen, or it may take another name if it is intended to augment the Chorus Reeds. The 1 3/5′, if not too dominating, can contribute a brassy effect, but it is frequently absent from this mixture, which is mostly fifth- and octave-sounding ranks. Since *each pipe* in this stop sounds from twenty to thirty partials, the brilliance can be increased considerably by making the chords more close-fingered and also by adding notes. It is a property of brass tones to sound more natural partials closer together than flue pipes can sound. The octave coupler might be added if the mixture is in tune. This stop never makes quite the same effect on the ear as a Clarion 4′, since the reed tone is more sudden in impact on the ear, and also has the property of sounding many transient partials throughout its *steady* tone. This is a most usable addition to loud Reeds. Middle C speaks at these notes:

Example No. 1		Example No. 2		Example No. 3		Example No. 4	
III		III		IV		V	
C^3	2′	G^3	1 1/3′	C^4	1′	C^4	1′
G^2	2 2/3′	C^3	2′	G^3	1 1/3′	G^3	1 1/3′
C^2	4′	C^2	4′	C^3	2′	E^3	1 3/5′
				C^2	4′	C^3	2′
						C^2	4′

CLEAR FLUTE. An open wooden Flute of 4′ on the manuals. It is sometimes made from metal stock. In tone it resembles a completely unimitative timbre inclining to the 4′ Hohlflöte, its mouth being inverted (smooth on the outside, beveled on the inside). The scales vary somewhat, the larger giving a louder and less bright effect, the smaller a less loud and slightly brighter timbre. Some examples are strong in the 2′ (second) harmonic. This is an ensemble Flute, suitable for addition to any other flues that can absorb its tone, such as the Diapasons, Gemshorns, other open Flutes, and Strings. It can also serve as a solo Flute, perhaps played an octave lower to make a "unison" tone. As in all flue and Reed stops, the top notes of the rank are made from *open metal* pipes of as similar intonation as is possible to create. Since this is a 4′ Flute, the middle C pipe is about one foot in speaking length; at C^4 or C^3 the metal pipes would begin, depending on the habits of the builder. Compare this Flute with the Clarabella.

COMPENSATING MIXTURE. A pedal mixture designed in each organ to sound the pitches and tone qualities that are needed to complete the ensemble. Since the function of the pedals is for the playing of melody and polyphonic parts as well as bass parts in the music, this stop may be needed to make the pedals a complete tonal entity, suitable to be heard with the manual parts. The ranks may extend to the top of the compass unbroken in pitch, as in most pedal Mixtures. The pitches are usually high, and the tone quality similar to that of the Diapasons, Gemshorns, or even open Flutes, according to the need. Here are III-, V-, and VI-rank examples speaking from the low CCC key:

Example No. 1		Example No. 2		Example No. 3	
III		V		VI	
C^1	2′	C^2	1′	C^3	1/2′
G	2 2/3′	G^1	1 1/3′	C^2	1′
C	4′	C^1	2′	C^1	2′
		G	2 2/3′	G	2 2/3′
		C	4′	E	3 1/5′
				C	4′

CONCERT FLUTE. An open wooden Flute of 8′ or 4′ on the manuals, intended to resemble the orchestral flute in timbre. In many examples the tone is really louder and smoother than in the prototype. Many different pipe structures have been used for its construction, but the traditional form is an open harmonic Flute, topped by metal pipes. In the 4′ rank, which is more common, there are 36 wooden pipes, and in the 8′ there are 48 wooden pipes, both topped by the metal pipes, voiced to continue the wooden pipes without any obvious break in loudness or tonality. The 8′ rank is given stopped wooden pipes in the bass for just one octave even by orthodox builders, although a purist might question this procedure on the grounds that the open overtone structure is broken, but it is a question whether the difference is really harmful. Open pipes might be substituted without question, since the harmonic bass pipes are not effective. This is both an ensemble and a solo stop. Most examples are not so imitative as those special efforts by builders to imitate the orchestral flute; only a few are successful. This stop-name has been used on a few organs for a large-scale Clarabella (open) and a Tibia Clausa (stopped). This is a misuse of the organ's terminology.

CONE DIAPASON. A Foundation stop of 16′, 8′, or 4′ on the manuals, and 16′ or 8′ on the pedals. It has the essential tone of the Diapason: a strong fundamental and a harmonic series developed to just below the point where dissonant harmonics (not spurious inharmonics) enter the tone. Many examples of this stop are moderately soft, and mixture ranks are frequently formed by it. Its unique feature is that the otherwise

cylindrical pipes are made just slightly conical in shape for their whole
speaking length. This form prevents many of the higher-pitched harmonics
from being created, and places the energy of the air column more in the
lower chord of harmonics. Those eliminated by this shape are between
approximately the sixteenth and twenty-third, varying, of course, with
scale and wind pressure. The second and fifth harmonics (4' and 1 3/5'
from an 8' rank) are almost always noticeably strengthened by a conical
flue pipe. Nor is the taper so great that the even-numbered harmonics are
eliminated, but the odd-numbered are somewhat strengthened, presenting
a clear, full tone. The stronger odd-numbered harmonics develop a luminous, clean, but not "cold" tone that is of easy blend with all types of
stops. To say the tone is "reedy" or "stringy" does not describe this
timbre, these two effects demanding a great number of high-pitched
partials.

In the treble notes these pipes, even at large scale, have a bell-like
clarity without that fringe of shrillness sometimes heard from cylindrical
ranks. The bass pipes are strong in fundamental ground tone and perhaps
seem a little duller to the ear, but they contribute powerful components
to the ensemble that are very valuable. The conical Foundation ranks are
not superior to the cylindrical pipes in the Diapason Chorus, because their
sparsity of harmonics will not mesh so well with ranks higher in pitch,
such as an 8' with a 4', or a 4' with a 2 2/3' rank. Thus the façade of tone
cannot be erected altogether by this type of Diapason. Sometimes just the
mutation pitches are conical, being perhaps three-quarters to seven-eighths
of the mouth-line diameter at the pipes' tops. Even the tuning collars are
conical in form too. See DIAPASON. Synonyms: SPITZ DIAPASON, SPITZ-
PRINZIPAL.

CONE GAMBA. A Gamba formed with conical open metal pipes instead of cylindical pipes, as in the regular Gamba, at 16', 8', or 4' on the
manuals, and 16' on the pedals. It has less keenness and impact on the
ear than any other form of Gamba. This shape of pipe removes many of
the higher-pitched overtones from these slender air columns, and somewhat increases the fundamental's strength, as well as the octave harmonic's. This makes a milder String tone and one with no peaking (in
loudness) in particular partials, although it does not wipe out the essence
of the String's timbre. This is a true *String Copula*, with better blend
and less keen quality than most Gambas. It forms a céleste and can at
times be an accompaniment or a solo voice. See BELL GAMBA, GAMBA.
Synonym: SPITZGAMBA.

CONE GAMBA CÉLESTE. A String stop of undulating tone, at 8'
manual pitch, composed of two ranks of Cone Gamba pipes of slender
scale. It can be anywhere from big and assertive in tone to delicate and
soft, like the Spitzflöte Céleste. It has a certain firmness not heard in
other String célestes and is only mildly bright, and more usable with other
Strings and all flues if tuned to beat slowly. The *normal-sharp* and *normal-
flat* patterns of pitches are both heard. See CÉLESTE, CONE GAMBA.

CONE GEDECKT. A half-covered wooden Gedeckt of 8' manual pitch. In the stopper of each pipe, except those at the extreme ends of the compass, is a small cylindrical (brass) rohr, or chimney, which admits just a vestige of the even-numbered series of harmonics not customarily heard from a stoppered pipe. In this particular variety of *Rohrgedeckt* these chimnies are flared outward, a few with even the curvature seen in a trumpet's bell. Pyramidal, straight, and inverted-pyramidal pipes have all been used for this stop, and also chimnies of conical, cylindrical, and inverted-conical shape, making *nine* possible forms for this stop. Practically speaking, the audience could hardly hear the difference between the timbres of these forms. In fact, the organist must concentrate on the differences between a Gedeckt and a Rohrgedeckt. In an unusually reverberant room these subtle differences may perhaps be heard. Increasing the diameters of the rohrs would add a few more partials to the tone, but this stop must remain essentially a dull tone. See GEDECKT, ROHRFLÖTE.

CONICAL FLUTE. An open metal Flute of 16', 8', or 4' manual pitch, and 16' or 8' pedal pitch. This medium to large-scale spotted metal rank sounds with a noticeable fundamental and a strong chord of lower-pitched (easier-to-hear) partials down near the fundamental. The fringe of brightness typical of a cylindrical pipe is removed by this pipe-shape. In the bass range this is a tone builder; in the high treble it is clean and bell-like; in the middle range it is an ideal Copula, accompaniment Flute, and inconspicuous support for any flue combination. It is not a colorful Flute, but an ideal adjunct for other flues. See PYRAMID FLUTE. Synonym: FLÛTE CONIQUE.

CONTRABASS. The narrow-scale orchestral bass String, at 16' manual

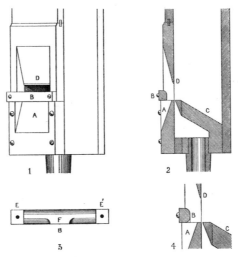

Orchestral String "Double Bass" in wood form at CCC. 1 is front view, 2 is an interior view, 3 is detail of harmonic bridge, and 4 is detail of mouth area where sound waves are originated. A is lower lip, B is the bridge, C is block, D is upper lip. E is used to show ends of bridge for attachment to pipe, and F is harmonic-creating ridge on bridge.

pitch, and 32′ pedal pitch. It is cutting, bright, thin, and pungent even in this deep bass range, although these longer air columns lack the same flexibility for creating many of the higher-pitched components. The Geigen, Violone, and Diapason basses are much larger-scaled than this String. The overtones of this stop — and it sounds practically no fundamental ground tone — are quite dissonant from even their own fundamental's pitch because of the excessive friction inside the pipe, but this creates a tone that is in keeping with the manual ranks of Viols that this stop is intended to support. Although perhaps not enclosed in the String Organ, this rank of slender spotted metal pipes sounds best with the célestes and keen timbres of all kinds of Viols and Muted Viols. The Fagotto at 32′ or 16′ is also an excellent bass for Strings. The Contrabass may be removed from the Crescendo Pedal by a special piston. Naturally certain examples of this bass are more brilliant and rubbing than others; any sort of tone can be designed and voiced by an organ builder. An infinite number of hybrid tones are practical between the mild and keen Strings. In fact, it might be said that all String stops are really mitigations of *the* String timbre. Diameters at the CCCC pipe range from 7 to 3.5 inches, and at CCC from 5.5 to 2.75 inches. Wooden specimens are milder in tone and may have that wood-like bass viol sound that adds to the sense of reality. See CONTRA VIOLONE, GROSSFLÖTE, VIOL D'ORCHESTRE. Synonyms: BASS VIOLIN, CONTRA VIOLONE, CONTRE VIOLE, DOUBLE BASS, VIOLIN BASS, VIOLONE.

CONTRA BASSOON. A low-pitched imitative Reed of 32′ or 16′ on the manuals, and 32′ on the pedals, lighter in tone than the Fagotto or Fagottone usually are. See FAGOTTO, FAGOTTONE, ORCHESTRAL BASSOON.

CONTRA BOMBARDE. A penetrating deep-toned Chorus Reed of 16′ on the manuals, and 32′ on the pedals. These pitches sound an octave below the unison's pitches on manuals and pedals, the term *Contra* signifying that a rank of pipes speaks below the normal (unison) pitch. These big Reed pipes are unenclosed in most cases to permit them to form their very long sound waves without obstruction. Sometimes they are laid horizontally on a wall or against a ceiling, because height may be unavailable. In this case advantage may be taken of the fact that if their tops point directly out towards a long nave or other air space, the fundamental as well as overtones will not be obscured so quickly.

This bass has a percussive effect on the ear. *Each* sound wave is formed more quickly than by deep flues of the same pitch. This faster impacting of the air molecules (which is theoretically called *intensity*, not loudness) imparts a greater sense of animation to the bass line of notes and also a cleaner impression of the exact pitch being heard. The Contra Diaphone does the same thing, although much more so and with practically no overtone structure. This Bombarde is brass-like but not coarse or dissonant, as are some bass Reeds. Starter pneumatics insure that the tone, although from very long reeds, will come promptly when the organist presses the key. Bass organ Reeds sometimes take a whole second to accelerate into their steady tones, making them rather useless to most music. This stop, in its most modern form at least, speaks quite promptly.

The ear cannot quite count the low number of cycles that comes from the low CCCC pipe of the Bombarde. This long reed swings back and forth only 16.3 times *in a second* in order to make this note. This profound bass stop satisfies the listener by carrying the ear right down to the lower threshold of hearing, as the high-pitched Cymbal or Twenty-second carries the ear upward to the top threshold. Hearing both limits of pitch-sensation orients the listener to the complete yardstick of pitch so that he interprets *all* pitches more accurately, *in both overtones and fundamentals,* and therefore hears timbres in their true value. This stop's pipes are of both metal and wood, and resemble the Contra Tuba's. See BOMBARDE, TUBA.

CONTRA BOMBARDON. A Chorus Reed of 16′ manual pitch, and 32′ pedal pitch, with moderately loud, brass-like tone similar to a more intense form of the Fagottone, capable of supporting Reeds from *f* to *ff*. See BOMBARDON.

CONTRA BOURDON. See MAJOR BASS.

CONTRA DIAPHONE. A valvular Foundation stop of 16′ manual pitch, and 32′ pedal pitch, one example sounding in the Midmer Losh organ in the Atlantic City Convention Hall at 64′ from full-length resonators, mitered in just a few of the longest pipes. The Contra Diaphone yields the ultimate in intensity of fundamental tone. The flexible pallet spring may be made to give some octave and super-octave overtone as desired, but this bass is most valued for its pure fundamental, smoothness, evenness, quickness of speech, especially between CCCCC and CCC, and the absence of the murmuring heard in some big Reeds. The two largest organs in the world, the one just mentioned and the John Wanamaker organ, Philadelphia, have several ranks of Diaphones to support their pedal and manual divisions, from the thunderous at 32′, to the very soft at 16′. Most of them play from the pedals, not the manuals, and some very high wind pressures are used. See DIAPHONE.

CONTRA DULCIANA. A very soft Foundation stop of 16′ on the manuals, and rarely at 32′ on the pedals, forming the proper bass line for the diminutive Foundation stops, such as the Dulciana. This 16′ will not take the attention from the accompaniment or solo part. The tone is unobtrusive and gentle on the ear, but, none the less, distinct in pitch, and not too easy to absorb. The 32′ is louder than the 16′ or 8′. See DULCIANA.

CONTRA FAGOTTO. A light-toned and neutral-colored Reed bass of 16′ on the manuals, and 32′ on the pedals, coming from pipes similar in design to the Fagotto. The chief point of versatility of this bass is its *distinct pitch impression* as well as its moderately developed overtone series, which keep it from standing apart from the other stops, either flue

or Reed. Its evenness of volume, cleanness of timbre, and even the usefulness of the 16′ manual rank as a solo tone make it one of the most valuable
of stops. It has been used on the Great in place of the heavier-toned
Double Diapason. In small organs the 8′ might be extended downward as a
16′ pedal bass. See FAGOTTO.

CONTRA GAMBA. A String bass of 16′ on the manuals, and 32′ on the
pedals, of rich, brilliant, but not especially loud tone. Even though mitered,
its long slender open metal pipes provide a pedal tone with point and a
clear pitch line. See GAMBA. Synonym: GROSSGAMBA.

CONTRA OBOE. An imitative Reed stop of 16′ on the manuals, and
32′ on the pedals, forming a suitable bass for light Reed choruses, but less
versatile than the Contra Fagotto at both pitches. The nasal, thin, pungent
tone extends down to about GG. See OBOE, ORCHESTRAL OBOE. Synonym:
DOUBLE OBOE.

CONTRA POSAUNE. A loud and brilliant Chorus Reed of 16′ on the
manuals, and 32′ on the pedals. It is louder and heavier than the Contra
Trombone in many examples, but has the basic timbre of this stop. The
free and blatant tone of the Trumpets is in some ranks, although this
bass Reed is less brilliant than the Ophicleide and less weighty in tone
than the Contra Bombarde. Softer forms are voiced for the smaller organs.
See POSAUNE.

CONTRA PRINCIPAL. See DOUBLE DIAPASON.

CONTRA SAXOPHONE. An imitative bass Reed of 16′ manual pitch,
and occasionally 32′ pedal pitch, particularly in the Continental organs.
This bass line of the orchestral counterpart is a poor imitation. This
highly variable, breezy, fluty tone with its peculiar initial harmonics and
unstable pitch is quite impossible to imitate by the steady wind supply of
the organ. Labial pipes have been used with some success, particularly
above CCC. They also have the advantage of standing in tune longer than
the reed pipes. The reedless Oboe and Clarinent are also quite good imitations, but, of course, these ranks do not have the same harmonic structures
as either the Reed stops or the instruments they imitate. This windy, light-
toned Reed is valuable in bass or solo line. See SAXOPHONE.

CONTRA TROMBONE. A Chorus Reed of loud and assertive tone, at
16′ on the manuals, and 32′ on the pedals. A 64′ Reed (not diaphonic)
octave is in the Wm. Hill & Son and Norman & Beard Organ in Town Hall
Auditorium, Sydney, Australia, sounding from wooden resonators. The
Contra Trombone is bright and brass-like in tone even in the lowest
pitches. It lacks the éclat and freely vibrating sound of the Trumpet type
of tone, but also is less heavy in tone than the Contra Bombarde. Half-
length resonators, which are not too commonly seen, strengthen the octave
harmonic and other higher partials. Wood, rolled zinc, or pipe metal with
spotted tops can be seen in the pipes of this stop, with all spotted metal in
the shorter pipes. See TROMBONE.

CONTRA TRUMPET. A very loud and brass-like Chorus Reed of 16′ on the manuals, and 32′ in the few profound pedal ranks that exist under this name. The free-toned, brilliant, and even light vibrations that come from this fiery Reed have none of the heaviness of the Bombarde or the firmness of pitch heard in the Tuba tribe of stops. Some examples are *Trompettes* with narrow flaring pipes; others are the more subdued form of *Trumpets*. This is the proper bass for the manual Trumpets. See TROM-PETTE, TRUMPET. Synonym: DOUBLE TRUMPET.

CONTRA TUBA. A loud, penetrating, firm-toned Chorus Reed of 16′ on the manuals, and 32′ on the pedals. The rolling and brassy tone that comes from these long inverted-conical pipes (sometimes made from wood) is quite brilliant, but has varying degrees of clang-tone in the many examples heard. This stop is designed to sound well with the Tubas of the manual divisions of the same organ. It can support the Trumpets and other Reed stops. Its distinguishing mark is its firmness of pitch, although most examples lack the heavy ground tone of the Contra Bombarde. The 16′ manual rank is heard only in large organs. See TUBA. Synonyms: DOUBLE TUBA, TUBA PROFUNDA.

CONTRA VIOLA. A manual String of 16′, frequently on the Choir Organ. The pedal 32′, if it existed, might be called a Contra Violone. Organists particularly value this sub-unison String for its cleanness of pitch as well as that mild stringy timbre the true Viola stop always displays. It blends well with Diapasons and String stops as well as with the diminutive Foundation ranks, like the Dulciana, Dolce, and Gemshorn. It rarely appears in an organ with the 8′ rank, unless in a special chorus of Viola stops. Ranks vary somewhat in loudness, and are spotted metal down to CCC. See VIOLA.

CONTRA VIOLONE. A bass String of 16′ manual pitch, and 32′ pedal pitch, sounding with a neutral tone quality usable with any flue ranks of any division, except the softest. Even the Diapasons are enhanced by the mild, incisive, but not keen, quality in this deep bass. It is given varying amounts of string-like tone, but almost all examples are strong in the fundamental, with moderate overtone development. Most ranks are little brighter than a Geigen. Wood pipes are usually less bright than cylindrical metal ranks, and less stringy, but this is more a matter of scale, mouth cut-up, and wind pressure than material. A brilliant tone can be given to the wooden pipes and a very dull tone to the metal pipes. All dimensions equivalent, the wooden Violones are more likely to have a resonant tone and also that warm, rich formant so much admired in them. Some ranks have been in operation for centuries in the older organs in Europe, many rebuilt time and again into a new scheme. Currently, the Violone is likely to be of spotted meal, perhaps just in the mouth section in the 32′ octave, voiced only moderately stringy, and somewhat loud, with a moderate scale. The *Contra Violone* is regarded as a synonym of *Contrabass*, but, unlike most other synonyms in this book, each is written up separately. See

CONTRABASS, VIOL, VIOLONE. Synonyms: BASS VIOLIN, CONTRABASS, CONTRE VIOLE, DOUBLE BASS, VIOLIN BASS, VIOLONE.

CONTRE VIOLE. See CONTRABASS, CONTRA VIOLONE.

COPULA. A stop intended to bind together the tones of other stops. It is frequently a stopped Flute, perhaps one of the Quint Flute series. It has an 8' or 4' manual pitch, and a 16' or 8' pedal pitch. It is intended for a particular function, like holding together in a more unified tone

1. bright and dull stops;
2. loud and soft stops;
3. low-pitched and high-pitched stops;
4. 8' and 4' stops with mixtures;
5. coarse and smooth-toned stops;
6. Reed and flue stops.

The Gemshorn and Erzähler can hold together the bright and dull registers, or the low-pitched and high-pitched. The 4' Koppelflöte improves the unity of sound in a Positiv ensemble, and is sometimes the only 4' stop in this division. The Nachthorn 4' or Quintaten 4' are also not unusual here. Loud and soft stops blend with the Bourdon 8' or 4' in many cases, perhaps with both pitches. The best binder for the mixtures and unisons is the stop-pitches between their pitches: the Octave, Twelfth, and Fifteenth. The Twelfth can hold the higher pitches to the unison-Octave combination. The Major Open Flute or Hohlflöte can give unity of tone to a poorly designed Diapason Chorus if it is not too loud. The train of harmonics in each one of these open Flutes represents the whole complement of pitches in the Chorus. The Clarabella or Gedeckt may smooth the rough, peaked overtones of any coarse register, and the Quintaten or Quintadena may hold together the softer flue choruses, perhaps in some organs the louder ones too. The best bond between the Reeds and flue stops depends upon the loudness of the Reeds and also their degree of brilliance, but the powerful *open* Flutes with their complete complement of harmonics are the best binders in many cases. The Tibia Plena, Stentorphone, and Major Open Flute can do much to hold together the whole ensemble, since they mesh their harmonics with those of the other stops drawn. Each of these three stops has this set of harmonic-pitches *in its 8 tones:* 8', 4', 2 2/3', 2', 1 3/5', 1 1/3', 1 1/7', 1', 8/9', 4/5', 8/11', and 2/3', etc. The precise pitches may vary a little, especially under higher wind pressure, but most components sound near the individual ranks' pitches and also quite near the harmonics of other flue and Reed stops. Pedal Copulas are important, but are in few organs. But the Bourdon, Nachthorn, Cone Flute, Bass Flute, and other stops can serve as pedal Copulas. Many stops have the Copula function without its name. Effective Copulas must stay in tune to fulfill their function. Some Copulas are used to hasten the speech of slow Reeds or bass pipes, covering up the waiting period, yet not giving a distinctive color of their own. Some 4' manual stops, the 4' Koppelflöte and Orchestral Flute particularly, repeat the same overtones an octave higher than the 8', and thus have the Copula function. See GEDECKT, KOPPELFLÖTE.

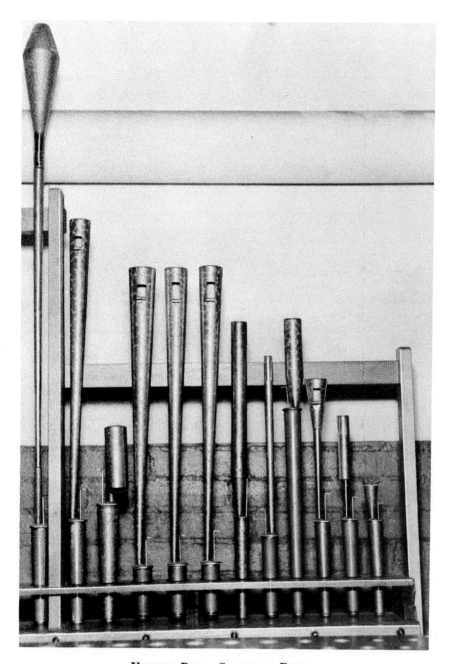

VOICING ROOM SPECIMEN PIPES

A rack of Reed pipes photographed in one of the voicing rooms of the Aeolian Skinner Organ Company. This set of pipes, always in front of the voicer, helps him to adjust and tune new pipes to the standard of these pipes. All speak from the middle C key. From the left:

English Horn 16′	Clarinet 8′
Fagotto 16′	Krummhorn 8′
Rankett 16′	Vox Humana 8′
Trompette 8′	Hautbois 4′
Trompette (smaller scale) 8′	Rohrschalmei 4′
Trompette (shallot variation) 8′	Fagotto (short) 4′

Courtesy: Aeolian Skinner Organ Company.

COR ANGLAIS. See ENGLISH HORN.

COR d'AMOUR. See CORNO D'AMORE.

COR de BASSET. See BASSET HORN.

COR de CHASSE. See WALDHORN.

COR de NUIT. See NACHTHORN.

CORNET. A compound stop composed of two or more ranks that go to the top of the compass unbroken in pitch. A mixture is also a *compound* stop, but its ranks traditionally break the pitch-succession one or more times before the top of the scale is reached. Therefore, in both of these types of stops the finger depressing one key sounds two or more pipes. In the pedals there are also Cornet and mixture stops. Since many pedal mixtures, because of their short, low-pitched compass, do not break in pitch, the terms are used with more freedom than in reference to the manuals. The function of the manual Cornet is to sound in a clear, prominent tone the chief melody of the music, a hymn, or a plainchant. Usually a third-sounding rank (the 1 3/5' or 4/5' on the manuals, and the 3 1/5' or 1 3/5' on the pedals) is present in this stop to contribute just a little sharpness to the tone, and to point up the timbre of the whole stop. The 4' and 2' should not dominate the timbre, as they do in some mixtures. The commonest design of pitches is illustrated in Example No. 3 below. The organ's size, number of Cornets, and musical function determine the number of ranks, loudness, scaling, pipe material, and general effect of the whole stop. Although ideal for the solo function, this is not usually on the Solo manual, but on the Great and Choir in many cases. In this, the most eminent compound stop in the organ, the ranks should all sound with a singleness of effect. No. 2 is called the "basic" Cornet.

Through the centuries of organ building this stop has been given the choice position on the front of the windchest, or even out in front of the whole organ screen, and unenclosed. Higher-pitched pipes make weak sounds in comparison to bass pipes, chiefly because the air in the pipe is *lighter in weight,* sometimes even 200,000 times lighter. Although the smaller pipe speaks more quickly, it cannot move the tons of air in any building so effectively. Further, higher-pitched sounds travel out *directly in front* of the mouths of the smaller pipes, and can be quickly absorbed by just the air itself. Higher-pitched overtones are also subject to these general laws of physics. If a long nave is to be traversed, the sounds must be loud, sharp, and telling to the ears. Even in front of the organ fully fifty per cent of the sound is lost, and this lost portion is the more important in establishing tone quality. Even *one* reflection is fatal to some overtones.

The Cornet combines well with other stops, especially louder Reeds and flues. In fact, it is sometimes said to resemble a Reed itself, owing to the closeness of its pitches, and therefore also its overtones. Some examples of this stop follow, with the notes sounded from middle C:

Example No. 1	Example No. 2	Example No. 3	Example No. 4
II	III	IV	V
C³ 2′	E³ 1 3/5′	E³ 1 3/5′	E³ 1 3/5′
G² 2 2/3′	C³ 2′	C³ 2′	C³ 2′
	G² 2 2/3′	G² 2 2/3′	G² 2 2/3′
		C² 4′	C² 4′
			C¹ 8′

Design No. 3 is repeated in the following series of pitches. It is usable on either manuals or pedals. It is, perhaps, the most typical Cornet:

32′ series	16′ series	8′ series	4′ series
IV	IV	IV	IV
6 2/5′	3 1/5′	1 3/5′	4/5′
8′	4′	2′	1′
10 2/3′	5 1/3′	2 2/3′	1 1/3′
16′	8′	4′	2′

Four examples of pedal Cornets follow, with notes from the low CCC key:

Example No. 5	Example No. 6	Example No. 7	Example No. 8
III	III	VI	VI
C¹ 2′	E 3 1/5′	C¹ 2′	G¹ 1 1/3′
G 2 2/3′	C 4′	G 2 2/3′	C¹ 2′
E 3 1/5′	GG 5 1/3′	C 4′	G 2 2/3′
		GG 5 1/3′	C 4′
		CC 8′	GG 5 1/3′
		CCC 16′	CC 8′

The Sesquialtera's pitches may be the same as those in a Cornet. However, the former's ranks are more likely to be broken in pitch and their timbre less solo-like and dominant in tone.

CORNET DE RÉCIT. A manual Cornet of unusually prominent tone, sometimes referred to as a *Solo Cornet*. It may or may not be placed high up in one of the upper tiers of pipes, but it is frequently *mounted* in front of the rest of the organ to give it some additional tonal advantages and to make more room for the other pipes. Since this is frequently a solo stop, it may be enclosed, perhaps in the Swell Organ. This name may refer to the more loudly voiced of two Cornet stops or to the Solo Organ's Cornet. It may be under higher wind pressure than the rest of the organ. As many as fourteen ranks have been used for this stop. A large example of VIII ranks follows, speaking from the middle C key:

	VIII	
(sounds on the 26th note)	G⁴ 2/3′	(fifth-sounding rank)
(sounds on the 22nd note)	C⁴ 1′	(octave-sounding rank)
(sounds on the 19th note)	G³ 1 1/3′	(fifth-sounding rank)
(sounds on the 17th note)	E³ 1 3/5′	(third-sounding rank)
(sounds on the 15th note)	C³ 2′	(octave-sounding rank)
(sounds on the 12th note)	G² 2 2/3′	(fifth-sounding rank)
(sounds on the 8th note)	C² 4′	(octave-sounding rank)
(sounds on the unison note)	C¹ 8′	(unison-sounding rank)

The upper two ranks would break back once in pitch because of their high frequencies. See CORNET.

CORNET des BOMBARDES. A compound manual stop composed of several ranks of loud Open Diapason pipes of metal. It is designed as a supplement to some particular division of loud Chorus Reeds or flue stops, such as the Solo, Fanfare, or Stentor. Pitches above the 1 3/5′ or 1 1/3′ are sometimes broken back in spite of the rule to carry Cornet ranks upward without breaks in pitch. *Stentor Cornet* or just *Harmonics* are also usable names. Four examples follow, with notes from middle C:

Example No. 1 III	Example No. 2 III	Example No. 3 III	Example No. 4 III
E^3 1 3/5'	C^4 1'	G^4 2/3'	C^5 1/2'
C^3 2'	G^3 1 1/3'	C^4 1'	G^4 2/3'
G^2 2 2/3'	C^3 2'	G^3 1 1/3'	C^4 1'

See CORNET.

CORNET des VIOLES. A compound manual stop composed of several ranks of Strings, either keen and brilliant, like the Viole d'Orchestre, or mild and soft, like the Viola or Salicional. It frequently is given the function of extending the String Organ upward in pitch as well as creating brightness. It has ensemble and also solo functions. The notes from middle C are:

Example No. 1 III	Example No. 2 III	Example No. 3 III	Example No. 4 V
C^3 2'	C^3 2'	E^3 1 3/5'	C^3 2'
C^2 4'	G^2 2 2/3'	C^3 2'	G^2 2 2/3'
C^1 8'	C^2 4'	G^2 2 2/3'	C^2 4'
			C^1 8' (sharp)
			C^1 8' (normal)

See CORNET.

CORNO CLARION. A soft solo Reed of 4' on the manuals, with a tone that resembles the 8' Corno d'Amore. They are rarely in the same organ, although this octave stop is designed as a treble for the Corno d'Amore. It will sound the "unison" notes if struck an octave lower than normally. This is a delicate, somewhat obscured, quiet voice with a tone quality that is horn-like and mildly reedy. It is a Swell Organ stop in the few examples one sees in a lifetime. It can be drawn with other soft Reeds, like the Orchestral Oboe or Horn, or with the Dulciana, Dolce, Viola, or a soft open Flute. An open Flute of 4' would enlarge its tone. Probably it would be more economical to indicate an 8' Corno d'Amore in the specifications, and use the 4' intramanual coupler and 8' unison-off tablet to obtain this tone. See CORNO D'AMORE.

CORNO d'AMORE. A solo Reed stop of 8' on the manuals, having a warm, "singing" sound of unusual sweetness for a Reed stop. It is soft and not at all pungent, like the Oboe, or plaintive, like the Musette. Some examples have a considerable body of tone, but most sound like a soft horn inclined towards a smooth voicing. The better specimens have a noticeable amount of inner resonance, but this is unfortunately something one pipe can have and not another. This *resonance* comes from a maximum of interplay between *all* the pipe's dimensions, the sound wave meeting as little inner friction as possible. This produces a surprising strength in the tone, sometimes as great as four to six times that expected, and without any hardness or brittleness. Smoothness in this stop comes from the absence of peaked harmonics. This Horn reinforces the softer flue stops in ensemble. It may be a Solo or Echo stop. Small-scale resonators with full caps and wide slots are often found. Synonym: COR D'AMOUR.

CORNO di BASSETTO. See BASSET HORN.

CORNO di CACCIA. See WALDHORN.

CORNO DOLCE. A solo Foundation stop of 16′ or 8′ on the manuals that suggests the sound of a soft and delicate horn, although this is a flue stop. This is also a useful accompaniment stop, and can enter into combination with all flues. It quickly loses its identity in combination, because its overtones are readily absorbed by even the Dulciana's train of overtones. Such a delicate overtone structure is best displayed as a soft solo stop, with, perhaps, a Dolcan or Echo Dulciana accompaniment. It usually has slightly flared inverted-conical walls to give it a few additional even-numbered components. Some builders actually make it straight-walled or even somewhat conical (about 5/6 top diameter to 6/6 mouth-line diameter). The scale is moderate or even large, and the metal spotted with tin crystals. Making the scale too small or the mouth-line too low would introduce some of the string partials into the tone. Keeping the tone horn-like is a matter of proportioning the scale, wind pressure, and mouth height, as well as some other dimensional features. Wooden examples of great beauty exist in some older organs.

CORNO FLUTE. A soft Flute stop of 8′ manual pitch having the basic timbre of many open Flutes, but with some of the Horn's upper partials added in this species. Compared to the Corno Dolce, not specifically a Flute, this stop is rounder and less horn-like in timbre, although of about the same dynamic value. It can be used as ensemble tone, accompaniment, or a soft solo register. There is a mellowness and warmth to the tone that comes from several of the noticeable lower harmonics. In spite of the moderate scale it has some ability to surround another tone and influence the timbre of most combinations. The pipes are either wood or metal, and flared outward a little towards their tops to produce an additional openness of timbre. This is either a Swell or Great Organ voice, and is frequently seen in small church organs. This stop, like many other flues, well illustrates the fact that playing two or more notes in a chord wipes out the timbre by massing overtones. Polyphonic music is so vital in tonality because its single-note pattern permits individual colors to be heard more as individual tones.

CORNOPEAN. A moderately loud Chorus Reed of 8′ or 4′ on the manuals, yielding the sound of a Trumpet. Cornopeans are used in small divisions of the organ where a Trumpet would be too assertive, and yet where some degree of éclat and a chord of strong lower-pitched overtones is useful. There are many degrees of brightness in the tones of the Cornopeans; a few are very dull, but most have quite a bit of the bright quality expected from a reed with inverted-conical resonators. Probably one-half the number of overtones heard in a Trumpet sound from this stop. A little horn quality creeps into some examples as well. The tone is most useful when it is kept neutral in color so that it can be blended with the flues, perhaps of the Choir Organ, where this stop is sometimes found. It is of course a solo stop and is more expressive if a tremulant and swell shades are provided for its sound. Liveliness of tone and a limited brilliance are its chief contributions to the organ. It has been suggested that a Fagotto-like bass adds to its usefulness.

CREMONA. This stop-name is associated with the Clarinet, sometimes a Clarinet Flute. It can be a mild Violin or Viola of 8' manual tone. It has been used for many years by reed organ manufacturers to indicate a mellow tone.

CROMORNE. See KRUMMHORN.

CYMBAL. A brilliant mixture stop on the manuals, occasionally on the pedals, composed of open metal Foundation pipes, sometimes designed as Geigen or Echo Geigen Diapasons. Its function is to add a harmonically full and closely pitched extension in the treble range to any Reed or flue combination. It is so popular with organists that a very large organ recently had included in it three specimens — on the Great, Choir, and Pedal. Many forms have been created, some with an overwhelming sound, others as a soft texture of tone almost unnoticeable. Although it frequently comprises only high-pitched octave and fifth-sounding ("Quint") ranks, the third-sounding pipes are also heard. It may be topped itself by a high-pitched Acuta or Scharf. Some examples seem to be reedy in timbre, especially when played in close-fingered chords. Power from the smaller air columns is quite impossible to obtain, at least for the louder examples, so builders may add additional ranks in each succeeding octave as the scale is ascended. Thus *Cymbal III to VI* can indicate three ranks below middle C and an additional rank for each octave above. Other patterns in number of ranks are also used. Breaking the pitch back as the scale ascends, sometimes twice in an octave, further complicates the design.

Unusual scales of pipes that progress irregularly through the compass have been experimented upon and some have added unusual results in clarity and greater usefulness in parts of the compass where the usual scaling does not show up well. Conical pipes are not uncommon, and may be employed at 2 2/3', 1 1/3', and 2/3', perhaps throughout the whole mixture. They do not form some of the higher-pitched partials that are dissonant to the scale's notes, and they strengthen the lower-pitched partials without becoming fluty. Since great brilliance may be desired, it is a matter of taste whether or not such pipes are used. Pure tin, although a luxury, imparts a formant to the tone that is silvery and clean to the ear. There seems to be no substitute for it. Spotted metal of good quality is usually heard; it makes a completely satisfying tone. Between these two grades of tin alloy are several qualities of white alloy that can be seen in some sets of exposed pipes. Cymbal pipes should be mounted in the open in order to be properly heard. Placing them even a little way back in a swell chamber wipes out this stop's power to lift the effect of the ensemble. After all, opening and closing the swell shutters in front of this high-pitched and consequently easily absorbed series of pipes does little to give it expression. Swell shutters mostly dull the timbre of bright stops.

The organist uses the Cymbal to bind the Chorus Reeds to the flues, to make the Trumpets and Tubas more brass-like, and build up to a peak the vertical line of pitches. It is seldom used alone, but alone with the 4' coupler it can simulate a Trumpet when played in chords without the tremulant. The Plein Jeu, which suggests this mixture by its sweeping range of pitches, makes a rich mat of Diapason tone; this forms many patterns of brightness, depending upon other stops combined with it, not loud in all cases. The Cymbal surpasses the Acuta in compass; it lacks the soft, bell-like timbre of most Carillons; it is usually pitched above the Fourniture and may be smaller in scale than this stop. It can seem animated in tone when played staccato, and can be depended upon to swell out legato chords in a broad, satisfying manner. Coming from many points of source, the sound imparts *quality* to other stops, since the ear usually interprets many instruments or organ pipes sounding together as being superior in timbre. The tremulant changes its character considerably, giving a new series of initial partials not heard when the notes are struck. Couplers, 16' and 4', spread the whole mixture out an octave in each direction, duplicating keys struck, but not, as every organist knows, the timbre heard from the mixture without the couplers. It can be drawn to other manuals an octave higher, as by a Choir to Swell 4' coupler. It speaks on the Sforzando piston and from one of the last circuits closed by the Crescendo Pedal. A favorite piston combination, sounding much like a small Positiv ensemble, is Diapasons 8', 4', 2 2/3', 2', and Cymbal. If anyone questions the desirability of having mixtures in an organ, and there are some persons who do, he should pay a visit to St. Thomas's Church and Riverside Church in New York City, or the Salt Lake City Tabernacle, Utah, and hear the masterpieces created by the late Donald Harrison of the Aeolian Skinner Organ Company. He realized as fully as any builder can that a mixture is a custom-designed work of art, technically perfected and fully usable with a variety of other stops in the organ.

Cymbals have a greater variety of pitches than other compound stops. They can be designed for 4', 16', or any other series of pitches. The following manual examples, sounding from the middle C key, are based on the unison:

Example No. 1 III		Example No. 2 III		Example No. 3 V		Example No. 4 V	
G⁴	2/3'	C⁴	1'	C⁵	1/2'	G⁴	2/3'
C⁴	1'	G³	1 1/3'	G⁴	2/3'	C⁴	1'
G³	1 1/3'	C³	2'	C⁴	1'	G³	1 1/3'
				G³	1 1/3'	E³	1 3/5'
				C³	2'	C³	2'

Cymbals that create unusual forms of brilliance follow. Their pitches are to be found in large organs, perhaps in an ancillary Bombarde division. All of these ranks are tuned as natural harmonics of the 8' series. They contain unusual stop-pitches heard more often in Continental Europe than in America. Only the 8/11' in No. 7 is very dissonant, and it would broaden a sweeping and very full-toned Chorus of flues or Reeds. It is the eleventh harmonic of the 8' series. The 8/9' and the 1 1/7' are useful in full organs, and sometimes as mutation stops with the 4', 8', or 2', etc. These last two unusual fractions are not nearly so dissonant when used with taste as thin-toned Viols:

Example No. 5		Example No. 6		Example No. 7		Example No. 8	
V		VI		VI		VI	
C⁴	1'	C⁵	1/2'	C⁵	1/2'	D⁴	8/9'
B♭³	1 1/7'	G⁴	2/3'	G⁴	2/3'	C⁴	1'
G³	1 1/3'	C⁴	1'	F⁴	8/11'	B♭³	1 1/7'
E³	1 3/5'	G³	1 1/3'	E⁴	4/5'	G³	1 1/3'
C³	2'	E³	1 3/5'	D⁴	8/9'	E³	1 3/5'
		C³	2'	C⁴	1'	C³	2'

These three pedal Cymbals would speak these notes from the low CCC key.

Example No. 9		Example No. 10		Example No. 11	
V		V		V	
C³	1/2'	G²	2/3'	C²	1'
G²	2/3'	C²	1'	G¹	1 1/3'
C²	1'	G¹	1 1/3'	C¹	2'
G¹	1 1/3'	C¹	2'	G	2 2/3'
C¹	2'	G	2 2/3'	C	4'

The typical mixtures in each division that follow show how versatile is this compound stop:

CHOIR: Grave II, Acuta II, *Cymbal III*
GREAT: Cornet III, Dulciana VI, *Cymbal IV*, Scharf III
SWELL: Plein Jeu V to VIII, Sesquialtera II, *Cymbal V to VII*
SOLO: Grand Chorus V to VIII, Cornet III, Harmonia Aetheria IV
ECHO: Mixture III, Viole Mixture V, *Echo Cymbal IV*
POSITIV: Fourniture IV, Carillon III, *Cymbal III to IV*
BOMBARDE: Stentor Mixture VI, *Harmonic Cymbal V*
PEDAL: Grand Mutation IX, Cornet IV, *Cymbal V*

Synonym: ZIMBEL.

DIAPASON. The most basic tone in the organ, and the most important member of the Diapason Chorus. The Diapason is a *Foundation* stop, heard in all divisions of the organ, and is the tone quality and dynamic value from which all other stops are classified. Its stop-names refer to *pitch* rather than timbre, as, in the manuals: Double Diapason 16', Diapason or Open Diapason 8', Octave 4', Super Octave or Fifteenth 2', and Super Super Octave or Twenty-second 1'. Important pedal names are: Contra Diapason or Double Diapason 32', Diapason 16', Octave 8', Fifteenth 4', Twenty-second 2', and Twenty-ninth 1'. Mutation and mixture ranks, including the Twelfth, Tierce, and Larigot, are almost always some form of Diapason (or Geigen), at least when given the above names. Hybrids with Strings or Flutes may also be included.

The *open metal* Diapason permits the organ to be an individual musical instrument, sounding a tone that is unique, but completely usable throughout the whole musical spectrum from the lowest bass to the highest treble. Other instruments lose their timbres after traversing a range of two or three octaves; the Diapason keeps its timbre throughout most of the

organ's compass. Its tone is necessary to a great deal of the organ's literature. The refreshing and vital quality of this stop as made in the pre-Bach
era is now returning in some installations, often with the *tracker action*
that permits a variety of finger accelerations and masses of hand weight
to vary the combinations of *initial partials*. These Diapasons hold the
listener's interest and do not grow tiresome. Baroque Diapasons are
moderately loud, sometimes soft, and frequently on low wind pressure.
Their pervading, rich effect on the ear seems always to come with a new
tone color. Each phrase sounds with a *new tone,* although still from the
same Diapason pipes, making the harmony and melody a thing by itself.
The ideal speed of the valve permits enough initial partials to "spit,"
attracting the attention of the ear to each note separately, and enhancing
the balances in the harmony. Smooth articulation would dull each note's
effect. The organist and listeners hear different timbres from various positions in a church from the same Diapason. But of more import is the
fact that any stop heard more loudly reveals more overtones, and therefore
gives a brighter, or less dull, impression. Initial partials will not be heard
well, say, 100 feet from the pipes because most are relatively soft and
high and of short duration.

The Diapason, by itself or with the Octave, has the characteristic
sound of the church organ, although the well-known *peal* does not depend
so much upon its tone as upon a variety of acoustical factors. Combined
with Flutes, Strings, or Reeds, the Diapason forms the base-tone upon
which limitless varieties of color can be placed. There remains the strong
feeling among organists that a combination of stops sounds better if it is
being transported to the listener's ear by the ground tone of a Diapason.
This factor may depend upon easy identification of pitch and the moderate
overtone development. Physically, it derives from the fact that higher
pitches and weaker sounds actually travel as mitigations of the *heaviest
fundamental*. The Diapason gives a sense of security, musically speaking,
with its firm pitch and non-fluttering overtones. Diapasons need not be
dull and boomy to fulfill these functions. The modern trend towards a
shining, clean, luminous timbre does not impair the functions of the
Diapason in any way; rather, it enhances it for all combinational work.
The *English Diapason,* sometimes so labeled on a draw knob, inclines
towards a silvery, ringing sound that must be heard to be fully appreciated. It sometimes serves as the Choir Diapason. The *Italian Principal*
sounds from a moderate-scaled rank with narrow mouths, making a somewhat fluty and small-voiced timbre. A few examples are very large-scaled.
Many players look upon it as an ideal 4′, 2′, or 1′ element in ensembles.

Theoretically, Flutes, Strings, Reeds, mixtures, and mutation stops are
merely supplements to the Diapason tone. Without the Diapason these
groups of stops would lose much of their usefulness. The Flutes would
become dull, the Strings would sound dissonant, and the Reeds would
grow strange to the ear. Other stops would have no reason to exist, and
all the organ would sound novel. The ear automatically goes back to its
memory of the Diapason's pitch and tone quality to be re-oriented. Even the

volume of the Diapason is a standard for other stops. The average Diapason sounds at f.

The steady, smooth roll of sound that comes from the Diapason or Principal has been so well devised by many centuries of builders that the ear finds in it an ideal tone. It is midway between dull and bright; it is a big tone that is easy to hear; its dozen or so harmonics cleanly state the pitch for both singers and listener; its harmonics are not strong enough to destroy tone quality or mask the singer's voice. Especially in the ecclesiastical function is the Diapason important. It sounds sober and a little formal, yet remains animated and striking in tone. The well-made specimens are always *resonant*. The fifty or so dimensional features that must be adjusted by the designer, voicer, and finisher all contribute to the rich fabric of sound so satisfying to listeners. The single essence that attracts one to this peculiar timbre is *balance between its partials*. Other stops do not have this almost unbelievable balance; they emphasize some harmonic at the others' expense, as the Viols the fourth, or big Flutes the first, or the Reeds several at once. This subtle beauty of well-balanced resonances is, unfortunately, very easily wiped out by walls and ceiling.

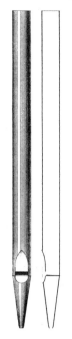

Diapason or Principal showing famous "bayleaf" shape of lip, developed for beauty in visible pipes but not necessary for the true tone.

A particular plaster or angle of reflection can be "tuned" just right to absorb that parcel of the eleventh or sixteenth harmonic, for instance, which the designer tried so hard to place in the tone. Overly absorbent rooms make the Diapasons fluty in effect. The same rooms also permit the bass to overbalance the middle and treble ranges. Reverberant rooms do not make the Diapason brighter than it naturally is. Of all stops the Diapasons are the easiest to mutate, because their valuable overtones taper so quickly in loudness in proportion to their prime tone.

The Diapason is considered a dull tone. It has fewer than one-quarter the overtones of the Tuba Magna, and one-half those in loud open Flutes. It is therefore a source of contrast with bright stops. It is voiced to display its tones best in chords, which, of course, aggregate harmonics into another sound from that heard from just one note. In fact, each chord-pattern carries with it, simply by the notes that it contains, a sort of "formant" for the tone color. The Diapason displays these patterns of notes better than other stops. Brilliance is achieved by building up a "vertical" façade of notes, perhaps also using more notes per chord or couplers. With Octaves, mutations, and mixtures, this is the *Diapason Chorus*. Harmonics in each rank in the Chorus do not intrude on those in a higher rank. The *basic* Chorus is formed as:

Manual Chorus		Pedal Chorus	
Fifteenth	2′	Fifteenth	4′
Twelfth (Nasard)	2 2/3′	Twelfth (Nasard)	5 1/3′
Octave	4′	Octave	8′
Diapason (unison)	8′	Diapason (unison)	16′

On the manuals the 1 3/5′, 1 1/3′, and 1′ may be added. On the pedals the 3 1/5′, 2 2/3′, and 2′ will provide a tone with more point. Many other higher-pitched ranks, mostly in mixtures, exist to supplement the tones of the Diapasons on both manuals and pedals. The 8′ Diapason never masks its 4′ Octave in either brightness or loudness. The 4′ Octave should never take the listener's attention from the notes being played. In the Diapason Chorus each *pitch* (as a single *pipe, note* in a chord, or *partial*) is a tonal entity for the ear to hear and analyze in relation to the whole sound. There are countless varieties of blend in the Chorus, but each blend should establish a *unity of tone* in the mind of the listener, not a series of stops and notes, or a mass of tones, as heard from the brighter stops. The true pleasure of listening to the Diapason Chorus* comes from being able to follow the interweaving of the integral pitches with the melody and harmony. Beauty of infinite variety can be achieved only when the parts can all be cleanly distinguished. An amorphous mass of partials is string-like.

The meshing together of the ranks in the Diapason Chorus is accomplished by duplication and reinforcement of one rank's harmonics by the next rank's harmonics. All harmonics are, of course, not duplicated, but enough to bind together the ranks. Since the harmonics are cut off by the voicer before they become dissonant with the notes of the scale (that is with the lower harmonics of another rank also), the accumulation of all harmonics never reaches the point of discord heard even in a mild Viola; it is simply *a huge vertical tower of on-pitch harmonics.* Such a shining and clean façade of tone has power to arrest the attention of the listener to an even greater extent than the loudest Bombarde Chorus. It is not a climax sound, but it is for a steady diet of the ear the ideal sound. It demands that the listener *think* about the notes of the music: the harmony, melody, and timbre. This sound is accomplished by keeping the organ in tune, drawing reasonably complete combinations, and avoiding types of Diapasons (like those that are too stringy) that make the ear lose interest in them as components in the structure of tone.

Since organists frequently add the *octave* and *sub-octave* couplers, particularly in the smaller organs, to the Diapason Chorus, a list is given below of the aggregate number of stop-pitches heard from only one rank each of 8′, 4′, 2 2/3′, and 2′ Principals with these couplers:

			4′		2′	1 1/3′	1′
	8′		4′		2′		
	8′		4′	2 2/3′			
16′	8′	5 1/3′	4′				

*The Diapason Chorus is a work of artistic judgment. As in oil painting and all other art forms, there is not one ideal to be achieved. Each creator of the *Chorus* will produce the tonal effects he thinks right.

Notice the *Copula* effect of the three 4′ pitches of Principals. Increased complexity of tone for the ear to analyze would follow the addition of a IV-rank Fourniture of, say, 4′, 2 2/3′, 2′, and 1 1/3′. The organist must realize that it is of the greatest importance to understand the principles of harmony in order to make a pleasing and purposeful improvisation from complex tones. *Each note* added to the music brings a new timbre (tone quality) of its own. Thus chord construction must be studied to show the Principals' most marked effects. Pedal notes must be considered too.

Since the Diapasons have a very limited number of partials (most of which can be called true *harmonics*), the upper part of the train where distinct dissonance exists is not reached in their tones. In the average Diapason of, say, sixteen partials, the lower eight are almost all on the notes of the scale. The upper eight are mostly off the notes of the scale, but these are extremely soft compared to the lower eight. Perhaps just the lowest three, two, or even one harmonic may be audible when consciously listened for, but all present affect the tone to some extent. In a String stop the dissonant partials may account for one-half the effect of the timbre; in a Diapason or stopped Flute the dissonant partials may account for even less than one per cent of the timbre. The 8′, 4′, 2 2/3′, and 2′ ranks duplicate the pitches of the lowest four harmonics in just the 8′ rank (the 2 2/3′ being slightly off true pitch). It can be seen that the brighter Diapason is brighter precisely because it has the three upper of these components louder in proportion to the 8′ component. Additional higher-pitched components also exist, but not all are duplicated as individual ranks each with its own pitch. Pitches of stops are determined mostly by the harmonics. The Diapason, being a cylindrical flue, emphasizes to some extent in each pipe the odd-numbered harmonics, not always noticeably, however.

Unenclosure is to be preferred for the main flue Chorus of an organ, except in a small residence or church organ. A prominent position in the chamber is also desirable. These factors keep the delicate and easily absorbed harmonics intact for the ears of the audience. Structurally, the Diapason is an open, round, metal pipe of low mouth cut-up. It has fairly thick walls in even the middle register, and pipe metal with a great deal of lead is frequently used. Recently the trend has been to the spotted metals, which appear with about thirty-five percent tin in their alloys. Such Diapasons have a better blend, although they may not be louder. Rolled zinc is preferable in only the 32′ octave, where overtones are fewer in number. The 16′ rank on manuals or pedals and the 8′ manual rank may also be either pipe metal or spotted metal. If several 8′ ranks are in a division, they can be graduated in loudness and brightness. The higher pitches are usually all spotted metal or even pure tin in a few cases. Mouth proportions vary with scales and wind pressures, but the average cut-up (that is, mouth-height in proportion to mouth-width) is around one-fifth to one-fourth. Higher mouths give fewer overtones and more fundamental. They also give less power in the higher overtone range. The upper lip is built to be rigid in order to prevent spurious tones from entering the complex. Harmonic bridges are found in most deep pipes to hasten and also steady the lower-pitched harmonics. Ears may or may not be used, but a few builders use them to steady the volume of sound and also to hold bridges when present. The small treble pipes never have bridges or ears because their small air columns speak so quickly that steadiness is not a question. Movable tin-plated steel collars at the pipes' tops tune the pipes, upward to flatten, downward to sharpen. Slotting makes some harmonics louder, giving the Keraulophone coloring, or even a stringy sound. The CCC metal pipe ranges in scale from 15 to 7 inches, usually larger for the same pitch on the pedals. The CC manual pipe varies between 8 and 5 inches, with 6.25 to 5.25 an average. Secret scales are sometimes brought from Europe, but most of the American builders prefer to use their own. A full supply of wind is necessary for that "plump" resonant tone so much admired. Classical and Baroque instruments may use very low pressures to give their Diapasons less-forced harmonics on truer pitches. These also have somewhat more pronounced initial harmonics, owing to shallow nicking or no nicking at all, that increase the degree of blend with all stops and also with the flue Chorus. Very loud tone can be forced from Diapasons with double languids, the space between the languids being connected to an outside opening in the pipe's back.

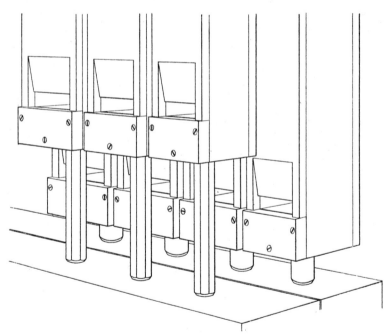

A Diapason 16′ showing manner of building up pipes to ensure that the long sound waves will not be hampered in expanding from the mouths.

Any degree of loudness, irrespective of brightness (many overtones), can be voiced into a Diapason, and vice versa. Diapasons that move the huge volumes of air in a cathedral with a high ceiling need more wind and larger scales than in small churches. Actually, both Diapasons can be given a voicing that will make them sound with the same loudness and brightness. The prime factors affecting the overtone structure of a Diapason of any pitch (and all *flue* pipes) are *scale, cut-up* of mouth, *wind pressure,* material, width of mouth in proportion to circumference, and sharpness of the upper lip. The first three factors outrank all others. Other factors that are important are nicking of the languid and inside the lower lip, shape of the pipe's body, and position of the upper lip in relation to the stream of wind coming from the foot. Theoretically, upon raising the wind pressure, the mouth must be raised too to maintain like timbre. Also, wider-mouthed and higher-pitched pipes speak more quickly; this is especially true of mixtures. All of these physical considerations color the many ranks of flues included in every organ. Diapasons are halved in diameter at the fourteenth to sixteenth pipe (counted from any lower pipe). By knowing on which pipe the halving occurs, the builder can figure out the dimensions of a whole rank of pipes of even tone, if he has one sample pipe.

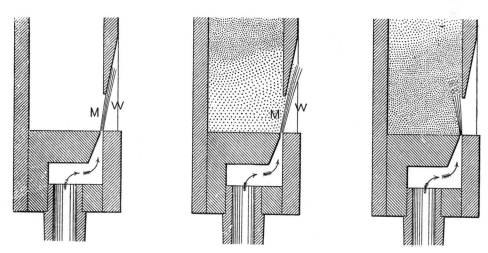

Flue pipe (either open or stopped) forming a sound wave. Left, wind-reed (or "wind-sheet"), W, is just beginning to disturb equilibrium of pressures in the enclosed air column by blowing a little outside the mouth, M; center, wind-reed vacuums air from lower portion of pipe, forming *condensation* of wave; right, atmospheric pressure forces some air back into body of pipe, forming *rarefaction* of wave.

The *Schulze* Diapason, named for one of the early English builders (who had come from Germany), is still venerated by builders and organists alike because of its ideal tone. Several magnificent examples of this Diapason are still to be heard in England. Voicers have sought to imitate its tone for many years. Careful measurements, comparison by ear, analysis of its harmonics, and plain guessing have all failed to make an exact copy. The formant of the windchest as well as the pipes themselves seems to contribute much to the tone quality. The tone is animated, "vital," and seems brighter than the best of the regular Diapasons. Undoubtedly this Stradivarius holds much the same secrets of tonal eminence as the famous violin: a particular pattern of *internal resonances* which vitalizes the ear without actually being louder or more brilliant with overtones. Physically, both the violin and the Diapason jump into vibration *in fewer thousandths of a second* than other specimens of their kind. This shortening of the initial period and the steady harmonic structures account for part of the tonal difference. Other factors may still remain secrets. Noel A. Bonavia-Hunt of England has had extensive experience in building and voicing Diapasons of the Schulze design. He relates many interesting facts in the case in his unusually complete book on the organ, *The Modern British Organ.* See Bibliography, DOUBLE DIAPASON, FIFTEENTH, GEIGEN DIAPASON, OCTAVE, TWELFTH, WOOD DIAPASON. Synonym: OPEN DIAPASON.

DIAPASON MAGNA. A large-scale, loud *solo* Diapason of 8′ manual pitch, sounding less dull in tone than the average large-scale Diapason. It is somewhat against the logic inherent in the Diapason's harmonic structure to say that a *solo* Diapason can be voiced. *Diapason* means a firm fundamental and only a modicum of harmonics, usually fewer than twenty. Loud Diapasons can, of course, be made for special buildings or choruses, but the brilliant tone (many harmonics) of a solo flue, if given to a Diapason, at once classes it as a kind of Stentorphone or loud open Tibia. Nevertheless, the names are convenient, especially in the larger organs which have to have a variety of stop-names. Following is a classification usable for louder Diapasons:

Chorus Diapasons	Solo Diapasons
Grand Diapason	Diapason Magna
Major Diapason	Diapason Phonon
Stentor Diapason	Diapason Sonora

Interchange of these names is inevitable, of course, and just *Diapason* is always usable. This stop is less bright than the Diapason Sonora and Stentorphone (classified as a Flute), nor is it so loud as they are. Any of these Diapasons or the Stentorphone can be flared outward towards their tops to build up even-numbered components — that is, a fuller tonality. Slotting has been seen also in this type of flue, particularly in very large organs. It provides additional components, giving either the Diapason-Horn or the Diapason-String approach. The Diapason Magna may sound alone, be a base-tone for Reeds, or combine. See DIAPASON, DIAPASON SONORA.

DIAPASON PHONON. A large-scale and loud Diapason at 8′, rarely 4′, on the manuals, and sometimes at 16′ on the pedals. A roll of pipe metal around the outside and inside of the upper lip of this rank gives it a pervasive, dull, round tone that is unfit for use as a base-tone for any type of Diapason Chorus. It varies in scale and volume among the many examples still playing in organs, but this stop cannot be heard leaving or entering the chords, rather it sounds like an aggregate of harmonics in *one note.*

The Phonon is unfit for the music of the polyphonic school, hymn tunes, or the soprano-alto-tenor-bass type of music. The normal Diapasons are designed to make every note of the chords stand out individually, yet blend into the whole sound; this the Phonon cannot do. On the solo manuals of theater, residence, and concert organs the Phonon finds its proper place. Its big, round, very resonant tone can be a temporary relief from too many Trumpets and Gambas, and even Tibias, following along the notes of the melody. It is a stop that often produces an intense emotional effect. It is a product of that school of organ building which early in the present century believed in accenting some particular harmonic element in a tone in order to satisfy the organists' desire for still another 8' unison solo rank. In this particular stop the fundamental receives much of the physical energy that might go into a reasonable train of lower overtones, as is heard in the Diapason Magna and Diapason Sonora, both solo stops. See DIAPASON.

DIAPASON SONORA. A solo Diapason of unusually loud tone and large scale, at 8' on the manuals. Compared to the Diapason Magna, this Diapason is more brilliant with harmonics, although not quite to the point of being a Stentorphone. Its intense and dominating fundamental is accompanied by a whole series of harmonics, which make it a solo stop of prime magnitude. It is an excellent base-tone for the Tubas and can firm the pitch of any other stop added to it. It is at home alike on the theater and concert organs and the big church instruments, although perhaps not under this name. It is not primarily a chorus Diapason, its tone being too brilliant for proper blending with the Octave, Twelfth, etc. See DIAPASON, DIAPASON MAGNA.

DIAPHONE. A valvular Foundation stop of 16' or 8' on the manuals, and 64', 32', or 16' pitch on the pedals. It was invented near the turn of the century by Robert Hope-Jones, who is said by several writers on the organ to have heard a loose pallet jump into vibration, making a magnificent and deep bass tone. The placing of a resonator on the top of such a pallet does much to control the frequency (pitch) of the vibration, and also steadies its volume. Diaphones have been made ever since, and placed in all types of organs except those that imitate the pipe structures and tones of the early period of Continental building. The Diaphone just escapes the criticism leveled by some against stops that speak with a pronounced ground tone (fundamental) but without sufficient overtones for blend. The chief function of the Diaphone in almost every model built is to furnish that which no other bass stop can furnish: a completely satisfying, really profound bass tone between CCCCC and C^1, not diminished in volume by the tendency of all *big* vibrating bodies to jump quickly into their octaves. Being essentially a *bass* stop with a specialized function to perform makes the Diaphone unique among bass ranks. Onto its heavy roll of tone can be placed sufficient 32', 16', or 8' ranks to unify its effect with any combination of stops.

The manual Diaphones seem to have no particular advantage over the bigger flue stops. Because they have a higher frequency of vibration, there is greater probability of their going off pitch. John Compton, of England, did a great deal of experimenting with the tone qualities of Diaphones and also did much to improve them mechanically. He was able to produce a Tibia, Horn, Diapason, and String, which represent all the four families of organ stops. Many organs built by his factory have noteworthy examples of Diaphones of various pitches in them. Theater and concert organs in America also have had many examples, the long pipes sometimes laid horizontally above the ceiling. Splendid, indeed, was the theater organ of the 1920s which had a 32′ stop. There was no doubt about the organist's ability to produce thunder from such a pedal! Many church instruments have had this pedal stop, the congregation no doubt believing they were hearing a Diapason of deep tone, for a great many Diaphones are designed to supplement the flue chorus of an organ, even being called *Diaphonic Diapason*, which is somewhat of a contradiction in terms.

In the case of the 16′ pedal rank, the listener (even the organist) could probably not tell the difference between a Diapason 16′ and a Diaphone 16′ unless it were of the very loud variety, since many Diaphones are voiced simply to support the ensembles of the organ without a spectacular roll of sound. It is almost always in the 32′ that a Diaphone identifies itself to the listener, and then usually in the largest organs. The spectacular, thunderous variety make their sound from very long, heavy-walled (three-inch) pipes of maple or firwood, perhaps under twenty inches of wind pressure. Most Diaphone pipes, like reed pipes, are formed as tapered tubes that act as (mitigated) exponential horns. The inverted-pyramidal pipes of the Diaphone are usually square, but they may be rectangular in cross-section to enable them to sit closer together.

The advantages of the Diaphone are chiefly in the bass range. The Diaphone speaks very promptly, even the low CCCCC pipe of the Midmer Losh Organ in the Convention Hall in Atlantic City, New Jersey. A flue pipe of this profundity, either stopped or open, would require at least one or two seconds to compact the air and eject its sound wave. Another advantage is the percussive effect on the ear of this stop. *Each* sound wave, and there are 16.3 per second at the low CCCC of the 32′, is made more suddenly than in any flue or Reed stop, even the Bombarde. This percussive compacting of the air-wave sounds on the ear with an unexpected vigor, enabling it to penetrate any other musical effect known. Evenness and smoothness of voice keep the Diaphone from sounding rough, even by itself. Carrying power and purity of fundamental are also advantages. See CONTRA DIAPHONE. Synonym: DIAPHONIC DIAPASON.

DIAPHONIC DIAPASON. See CONTRA DIAPHONE, DIAPHONE.

DIAPHONIC HORN. A loud foundation stop of 8′ on the manuals, and 16′ on the pedals, invented by Robert Hope-Jones. Its tone has considerably more overtone structure than the Diaphone. Its pipes are inverted-conical and the flexible spring of the pallet is adjusted to impart some of its partial vibrations to the air column of the resonator. See DIAPHONE.

DOLCAN. A very soft but distinctly voiced Foundation stop of 16', 8', or 4' on the manuals, resembling the Dulciana in tone quality, but much softer although a little brighter in tone, owing to its inverted-conical open spotted metal pipes of small scale. It is not so soft as the Flauto Dolcissimo or Vox Angelica, nor is it up to the dynamic level of the Echo Dulciana. This beautiful and sedate tone may be used for background playing or as an accompaniment to the softest of stops, like the Corno d'Amore, Echo Open Flute, Viola d'Amore, or Echo Gamba. It can mutate the Vox Humana's timbre or dilute a soft String céleste. See DULCIANA.

DOLCAN CÉLESTE. An unusually soft Foundation stop made from Dolcans of 8', one *normal* in pitch, the other either slightly *flat* or *sharp*. It is even softer than the Dulciana Céleste, and, like that stop, forms a useful accompaniment or background effect

Dolcan pipe at tenor C. This inverted-conical pipe sounds all of the harmonic train, giving a little more strength to the even-numbered harmonics than a cylindrical pipe.

for other stops or the softer portions of the church service, such as a prayer. It is usually tuned to undulate quite slowly to maintain its timbre. See CÉLESTE, DOLCAN, DULCIANA CÉLESTE.

DOLCE. A soft or moderately soft Foundation stop of 16', 8', or 4' manual pitch. This near-Diapason is not so soft as the Dulciana or Dolce Flute, but it is softer than the Gemshorn or many Quintatens. It is never string-like, although a great many partials come from its inverted-conical open metal pipes. While it is not a Corno Dolce, the horn-like sound may come from certain specimens, and the luminous, clear effect of the Gemshorn is impossible to this shape of pipe. However, a few builders make their Dolces cylindrical or slightly conical in form, thereby increasing the second harmonic and decreasing the warm, high-pitched even-numbered harmonics. This is an ideal accompaniment for many solo stops, like the Philomela or 'Cello. It is a soft solo voice and a source of bright tone for other soft stops that may be dull as well. The 8' Dolce and the 8' 'Cello together make a beautiful solo String of unusual "plumpness" and broadness of tone. The hybrid *'Cello-Dolce* is also a useful solo and ensemble stop, but rarely heard. The Dolce forms whole choirs of stops like the Dulciana. A few ranks are of wood. See DOLCAN, DOLCE CORNET, DOLCE FLUTE, DOLCETTE, DOLCISSIMO.

DOLCE CORNET. A soft compound manual stop made from several ranks of specially designed Dolce pipes, the fifth-sounding being softer than the octave-sounding. This is a useful accompaniment and timbre-creating stop. It may also be designed as a solo stop. Middle C speaks these notes:

Example No. 1	Example No. 2	Example No. 3	Example No. 4
III	III	IV	IV
C^3 2′	E^3 1 3/5′	C^3 2′	C^4 1′
G^2 2 2/3′	C^3 2′	G^2 2 2/3′	G^3 1 1/3′
C^2 4′	G^2 2 2/3′	C^2 4′	C^3 2′
		C^1 8′	C^2 4′

See DOLCE.

DOLCE FLUTE. A very soft open metal (or wooden) Flute of 8′ or 4′ on the manuals, traditionally made from slightly inverted-conical pipes, like the Dolce, but usually seen nowadays as slightly conical open thick pipes of spotted metal. The mouth is very narrow to soften the tone and dampen some harmonics of the train. It is less likely to suggest the string-like timbre than is the Spitzflöte. See DOLCE. Synonyms: FLAUTO DOLCE, FLÛTE DOUCE.

DOLCETTE. A very soft Foundation stop of 4′ manual pitch, voiced to give a diminutive octave of Dolce tone. At this pitch the tone is simply an overlay of soft partials to be added to other stops, but played an octave lower than normal it sounds as a type of Dolce. See DOLCE, DOLCETTE FLUTE.

DOLCETTE FLUTE. A very soft Flute of 4′ manual pitch, voiced to give the octave of the Dolce Flute. This stop is very delicate in tone and easily absorbed by another stop. It adds a little timbre to the Vox Humana, Dolce Flute, Dolcan, or Dulciana Céleste. See DOLCE FLUTE, DOLCETTE.

DOLCISSIMO. An extremely soft Foundation stop of 8′ manual pitch, voiced to give a tone of unusual delicacy and sweetness. It is so soft that it may be called a *Vox Angelica*. This *Echo Dolce* tone comes from inverted-conical or conical pipes of metal, although wood may easily be used for this accompaniment or ensemble stop. See DOLCE, DOLCE FLUTE, FLAUTO DOLCISSIMO.

DOPPELFLÖTE. A wooden *stoppered* Flute of 16′, 8′, or 4′ manual pitch, with two mouths per pipe, hence *Double Flute*. The 4′ rank is especially valued by organists, and is most useful as a Solo Organ combinational stop.

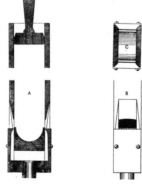

Doppelflöte with two mouths on opposite sides of pipe. A is interior cross-section, B is front view showing a mouth on the narrow side, and C is a transverse section through mouth area. Notice large wind-way in foot.

The tone resulting from this unusual construction is one of marked fullness and some penetration, but not with the heavy effect of the Bourdon. There is a well-rounded, strong, liquid timbre in this Flute that seems to suggest the idea of motion in its notes. It is not a bright tone, since it is generated in stopped pipes, but it is easy to hear efficiently, and it is of marked intensity even in the highest pitches. It is a solo stop at any pitch, and also an adjunct to any other solo stop, such as the Rohr-flöte, 'Cello, or Major Open Flute. It fills out without dulling these and other tones. Some specimens have heavy walls, and mouths on adjacent sides. An open Doppelflöte may be called a *Seraphonflöte*. ―

DOPPELGEDECKT. A stoppered wooden Flute of 16' or 8' on the manuals, of smaller dimension than most Doppelflötes, and also possessing two mouths per pipe. This is a rectangular Flute in cross-section, the mouths being on the narrow sides. This creates a deeper and softer tone than that of the Doppelflöte. Nor is the tone so full and liquid. It has more of the ensemble function, combining with one or even several other stops to give a strong fundamental and a timbre of more prominent dimensions. See DOPPELFLÖTE.

DOPPELROHRBORDUN. A half-covered Flute of 16', 8', or 4' on the manuals and pedals, resembling the Doppelrohrgedeckt in structure, but with a heavier and louder tone than that stop. It contributes fundamental prime tone and a few of the lower-pitched overtones to any other stops without imparting character of its own to the combination. It is usable with both solo and ensemble stops, and the pedal combinations. All of the above pitches can be used to build up prominence in the pedals, perhaps from one rank of pipes. Scale and volume vary in this stop. See DOPPEL-ROHRFLÖTE.

DOPPELROHRFLÖTE. A half-covered solo and ensemble Flute of 8' or 4' on the manuals, having the physical features of both the *Doppelflöte* and the *Rohrflöte*. The double mouths of the Doppelflöte emit a strong fundamental and a few of the lower-pitched odd-numbered harmonics. The rohr of the Rohrflöte gives a soft overlay of even-numbered harmonics, making this timbre just a little "open." This large-scale wooden rank is really a stopped Flute in tone. However, it approaches some distinction in tonality by its liquid and pervading voice, which is moderately loud. It is one of the most useful of solo voices and can also fill out the timbres and firm the pitches of many other flue stops. See DOPPELFLÖTE, ROHRFLÖTE.

DOPPELROHRGEDECKT. A half-covered wooden Flute of 8' or 4' on the manuals, and 16' or 8' on the pedals, yielding a tone of greater harmonic texture but less volume of sound than the Doppelrohrflöte, because it is of smaller scale. It is also softer and of smaller scale than the Doppel-rohrbordun. It is not of a liquid and penetrating tone but can sound by itself as a placid and dulcet solo voice at either 8' or 4'. With other flue stops it has the same function as the Doppelrohrbordun. It can be designed in a great variety of tone colors and volumes, some of the Echo form, others quite loud. Its pipes have both rohrs and the double-mouthed structure, making a stopped tone that is round but not dull. See DOPPELROHRBORDUN, DOPPELROHRFLÖTE.

DOPPELSPITZFLÖTE. An open wood (or metal) Flute of pyramidal shape, at 16′, 8′, or 4′ on the manuals. There are two mouths in each pipe of this stop. It is moderately soft and has elements of both the Flute and String in it. The lower-pitched overtones are made brighter than the higher-pitched, and the fundamental prime tone is noticeable. This is an excellent binding tone between Flutes and Strings, and Diapasons and Strings. It has the true Copula function. It is also an accompaniment stop. The metal specimens are a little brighter and easier to make than the wooden. See SPITZFLÖTE.

DOUBLE BASS. See CONTRABASS, CONTRA VIOLONE.

DOUBLE DIAPASON. The bass of the unison Diapasons on manuals and pedals, at 16′ manual pitch, and 32′ pedal pitch. The term *Double* indicates that a stop sounds an octave lower than the unison pitch. The timbre of this stop is like that in the unisons, although any bass tone seems less pointed because its whole series of overtones is limited in number.

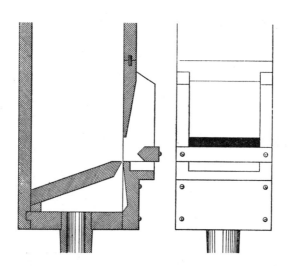

Pipe of the 32′ Pedal Double Diapason. The interior view at the left shows a bridge. At the right an exterior view shows same bridge from the front.

The bass overtones are in the range of pitch where the bigger air columns cannot form them in so great a number as in the middle range. It is for this reason that the Contra Fagotto and Contra Bombarde on the pedals are so useful. Each of these Reeds can give some added definition of the pitch plus some timbre. The fundamental becomes heavier in both the 32′ and 16′ Diapasons as the musical scale is descended, causing fewer overtones to be heard. If the scale of the pipes is larger than average, the fundamental may sound with an unusual impact upon the ear. If it is smaller than average, the string-like overtones may begin to make themselves plain. Indeed, many Double Diapasons are purposely designed to inject some of the string-like sound into the bass because it is clean in pitch, holds the harmony well, and is somewhat pointed in tone. If a deep pedal String stop is also present, there is less need to do this. Smaller organs that have less variety in their bass stops are most likely to be given these *hybrid* tones by the builders. Higher mouths and larger scales may make this deep stop a little fluty.

The Double Diapason is the proper bass for the Chorus of Diapasons on the pedals. It is not always heard, however, for the Gemshorn, Flute Ouverte, Fagotto, Bombarde, or Bourdon may be used. At the lowest pedal pitches these stops do not damage the tone, since the ear hears deep pitch with less precision in frequency and volume than in the middle range. The harmonics of these stops (except the Bourdon) are on the same pitches as those of the Double Diapason. The Fagotto 16′ is preferred by some organists on the Great because of its easy blend and clean pitch, especially in chords. But a very large organ has use for the Double Diapason. Traditional names for the *sub-unison* series of Diapasons follow:

Manual		Pedal	
Octave Diapason	4′	Octave Diapason	8′
Quint Diapason	5 1/3′	Quint Diapason	10 2/3′
Diapason (unison)	8′	Diapason (unison)	16′
Double Diapason	16′	Double Diapason	32′

The sub-octave coupler cannot be depended upon to add the lower pitches for all notes in a chord, because keys depressed beyond the range of one octave may duplicate orders to the pipes. Very large organs have complete Diapason Choruses for all of the important series of stop-pitches. This requires a great deal of space and a tremendous outlay of funds. The Midmer Losh organ designed by Senator Emerson Richards for the Atlantic City Convention Hall has the most complete set of Diapason Choruses in the world. Its 33,112 pipes and 22 tonal divisions are controlled by a console of seven manuals and 1250 stop keys. The Great Organ alone has eleven 8′ Diapason ranks. The low CCCC open zinc pipe of one of its cylindrical Double Diapasons is 38.5 feet long and 24 inches in diameter, made from metal 5/8 of an inch thick. It is unmitered and stands at the left of the stage.

In the John Wanamaker organ in Philadelphia is the largest Double Diapason pipe in America.* It too sounds at low CCCC; it is 32 x 27 inches in cross-section, three inches thick, and over 32 feet long, and required 1735 pounds of sugar pine in its building. The Atlantic City organ has *ten* 32′ ranks, and the John Wanamaker organ has *eight* 32′ ranks. Such large Diapasons as these are needed to move the hundreds of tons of air in the great buildings in which these organs play. Most Double Diapasons

---

*Two other noteworthy examples of this stop are in the Austin organ in First Methodist, Asbury Park, N. J., and the Longwood Gardens (Kennett Square, Pa.) organ, built by the Aeolian Company, rebuilt by Moller. Both form excellent acoustic 64′s.

are designed on a less grand scale. See DIAPASON, GROSSFLÖTE. Synonyms: CONTRA PRINCIPAL, DOUBLE OPEN DIAPASON, SUB PRINCIPAL.

DOUBLE FLUTE. A manual 16′ Flute, and pedal 32′ Flute, of either open or stopped construction. The manual stop may be a *Doppelflöte*.

DOUBLE GEMSHORN. A Foundation stop of 16′ manual pitch, and 32′ pedal pitch. The 32′ manual form also exists in a few organs. It is the proper bass for the Gemshorn Chorus, and its luminous, clean-toned chord of lower-pitched harmonics is sometimes preferred to the Double Diapason of heavier quality. It blends unusually well with all manual combinations. Its long pipes are conical, rather than cylindrical like the Diapasons, but are sometimes made from wood. See GEMSHORN. Synonyms: GEMSHORN-BASS, GROSSGEMSHORN.

DOUBLE MELODIA. An open wood Flute of 16′ on the manuals, with a tone that resembles in its upper compass the manual Melodia. From CCC to CC it becomes quite heavy in some examples, and loses character. Since this is a bigger rank than the unison, it is not so mellow and does not approach the imitative quality. See MELODIA.

DOUBLE OBOE. See CONTRA OBOE.

DOUBLE OPEN DIAPASON. See DOUBLE DIAPASON.

DOUBLE SALICIONAL. A bass String of 16′ on the manuals, and 32′ on the pedals. The 32′ rank is not so common in organs, and may be known by another name, such as *Contra Violone* or *Bass String*.* This stop is less keen and loud than the unison Salicional, but more subdued than the Gamba tribe. It has fewer uses than a Contra Viola, which is really string-like but quite mild in tone. See SALICIONAL.

DOUBLE STRING. A stop-name used in a few unit organs to indicate a 16′ manual String. It is likely to be orchestral in voicing. This name is also used for the *Bass Violin* stop. See CONTRABASS, CONTRA VIOLONE.

DOUBLE TRUMPET. See CONTRA TRUMPET.

DOUBLETTE. A manual stop composed of two ranks of Diapason pipes, of different pitches, and voiced to create timbre for any flue chorus. The two ranks are designed to sound well with each other and to augment each others' tones. They may or may not have separate stop controls. They may be extended throughout their compasses without a pitch break. A variety of dynamic values is used for examples of this dual stop. This name may indicate a Fifteenth (Super Octave) 2′ with a very bright tone.

*No confusion between manual and pedal names of stops should occur if it is remembered that for the *same name* the pedal pitch-indication is a number twice as large as that used for the manual pitch-indication. There are two invariables among the many factors in stop-names: the *definition* of the name itself and the names of the *notes* of the scale as is indicated by their pitches. For example: a Salicional always has a characteristic tone quality, and the note called CC always has 65.41 cycles in a second.

Some examples are listed below, sounding from middle C:

Example No. 1	Example No. 2	Example No. 3	Example No. 4
II	II	II	II
C^3 2'	C^4 1'	G^2 2 2/3'	C^3 2'
C^2 4'	C^3 2'	C^2 4'	G^2 2 2/3'

No. 1 and No. 2 are octave-sounding ranks. No. 4, sometimes called a *Grave Mixture*, is probably the oldest pitch combination known in a compound stop. Doublettes for the pedals also exist, like 5 1/3' and 4', or 10 2/3' and 8'.

DOUBLE TUBA. See CONTRA TUBA.

DOUBLE VOX HUMANA. On the manuals, this 16' pitch of the Vox Humana is usually seen only in the larger theater organs, perhaps with a whole Vox Humana chorus of 16', 8', and 4'. Other organs depend upon the sub-octave coupler to obtain it at the 16' pitch. The 16' pedal Vox Humana should be referred to simply as *Vox Humana*. It is useful as a timbre creator with the lighter-toned flue ranks. Without the tremulant, this example of the Schnarrwerk of the short-resonator Reeds is useful in creating a contrasting tone in countermelody. It may sound alone or with another stop on manuals or pedals. This thin, covered, somewhat plaintive tone has the same functions as the Rankett and Regal. At this pitch the less guttural timbre is easier to blend. See RANKETT, REGAL, VOX HUMANA.

DULCET. A soft Dulciana at 4' on the manuals, intended to supply the octave form of the Dulciana or Dolcan. It may be called a *Dolcette* or *Echo Octave*. With both 8' and 4' Dulciana tone available on one manual, the organist has a very valuable accompaniment or background combination. With or without couplers these two small-scaled diminutive Foundation ranks make a beautiful light-toned sound that is especially effective in chords. They may be played in contrast with other stops, like solo Flutes or Strings. The addition of a soft stop, such as the Harmonika, Echo Open Flute, or Dolce Flute, makes the combination even more useful. Soft accompaniment stops, which are often diminutive Foundation tones, are one class of which the American organ might have more. The Dulciana and Dulcet are soft, easy to hear, very satisfying as tone qualities, and carry some distance. They also blend, as accompaniments, with all stops. See DULCIANA.

DULCIAN. An imitative Reed of 16', 8', or 4' on the manuals, and 32' or 16' on the pedals, in timbre a reedy but not piercing tone, in most examples neutral rather than nasal, whining, rattling, or thin. Probably the most marked effect on the ear of this stop is simply a reedy brilliance. Capping the short pipes seems to impart a distinction to the tone. Some builders do this; others leave the pipes' tops open or partly capped. Capping of course dampens many of the highest and weakest higher partials, making the tone less brilliant. This Reed is less windy and piping than the Rankett, more brilliant than the Musette or Oboe, and not so loud as most Regals. A few Dulcians have a slight amount of metallic glitter in their tones, and some even an interesting little twang-like effect that sounds just when the reed is actuated. Many examples are quite soft;

others are inclined towards *mf*.

(It should be noted that even in this short description there are at least one hundred different varieties of Dulcian tone implied. In order to form a clear mental pattern of this tone it would be necessary actually to hear a Dulcian stop in an organ, perhaps several for comparison. Word-descriptions of any pitch, dynamic value, or tone color are inadequate unless accompanied by the aural experience.)

The functions of the Dulcian are similar to those of the Regal and Rankett, although this stop is better able to sound alone, without flue stops, than those two Reeds. It is equally useful on manuals and pedals. Its chief function is to draw the listener's attention to a particular line of notes. It might be called a device for emphasis, as well as an adjunct to the less-bright flue tones of the organ. It is heard in Baroque as well as Classical organs of all sizes.

The Dulcian's pipes are made from spotted metal or pure tin if the maximum bright tone is desired. They are very short in many examples, being from one-eighth to one-quarter of the Trumpet's unison length, breaking back and repeating the same lengths in the lower octaves, as many short Reed ranks do. The design of the shallots and reeds has as much to do with the tone as the resonators, perhaps more. Resonators are inverted-conical, cylindrical, or a combination of both. The examples of manual or pedal choirs of light-toned Reeds that follow may be played as a group or the stops may be drawn alone or with soft flues:

Rohrschalmei	4'		Oboe Schalmei	4'		Dulcian	4'
Fagotto	8'	or	Dulcian	8'	or	Oboe	8'
Dulcian	16'		Barpfeife	16'		Clarinet	16'
						Fagotto	32'

See RANKETT, REGAL. Synonym: DULZIAN.

DULCIANA. A soft Diapason-like stop, sometimes called an *Echo Diapason*, at 16', 8', or 4' on the manuals, and 32', 16', or 8' on the pedals. It is frequently found in the Great Organ of both small and large instruments. If an organ has but three ranks, it is quite sure to include this stop. It serves as an accompaniment for the Swell Organ's Flutes and Strings. It may be used for a background tone, as during a prayer, although it encounters competition from the Spitzflöte Céleste, Echo Dulciana, and Viola Aetheria in this function. The swell shades can reduce it to any required volume of sound. It is not a stop that loses character in traveling distance, as do the Gedeckt and Viola d'Amore, although it has fewer overtones than the Erzähler or Conical Flute. It is always a source of soft timbre for other stops, like the Melodia, Gedeckt, Gemshorn, or Dolce. It is not properly string-like in tone, but rather silvery, neutral-colored, and sedate. The CC pipe is around 3.7 to 2.9 inches in diameter (inside measurement). Pure tin ranks of great beauty exist, but these pipes are usually of spotted metal.

Evenness of tone and a resonant singing quality are physical characteristics that make this stop usable in even the major flue Chorus of the organ, although it is soft. It forms a céleste, but a better use of funds is a chorus of Dulcianas of normal pitch:

Dulciana	2′		Dulciana	2′
Dulciana	2 2/3′	or	Dulciana	2 2/3′
Dulciana	4′		Dulciana	4′
Dulciana	8′		*Dulciana	5 1/3′
			Dulciana	8′
			Dulciana	16′

Choruses of soft *diminutive Foundation* stops are of much usefulness on the Accompanimental, Choir, Great, or Echo Organ. They blend well with all other flues, including the Diapason Chorus, Strings, and mixtures. They make a great variety of accompaniments for the singers, instrumental soloists, and solo stops, including Reeds. They are one of the most valuable tonal adjuncts in the small church organ, and also certain divisions of the larger organs. They can dilute the Strings' keenness, build up timbre without being conspicuous, and serve as mutation stops. They fulfill the basic tenet of organ tone: *unity of effect*. The following diminutive Foundation ranks all are usable, perhaps in different combinations, for the above choruses:

Dolcan	Echo Geigen Diapason
Dulciana	Echo Gemshorn
Echo Diapason	Erzähler
Echo Dulciana	Nachthorn

DULCIANA CÉLESTE. An undulating manual stop of 8′ composed of two ranks of Dulciana pipes, sometimes voiced especially for the céleste function. Since this is a dull céleste, it is more useful at a slow undulation, which will impair its timbre and the timbres of other stops less. It is usually *normal-sharp*, but *normal-flat* is also heard in some examples. The *sharp-flat* pattern does not leave a *normal* rank free for combination. This sedate, quiet, somewhat colorless stop makes an ideal background and accompaniment tone, perhaps in the quieter parts of the church service. In the 88-rank String Organ of the John Wanamaker organ, Philadelphia, 21 ranks of Dulcianas are used to dilute the keenness and build up the tone, mostly as *normal-flat-sharp* ranks. Thirty special pedal ranks, some Dulcianas, support this String Organ. See Céleste, Dulciana.

DULCIANA CORNET. A compound manual stop formed from several ranks of Dulciana pipes, perhaps also Dolcan, Dolce Flute, and soft Dolce ranks at some of the pitches. Only octave- and fifth-sounding ranks are generally included, since this is not a solo stop of pointed tone. It may sound as a background, accompaniment, or timbre-creating tone, depending upon the way the organist uses it. Chorded, it builds up a soft but bright mass of tone, useful either by itself or with other flue stops. The céleste quality cannot wholly be kept out of it, its multitude of higher partials being increased by couplers, tremulant, and the number of notes in a chord. All ranks may have separate stop controls, making available many new sources of mutation and octave-sounding stops. It is more useful if enclosed. Fifth-sounding ranks are softer than the octave-sounding ranks. Middle C would speak at these notes in these two examples:

*Belongs to 16′ series.

Example No. 1		Example No. 2	
IV		VI	
C^4	1'	C^4	1'
G^3	1 1/3'	G^3	1 1/3'
C^3	2'	C^3	2'
G^2	2 2/3'	G^2	2 2/3'
		C^2	4'
		C^1	8'

See CORNET, DULCIANA.

DULCIANA FLUTE. A soft open Flute of 8' or 4' on the manuals, with a tone that is a hybrid between a small-scale open metal Flute and the diminutive, silvery effect of the Dulciana. The mouth cut-up is higher than in the Dulciana, making a tone of fewer harmonics. The pipes are cylindrical. This Flute forms accompaniments for other soft stops.

DULZIAN. See DULCIAN.

DULZIANREGAL. A short-resonatored Reed of 16', 8', or 4' on either manuals or pedals, making a soft but brilliant reedy timbre, sometimes very metallic as well, useful in flue combinations. See DULCIAN, REGAL.

ECHO. See ECHO FLUTE.

ECHO BOURDON. See BOURDONECHO.

ECHO 'CELLO. A String stop of soft tone, at 8' on the manuals, voiced to have much of the harmonically full, rich, warm timbre in the rank of normal scale. It has none of the *muted* sound, since this would dampen the *number* of harmonics in the tone. This is the complete 'Cello tone, except that it is at *piano* instead of *mezzo forte*. However, it is only natural that a few harmonics at the top of the train will disappear as the stop becomes softer, but these may make little difference. This is a soft solo stop of great beauty. It can form a céleste, but is a little too string-like for most Choir Organs; it is more usable on the Swell, Echo, or String. Either wood or metal pipes may be seen in this stop. See VIOLONCELLO.

ECHO CLARABELLA. A soft open Flute of 8' or 4' on the manuals, with a smooth, fluty tonality, but not the dullness of the Gedeckt tribe of stops. This is frequently an Echo Organ stop, and has combining, solo, and accompaniment functions. Most ranks are of wood. See CLARABELLA.

ECHO CLARION. See OCTAVE OBOE.

ECHO CORNET. A soft compound stop on the manuals, designed either to resemble the Cornet or to produce an accompaniment background in the form of a mixture. The pipes are Dulciana, Echo Diapason, or most usefully, Echo Geigen in tone. There may be no breaks in the pitch, and the third-sounding Tierce may be included. It is useful in the Processional or Echo Organ, being quite soft for the Choir. If used for the Cornet function, it should be unenclosed. Middle C would speak at these notes:

Cornet Example No. 1		Cornet Example No. 2		Accompaniment Example	
III		IV		V	
G^3	1 1/3'	C^4	1'	G^3	1 1/3'
C^3	2'	E^3	1 3/5'	C^3	2'
G^2	2 2/3'	C^3	2'	G^2	2 2/3'
		G^2	2 2/3'	C^2	4'
				C^1	8'

See CORNET, DOLCE CORNET, DULCIANA CORNET.

ECHO DIAPASON. A Foundation stop of Diapason tone quality, at 16′, 8′, or 4′ on the manuals, having less volume of sound than the normal Diapasons. Few examples have a smaller number of harmonics than normal, but most are a little smaller in scale. Some examples are unusually soft, but this name is not proper on the Dulciana or Dolce. It has the same functions as the bigger Diapasons, and is found at all mixture pitches and mutation pitches, perhaps in the Geigen form. See DIAPASON, GEIGEN DIAPASON.

ECHO DULCIANA. An extremely soft Foundation stop of 16′, 8′, or 4′ on the manuals, similar to the Dulciana in timbre, but much softer than the Dolce or Dolce Flute. This stop represents the problem inherent in all soft registers: Do the voicing and acoustics of the organ chamber make it possible to hear the tone quality of the stop? This particular diminutive Foundation stop is relatively easy to hear, and is very useful in accompaniments and as a soft céleste. See DULCIANA.

ECHO DULCIANA CÉLESTE. One of the softest célestes in the organ, at 8′ on the manuals, and composed of two ranks of Echo Dulciana pipes, usually *normal-sharp,* and very small in scale. It may be called an *Echo Céleste* or a *Vox Angelica.* It is a soft accompaniment or background tone to contrast with soft Flutes and Strings. See CÉLESTE, ECHO DULCIANA.

ECHO FLUTE. A very soft open, stopped, or half-covered Flute of 8′ or 4′ on the manuals, made from either wood or metal. These twelve combinations of form and material of pipe indicate that there is no standard pattern for this Flute. See ECHO OPEN FLUTE, ECHO STOPPED FLUTE, Synonym: ECHO.

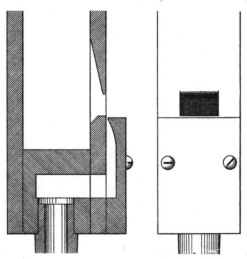

A soft Flute, sometimes designated as *Orchestral.* The Echo Flute can be made in this form, since the inverted upper lip gives the tone enough overtone-structure to carry well to the listener.

ECHO GAMBA. A very soft String of subdued keenness and small scale, at the 8′ manual pitch. The regular Gamba timbre is not too apparent in this stop, because the smaller scale reduces the quantity of prime tone (fundamental). It forms a contrast with light Flutes and Strings. See GAMBA.

ECHO GEDECKT. An unusually soft form of Gedeckt, at 16′, 8′, or 4′ manual pitch, made from either wood or metal pipes. It sounds almost pure fundamental, and can furnish this ground tone to such soft stops as the Echo Gamba, Dulciana, or Dolcan. It is a poor accompaniment stop because its pitch is not apparent even to listeners close to the organ. See GEDECKT.

ECHO GEMSHORN. A very soft Foundation stop of 8′ or 4′ on the manuals, yielding a delicate, clear, somewhat silvery Gemshorn tone, but much reduced in volume. This stop enters into combination with any other flue stop, and is an ideal soft accompaniment, perhaps for an Echo Oboe or Orchestral Flute stop. It is formed like the bigger Gemshorn. See GEMSHORN.

ECHO HORN. A Reed stop of 8′ manual pitch, resembling the Orchestral Horn stop (called *French Horn*) or brighter Waldhorn in timbre, but considerably softer than either. This name is not synonymous with *Fernhorn*, which is an Echo *Nachthorn*. In residence and theater organs the voicer may inject a little of the pungent Krumet quality. See FRENCH HORN, WALDHORN.

ECHO MIXTURE. A compound manual stop made from soft Diapasons, perhaps Echo Geigens, Dulcianas, or even Echo Dulcianas, occasionally designed to resemble a Fourniture, Cornet, or some other type of multiple-rank stop. Or it may be simply a series of needed harmonic-pitches, as in a Choir or Echo Organ. It has accompaniment and background uses, as well as being a soft timbre creator or tone builder. As in most mixtures and Cornets, the pitches in any one note usually leave no gaps in the train of harmonics, as would be seen between 4′ and 2′, for example, if the 2 2/3′ were omitted. These examples, increasingly bright from left to right, sound from middle C:

Example No. 1 III		Example No. 2 IV		Example No. 3 V		Example No. 4 VI	
C^3	2′	E^3	1 3/5′	C^4	1′	C^4	1′
G^2	2 2/3′	C^3	2′	G^3	1 1/3′	G^3	1 1/3′
C^2	4′	G^2	2 2/3′	C^3	2′	E^3	1 3/5′
		C^2	4′	G^2	2 2/3′	C^3	2′
				C^2	4′	G^2	2 2/3′
						C^2	4′

ECHO NACHTHORN. A very soft Foundation rank of 8′ or 4′ on the manuals, sounding a fluty but not round-toned timbre that suggests the bigger stopped metal pipes of the Nachthorn. The regular Nachthorn is usually quite soft, so this variety of stop is useful with only the very softest stops, like the Dulciana, Echo Dulciana, Flauto Dolcissimo, or Echo

Viola. Its placid, quiet voice makes a beautiful solo stop. See NACHTHORN. Synonym: FERNHORN.

ECHO OBOE. A small-scaled imitative Reed of 8' on the manuals, sounding with a gentle, plaintive, nasal voice, similar to that of the larger Oboe ranks. Its smaller scale gives it a pointed, reedy, soft timbre that is still easy to identify as a variety of the Oboe species. In some ways it is a more realistic imitation because it is not so loud and is less sharp in tone. It is a solo stop on any manual, such as the Echo, Solo, or Swell. Small-scale labial pipes have made this tone with some success, but they lack the initial "spit" of harmonics so necessary for identification of this tone color and the other "woodwinds." See OBOE, ORCHESTRAL OBOE.

ECHO OPEN FLUTE. A wood (or metal) Flute of various shades of color, sounding at 16', 8', or 4' on the manuals. Being an open Flute, it may represent either the Clarabella (beveled lip) tone or the Hohlflöte (inverted lip) tone. The first is likely to be smooth and bright, the second strong in the second harmonic (the octave). This is a solo or combinational Flute for any division. It can be a mixture component or a mutation rank. Its blending ability is never in question, and its dynamic quality of unusual softness makes it usable with all other stops. The 4' rank can add a little bright tone; the 8' rank can be used to deepen soft Strings and Dulcianas; the 16' rank, rarely seen, is a tone builder with such stops as the soft diminutive Foundation ranks and the soft Strings. This stop-name may refer to *Echo Flute*.

ECHO STOPPED FLUTE. A wooden or metal Flute of various shades of color, sounding at 8' or 4' on the manuals. It is usually designed as a small-scale Gedeckt, although large-scale Gedeckts can also be very soft. It is softer than the Echo Open Flute, having but half that Flute's harmonic train. It is a useful but soft Copula. It can add the prime tone to any soft stop, such as the Echo Gamba or Dolcan. It is a poor accompaniment. It may be a *Fernflöte* or *Echo Flute,* or even a soft *Doppelgedeckt.*

ECHO TIBIA CLAUSA. A stopped Flute of solo quality, at 16', 8', 4', or 2' manual pitch. It has the "pure" fundamental of its larger-scaled counterpart, but not its "sweetness" or intensity of tone. However, the tone quality of this Tibia is somewhat liquid and smooth, without any obvious third harmonic. High cut-up, leathered or leaded lips, thick, smooth walls, and beveled mouths make this *Echo Tibia* a useful solo tone on the Swell, Solo, or Echo. *Flautino* may be the 2' pitch. See TIBIA CLAUSA.

ECHO TRUMPET. A small-scaled Reed of 8' manual tone. This Trumpet lacks the characteristic big-toned effect of the parent stop, and also much of its éclat and brilliance. Although not a muted, thin-toned Reed, it is unassertive and only moderately loud. It is as bright in tone as the Cornopean, but not quite up to the dynamic of that stop. It is useful in solo and ensemble playing, and as a contrast to other Trumpets. It may be on the Choir or Echo when a loud Reed is not wanted. Synonym: PETITE TROMPETTE.

ECHO VIOLA. A mild, soft String of 8' manual pitch, sounding like the Viola of regular scale, although this too is a mild and soft stop. This diminutive Viola is delicate but definitely string-like in tone color. It is an accompaniment for soft solo stops, like the Corno d'Amore and Echo Open Flute, and a dilutant for brightness in the Echo Violin Céleste. It too can form a quiet céleste of mild tone, unique because it is at the same time stringy, soft, and not keen. The *Viola Aetheria* is even softer. See VIOLA.

ECHO VIOLIN. A String of soft orchestral tone color, at 8' on the manuals, representing the Viole d'Orchestre timbre, but in softer form. The incisive brilliance, keenness, and cutting tone quality of the orchestral String stops are all present in this stop, but greatly reduced in intensity, because making any bright stop an *Echo* stop automatically wipes out of existence some of its highest-pitched overtones. This, in turn, limits the dissonance in the tone, without damaging the basic color of the timbre. Its prime tone (fundamental) is inaudible, and the fourth harmonic the loudest component, as in many bright Strings. This stop is brighter and softer than the Muted Violin and Aeoline. See VIOL, VIOLE D'ORCHESTRE.

ECHO VOX HUMANA. A soft Reed stop of 8' manual pitch, similar in tone to the Vox Humana, but more muffled and softer. This stop is sometimes labeled *Vox Mystica*. It may be placed in an inner swell box for additional softness. It sounds as just a whisper of extremely high overtones. Its tenuous, soft timbre is most effective in chords near the middle of the keyboard. Here it may seem to give no sense of pitch at all. It sounds well combined or by itself, and with the tremulant. See VOX HUMANA.

EGYPTIAN HORN. A solo Reed of 8' on the manuals having a tone color that resembles an intensely brassy and *also* very reedy Trompette of moderate volume. It is somewhat thin in voice and there is a mere suggestion of the Basset Horn quality in it. The high and blatant harmonics are pointed up, although the fundamental prime tone is audible. It is a solo stop for the unusual effect, and an ensemble stop for the louder Reed combinations. There are not many examples around, but there is one in the Midmer Losh organ in the Convention Hall, Atlantic City, designed by Senator Emerson Richards. It is in the Gallery IV division, which is made up altogether of very bright Reeds. It is on 25 inches of wind and has exponentially curved resonators of very slender scale, the flare being mostly at the top of the bells. (This division also contains Saxophones of 16', 8', and 4', a Euphone, Horns, Oboes, and a Musette.)

EIGHTEENTH. A very rare rank of pipes of Foundation tone at the unusual pitch of 1 5/11' on the manuals, and 2 10/11' on the pedals. It speaks two octaves and a fourth above the keys depressed, that is at F^3 from middle C, and at F from the pedal low CCC key. It is not a common harmonic of any series of pitches, and is of use only in a very complete *Harmonic Chorus,* an ancillary that includes stop-pitches for all regular pitch-positions as well as many of those in between. The manual pitch is between the 1 3/5' and the 1 1/3' stops. See ELEVENTH.

ELEVENTH. A very rare rank of pipes of Foundation tone at the pitch of 2 10/11′ on the manuals, and 5 9/11′ on the pedals. It sounds one octave and a fourth above the key depressed, which is at F^2 on the manuals from the middle C key, and at FF on the pedals from the low CCC key. It is not a natural harmonic of any series, and is of limited usefulness on even the largest organs, and then only in an ancillary Harmonic Chorus. It sounds one octave below the Eighteenth on manuals and pedals. It gives a dissonant effect and a close-toned brilliance to any loud Reeds or a flue combination, and also makes some clang-tone which may be brass-like in effect. The 2 10/11′ sounds between the 3 1/5′ and the 2 2/3′ on the manuals. See EIGHTEENTH, NINTH.

ENGLISH HORN. An imitative Reed stop of 8′ on the manuals, sounding like its orchestral counterpart. Its round-toned, plaintive, expressive tone quality can have a strong emotional effect on the listener, unlike the nasal, thin Orchestral Oboe, which is more symbolic of gaiety and lightness of mood. Although the English Horn lacks the piquant and sometimes grotesque sound of the Oboe tribe, it still has a little of the pastoral quality in its tone. Some specimens are even melancholy in their upper bass range. The more realistic ranks are not too loud and a little on the small side in scaling. They are usually voiced for ensemble as well as solo playing, since this is frequently a Choir stop, but probably not so versatile as the Fagotto. English Horn, Clarinet, Orchestral Oboe, and French Horn form the "Big Four" group of orchestral Reeds.

English Horn middle C pipe. 1, inside boot; 2, general form of pipe.

The unison-length resonators are inverted-conical in form with double-belled tops, the upper bell being inverted. The sound is emitted through a hole in the center of each pipe's top. Synonym: COR ANGLAIS.

ENGLISH POST HORN. A Reed stop of 8′ pitch on the manuals, yielding a brilliant, loud, somewhat blatant Trompette tone. This stop also has definite horn-like characteristics as well as a freely vibrating sound. It can serve as a solo or ensemble tone, and is usually heard in concert and theater organs of some size. It has its full share of clang-tone and a peculiar variety of mellowness which comes from several of the lower-pitched partials sounding almost as loud as their fundamental. The full-length resonators are slightly inverted-conical for one-half their lengths, the upper halves being of even greater taper outward towards their tops. Those of better quality are made from spotted metal rich in tin content to ensure a flood of higher-pitched partials, the source of brilliance in any organ stop. Synonym: POST HORN.

ERZÄHLER. A Foundation stop of 8′ or 4′ on the manuals, invented by Ernest M. Skinner. It serves as a binding tone between bright and dull stops, high-pitched and low-pitched stops, and the unisons and the mutations and mixtures. It fills in the lower-pitched overtones so completely that cohesion of tone is achieved. The fundamental and octave components are both noticeable. The rest of the train of overtones contains elements of the String, open Flute, and Foundation stops, without any color-forming fringe of the very high-pitched overtones. It points up the pitches of the stops being played instead of masking them and making them lose character. It is probably the most valuable single adjunct to the tones of all stops that exists in the organ. It does not destroy timbre in another stop,

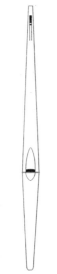

A conical Erzähler

rather it supports it by giving it additional strength. Nor does it make the tone colors more vivid, as does the Gedeckt. It is available in many degrees of loudness and scale. It is heard from most divisions. It is an ideal accompaniment. The 8′ and 4′ together can accompany most stops adequately. Two ranks of each of these pitches (not as a céleste) can be very useful on both Choir and Great. These spotted metal pipes are conical and more pointed than a Gemshorn in relation to an equivalent mouth-line diameter. The *Echo Erzähler* is a very useful stop, having most of the functions of this stop. See ERZÄHLER CÉLESTE, GEMSHORN.

ERZÄHLER CÉLESTE. An undulating 8′ manual stop of Foundation tone, made from two ranks of Erzähler pipes, tuned most usefully in the *flat-sharp* pattern of pitches, since this impairs the pitch of the other stops less in the ear of the listener. It is not too unusual to hear a *Foundation* stop in céleste form, because there are many *diminutives* in this tonal family that make useful accompaniments when undulating very slowly, perhaps one-half to two beats in a second, between two of their own ranks. This neutral-toned and somewhat bright stop makes a good accompaniment for either vocal or organ solo. A single 4′ Erzähler rank added to this céleste increases its usefulness with the louder solo stops, since it gives more pitch-support and a little more penetration. See CÉLESTE, ERZÄHLER.

ETHEREAL VIOLIN. An extremely brilliant String of 8′ manual pitch, sounding like a very soft but luminous form of the Viole d'Orchestre stop of louder tone. It is neither muted nor reduced to unusual softness. In spite of this stop's ability to sound between forty and fifty overtones from each one of its narrow spotted metal pipes, it has a dynamic value around *piano*. This tone has a delicacy and refinement not sensed in most of the organ's Viols. It is less soft than the Aeoline. It is brighter (has more

Making Spotted Metal

MAKING SPOTTED METAL

A workman rolling up a long sheet of flexible spotted metal after it has been poured as a molten alloy and cooled on this flat table top. The spots, which appeared slowly as the mass cooled, are a natural effect of mixing tin and lead together. All pipe metals are made in different thicknesses and in several proportions to satisfy the need for different timbres and sizes of pipes.

overtones) than the Salicional, Gamba, Echo Gamba, Muted Violin, or Echo Violin. It is not an accompaniment stop in most organs, but makes a contrast to other less-bright sounds. It is in the Echo, String, or Swell of some instruments, usually as céleste. See VIOLE D'ORCHESTRE.

ETHEREAL VIOLIN CÉLESTE. An undulating String stop of 8' manual pitch, composed of two, three, or more ranks of Ethereal Violin pipes. This tone is attractive because it is soft in contrast to its unusual brilliance. Its shimmering, delicate, lustrous effect is one of the most beautiful obtainable among the Strings of the organ. See CÉLESTE, ETHEREAL VIOLIN, VIOLE CÉLESTE.

EUPHONE. A Reed stop of 16' or 8' manual pitch, and 16' pedal pitch, sounding with a muffled, reedy, somewhat pungent tone. The brass-like quality can be sensed in a few examples. See EUPHONIUM.

EUPHONIUM. A rare stop-name indicating the large orchestral Tuba, at 16' on manuals and pedals. This stop-name is not synonymous with *Euphone*.

FAGOTTO. One of the most versatile of all imitative Reed stops, at 16', 8', or 4' on the manuals, and 32', 16', or 8' on the pedals. A few examples are voiced to imitate the orchestral bassoon, but the Orchestral Bassoon is usually a brighter organ stop than the Fagotto. The Fagotto lacks the mournful quality of the Krummhorn and the acidity of the Schalmei. Nor is it round in tone, Clarinet-like, or piercing, like the Musette. Some ranks of pipes approach a "woody" tone, and a few have a grotesque or pungent

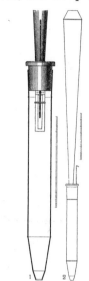

Euphone tenor C pipe. 1 shows view inside boot, 2 the form of the pipe.

effect on the ear. The Fagotto is properly reedy, mildly bright, not too distinct as to color, and always of *clean pitch*. It carries its timbre evenly throughout its entire compass from bass to treble. It blends without asserting its own individuality, and it also forms a solo stop of distinction, although usually not on the Solo Division. The 16' manual rank has been substituted for the sub octave on many different manuals, even the Great, and it is a favorite in the 16' - 8' - 4' light-reed choruses, three examples of which are given below, usable on manuals or pedals:

Fagotto	4'		Schalmei	4'		Musette	4'
Fagotto	8'	or	Oboe	8'	or	Clarinet	8'
Fagotto	16'		Fagotto	16'		Fagotto	16'

The pedal ranks are voiced with a little more fundamental than the manual ranks, and also less brightness. They make an ideal combination with the Gemshorns, Diapasons, or Violones for establishing a clear pitch line of pedal notes. The very slender resonators are inverted-conical in shape, made from spotted metal, and of unison length in almost all specimens, but the half-length are known; these stimulate the second harmonic of the series, the unison-length stimulating the fundamental. If fully capped, the sound emerges from a long, narrow slot near the top of each pipe. The partly capped or fully open type give a brighter tone with more higher partials. Wooden resonators are not unknown. The Fagotto being a moderately soft stop, it is better to leave the bass pipes, as from CCCC to GG, unenclosed to preserve the fundamentals.

FAGOTTONE. A Reed stop of 32′ on the pedals, and sometimes also on the manuals at this profound pitch. It sounds with a reedy, distinct quality that is valuable in combination or alone. Although it is soft, it is not dull in tone, and has the advantage of a clear statement of the pitches. The pedal flue stops are frequently made much more usable by this Reed, especially if they are crowded or too dull in tone. See FAGOTTO.

FANFARE. A very brilliant and loud Chorus Reed of 8′ on the manuals, produced by a variety of pipe forms: Trompette, Trumpet, Ophicleide, or Brass Trumpet. It is a solo stop as well as a source of power and brass-like overtones for the bigger ensembles. It is probably most impressive when played in contrast to the full organ. Fanfares are most realistic when chorded and without the tremulant. Some examples are unenclosed to give a free sound unabsorbed by organ chamber walls. A few are mounted horizontally, and these should be referred to by the name *Trompette en Chamade*. Probably *Trumpet Fanfare* would be a more explicit name for this stop. See BRASS TRUMPET, TROMPETTE, TROMPETTE EN CHAMADE, TRUMPET.

FAN TRUMPET. See TROMPETTE EN CHAMADE.

FELDFLÖTE. See WALDFLÖTE.

FERNFLÖTE. A very soft Flute of 8′ or 4′ on the manuals, sounding from stoppered pipes in most examples, although the open pipes are sometimes used for this stop. See ECHO FLUTE, ECHO OPEN FLUTE, ECHO STOPPED FLUTE.

FERNHORN. See ECHO NACHTHORN.

FIELD TRUMPET. See TROMPETTE MILITAIRE.

FIFE. An open metal Flute of 2′ or 1′ manual pitch, yielding a loud and sometimes shrill tone similar to that of the marching fife. This is not a common name for an organ stop, there being a wide variety of high-pitched ranks that sound with as much penetration but with better blend and a timbre that chords with less accumulation of dissonance. The Blockflöte, Sifflöte, Piccolo, and conical Foundation ranks are all more useful to the organist.

FIFTEENTH. A Foundation stop of Diapason tone, speaking at 2′ on the manuals, and 4′ on the pedals. It sounds at the note two octaves above the key depressed on both manuals and pedals. It corroborates the fourth natural harmonic when added to the unison stops. Its effect is one of brilliance in any combination, since it duplicates at higher pitch most of the harmonics of the unison and octave Diapasons. It is one of the most frequently seen mixture components, and it is the first rank met with in ascending the ladder of stop-pitches that seems to be really high. It is also the highest-pitched stop on many smaller organs. It may be in the form of the *Piccolo* on the Swell, since smaller organs frequently have only 8' and 4' stops on the Great. It is the Super Octave of the basic Chorus or Diapasons. This basic Chorus on the *manuals* is as follows:

(fourth harmonic)	Fifteenth	2'	(octave-sounding rank)
(third harmonic)	Twelfth (Nasard)	2 2/3'	(fifth-sounding rank)
(second harmonic)	Octave	4'	(octave-sounding rank)
(first harmonic)	Diapason	8'	(unison-sounding rank)

The basic Chorus of the *pedals* is as follows:

(fourth harmonic)	Fifteenth	4'	(octave-sounding rank)
(third harmonic)	Twelfth (Nasard)	5 1/3'	(fifth-sounding rank)
(second harmonic)	Octave	8'	(octave-sounding rank)
(first harmonic)	Diapason	16'	(unison-sounding rank)

On the pedals the pitch indication is one octave below that of the manuals. Pedal stops of the *same name* always have pitches that are numerically twice as large as manual stops. For example, the *unison* of the pedals is arbitrarily set at 16' (for every note on the keyboard), whereas the manual's unison pitch (like the piano's) is set at 8' simply because *an open pipe eight feet long makes the pitch for the note of CC,* the bottom note on the manuals. All other stop-names are adjusted to these unison pitches, the Tierce, for example, which is at 1 3/5' on the manuals, being twice this number, or 3 1/5', on the pedals. It might be helpful to think of the pedal keyboard as containing just the bottom 32 notes of the manuals. An 8' (or a 16') stop drawn on *both* manuals and pedals will sound the same pitch if bottom keys are depressed. However, since it is convenient to have the pedals at a deeper pitch than the manuals, the organ is made to sound the note an octave lower for the *same stop-name* than it does on the manuals. We are comparing here equivalent keys, of course, like the two bottom keys mentioned above. Or we might compare the third or thirtieth keys, or any keys.

Fifteenths are customarily a little smaller in scale than their Octaves, but a few are made larger, and slightly conical, to give them less "hardness" of tone and more penetration in the Chorus. The Great and Swell may also have Flutes, Gemshorns, Strings, etc. of 2'. A soft 1' may be needed to supplement the 2' ranks, and to help the mixtures "sit" on the Fifteenth's tone. See DIAPASON, TWELFTH. Synonym: SUPER OCTAVE.

FIFTH. See QUINT.

FLACHFLöTE. An open metal Flute of 8', 4', 2', or 1' on the manuals, sounding from pipes of large or moderate scale, shaped like either the Conical Flute or simply a cylindrical metal Flute with open truncated portions on the tops. The low mouth cut-up provides a rich and moderately loud train of harmonics, the higher-pitched dampened by the pipe shape. See CONICAL FLUTE.

FLAGEOLET. An open metal Flute of 2′ or 1′ on the manuals, with a moderately soft tone of round rather than bright quality. It is not so loud or harmonically developed as the Piccolo or Blockflöte. It is used in soft flue ensembles or occasionally as a solo stop.

FLAGEOLET HARMONIQUE. An open metal Flute of 2′ or 1′ pitch on the manuals, constructed from double-length pipes, a hole being pierced near the middle of each. This Flute is louder and even rounder than the Flageolet, giving some sense of fullness and "plumpness" of tone. It has the same uses as the Flageolet. See FLAGEOLET, HARMONIC FLUTE.

FLAUTADA. A Foundation stop of 32′, 16′, or 8′ on either manuals or pedals, the 32′ manual rank being somewhat unusual. It is formed from open, large-scale, heavy-walled wooden pipes that yield a tone of great weight and loudness. It is a Principal-Flute hybrid. See DIAPASON, WOOD DIAPASON.

FLAUTINO. An open metal or wood Flute of 2′ manual pitch, voiced to sound a pure, unassertive, smooth tone of less strength than most other 2′ Flutes. The unit organ's *Flautina* is often a Tibia Clausa of 2′ pitch.

FLAUTO AMABILE. See AMOROSA.

FLAUTO d'AMORE. See FLÛTE D'AMOUR.

FLAUTO DOLCE. See DOLCE FLUTE.

FLAUTO DOLCISSIMO. An extremely soft metal or wood Flute of 8′ or 4′ manual pitch, made from pipes that flare gently outward towards their tops, somewhat like the Dolce. *Dolcissimo* refers only to a Dolce. See DOLCE FLUTE.

FLAUTO MAJOR. See MAJOR OPEN FLUTE.

FLAUTO MIRABILIS. A Flute of open metal or wood, at 8′ or 4′ manual pitch, sounding with a tone of unusual loudness and brilliance, but not equal to the Stentorphone or some Tibia Plenas in power. Its large scale and low mouth cut-up give it clarity and penetration for either solo playing or ensemble use. It may be on the Great, Swell, or Solo Organ.

FLAUTO TRAVERSO. See ORCHESTRAL FLUTE.

FLÖTENBASS. See BASS FLUTE.

FLÜGELHORN. A solo reed of 8′ manual pitch, voiced to imitate the orchestral prototype. It has some of the warm timbre of the Horn stop and the mild brass overtones of the Trumpet. This tone may be mellow in some specimens. Although rare as an organ stop, it is a beautiful and useful voice. It can be used to build up ensembles of light brass tone.

FLÛTE à BEC. A Flute of 4′, infrequently 8′, on the manuals, with a soft whistle-like timbre meant to imitate the old instrument of this name (the recorder). The pipes are open, usually metal, and small in scale. See BLOCKFLÖTE.

FLÛTE à FUSEAU. An open Flute of 8′, 4′, or 2′ on the manuals, with a moderately bright but soft tone formed from half-covered or conical pipes.

FLÛTE à PAVILLON. See BELL DIAPASON.

FLUTE BASS. See BASS FLUTE.

FLÛTE CÉLESTE. An undulating Flute stop of 8′ manual pitch, made from any Flute well-developed harmonically and somewhat on the soft side. A prominent fundamental damages this delicate, subtle tone quality. The pattern of pitches is *normal-sharp, normal-flat,* or *sharp-flat,* the first two giving the organist a stop for other combinations. A slow undulation blends more easily with other soft stops, and wipes out less of this Flute's timbre. The Spitzflöte has become almost synonymous with this name, but the Dolce Flute, Viol Flute, and other forms may also be used. This is a background tone and an accompaniment stop. With the Quintaton, Nachthorn, and Clarinet it forms a variety of effects. See CÉLESTE, SPITZFLÖTE CÉLESTE.

FLÛTE CONIQUE. See CONICAL FLUTE.

FLÛTE d'AMOUR. A soft and delicately voiced open or half-covered solo Flute of 8′ or 4′ on the manuals, with a tone characterized by an unusual proportion between several of its lower-pitched harmonics as well as a great amount of inner pipe resonance. This *resonance* has a "plump" effect on the ear that the listener interprets as "bright" or "string-like," although the number of overtones does not warrant the use of these words.

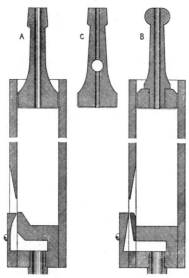

Flûte d'Amour in three forms: A shows rohr carved from a solid stopper, C shows opening cut across rohr, and B shows a variation of A, not solid.

It is a soft accompaniment stop and a beautiful and subtle-toned solo stop that is long remembered by all who hear it under good conditions of acoustics. Rohrs on the wood examples or conical tops on the metal ranks help to give strength in the lower part of the harmonic train. Synonym: FLAUTO D'AMORE.

FLÛTE DOUCE. See DOLCE FLUTE.

FLÛTE HARMONIQUE. See HARMONIQUE FLUTE.

FLÛTE NASARD. A stopped (sometimes open) Flute of 2 2/3′ manual pitch, and occasionally at 5 1/3′ on the pedals, formed as a Gedeckt. See TWELFTH.

FLÛTE OUVERTE. An *open* Flute, of wood in many examples, at 8′ or 4′ on the manuals, and 32′, 16′, or 8′ on the pedals. It is more often heard from the pedals, and indicates a thick-walled, smooth-toned, large-scaled stop of moderate brightness and any volume suitable for the other stops.

FLUTE QUINT. A manual 5 1/3′ and a pedal 10 2/3′ Flute constructed as either a large-scale Gedeckt or open Flute-Diapason hybrid. See QUINT.

FLÛTE TRIANGULAIRE. An open wood Flute of triangular cross-section and wide mouth, at 16′ or 8′ on the manuals, usually the latter. The tone is hollow and dull and not so prominent as that from the Hohlflöte. The octave harmonic is strong, as well as the fundamental. Its firm, quick, neutral-colored speech can support the Diapasons and other flues well. Although the Diapasons need no adjuncts of any kind, it is to be admitted that many organists think Diapasons "sound better" when a smoothing Clarabella, Hohlflöte, or Flûte Triangulaire is combined with them. Sometimes just an open 4′ Flute serves this function, and adds a little brightness of tone as well. Both the 8′ and 4′ open Flutes might be added to good effect in some combinations. Undoubtedly, the softer, higher-pitched overtones are absorbed in the more

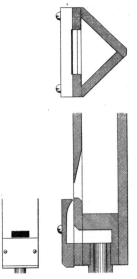

Specimen pipe from a 4′ wooden Flauto Traverso. Cross-sectional view of pipe shows a triangular shape, somewhat less full of overtones.

acute angles of these pipes. The decrease in scale caused by building only three walls tends to increase the number of higher overtones. Probably the decrease in scale overrides the effect of the absorbing sharp angles, at least in the smaller scales and smaller high-pitched pipes of the stop. This tone is subdued compared to that of a quadrangular Hohlflöte. See HOHLFLÖTE.

FOREST FLUTE. A stop-name used to refer to a variety of Flute tones at either 8′ or 4′ on the manuals. The smaller-scaled Waldflöte or Orchestral Flute fulfills this definition in tone, but this *Flute de Bois* sounds other elements as well. The full-toned, smooth effect of the Clarabella is in it, as well as some horn-like overtones; other examples are said to have a "woolly" indistinct timbre. It has also been made at 2′ and 1′, and heard in all divisions as a solo or ensemble voice. A well-polished upper lip or pipe-front of hardwood with rounded shape aids in making this unique tone quality.

FOURNITURE. Probably the most important single Mixture on a large or small Great or Choir division, speaking from fifth- and octave-sounding pipes, rarely third-sounding.† It extends *upward* harmonically the tone of the flue Choruses, adding, of course, a little brilliance as well. It enhances pitch-definition and that needed sonorous quality in the Chorus's treble notes. It is an *extension of the Diapason timbre*, less great in range than most Plein Jeus of orthodox pattern. Pitch breaks, loudness, timbre, and number of ranks vary with each example. Some examples adhere to the traditional dull-toned high pitches and brighter lower pitches, perhaps with conical pipe-tops. Mixtures are always carefully custom-designed. Many times only the 8′, 4′, 2 2/3′, and 2′ Diapasons and the Fourniture are drawn together to produce a small Diapason Chorus. In some newer organs the tin-white pipes of this and other mixtures can be seen standing in front of the organ screen. Here they are not only beautiful, but can sound full-toned and unobstructed as part of the air-mass of the listening chamber. Notes for middle C and the low pedal CCC keys are given in these examples:

Example No. 1		Example No. 2		Example No. 3		Example No. 4	
III		IV		VI		VI	
C^4	1′	C^4	1′	G^4	2/3′	G^4	2/3′
G^3	1 1/3′	G^3	1 1/3′	C^4	1′ (soft)	C^4	1′ (soft)
C^3	2′	C^3	2′	G^3	1 1/3′	G^3	1 1/3′
		G^2	2 2/3′	C^3	2′ (loud)	C^3	2′ (soft)
				G^2	2 2/3′	G^2	2 2/3′
				C^2	4′ (soft)	C^2	4′ (loud)

Example No. 5		Example No. 6		Example No. 7		Example No. 8	
VI		VI		(Pedal)		(Pedal)	
				III		IV	
C^4	1′	C^4	1′	C^1	2′	C^1	2′
G^3	1 1/3′	G^3	1 1/3′	G	2 2/3′	G	2 2/3′
C^3	2′	E^3	1 3/5′	C	4′	C	4′
G^2	2 2/3′	C^3	2′			GG	5 1/3′
C^2	4′	G^2	2 2/3′				
*G^1	5 1/3′	C^2	4′				

*Belongs to the 16′ series.

Organists add the *octave* and *super-octave* couplers to a combination containing one or more mixtures quite frequently. To make graphic the complexity of stop-pitches heard when adding these *two* couplers to Example No. 3, and depressing the middle C key alone, this listing follows:

1) one pitch at 8′
2) one pitch at 5 1/3′
3) two pitches at 4′
4) two pitches at 2 2/3′
5) three pitches at 2′
6) three pitches at 1 1/3′
7) two pitches at 1′
8) two pitches at 2/3′
9) one pitch at 1/2′
10) one pitch at 1/3′

It would be profitable for the student of the organ to work out the names of all the notes (CC, G^3, etc.) that would be sounded in the chord composed of tenor C, tenor G, middle E, and middle B♭ from this mixture example and the two couplers.

Assume no pitch-breaks in the example.

FOURTEENTH, FLATTED. A rank of Foundation pipes at the unusual pitch of 2 2/7′ on the manuals, and 4 4/7′ on the pedals, the "Sep-

†Tierces, because of acute tone, are more useful if on separate stop keys.

tièmes" of the *sub-unison* series. This stop speaks one octave and a flatted seventh above the keys struck, which is B♭² from middle C key, and BB♭ from low pedal CCC key. It may be heard in a large Grand Chorus mixture or some other compound stop, but not as a separate stop key. It is peculiar to the largest of organs that attempt to have a complete set of harmonic pitches for the many series of stops, such as 16′, 8′, 4′, etc. On both manuals and pedals it can add richness of timbre in loud, heavy combinations.

FRENCH HORN. An imitative Reed stop of 8′ on the manuals but not the pedals. It is intended to imitate the orchestral prototype. It is chiefly a *solo* stop, but can be used in light Reed and flue ensembles. This Reed requires moderately high or high wind pressure to assume its normal timbre. It lacks the well-defined pitch-line of a bright Reed. This is a difficult instrument for the organ builders to imitate, but several, notably Ernest M. Skinner, have produced realistic examples, even to the characteristic "bubble" in the tone. The peculiar proportion of harmonics in this Reed is easily damaged by absorption, the result often being a neutral, fluty sound. Consequently, the French Horn stops that sound in hard-walled churches of some height

French Horn, capped, and with slot for the emission of the sound waves. This is in the proportion of the tenor C pipe. Observe the 12-inch rule at the right.

always make a better impression. The human elements of breath control and holding position are not in the organ stop, nor is the particular series of initial harmonics given by the lips. Nevertheless, this is one of the better imitations. The tone is smooth (without peaking in the loudness of the harmonics), brass-like (of strength in all lower six or eight harmonics), and with just a suggestion of clang (beating between certain harmonics). It is the *stopped* tones of the horn that are imitated. The middle range, from G to G¹, is the most realistic. The *open* Horn tones come from the *Waldhorn* stop.

The resonators are unison-length, capped to dampen the unwanted high partials, and have slots near the pipes' tops to emit the sound. Like most Reeds, they are inverted-conical, and of wide flare. The shallots are closed to subdue the reeds' vibration into higher partials of the train. A thick-walled labial stop of wood can imitate this Horn, but it lacks the more realistic initial sounds. The name *French Horn* properly belongs to the hunting horn of the forest, but this sound is made by the Waldhorn in the organ, and *French Horn* has come to indicate the orchestral horn. Synonyms: HORN, ORCHESTRAL HORN.

FRENCH TRUMPET. See TROMPETTE.

FUGARA. A String stop of the Gamba type, at 4′ on the manuals. It has a bright, keen, penetrating quality, usually on the loud side. Some examples are really Diapason-String hybrids. Its function is to create a rich and brilliant treble line for the melody, countermelody, or chords of the division in which it is included, which is frequently the Great or Swell. A few examples are mild. The *Gemshorn Gamba* of 4' is often of better blend than the open metal cylindrical Fugara. The latter may be a large-scale String and is brighter in tone if made from spotted metal. See GAMBA.

FULL FLUTE. A 4' manual Flute of loud or moderately loud tone, constructed as open metal or wood pipes which sometimes resemble the Principal Flute. This is a solo and ensemble Flute of large scale and impressive tone, found in the Great, Swell, or Solo division. It adds brilliance and considerable firmness to any other loud Reed or flue stops. The name has also indicated a large-scale stoppered rank of the same pitch.

FULL MIXTURE. A manual and pedal mixture of large-scaled Diapasons intended to supplement the ensemble of any division in the organ. Some examples make a full ensemble by themselves. Reed and flue choruses are both aided by this stop, since it is composed of loud, bright, neutral-timbred Foundation ranks covering a wide range of pitches. It is less loud than the Stentor Mixture. Middle C and the pedal's low CCC key sound these pitches:

Manual 16' series VI		Manual 8' series VI		Pedal 32' series VI		Pedal 16' series VI	
C^3	2'	C^4	1'	C	4'	C^1	2'
G^2	2 2/3'	G^3	1 1/3'	GG	5 1/3'	G	2 2/3'
C^2	4'	C^3	2'	CC	8'	C	4'
G^1	5 1/3'	G^2	2 2/3'	GGG	10 2/3'	GG	5 1/3'
C^1	8'	C^2	4'	CCC	16'	CC	8'
C	16'	C^1	8'	CCCC	32'	CCC	16'

GAMBA. An unimitative String stop of 16' or 8' on the manuals, and 32', 16', or 8' on the pedals. This well-known and very useful solo and ensemble String is voiced to sound with a clear, brilliant, incisive tone of moderate loudness. Its parcel of overtones is louder than that of the Salicional, and it has more fundamental than that stop, but is not quite so loud as the 'Cello or Violin Diapason. Being of less-small scale than the orchestral Viols, its pipes sound with much less of the keen, pungent, cutting timbre than those stops. The modern Gamba is a good combinational stop, not masking other tones so much as the older, coarser forms do. The pipes have a very high tin content and a moderately large scale for a String. The *Viola da Gamba* is imitative of the old instrument of the same name, but the Gamba of the modern organ is not so light-toned and has a more noticeable fundamental prime tone. This String, like others,

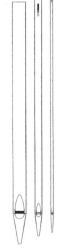

A diagram to show different scales of pipes of the same pitch. Left, a Principal; center, a normal String pipe; right, a Viole d'Orchestre.

should sometimes be played alone as a contrast to the many large-scaled and less bright stops. Following is a list of the most common String stops arranged from top to bottom in order of increasing brightness (number of overtones). The brightness of a String indicates to the organist its potential in combinations, more than does its relative loudness. A continuation of this scale into the realm of the Foundation stops can be seen under GEIGEN DIAPASON:

Violone (8')
Viola d'Amore
Muted 'Cello
Cone Gamba
Viola (average specimen)
'Cello (wood)
'Cello (metal)
Salicional
Gamba
Aeoline (a soft stop)
Ethereal Violin (a soft stop)
Viole d'Orchestre

See BELL GAMBA, CONE GAMBA, VIOLA DA GAMBA.

GAMBA CÉLESTE. An undulating 8' String stop on the manuals composed of two ranks of Gambas. On the Solo Organ this céleste can be quite loud and pungent, and may even rival the 'Cello Céleste in power, but it lacks that stop's warm, assertive, orchestral tone quality. It makes a very brilliant céleste and may be heard from the String Organ with the Viole Célestes. It makes a definite contrast with all other String célestes because it is both loud and bright-toned; most of them are *soft* and bright. It is useful in playing episodic passages that demand a tone of special contrast. It blends less easily than the Voix Céleste, but more easily than the Viole Céleste. See CÉLESTE, GAMBA.

GAMBETTE. A Gamba of 4' octave pitch on the manuals, somewhat smaller in scale than either the Fugara or some Diapason-String hybrids at this pitch. It is the proper Octave for the unison Gamba of 8'. It is voiced to blend with the unison Gamba without destroying its pitch-impression. It may be in a Swell or String Organ. Various pipe-forms have been made for it, each having some tonal advantage, since the conical form remains keen but lacks all tendency towards dissonance or shrillness. The Gamba 2' also is sometimes seen. See FUGARA, GAMBA.

GEDECKT. A *stopped* Flute of 32', 16', 8', or 4' on the manuals, and 32', 16', 8', or 4' on the pedals. The pipes are usually of wood to ensure a pleasing formant and a resonant tone, but thick metal is sometimes used. High mouths create tones of comparative purity of fundamental but slow the speech; lower mouths inject a little more *Twelfth* (assuming the unison pitch). The only purer Flute is the *Tibia Clausa*. The *Lieblichgedeckt* has a smooth, round tone that is generally also soft. The Gedeckt blends well, even with Strings, because it is not intense or loud. It blends also with open or stopped Flutes. It is chiefly a combining stop, and its main function is to offer a fundamental suitable for ensembles of both soft and moderate dynamic levels. Secondary functions include diluting the too-prominent partials in another stop, solo playing, contrast with bright stops like the Gamba, and the sounding of a pervading, gentle bass in the pedals. It is also well-known as one of the most useful Copulas. It is not an ideal accompaniment stop.

The Gedeckt may be in any division, even the String Organ if it is of small scale. The Choir finds use for it as a support to the ground tone at the unison pitch. On the Positiv it can make a "pure" tone at any of the octave-sounding or mutation pitches, such as 2′ or 2 2/3′. The Bourdon may be preferred for the Great, but the Gedeckt's round, liquid tone may travel outward from the Solo Organ either alone or in combination with another flue in need of a firmer pitch or a deeper tonal dimension. It is also heard from the Swell and Echo Organs at either 8′ or 4′. The pedal examples, of larger scale than those of the manuals, are useful with the Vox Humana, soft diminutive Foundation stops, like the Dulciana and Dolcan, and as a source of ground tone for any other stop. This stop is sometimes unified in the smaller church organs. Since this

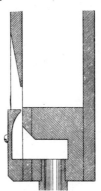

Mouth portion of a Gedeckt pipe. This specimen has a relatively low mouth cut-up, giving it some additional third harmonic, proportional to the wind.

Flute is not valuable in building a vertical line of tone, as are the Diapasons and Gemshorns, this can be a useful source of many stop-pitches, such as the 4′, 2 2/3′, 2′, or 1 3/5′. Treble pipes are soft-toned and open.

Many varieties of Gedeckts exist, some mostly aids to other tones, like the *Stillgedeckt* and the *Gedeckt* itself, and others conspicuously beautiful solo voices, like the *Schöngedeckt* and *Singengedeckt*. The *Echo Gedeckt* and *Lieblichgedeckt* are useful for many solo and ensemble functions. There are many other varieties beside these, with some interchange of names and tone qualities. The well-known experiment of multiplying Gedeckt ranks of many pitches in order to simulate other stops fails because these ranks never go high enough, are tuned by hand rather than natural law, and are not accurately adjusted in volume. Neither do they simulate *initial* harmonics.

If these wooden pipes are rectangular, the mouths are cut on the narrow sides to increase depth of tone and that truly velvety quality so much admired by many listeners. The upper corners of the mouth may be arched to eliminate a few even-numbered harmonic traces. This Flute covers more of the eleven-octave compass of the pipe organ than most stops, but, of course, is made from small open metal pipes in the high treble notes, the break in timbre between the stopped wood and the open metal being imperceptible in most specimens. The scale of the CC pipe is around 3.5 x 3 to 6 x 4 inches. The low pedal CCC pipe varies from 10 x 7 to 15 x 11 inches, and the very large CCCC pipe is about 20 x 17 inches. Capped metal ranks also make the Gedeckt's tone, without the wood's resonance. See COPULA.

GEDECKTFLÖTE. A Gedeckt of 4' on the manuals, useful as a soft source of the octave in combinations. See GEDECKT, LIEBLICHGEDECKT, SCHÖNGEDECKT.

GEDECKTPOMMER. A stopped metal (sometimes wood) Flute of 16' or 8' on manuals and pedals. Its third harmonic, made prominent by over-blowing, can be as loud as its fundamental. In a heavier flue combination this stop creates some cleanness of ensemble and a clearness of pitch impression, both of which are most useful in identifying the notes of the music. It thus has the function of the *Quint Flute* series. It is a Copula as well. It can have a louder third harmonic than the Quintadena, in relation to its prime tone, and its fifth harmonic may also be heard. See ROHRPOMMER. Synonym: POMMER.

GEDECKTQUINTE. A large-scaled Gedeckt of 5 1/3' on the manuals, and 10 2/3' on the pedals, pitched at the third harmonic of the sub-unison series of stops. A sub-unison stop should be drawn with it. See GEDECKT, QUINT.

GEDECKT TIERCE. A small-scaled Gedeckt of 1 3/5' on the manuals, and 3 1/5' on the pedals, sounding the fifth harmonic of the unison series of stops. It is of more use on the pedals because in the manual rank many pipes are of open form. This useful mutation is a *mild* Tierce. See GEDECKT, TIERCE.

GEDECKT TWELFTH. A 2 2/3' manual and 5 1/3' pedal Gedeckt sounding the third harmonic as a soft Flute *Twelfth*. See GEDECKT, TWELFTH.

GEIGENBASS. A Foundation stop of Diapason tone, at 32' or 16' on the manuals, and 32' on the pedals. The 32' manual stop is heard on the Great of a few large organs, mostly in Europe, and then sometimes only down to tenor C (below middle C). This permits the 32', and also 16' and 8', to be available on the pedals. The 16' manual Geigen is preferred by some organists because it is usually of better blend, being somewhat stronger harmonically than the average Diapason. This "Double" on both manuals and pedals has a strong fundamental and never assumes the harmonic development of the Violone or Violin Diapason. Wooden pipes are sometimes seen, and they can give a superior tone. See DOUBLE DIAPASON. GEIGEN DIAPASON.

GEIGEN DIAPASON. A Diapason of more than normal loudness in its overtone series, rarely superior in the *number* of overtones to most open metal Diapasons of equivalent pitch. This Foundation stop sounds at 32', 16', 8', or 4' on the manuals, and 32', 16', or 8' on the pedals. It is not at all string-like in spite of this name, nor does it deserve the adjective *bright;* it merely has an *extension in loudness* of the regular Diapason overtones, plus, in some ranks, fewer than six additional overtones. It blends well with all stops, even Reeds, and is considered to be superior at the higher pitches (above 8′) by many organists. Mixture and mutation ranks are frequently Geigens. This may be the second or third Diapason on the Great or Choir at 8′.

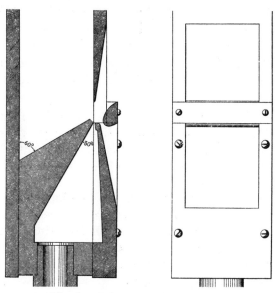

Wooden Geigen Diapason at CC.

A list of "Diapasons" is arranged below in order of increasing brightness from top to bottom:

Wood Diapason (dull)
average metal Diapason
Schulze Diapason
Echo Geigen Diapason
Geigen Diapason
Viola Diapason
Salicional Diapason
Violin Diapason
Gamba Diapason
Violone (a String) (bright)

See DIAPASON, GEIGENBASS. Synonym: GEIGEN PRINCIPAL.

GEIGEN FIFTEENTH. A Geigen Diapason of 2′ manual and 4′ pedal pitch. This Super Octave adds a brighter-than-average "top" to the 8′, 4′, 2 2/3′, and 2′ basic choir of Diapasons. It is frequently heard in mixtures and is also heard as a separate stop. See FIFTEENTH, GEIGEN DIAPASON. Synonym: GEIGEN SUPER OCTAVE.

GEIGEN OCTAVE. A Geigen Diapason of 4′ manual pitch, and 8′ pedal pitch, sounding what many organists consider to be the superior Octave, because it imparts liveliness, great clarity, and a "fiery" quality to the unisons without also giving the string-like sound. See GEIGEN DIAPASON, OCTAVE.

GEIGEN PRINCIPAL. See GEIGEN DIAPASON, PRINCIPAL.

GEIGENREGAL. A brilliant but light-toned 8′ or 4′ manual and pedal Regal, emitting a string-like series of partials from short, small-diametered resonators. The timbre is reedy and very thin. See REGAL.

GEIGEN SUPER OCTAVE. See GEIGEN FIFTEENTH.

GEIGEN TWELFTH. A Geigen Diapason of 2 2/3′ manual pitch, and 5 1/3′ pedal pitch, forming one of the most useful Twelfths in the organ. Being bright but not stringy, it gives a unique variety of the "quinty" effect to any ensemble. See GEIGEN DIAPASON, TWELFTH.

GELINDGEDECKT. A very soft and pure-toned Gedeckt of small scale, at 16′, 8′, or 4′ on the manuals. See ECHO GEDECKT, GEDECKT, LIEBLICH-GEDECKT.

GEMSHORN. A Foundation stop of 16′, 8′, or 4′ on the manuals, and 32′, 16′, 8′, or 4′ on the pedals. This near-Diapason does not have the functions of the Diapason, but it is a clean-toned, neutral-colored fabric of the harmonics natural to open metal pipes of *conical* shape. Some ranks are delicate in tone, although many examples are as big at the mouth-line as the Diapasons that they may sit next to. The harmonics from approximately the twelfth to the twenty-fourth are damped by this pipe-shape. The second, fourth, fifth, seventh, and ninth are stimulated by this pipe-shape. The timbre is fine, silvery, and escapes hardness, and even suggests brightness. This beautiful singing tone, frequently unnoticed, is often used in combination with Diapasons, Flutes, Strings, and Reeds. It is an ideal accompaniment for many solo stops, because it does not disturb the identity of the more colorful register. It makes the pitches in the accompaniment clear without adding any apparent weight of tone, but simply gives support and a little ground tone against which to contrast the solo stop. Using the octave and sub-octave couplers makes a broader range in the accompaniment without making it much louder. When added to an 8′ solo stop, either at 8′ or 4′, such as the Keraulophone, 'Cello, Gamba, or Flauto Mirabilis, it supplies missing or weak *lower* harmonics without becoming conspicuous itself. The Echo Gemshorn can have the same function.

The Gemshorn is an ideal Foundation stop for the Great or Choir, not duplicating the Diapason's effects in either accompaniment or ensemble. It is even a good accompaniment for a solo on the Diapason itself. It can build up the bright tones of the Swell, but it is not often in this division. It is a telling pedal bass, clear down to the 32′ octave, but does not have the heavy fundamental of many pedal flue stops. Nevertheless, it makes the pitches known clearly, and even provides a little of the rumble expected from an open pipe thirty-two feet long. Like all conical ranks, it is a good binder between bright and dull flue stops. The manual 16′ rank is preferred by some organists because it is not weighty in tone, yet makes the sub-octave pitches felt. Neither the metal nor the wood rank is a colorful solo stop by itself.

This stop varies in loudness, the Great Organ rank often being of considerable carrying power. *Echo Gemshorns* exist, and are heard in the

Choir or Echo Organ. An interesting contrast can be made with the Dolce, another Foundation stop, which has the *inverted-conical* shape of pipe. Its tones are opaque, full, warm, in opposition to the Gemshorn's, which are transparent, silvery, and almost luminous to the ear. Both are ensemble and accompaniment stops of much usefulness. Together on one division they may be combined, making a complete accompaniment tone, but one not too loud for many solo stops. This stop is frequently unified on smaller church organs, but it is more useful if four straight ranks are provided, especially since couplers are frequently used on these organs:

(two octaves higher)	Gemshorn 2′	(fourth harmonic)
(the twelfth note above)	Gemshorn 2 2/3′	(third harmonic)
(one octave higher)	Gemshorn 4′	(second harmonic)
(the piano's unison pitch)	Gemshorn 8′	(first harmonic; fundamental)

Placing this chorus of Gemshorns on the Choir or Great makes the very valuable 4′, 2′, and 2 2/3′ ranks available for separate combinations. The *Erzähler* is of conical form also, but frequently of smaller mouth-line diameter and top diameter as well. The conical *Spitzflöte* is of higher cut-up but about two-thirds top diameter, whereas the Gemshorn has a top diameter of about one-third the mouth-line diameter. *Baarpijp* refers to some type of Gemshorn or open Flute. See ERZÄHLER, SPITZFLÖTE.

GEMSHORNBASS. See DOUBLE GEMSHORN.

GEMSHORN CÉLESTE. An undulating 8′ Foundation céleste on the manuals, made from two ranks of Gemshorns, sometimes of smaller than normal scale. They may be *normal-sharp* in pitch design, but are more useful if *sharp-flat,* since this enables both ranks to sound nearer the normal pitch. A slow undulation offers more uses in combination and accompaniment, because it causes less impairment to the timbres of all other pipes. Only the brilliant, small-scale stops are adaptable to fast undulations. The timbre of this céleste can be clear and shining, sounding silvery in some examples. See CÉLESTE, GEMSHORN.

GEMSHORN FIFTEENTH. A Foundation stop of 2′ manual and 4′ pedal pitch. It has much of the Gemshorn's transparent and clean tone, but the overtones at this pitch are harder to hear, making this tone color less apparent. This fourth harmonic of the *Gemshorn Chorus* is useful with or without the other Gemshorn ranks. It may be on the Choir. It is never shrill or fluty in tone, but clear and neutral-colored, in spite of its pitch. It is useful with the stops of the String Organ, since a 2′ String is quite a bright timbre. It is not a substitute, however, for the regular Great Fifteenth. Its spotted metal pipes are of very small scale. See FIFTEENTH, GEMSHORN. Synonym: GEMSHORN SUPER OCTAVE.

GEMSHORN MIXTURE. A compound manual stop designed as a mixture and made from several ranks of Gemshorns of varying loudness and hue. The Erzähler and Conical Flutes are also sometimes used: This mixture of Foundation pipes is valuable as a tone builder, accompaniment, background, and source of separate ranks at many pitches. It sounds better without the 1 3/5′ Tierce, but this might be included for a particular reason. It may be called a *Gemshorn Cornet* when played as a solo voice, with or without the 1 3/5'. Pedal forms of compounded Gemshorns are less valuable than Diapasons. These examples show the same pitches at three different series. Middle C would sound at these notes, other keys in relative positions:*

16' Example VI			8' Example VI			4' Example VI	
C³	2'		C⁴	1'		C⁵	1/2'
G²	2 2/3'		G³	1 1/3'		G⁴	2/3'
C²	4'		C³	2'		C⁴	1'
G¹	5 1/3'		G²	2 2/3'		G³	1 1/3'
C¹	8'		C²	4'		C³	2'
C	16'		C¹	8'		C²	4'

See GEMSHORN.

GEMSHORN OCTAVE. An octave Foundation rank at 4' on the manuals, and 8' on the pedals, usually of smaller scale and softer voice than the unison Gemshorns. This delicate, clear, silvery timbre is an ideal soft second Octave for the Great or Choir Organ. It furnishes an inconspicuous layer of overtones, without hardness or loudness, to any combination of flues. It may be derived from a Gemshorn Chorus. See GEMSHORN, OCTAVE.

GEMSHORNQUINTE. A Foundation stop of 5 1/3' manual pitch, and 10 2/3' pedal pitch, made from Gemshorn pipes, sometimes of large scale. It should not be drawn without a 16' manual flue or a 32' stop on the pedals. It is a less penetrating and easier to use Quint than the normal Diapason Quint. See GEMSHORN, QUINT.

GEMSHORN SUPER OCTAVE. See GEMSHORN FIFTEENTH.

GEMSHORN TWELFTH. A Foundation stop at the Twelfth's pitch of 2 2/3' on the manuals, and 5 1/3' on the pedals, sounding from Gemshorn pipes. It is a moderately soft Twelfth in most examples, since it is of smaller scale than either the Octave or unison Gemshorns. It has all of the function of the Twelfth, and makes a useful Twelfth with the Strings, Diapasons, and all flues of light tone. It cannot be substituted for the regular Twelfth. It sometimes functions like the Copula. See GEMSHORN, TWELFTH.

GEMSHORN VIOLIN. A hybrid stop of String classification, at 8' manual pitch, sounding with both the brilliant timbre of the Viol and the transparent, clean timbre of the Gemshorn of smaller scale. This combination of tones creates a stop that is useful in many ensembles. It is a good 8' base-tone for the String division, perhaps as a *normal-sharp* céleste, and a suitable String for the Swell. It is a bright but rather inconspicuous accompaniment, and a source of timbre for other stops, such as the 'Cello Keraulophone, Viola, or the open Flutes. It forms a binding agent between the Viole d'Orchestre and the dull flues, like the Diapason or Gedeckts. See GEMSHORN, VIOL D'ORCHESTRE.

*Middle C and the low pedal CCC keys are used to illustrate examples of compound stops because it is felt that most organists think of timbre and pitch around these positions on the manuals and pedals. Breaks in pitch can be calculated from middle C as well as from the low manual CC key, from which point some organ books illustrate manual mixtures.

GERMAN FLUTE. An open metal Flute of 8′ or 4′ on the manuals, with a bright, ringing, harmonically full timbre that is not at all stringy or horn-like. Its pipes are usually formed from spotted metal and are both *harmonic* and *conical*. The harmonic form adds some resonance to the lower-pitched harmonics, and the conical shape removes the higher harmonics and brings out the stronger odd-numbered components, making the tone a little more pervading and expansive than it would otherwise be. If well-proportioned, the tone is an ideal solo as well as ensemble Flute, resembling the Orchestral Flute. See CONICAL FLUTE, HARMONIC FLUTE, SILVER FLUTE.

GERMAN GAMBA. A String stop of 8′ on the manuals, with a longer *initial*† period of harmonics than most Gambas, and some noticeable coarseness in speech, much desired by certain organists. A Gedeckt or open Flute of 8′ may be drawn with it to mask its slowness in speaking. See GAMBA.

GLOCKENFLöTE. See BELL FLUTE.

GLOCKENGAMBA. See BELL GAMBA.

GLOCKENSPIEL. See CARILLON.

GRAND BOURDON. A pedal mixture composed of several ranks of stopped wood, occasionally metal, Flutes, designed to build up the pedal tone to harmonic fullness. This is more satisfying to the ear. From just one pedal key a strong *chord* of notes can be heard, usually beginning at the 32′. This compound stop takes up much space, and is found only in an organ of some size. Ranks, like most pedal mixtures, do not break back in pitch, as the scale is ascended. The entire mixture may be made from wooden or metal ranks of *open* form. It is not desirable to unify all the pitches from just one long rank of pipes because even with the special unit-rank scales the balance of tone is not ideal. Also, even in the deep bass the difference in pitch between pipes tuned to the equal-tempered notes and those tuned to natural harmonics can cause some undulation. Four examples with notes from the CCC key:

Example No. 1		Example No. 2		Example No. 3		Example No. 4	
VIII		VIII		VIII		X	
*C¹	2′	C³	1/2′	C¹	2′	C²	1′
G	2 2/3′	C²	1′	G	2 2/3′	G¹	1 1/3′
E	3 1/5′	C¹	2′	C	4′	C¹	2′
C	4′	C	4′	GG	5 1/3′	G	2 2/3′
GG	5 1/3′	GG	5 1/3′	CC	8′	C	4′
EE	6 2/5′	CC	8′	GGG	10 2/3′	GG	5 1/3′
CC	8′	CCC	16′	CCC	16′	CC	8′
CCC	16′	CCCC	32′	CCCC	32′	GGG	10 2/3′
						CCC	16′
						CCCC	32′

*Ranks above 4′ can be soft *open* pipes.

GRAND CHORUS. A manual and pedal mixture composed of open Foundation pipes designed to build up the tone to the maximum extent in both body and brilliance. Even the 1/4′ can be seen in both manual and pedal examples. Some examples have two or even more ranks at the same

†Inital harmonics are *transient*, as are those that come and go from the steady tone. Entirely **different** transients sound in the dying-away period also.

pitch to increase the sound-sources. This stop has a variety of materials and unusual patterns for the breaks in the pitches, usually in the manuals, since pedal ranks are not likely to break in pitch. Occasionally the pipes are borrowed from a great variety of other stops, especially in the pedal examples. Three examples follow, with notes sounded by middle C and the low pedal CCC key:

Manual Example XIII		Pedal Example No. 1 XVIII		Pedal Example No. 2 XVIII	
C^5	$1/2'$	C^3	$1/2'$	C^3	$1/2'$
G^4	$2/3'$	G^2	$2/3'$	G^2	$2/3'$
E^4	$4/5'$	C^2	$1'$	E^2	$4/5'$
C^4	$1'$	G^1	$1\ 1/3'$	C^2	$1'$
Bb^3	$1\ 1/7'$	E^1	$1\ 3/5'$	G^1	$1\ 1/3'$
G^3	$1\ 1/3'$	C^1	$2'$	E^1	$1\ 3/5'$
E^3	$1\ 3/5'$	Bb	$2\ 2/7'$	C^1	$2'$
C^3	$2'$ (conical)	G	$2\ 2/3'$	G	$2\ 2/3'$
C^3	$2'$	E	$3\ 1/5'$	E	$3\ 1/5'$
G^2	$2\ 2/3'$ (conical)	C	$4'$ (wood)	C	$4'$
G^2	$2\ 2/'$	C	$4'$ (metal)	GG	$5\ 1/3'$
C^2	$4'$	GG	$5\ 1/3'$ (wood)	EE	$6\ 2/5'$
C^1	$8'$	GG	$5\ 1/3'$ (metal)	CC	$8'$
		CC	$8'$ (wood)	GGG	$10\ 2/3'$
		CC	$8'$ (metal)	$*EEE$	$12\ 4/5'$
		CCC	$16'$ (wood)	CCC	$16'$
		CCC	$16'$ (metal)	$*GGGG$	$21\ 1/3'$
		$CCCC$	$32'$	$CCCC$	$32'$

*Belongs to 64' series.
See GRAND BOURDON.

GRAND CORNET. A compound manual stop of the sub-unison series of 16' (or a pedal stop based on the 32' series) composed of loudly voiced pipes of open metal construction. This stop provides a brilliant and richly voiced source of timbre for addition to either the flue Chorus or Chorus Reeds of any division. One example with notes from middle C follows:

Manual Example
V

G^2	$2\ 2/3'$
$*E^2$	$3\ 1/5'$
C^2	$4'$
$*G^1$	$5\ 1/3'$
C^1	$8'$

*Belongs to the 16' series.
See CORNET.

GRAND DIAPASON. A full-toned and loud Diapason of open metal pipes at the unison 8' manual pitch, and sometimes at 16' pedal pitch. This name is sometimes given to the largest manual Diapason in scale in a whole series of Diapasons, as on a Great Organ, but this name does not indicate the solo type of Foundation tone. It is practically synonymous with *Major Diapason* and *Stentor Diapason*. The name *Chorus Diapason* has itself been used on a few stop keys. Here is this name in association with other *unison* names, as on a very large Great Organ, decreasing in brightness from No. 5 to No. 1:

Diapason No. 5	$8'$
Diapason No. 4	$8'$
Diapason No. 3	$8'$
Diapason No. 2	$8'$
Diapason No. 1	$8'$
Grand Diapason	$8'$

Octaves, Twelfths, Fifteenths, and compound stops would be provided for combination with these unisons. Such a series is necessary in a *very large* auditorium or cathedral for full intensity, as well as being desirable for better tone. Many sound sources, like duplicated first violins in an orchestra, are irreplaceable for better quality; they create the complex, constantly varying undulations needed for a "big," warm tone quality. See DIAPASON. Synonym: GRAND PRINCIPAL.

GRAND FOURNITURE. A brilliant and full-toned mixture stop on the manuals, designed to complete the chorus of harmonic pitches in the 16' or 8' series of stops. It is made from open metal Diapasons. It extends the Chorus upward in pitch, making a structure of sound that is rich and most typically organ-like in timbre. Pedal examples also exist. The Tierce of 1 3/5' is usually supplied by another mixture or independent. Middle C sounds:

16' Example VI			8' Example VI	
G^3	1 1/3'		C^5	1/2'
C^3	2'		G^4	2/3'
G^2	2 2/3'		C^4	1'
C^2	4'		G^3	1 1/3'
G^1	5 1/3'		C^3	2'
C^1	8'		G^2	2 2/3'

See FOURNITURE.

GRAND MIXTURE. A stop name that refers to a manual or pedal mixture of unusual completeness in its harmonic pitches. Its open metal (or wood) ranks add *a complete chord of harmonics* to any combination, solo or ensemble. It may be used alone or as an adjunct to flue or Reed tones. Its pitches are based on the unison open-pipe partials. The lowest eight are represented. Examples on other pitch series can be formed. Sounding from the middle C key and the pedal's low CCC key:

Manual Example VIII			Pedal Example VIII	
C^4	1'	(eighth harmonic)	C^1	2'
Bb^3	1 1/7'	(seventh harmonic)	Bb	2 2/7'
G^3	1 1/3'	(sixth harmonic)	G	2 2/3'
E^3	1 3/5'	(fifth harmonic)	E	3 1/5'
C^3	2'	(fourth harmonic)	C	4'
G^2	2 2/3'	(third harmonic)	GG	5 1/3'
C^2	4'	(second harmonic)	CC	8'
C^1	8'	(first harmonic; unison)	CCC	16'

For the student interested in ascending natural harmonics that climb even higher in the 8' series, here are the *ninth* to *sixteenth* complete. All would be tuned to the harmonics' pitches, not the scale's notes. A mixture with all sixteen does not exit in America, but even a Gamba of 8' *sounds every one from each pipe,* the dissonant 8/11', 8/13', and 8/15' very softly. Pedal equivalents exist for the 16' series, at the double pitches as above:

C^5	1/2'	(sixteenth harmonic)
B^4	8/15'	(fifteenth harmonic)
Bb^4	4/7'	(fourteenth harmonic)
A^4	8/13'	(thirteenth harmonic)
G^4	2/3'	(twelfth harmonic)
F^4	8/11'	(eleventh harmonic)
E^4	4/5'	(tenth harmonic)
D^4	8/9'	(ninth harmonic)

All ranks speaking together would sound reed-like; most mixtures sound the 2/3' and 1/2' in the lower compass. Much vitality of tone and some unusual staccato effects can be obtained from these pitches as diminutive Principals. Octave- and fifth-sounding ranks require no additional pitches to assimilate them into the tone; the more unusual pitches do require at least one octave-sounding rank to orient them.

Individual ranks in the above mixture are at different degrees of volume, perhaps also different in tone quality, in order to give the sound unity of effect. The octave-sounding ranks (16', 8', 4', 2', 1') are louder than the other ranks, the two unison ranks being the loudest. The fifth-sounding ranks (5 1/3', 2 2/3', 1 1/3') are less loud, and perhaps conical in form. The third-sounding ranks (3 1/5', 1 3/5') are quite soft to keep them from injecting too much sharp quality. The flatted-seventh-sounding ranks (2 2/7', 1 1/7') are very soft, perhaps Echo Dulcianas, to keep them from being "gritty" in the ear. See GRAND BOURDON, GRAND CHORUS.

GRAND PRINCIPAL. See GRAND DIAPASON.

GRAND QUINT. A Foundation stop of large scale and loud tone, pitched at 5 1/3' on the manuals, and 10 2/3' on the pedals, forming the third harmonic (the "Twelfth") of the sub-unison choir of pitches. This stop, which is a Principal or Diapason in most examples, should always be combined with louder ensembles including a 16' manual pitch and a 32' pedal pitch. It speaks at the interval of a fifth above the keys depressed on manuals and pedals, that is at G¹ from middle C, and GGG from the pedal's low CCC key. It is similar to the Quint in function. A few stops of this name speak at 10 2/3' on the manuals and 21 1/3' on the pedals, but the names *Gross Quint* or *Grossquintenbass* are more appropriate for them. *Grand* may refer to a large scale, prominent voicing, or to any one of the long series of the sub-unison pitches one octave below the normal meanings in a stop name. See QUINT.

GRAND VIOL. A String stop of 8' on the manuals, having a solo tone quality similar to the Orchestral Violin (Viole d'Orchestre) stop, but of much keener and more assertive effect than this stop usually has. It is also useful as the loudest unison rank of a String Organ, for it can blend with the brilliant and incisive stops of this division. Its cutting, pungent, loud tone is unsuitable for any of the organ's regular divisions (Great, Swell, Choir, Solo), because its dissonant harmonics (and inharmonics) would clash with the notes of the equal-tempered scale, as sounded by the fundamentals of other stops. Some of this clashing is pleasant and some unpleasant, and the amount tolerated must be judged by the musical function of the organ in question. The smaller scales of this String naturally have more dissonance within one pipe's tone than the larger scales. The scale of the 8' manual Violone is assumed by some specimens, and others have a scale so small at low CC that it is little more than one inch inside the pipe. Smaller scales induce hardness as well as dissonance, and have less fundamental with which to sound the melody's pitches. The pipes are constructed like those of the other Viols. See VIOLE D'ORCHESTRE.

GRAVISSIMA. See RESULTANT.

GROSSDOPPELGEDECKT. A large-scale stopped wood Flute of 16′ on the manuals and pedals. It is built with two mouths in each pipe, usually on opposite sides, in order to give a very round-toned, full sound which can be used as a base-tone for the building up of ensembles of stops. On the pedals it serves as a foundation for Diapason, Flutes, and Strings of louder tone, making them firmer in pitch and of more weight. It may be seen as the 16′ stop on a larger Solo Organ where it can give substance to many of the stops, making their timbres stand out in greater dimension and more obvious pitch. See DOPPELGEDECKT, GROSSFLÖTE.

GROSSFLÖTE. A large-scale open wood Flute of 8′ on both manuals and pedals. Most specimens have one mouth per pipe, but a few have two for the purpose of making the tone deeper and of greater *intensity*, but not necessarily louder. It is more useful in combination than by itself, since it provides a carrier sound wave of considerable intensity on which to transport tones of other stops, perhaps some distance. This function is also performed by the profound bass stops and 16′ manual stops. The fundamental also performs it for a series of overtones. There is less loss of the exact timbre and sense of true pitch, as well as the many degrees or volume, when higher and weaker sounds are transported to the ear by the deeper pitches. Details of the music are therefore heard more accurately when just the right amount of fundamental (or sub-fundamental) is heard.

This stop is midway between a dull and a bright tone, without enough harmonic development to make it individual. It does no damage to the solo Trumpets, Gambas, or Major Open Flutes that it sounds with. Of course it will impress its own sound on the softer stops, but it is not primarily designed for these, although examples do vary in loudness. Hardwood lips and shades at the tops are also used.

GROSSGAMBA. See CONTRA GAMBA.

GROSSGEDECKT. A large-scale Gedeckt of 16′ or 8′ on the manuals with a deep sound and substantial prime tone at both pitches. One company builds the mouths halfway up the pipe's body to achieve some additional resonance. See GEDECKT.

GROSSGEMSHORN. See DOUBLE GEMSHORN.

GROSS NASARD. See QUINT.

GROSS QUINT. See SUB QUINT.

GROSSQUINTENBASS. See SUB QUINT.

GROSSRAUSCHQUINTE. A compound manual stop composed of Diapason pipes, sounding the third and fourth harmonics of the sub-unison series. Middle C speaks at these notes:

$$\text{II}$$
$$\text{C}^2 \quad 4'$$
$$\text{G}^1 \quad 5\ 1/3'$$

See RAUSCHQUINTE.

GROSS TIERCE. See TENTH.

HARFENPRINZIPAL. A soft, delicately toned Diapason of 8' or 4' on the manuals, sounding noticeably both the fundamental and the octave harmonics. If played with a staccato touch, perhaps as arpeggios, these slow-speaking pipes might seem to give the gentle twang of a string. This stop may also take the form of an *Echo Geigen Principal*. The pipes are of small scale and the alloy rich in tin. See DIAPASON, GEIGEN DIAPASON.

HARMONIA AETHERIA. A manual mixture of soft and sedate tonality, creating a beautiful and delicately toned background, also serving as a source of harmonics for soft combinations. This is also an accompaniment stop, even the high-pitched ranks not disturbing the solo notes, since the whole mixture is designed and voiced to sound as a *unit of tone*. The pipes may be Echo Viola, Echo Dulciana, or especially voiced for this mixture, which may be called an *Echo Mixture*. Middle C sounds at these pitches:

Example No. 1		Example No. 2		Example No. 3	
V		V		V	
G^3	1 1/3'	C^4	1'	C^5	1/2'
C^3	2'	G^3	1 1/3'	C^4	1'
G^2	2 2/3'	C^3	2'	G^3	1 1/3'
C^2	4'	G^2	2 2/3'	C^3	2'
C^1	8'	C^2	4'	C^2	4'

HARMONICA. An open wooden Flute of 8' on the manuals, sounding like a hybrid between a very soft *open* Flute and an Echo Aeoline. It has a certain amount of brightness in spite of its soft quality, and is a little brighter than a Dulciana Flute. *Harmonika* may be a preferred spelling.

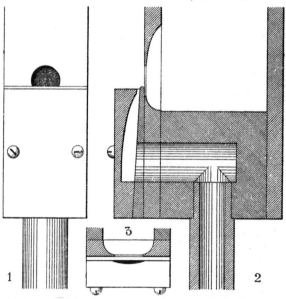

Harmonica or *Harmonika* pipe at middle C. The unusually small, round mouth creates Flute-String timbre of unusual softness. 1 is front view; 2 is interior side view; 3 is cross-section at mouth-line.

HARMONIC CLARIBEL. An open wood Flute of 8′ on the manuals, with a form quite like the Claribel's, but *harmonic* in length, each double-length pipe pierced near the middle by a small hole. This moderately loud Flute sounds with clarity and firmness of speech. It has fewer overtones than the unison-length variety. It is of excellent blend, and some examples can disappear into an ensemble of flues, at the same time lending smoothness, an even-pitch quality, and some strength in the lower overtones. It is a solo stop as well. The 4′ and 2 2/3′ ranks exist. See CLARABELLA.

HARMONIC CLARION. See CLARION HARMONIC.

HARMONIC CORNET. A compound Foundation stop on the manuals, made harmonic for greater penetration and cleanness of timbre. Its rich tones make prominent the chief melody of the music. It is a majestic and imposing solo stop. It gives brilliance to the Diapasons of the Chorus or the loud Trumpets and Tubas. Middle C would sound these notes on the manuals:

Example No. 1 III		Example No. 2 III		Example No. 3 III	
E^3	1 3/5′	E^3	1 3/5′	C^4	1′
C^3	2′	G^2	2 2/3′	G^3	1 1/3′
G^2	2 2/3′	C^2	4′	C^3	2′

See CORNET.

HARMONIC CYMBAL. An unusually brilliant and penetrating form of the manual Cymbal stop, made from open metal pipes of harmonic length. These pipes sound more brilliant at these high pitches because their trains of overtones are down nearer the threshold of audibility than those sounded by the unison-length pipes of the Cymbal. They are less dissonant and also of better blend with the louder Reed and flue stops. This is an ideal mixture for the Bombarde or Solo division and may also point up the altitude of pitch in a big Diapason Chorus, since these pipes are basically Foundation pipes. Middle C would speak these notes from these examples:

Example No. 1 VI		Example No. 2 VI	
C^5	1/2′	C^5	1/2′
G^4	2/3′	G^4	2/3′
C^4	1′	E^4	4/5′
G^3	1 1/3′	C^4	1′
C^3	2′	G^3	1 1/3′
G^2	2 2/3′	E^3	1 3/5′

These very high-pitched ranks will duplicate harmonics to the point of unusual loudness and even intense brilliance. This type of mixture is suitable only with the loudest of fanfares or flue ensembles. See CYMBAL, HARMONIC CORNET.

HARMONIC DIAPASON. A Foundation stop of 8′ manual pitch, creating this Diapason tone from large-scale, thick-walled pipes of loud voicing. The small hole in the wall of each pipe and the double-length form function as the Harmonic Flute, making a tone that is louder in total energy output but less bright than a unison-length pipe of 8′. Large-scale harmonic flues are usually quite dull, but intense, and opposite in effect from a Stentor-phone. The Harmonic Diapason can be used as a base-tone for the Solo or Bombarde Organ, where its firmness of tone and great body of sound build up the Tubas and Trumpets to an even more magnificent effect than they can achieve without a loud flue support. It is not conducive, of course, to the fanfare effect. A louder than normal Octave may accompany it. It is not considered a desirable support for the Diapason Chorus. By itself it is an impressive and penetrating solo voice peculiar to the larger and more complete organs. The pipes are unison-length in the bass range. See DIAPASON.

HARMONIC FLUTE. An 8′ or 4′ manual Flute of metal or wood construction formed from double-length pipes, pierced near the middle with a small hole, or even three holes vertically arranged. Some 2′ examples exist, but these may have another name, such as *Piccolo*. The tone quality is of solo stature and most useful in brightening an ensemble of flues without contributing some of the unwanted harmonics in the unison-length Flutes. Most specimens suggest the orchestral quality. The stop named *Orchestral Flute* is frequently a *harmonic* rank. The Harmonic Flute is light-toned, mildly penetrating, clear, and of a peculiar pervasive quality. It can be voiced towards the bright or less bright quality. It can be loud or soft in volume, the Great Organ type being of considerable power, the Solo Organ type sounding usually with less volume but more harmonic structure. It is in character mostly above middle C, perhaps G

Harmonic Flute. This example has a fairly large scale and the high mouth characteristic of most Flutes. Notice small hole halfway up body.

below middle C. Stoppered basses are commonly used. The pipes are over-blown to sound their second harmonics, which become the most audible constituent, the first harmonic sounding softly too, but not generally audible to the listener. The small hole aids the pipe to sound what may be considered the "fundamental" of one-half the pipe's length, i. e. the second harmonic of the whole length. The hole permits overblowing without unsteadiness of pitch or jagged edges on harmonics. Middle C thus requires a four-foot speaking length. It is not unusual for an organ to have two or more harmonic open ranks. The stoppered harmonic form in pipes also exists. See ORCHESTRAL FLUTE, ZAUBERFLÖTE. Synonym: FLÛTE HARMO-NIQUE.

HARMONIC GEDECKT. An 8′ or 4′ manual Flute, formed from Gedeckt pipes of harmonic form. It is more liquid and velvety than the

Gedeckt of normal length, therefore making a unique solo voice It sounds a penetrating but not loud carrier-wave for other solo stops as well, making these more colorful and vivid in timbre because their higher partials are transported with less loss of energy on this stop's wave. The Gedeckt can perform the same function. The pipes are approximately three times the length needed for regular stopped ranks of the same pitch, middle C therefore being around three feet, depending upon the scale. See GEDECKT, HARMONIC STOPPED TWELFTH.

HARMONIC OCTAVE. A Foundation stop of 4′ on the manuals, creating the Octave's tone from double-length open metal pipes. It is moderately large in scale and loud in tone, although not brilliant or shrill. Like all harmonic open metal pipes, it is inclined to a round flutiness rather than an edgy or hard tone. It is not intrusive in combination and blends well with loud unisons of all sorts. Two or three ranks of 4′ Diapasons all speaking together are generally considered to be superior to this stop in tone, although more expensive. See HARMONIC DIAPASON, OCTAVE, PRINCIPAL.

HARMONIC PICCOLO. A Flute of 2′ on the manuals, producing a very good imitation of the orchestral timbre, more realistic than the unison-length Piccolo. The scale is moderate and the pipes are wood or metal in construction. The timbre is round rather than brilliant with many partials, and liquid rather than transparent or cold. This is both a solo and an ensemble voice at the pitch of the fourth harmonic of the unisons. It is frequently heard from the Swell or Solo. See HARMONIC FLUTE, PICCOLO.

HARMONICS. This stop-name, like *Mixture,* is not explicit as to design, pitches, or timbre, but it usually indicates high-pitched ranks of open metal Foundation pipes voiced to augment the Diapasons or Flutes in any division, including the pedals. Manual and pedal examples follow, each group increasing in brightness towards the right. The notes indicated sound from the manual's middle C key and the pedal's low CCC key. The first four are for the manuals, the second group is for the pedals:

Example No. 1		Example No. 2		Example No. 3		Example No. 4	
III		III		III		III	
C^3	2′	C^4	1′	C^4	1′	C^4	1′
G^2	2 2/3′	C^3	2′	G^3	1 1/3′	G^3	1 1/3′
C^2	4′	G^2	2 2/3′	C^3	2′	E^3	1 3/5′

Example No. 5		Example No. 6		Example No. 7		Example No. 8	
IV		IV		IV		IV	
G	2 2/3′	C^1	2′	G^1	1 1/3′	C^2	1′
C	4′	G	2 2/3′	C^1	2′	G^1	1 1/3′
GG	5 1/3′	C	4′	G	2 2/3′	C^1	2′
CC	8′	GG	5 1/3′	C	4′	G	2 2/3′

HARMONIC STOPPED TWELFTH. A harmonic Flute of stoppered design of 2 2/3′ manual pitch, composed of pipes that are equivalent in length to those needed for an open rank of 4′ . This moderately soft but telling Twelfth is the favorite of some organists because it blends very well, at the same time penetrating the ensemble fully. Compared to the *Twelfth* of Principal pipes, it is duller, a little softer, and of better blend.

It is hardly a substitute for this pitch in the main flue Chorus, since it has too few partials to mesh with the 4′ and 2′ components. It is a useful mutation stop. It may accompany the regular Twelfth on any manual, sounding with it in the louder ensembles, or building up the softer Flutes and lesser Foundation stops. See TWELFTH. Synonym: HARMONIC TWELFTH.

HARMONIC TRUMPET. A Chorus Reed of 8′ manual pitch, having the timbre of a Trumpet but without some of the free-toned dissonance that characterizes the average loud Trumpet. This tone contains a lot of clang and a complete set of the brass-like harmonics, but its brilliance is of a different sort: its double-length (sometimes triple-length) resonators eliminate by absorption many higher-pitched inharmonics, at the same time augmenting the power by their greater length. Some rough undulations between partials that can be perceived in the unison-length pipes are not heard. However, this stop is still able to deliver a dazzling and stentorian fanfare sound as well as form the base for a Reed chorus. Organ builders can provide a Harmonic Trumpet that is less loud than those examples heard in the unusually loud divisions of large instruments. One can always be designed for any average-size four-manual organ. All stops are custom-designed and voiced for a particular organ. This is a solo stop of great power and emotional appeal. It is frequently heard from the Solo division of a large organ, or the Bombarde or Stentor division, these being designed to furnish the brass tone at all usable pitches. See TRUMPET.

HARMONIC TUBA. A very loud Chorus Reed of 8′ manual pitch, like the Harmonic Trumpet, furnished with double (or triple) resonators whose added length is designed to remove from the tone many of the very high partials that characterize these two Chorus Reeds when of normal unison length. The harmonic length, usually not in the bass octave, enables these pipes to maintain an even and steady pitch of both fundamental and most overtones, at least the lower-pitched ones. This is generally a louder Reed than the Harmonic Trumpet, and also one of heavier and firmer tone. Some of the freedom of vibration the listener can hear in the Harmonic Trumpet is not in this tone. In many specimens it is completely free from dissonance, at least of the noticeable sort, because of the damping action of the longer tubes. These tubes, called *resonators* in all reed pipes because they make the original vibrations of the thin brass reeds fully audible, are thick-walled to prevent their own absorption of the reeds' tones. In both of these harmonic Reeds they are of spotted metal for their full lengths. Ordinary pipe metal of high lead content would never resonate the highest overtones. Tin in the proportion of from 35% to 85% is needed in these Reeds, and in most other Reeds, because it permits the voicer to obtain a brighter tone with a resonator of average dimensions. These resonators are tuned by rolling the metal in the slot.

This Tuba is not so bright as the Tuba Mirabilis or the Tuba Magna, but is much brighter than the Tuba Sonora. Like the Harmonic Trumpet,

it is a solo and ensemble stop of great power and excellent blend with
flues as well as other Reeds. A Stentorphone or Tibia Plena, perhaps a
bright mixture, and 16' and 4' Chorus Reeds may be added to its voice as
a climax effect to the full ensemble of the organ. Very large organs have
several loud Reeds in their many divisions. See HARMONIC TRUMPET,
TUBA. Synonym: TUBA HARMONIC.

HARMONIC TWELFTH. See HARMONIC STOPPED TWELFTH.

HAUTBOIS. See ORCHESTRAL OBOE.

HAUTBOIS d'AMOUR. See OBOE D'AMORE.

HECKELPHONE. An imitative Reed of 8' on the manuals, having a
round and deep timbre somewhat like the color of the English Horn stop,
but this "Baritone Oboe" is of stronger volume and greater individuality.
Since it is quite rare as an organ stop, its position is usually in the Solos
of very large instruments. The medium-large resonators are shaped as two
inverted-conical sections: a very narrow one, two-thirds the unison length,
is at the bottom; one of wider flare, completing the unison length, sits
on the top and is capped, with a slot near the top for the emission of the
sound. The top diameter is not of unusually wide scale, but just a little
wider than the Fagotto. The brass reeds are tuned by spring-like wires,
the pipes by rolls of metal in the slots.

HELLFLÖTE. A manual Flute of 8' or 4' pitch, constructed of open
wood pipes. It is moderate in scale, sometimes on the smaller side, and the
tone is bright and loud. It furnishes any combination with the partials
needed to build up the tone. Timbre-creators are needed in all divisions
of the organ, even the Solo. This Flute, like many other open Flutes, is
able to furnish the whole series of lower-pitched harmonics, and a few
higher ones, in such a way that it does not destroy the general ensemble
color, but offers support to all the stops. Many other stops can do the
same thing, in varying degrees of brightness and volume of sound. The
choice of such a stop is often just a matter of the organist's taste, not a
matter of being correct. This stop is useful on the Great or Swell. It can
be a solo voice, or sound with a solo voice, such as the 'Cello or Major
Flute. See CLARABELLA, CLEAR FLUTE, HOHLFLÖTE, TIBIA PLENA.

HOHLFLÖTE. An open wood Flute of 8' or 4' pitch definition, having
a substantial, hollow tone of much use on the manuals for combining purposes. The unique train of harmonics, which makes this Flute of so much
value in combination with other louder flue stops (Diapasons, Flutes, or
Strings), is based on a loud fundamental and an almost equally loud Octave
harmonic. The third harmonic is not so noticeable, and the fourth harmonic
varies somewhat in different examples. The rest of the train of from
twenty to twenty-eight harmonics quickly tapers in loudness as its pitch
rises. The triangular form of this Flute has fewer harmonics than either
the square or rectangular form. It is preferred by some organists on the
Great because it gives strength of tone without brightness. The *inverted*
lips seen on most ranks of Hohlflöte pipes, including the Flûte Triangulaire,
give an added parcel of initial harmonics that sound from each pipe

before the steady tone is reached. Since the ear receives a great deal of its sense impression from the way any tone is accelerated, the Hohlflöte seems "brighter" than many other stops because these initial harmonics make a more obvious impression on it. They are off-pitch, peaked in loudness, and also a little on the order of a piping sound. They pick up the ear's attention sharply. In reality, the steady tone of this Flute is usually less than *bright*. The inverted-lip Flutes are arranged below according to average scale:

1. Flauto Traverso (Orchestral Flute) (small)
2. Melodia
3. Waldflöte
4. Hohlflöte (large)

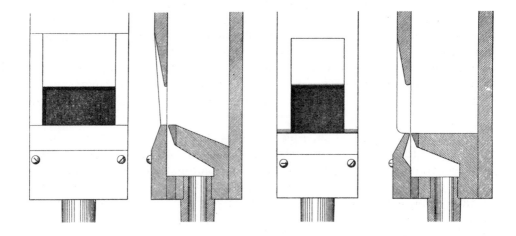

Two Hohlflöte pipes, both with beveled lips. These tenor C specimens show relatively high mouths, giving somewhat dull tones, and the substantial type of construction that characterizes good design in pipes, resulting in good timbre.

The moderately high mouths and larger scales of this Flute tend to make tones of duller quality but louder sound than the ranks of lower mouth cut-up and smaller scale. There are hundreds of varieties of this unusually versatile Flute in existence, from the *Echo* forms to the huge pipes that dominate their ensembles. Generalizations can hardly include them all. The 2' Hohlflöte of large scale is most useful in ensemble, and is a favorite of many organists. Wooden slides tightly screwed to the pipes' slots tune this open wooden Flute, upward to flatten, and downward to sharpen the pitch. Some Hohlflötes have beveled mouths like the Clarabella. *Flûte Creuse* refers to a Hohflöte. See WALDFLÖTE. Synonym: HOHLPFEIFE.

HOHLPFEIFE. See HOHLFLÖTE.

HOLZFLÖTE. An open *wood* Flute of 8' or 4' manual pitch, and 16' or 8' pedal pitch. This name is used for a variety of timbres and volumes. See WOODEN OPEN FLUTE.

HOLZGEDECKT. A stopped *wood* Flute of 8′ or 4′ manual pitch, and 16′ pedal pitch, resembling a large-scale Gedeckt in form, and louder than this stop in some examples. See GEDECKT.

HOLZPRINZIPAL. See WOOD DIAPASON.

HOLZRANKETT. A form of Rankett with *wooden* resonators of short length, speaking at 8′ or 4′ on both manuals and pedals. It is much less bright and more muffled in tone than the usual metal form. But it has the sibilant, reedy, covered tone of the metal resonators. A few specimens also have a peculiar droning sound. The flood of higher partials that comes from its thin reeds resembles those of many Regals in effect, but Regals are more likely to be metallic and there is none of the brilliant whine in this stop. Neither does it have the nasality of the Oboe or the piercing, small tone of the Musette. Upon hearing it, perhaps as a pedal line of notes in the polyphonic style, the listener is immediately alerted to the fact that its timbre is unique; it stands out, but, interestingly enough, it is not loud. The manual and pedal ranks are both usable alone or as adjuncts to the flues, such as the Diapason, Gemshorn, or open Flutes. See RANKETT, REGAL.

HOLZREGAL. A short-resonatored Reed stop of 16′, 8′, or 4′ on either manuals or pedals. Since its pipes are made from *wood*, it is less brilliant than the other Regals. It is brighter in timbre, however, than the Holzrankett, and even more likely to be droning, acid, pointed in brightness, or highly individualistic in some way in quality. Even these wooden pipes may be brilliant, but this variety of Regal mostly sounds with one of the softer tones of this group of stops. Since the metallic and scintillating effects of the metal resonators are not possible to it, there remains in most examples the audible piping and windy sound obvious in all of the Ranketts, Regals, and Kinuras. Its functions are to create individuality in some line of notes, usually with a soft flue, and occasionally to build up a bright tone. It is, like all other short-resonator Reeds, very much the artistic product of its voicer. See REGAL.

HORN. See FRENCH HORN.

HORN DIAPASON. A Foundation stop of 8′ on the manuals, and not often represented on the pedals. It has the essential tone of a Diapason, but with a strengthening of the lower overtones near the fundamental, which gives it what seems to be a brass-like, but not brilliant, timbre. Loud and penetrating examples exist as well as those that are quite dull and heavy in tone, but this stop does not become cloying, nor does it make an indistinct pitch-impression on the ear. Some churches that now use rebuilt theater organs have little else with which to accompany their congregations. It serves for hymns better than a Diapason Phonon, and can be further aided by the addition of open Flutes of 8′ and 4′, as well as a Viola, Gemshorn, and Cornopean. This Diapason is not sufficiently orthodox in timbre to serve as a base in the Classical Diapason Chorus, but many specimens do have that sort of full-toned, big, almost mellow effect which is usable in the Solo Organ. Slotted, thick-walled open metal pipes make this tone. Careful dimensioning of mouth parts will prevent a string-like character in the tone. See DIAPASON, DIAPASON MAGNA.

HUNTING HORN. See WALDHORN.

JEU de CLOCHETTE. A bright, delicately toned mixture on the manuals, formed from open metal pipes of high pitch and brilliant tone. This stop gives the effect of small bells sounding in the distance, especially when played staccato. It creates a charming effect with the softer Flutes or diminutive Foundation ranks, like the Dolce or Dulciana. It is effective with both 8' and 4' stops. It can be used by itself. The ranks of which it is composed are close together in pitch, therefore so are its overtones, making the bell-like effect more pointed. It can be chorded, like the Carillon, to be simply a source of bright timbre in soft combinations. Many excellent examples are to be heard in European organs, but very few in America. It may be unenclosed and in the Choir or Positiv. Five examples follow, with the notes indicated that would sound from the middle C key:

Example No. 1	Example No. 2	Example No. 3	Example No. 4	Example No. 5
II	II	II	II	II
E^4 4/5'	C^5 1/2'	G^4 2/3'	G^4 2/3'	C^5 1/2'
C^4 1'	C^4 1'	E^4 4/5'	C^4 1'	G^4 2/3'

JUBALFLöTE. See SERAPHONFLöTE.

KEEN STRINGS. A group of two, three, or more ranks of small-scaled 8' Viol pipes, tuned as a complex in some examples. The singular name refers to one normally pitched rank. See VIOLE CÉLESTE, VIOLE D'OR-CHESTRE.

KERAULOPHONE. A Foundation rank of 8' manual pitch, sounding with a moderately loud voice a hybrid tone between an open metal Flute and a Diapason. Horn-like character is given by some strength in the lower overtone range. It is heard from the Solo manuals of a few big church organs, but is usually associated with the organs of concert and theater use. A round or rectangular slot in the tuning collar of each open metal pipe injects additional partials, but they usually do not become string-like.

KINURA. A Reed stop of 8', sometimes 4', on the manuals that sounds from extremely short resonators of inverted-conical shape and extremely wide flare. Such resonators have almost no control over the motions of the reeds down in the boots of the pipes, and the resulting tone is a great mass of *inharmonic* as well as *harmonic* partials that merely approximate the pitches of the notes. The glittering mass of component tones heard from this Reed lacks the on-pitch effect of the Dulcian and Schalmei, which also have short resonators, because these components do not corroborate the fundamental's frequency in most cases. It is not a sharp or nasal tone. It does not have the covered, rattling tone of the Barpfeife. It does not suggest the pastoral or sylvan. It is merely a brilliant daub of tone that contrasts with other stops' effects, perhaps reminding the listener of a "bee in a bottle." As the "Regal" of the American theater organ, this stop has been heard by a vast number of listeners. Many ranks still exist behind the prosceniums, or in crates of old pipes in warehouses, where the amateur organ builder can still obtain them, or any other ranks he may want. See REGAL.

KLEINE MIXTURE. A soft manual mixture whose function is to create a body of tone of suitable timbre for building up the Accompanimental, Echo, or Choir Organ. It may serve as an accompaniment stop on any division, even the Great. Its structure may resemble the Echo Mixture, Dulciana Cornet, or Soft Mixture. It may extend the 4′ Chorus of flues as well as the unison Chorus. Echo Geigen Diapasons, Dulcianas, or any other diminutive Foundation stops may be used to compose its ranks. Four examples follow, with the notes sounded by the middle C key:

Example No. 1		Example No. 2		Example No. 3		Example No. 4	
IV		IV		IV		V	
C⁴	1′	C⁴	1′	C⁵	1/2′	C⁴	1′
C³	2′	G³	1 1/3′	C⁴	1′	G³	1 1/3′
G²	2 2/3′	C³	2′	G³	1 1/3′	*E³	1 3/5′
C²	4′	C²	4′	C³	2′	C³	2′
						C²	4′

*Since this is a *soft* mixture, this Tierce sounds less acute and pointed than most ranks of this pitch. It can be made as soft as may be needed.

KLEINERZÄHLER. A Foundation stop of 4′ on the manuals, frequently serving as the softer of two 4′ stops on the Great or Choir. These Erzähler pipes may be smaller in scale than the 8′ rank, and are of unusually easy blend with all families of organ tone. Sometimes *two* 4′ ranks speak from a single stop knob, although they are not tuned as a céleste. This device produces a sound of greater intensity without hardness of quality. This soft Octave fades into the tones of the other flue stops without being conspicuous, lending them a transparent, mildly bright tone. Occasionally this name may refer to a *soft* 8′ Erzähler. See ERZÄHLER.

KLEINFLÖTE. A manual 4′ Flute of tone quality similar to the stopped Lieblichflöte or Gedeckt. It is a very soft Octave for addition to other soft stops. It may appear in any division. See GEDECKT, LIEBLICHGEDECKT.

KLEINGEDECKT. A stoppered wooden manual Flute of 8′ or 4′ pitch, resembling any variety of Gedeckt, but not necessarily the same as the Kleinflöte. The prefix *Klein* may refer to either a 4′ stop of any species or a *softer* form of any 8′ stop. See GEDECKT, KLEINFLÖTE.

KLEINPRINZIPAL. A Foundation stop of 4′ pitch on the manuals, having in almost all examples the tone quality of a small-scale Octave, but not so soft as an Echo Diapason 4′. There are many times when an organist desires a soft Octave to add to the unison Diapason, Gemshorns, and soft ensembles without building them up to Chorus proportions. This Octave provides just such a slight extension in brightness, and is frequently found on the Choir or Positiv Organ. See DIAPASON, OCTAVE, PRINCIPAL.

KNOPFREGAL. A short-resonatored Reed of the Regal group, sounding at 8' and 4' on both manuals and pedals. It has a thin, brilliantly reedy, somewhat acid tone that comes from pipes rarely longer than four to six inches. The small knob-shaped structures on the tops of the narrow brass pipes are hollow, and each has an opening like a large sleigh bell in its top for the egress of the sound. This Regal is less muffled than some; however, tones and stop-names are not always consistent. See APFELREGAL, REGAL.

KOPPELFLÖTE. An open metal Flute of 8' or 4' manual pitch, with a tone color midway between a bright cylindrical metal Flute and a Gemshorn. Although it has a liquid and sylvan effect when played in melody, this Flute is not primarily a solo voice, but a combination stop intended to enhance the blend between other stops. The upper third or quarter of its speaking length is composed of a truncated conical section, either fully open or with a small hole in a built-up cap. The lower portion of the pipe is cylindrical. Spotted metal is used in all examples and an arched mouth of some height ensures that the Flute's overtones will be preserved.

Since this Flute sounds midway between a bright and a dull quality, it is an admirable accompaniment for many solo stops, such as the Basset Horn, Oboe, Krummhorn, or Schalmei. It can couple the Gambas to the Foundation stops or Flutes, bind mutation ranks to the unisons, hold the softer mixtures in a soft chorus, or sound the Octave in a Positiv ensemble. One of its most effective uses is to sound in rapid passages against a quiet background, like a Dolcan or Spitzflöte Céleste. This Flute is unique in tone and without imitations. It is a Baroque as well as a modern Flute tone.

KRUMET. A manual Reed of 8' pitch with a moderately loud tone that resembles more than anything else a hybrid between a nasal Clarinet and a Kinura of windy and piping effect. It is a theater-organ voice, and was introduced early in the present century to provide yet another 8' unison solo color for the enjoyment of moving picture audiences. Examples vary a great deal, some a little like the Vox Humana, others with a horn-like tone, perhaps called *Krumet Horn*. This Reed might be called a modern form of the Regal.

KRUMMHORN. A solo Reed of 8' manual pitch, sounding with a clean, vivid, reedy timbre that suggests the mournful and sedate aspects of the music. It is also valued as an ensemble stop, especially at 8'. It lacks the sweetness of the Basset Horn and the obvious fundamental tone of the Clarinet. It is not pungent, but it is highly distinctive, and useful in the music of all schools. The resonators are either full or half-length, and of varying diameter, some quite small, others large. The Baroque Krummhorn can sound almost like a Regal or even a Krummhorn Regal. Certain other examples are definitely *hybrids* with a Dulzian or Rankett. The very narrow types of Krummhorn, Schalmei, and other Baroque Reeds on very low wind pressures sound a whole gamut of soft but high-pitched overtones, and give much liveliness to the lines of notes in early music. Such Reed pipes stimulate the listener's attention by contrasting for him on

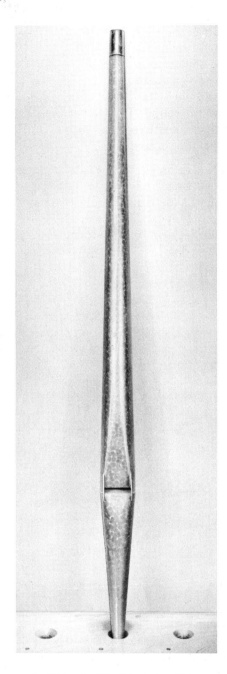

A Conical Foundation Pipe

Spotted metal Gemshorn for the tone B, showing low mouth and steel tuning collar at top. The tapered conical shape of this pipe dampens the higher-pitched harmonics, especially the even-numbered ones. Therefore a chord on this stop consists of components chiefly in the lower reaches of the train. This makes the conical Foundation rank very useful in all higher stop-pitches, such as 4', 2', and 1'. As a conical Principal this form of pipe can be heard at mutation pitches, like 5 1/3', 2 2/3', 1 3/5', etc. In chords the conical flue does not aggregate nearly so many very high-pitched overtones for the ear to sort out and assimilate into the form of the music.

Courtesy: Casavant Frères, Ltd.

BOURDON CCCC PIPE

This profound bass pipe is really over seventeen feet long from its foot, here clearly visible, to its stopper, above the top of the picture. Such a pipe, if necessary, can be built in many shapes to make it fit under rafters or ceiling. It can even be bent double, so that its stopper is right in front of its upper lip. Deep sound waves are not impaired by "mitering." A six-inch ruler can be seen on the right side below the lower lip. The wind-regulator is visible in the pipe's foot. The upper lip is arched to discourage even-numbered harmonics (the 16′ and 8′ of this 32′ stop). This larger scale discourages barking of the third harmonic, at 10 2/3′. Walls are over an inch thick and glued rigidly to prevent the pipe's structure from absorbing the most valuable fundamental. It purrs at only 16.35 cycles per second.

Courtesy: Wicks Organ Company.

each note an extended period of *initial* inharmonics and steady tone harmonics that follow. The M. P. Moller Organ Company has designed a Krummhorn that is especially bright and colorful. It has solid brass resonators, a heavy block, and sliding tuning collar. Synonym: CROMORNE.

LARIGOT. See NINETEENTH.

LIEBLICHBORDUN. A stopped Flute of 16′ or 8′ on the manuals, composed of wood pipes. It is softer than the Bourdon but lacks the Gedeckts' lightness of tone. Some examples have rohrs in their caps. See BOURDON.

LIEBLICHFLÖTE. A stopped wooden Flute of 4′ manual pitch, similar in tone to the Lieblichgedeckt. See GEDECKT, LIEBLICHGEDECKT.

LIEBLICHGEDECKT. A stopped wooden Flute of 16′, 8′, or 4′ on the manuals, and 32′, 16′, 8′, or 4′ on the pedals. It is typically a Gedeckt in every way except that it is sometimes softer but always conspicuously much smoother in tonality, many examples having less third harmonic than the Gedeckt. Scaling varies, but some examples are quite large and sympathetic in tone, rather than hooting or muddy. Other forms are actually smaller in scale than the average Gedeckt. It has the Gedeckt's functions. See GEDECKT.

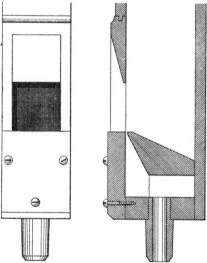

Square-mouthed Lieblichgedeckt.

LIEBLICHNASAT. A manual Twelfth 2 2/3′ made from the soft and dull tone of the Lieblichgedeckt. Some examples are open and made from Echo Principal pipes. See GEDECKT, LIEBLICHGEDECKT, TWELFTH.

LITURGICAL TRUMPET. A Chorus Reed of unison 8′ manual pitch, sounding with unusual brilliance but comparative freedom from the dissonant clang that characterizes most Trumpets and Trompettes. In its ideal form it is made from solid brass resonators of *exponential* shape, such as are seen in the *Gottfried Trumpet*. The polished, smooth bells of these pipes deliver the ultimate in number of overtones without overwhelming loudness. Sometimes a precious metal, like silver, is included in the alloy for some variety of timbre. This is a Solo Organ Reed in a few larger churches or cathedrals, and its cymbal-like tones may be heard at the Elevation in some rites. Occasionally the pipes are horizontal in the organ's screen, which allows them to sound their tones without loss of power into the great air spaces of the building. The Trompette delivers fewer overtones, more power, but more dissonance than this unusually clean and ethereal stop. See Brass Trumpet, Trompette, Trompette en Chamade, Trumpet.

LLENO. This Spanish word refers to a mixture stop.

LOCHGEDECKT. See Stillgedeckt.

LUDWIGTONE. An open stop of 8′ or 4′ on the manuals, formed from small-scale wooden pipes, each with two mouths, on opposite sides. It resembles the other softer Foundation stops in timbre. There is a partition down the middle of each pipe, really making two sounding air columns in each pipe structure. The two air columns of each pipe are both tuned off the normal pitch: one slightly *sharp*, and the other slightly *flat*. This creates a gentle and slow undulation that is unusually pleasant to the ear, and of great usefulness as an accompaniment tone to both other stops and singers alike. Since it is a relatively soft tone, the stops that it accompanies must not be on the loud side to sound appropriately with it. By itself it makes a background of soft and neutral-colored timbre that may be used between portions of the church service. Not only do the two tones from each pipe in this rank undulate with each other, but they also form an additional series of célestes with other softer stops, like the Erzähler, Dulciana, Dolce, Dolcan, Gemshorn, Aeoline, Spitzflöte, Quintaten, and Melodia. At the top of each pipe is a roll of pipe-metal by which tuning is accomplished, and therefore also the degree of beating is adjusted. This unique stop was invented by H. H. Holtkamp and A. G. Sparling. It is designed to sound at many dynamic levels, different patterns of undulation, and in some variation in tone quality. It is hard to imagine a more ideal accompaniment tone for either a vocal artist or a solo stop. It is mildly pervading but never obtrusive on the ear, and it relieves the listener of a too strict comparison between accompaniment and solo voice. It never destroys a solo stop's character of tone, but rather adds to it by furnishing a contrast in volume, timbre, and pitch. See Céleste.

MAGNATON. A diaphonic type of Foundation stop developed by the Austin Company to produce a firm, smooth, penetrating bass on the pedals at the 32′ pitch. It is suitable for both flue and Reed ensembles. Its valvular pipes are a bass extension of a large-scale, thick-walled flue Diapason of metal form. This mechanism was used only in the notes from CCCC to CCC. Thick brass reeds, rather than a Diaphone's pallet, vibrate against a very heavy wooden shallot. The resonators are of thick zinc. It is not now being built, and exists in just a few of this company's organs.

MAJOR BASS. The principal stopped bass of the organ, at 16' on the manuals in very few organs, and at 32' on the pedals. This name is also used for the *Double Diapason*, but *Principal Bass, Contra Diapason,* or *Sub Principal* are more accurate for this Foundation stop. *Sub Bass,* however, also refers to this Flute of deep pitch, and *Contra Bourdon* is frequently seen on consoles. The pipes are of large scale in most specimens, and of heavy-walled construction. This stop makes a well-diffused, penetrating sound that depends upon a large supply of wind. Its big, intense, but not always loud tone supports Reeds and flues alike. It gives dimension to the pitches of the music being played because it subjects the hearing mechanism to a range of from six to ten octaves *in the same chord,* overtones included. The function of this stop is to provide the profoundly deep vibrations to be contrasted with the middle and high pitches of the whole sound spectrum. It is only when the ear can hear (or remember) the effect of notes sounding over most, if not all, of the whole pitch range that the greatest pleasure in the music is possible. For example, middle C as a pitch is not fully appreciated until it can be *contrasted* with the great range of pitches the ear can hear. This is as true of overtones as it is of fundamentals. The Major Bass (Contra Bourdon) is the least expensive and least tall rank of pipes that goes down to the threshold of bass hearing. Its pipes are fairly wide, but only about sixteen feet in height, and the taller ones can be mitered severely. (The 64' Resultant is therefore possible from a set of stopped wooden pipes of around eight feet in height.)

The 16' Diapason and Violone, as well as stops of proper loudness at 10 2/3', 8', 5 1/3', and 4', should be added to the pedals with the Major Bass whenever possible adequately to build up the harmonics' pitches in this division. The 32' Bourdon does not stand apart from other stops because of its profound pitch; it is just on the end of the line of pitches. When funds and space are scarce, the Bourdon may be extended all the way from the 32' octave up to the 1', including mutations, for additional stops.

The huge and very tight stoppers in the bigger pipes are in some cases never moved again after installation. The ear identifies low pitches with so little efficiency that between CCCC and CCC (between 16.3 and 32.7 vibrations a second) the tuner may consider the pitches "in tune." The slow impacting of the air mass at these pitches makes a large scale necessary in order to fill a large building with the proper loudness of tone. It takes more energy to move the 600 tons of air in a cathedral than it does in a small church of 6 tons capacity. Since all people hear the deep notes with a wider range of *impression* than the higher pitches, there is a greater variety of tastes among organists in the matter of volume and tone quality of their bass pipes. See BOURDON, GROSSFLÖTE. Synonyms: CONTRA BOURDON, SOUBASSE, SUB BASS, SUB BOURDON, UNTERSATZ.

MAJOR DIAPASON. A large-scale and loud Diapason of 16' or 8' on the manuals, and 16', rarely 8', on the pedals under this name. This is a chorus Diapason, not a brilliant-toned flue for the fourth or fifth manual. It is usually accompanied by the *Major Octave,* and perhaps other Diapa-

sons. See DIAPASON, DIAPASON MAGNA, GRAND DIAPASON, STENTOR DIA-
PASON.

MAJOR FLUTE. See MAJOR OPEN FLUTE.

MAJOR OCTAVE. A powerfully voiced and large-scaled Diapason
Octave of 4′ on the manuals, and sometimes at 8′ on the pedals. It is
designed to sound with a very loud unison Diapason, such as the *Major
Diapason*. See OCTAVE.

MAJOR OPEN FLUTE. A large-scale and loud open Flute of 8′ or 4′
on the manuals, and 16′ or 8′ on the pedals,

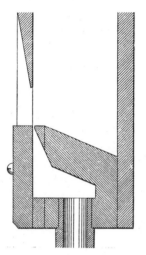

although perhaps under another name on
the pedals. It is a solo and ensemble Flute,
as likely to appear on the Great or Stentor
Organ as on the Solo. Alone, its brilliant,
strong, clear sound, perhaps with the 4′
coupler, makes a very usable solo voice. In
combination with louder Reeds or Diapasons
or other flues it lends a firm pitch, stability
of harmonic structure, and a whole chord of
partials that build *timbre* in the other stops
sounding with it. From *each* 8′ pipe the 8′,
4′, 2 2/3′, 2′, 1 3/5′, 1 1/3′, 1 1/7′, 1′, 8/9′,
4/5′, 8/11′, and other components can be
heard, *not individually*, since the ear makes
only a *generality* of these pitches, but as a
well-timbred chord of sound. Each note,

Mouth of a Major Open Flute.

coupler, and even stop at another than the 8′ pitch will augment this
tonal complex. It should be remembered that in this series of natural
harmonics only the octave-sounding harmonics actually speak right on the
true notes of the equal-tempered scale; the others closely approximate the
scale's notes. The ringing and brilliant tone of this open Flute is not so
individual in color that it damages other *stop's* tones. Many times it can
disappear into an ensemble of tone. Large scales need adjustment of
mouths and quantity of wind in order to prevent a dull tone. Many species
of wood are used for this Flute, each of which has its own formant of tone.
Maple, mahogany, birch, and even thick spotted metal have been used
The mouth cut-up is quite low to create many overtones of the series, and
the lips are beveled in most cases. Synonyms: FLAUTO MAJOR, MAJOR
FLUTE.

MAJOR PRINCIPAL. A large-scale Diapason of prominent tone, falling into one of the following classifications:

    a) the chief Diapason 8′ on any manual;
    b) the chief Octave 4′ on any manual;
    c) the chief Diapason 16′ on the pedals.

Occasionally the 16′ rank is made from wood. See DIAPASON, OCTAVE, PRIN-
CIPAL.

MELODIA. An open wood Flute of 8' on the manuals, possessing a warm, sometimes mellow, slightly hollow quality of tone. It is somewhat smaller in scale than the other inverted-lip Flutes. It is much depended upon by organists as an accompaniment in the Great Organ. It is also heard from the Solo in a few large organs. Although this moderately scaled rank never reaches the proportion of the Hohlflöte or Waldflöte, a little weight may creep into its tone. This beautiful stop can have a little of the imitative Flute timbre in its tone, and is sometimes sylvan and even liquid to the ear. A close resonance between its mouth cut-up and scale contributes much to its beauty. It is preferred by some organists to

Melodia with inverted lip.

the smaller-scaled Flauto Traverso of 8'. A few 16' examples exist, but these seem to be of less usefulness than a Rohrflöte. See HOHLFLÖTE, WALD-FLÖTE.

MELOPHONE. A Flute stop of solo quality, at 8' on the manuals, and formed from heavy-walled open metal pipes, sometimes wood. It is quite loud, and sounds as a hybrid between the horn's overtones and an open Flute. Good examples are sympathetic and warm in quality. A few are string-like or even bright. It is also a big-toned ensemble stop, of easy blend with Trumpets or Diapasons. It has a complete train of harmonics since its pipes are inverted-conical and the mouth cut-up is fairly low. It may be heard from the Solo chests of concert or theater organs, and also some church organs. A few examples have belled tops for one-third to one-half their lengths. The wooden ranks are slightly inverted-pyramidal in shape. *Mellophone,* of different spelling, refers to a brass-like, moderately loud Reed stop of 8'.

MENSCHENSTIMME. See VOX HUMANA.

MILITARY TRUMPET. See TROMPETTE MILITAIRE.

MINOR DIAPASON. A Diapason of smaller than normal scale and less than average volume of sound, at 16', 8', or 4' on the manuals, and 16' or 8' on the pedals. It may sound in contrast to a louder Diapason or imply a *Principal*. See DIAPASON, ECHO DIAPASON, PRINCIPAL.

MINOR OCTAVE. An Octave Diapason of smaller than normal and less than average volume of sound, at 4' on the manuals or 8' on the pedals. It may sound in contrast to a louder Octave or imply a *Principal Octave* 4'. It may appear on the Choir as its only Octave stop. See DIAPASON, ECHO DIAPASON, OCTAVE, PRINCIPAL.

MINOR OPEN FLUTE. A stop-name that refers to a variety of open Flutes of either metal or wooden construction, at 8' or 4' on the manuals, or 16' or 8' on the pedals. It may sound in contrast to a louder Flute on any division. In the Great of one very large organ *Tibia Minor* and *Tibia*

Major are used. Large unit organs usually make use of the Reed and flue names that they want to duplicate at different dynamic levels by adding *Major* and *Minor* to them. See MAJOR OPEN FLUTE, WOODEN OPEN FLUTE.

MINOR PRINCIPAL. A moderately loud, smaller-scaled Diapason of somewhat fewer than the normal train of harmonics and of either wood or metal construction, falling into one of the following three classifications:

    a) a second, smaller-scale Diapason 8' on any manual;
    b) a second, smaller-scale Octave 4' on any manual;
    c) a second, smaller-scale Diapason 16' on the pedals.
See DIAPASON, OCTAVE, PRINCIPAL.

MIXTURE. A general name that refers to two or more ranks of pipes drawn by a single stop control, differing from the *Cornet* by having its ranks break in pitch one or more times, perhaps in each octave, as the scale is ascended. The term *compound stop* refers to both types. On the borderline between these two types is the Rauschquinte, sometimes also the Sesquialtera, which may or may not break in pitch. (No reference is made in *Mixture* to a double-rank Principal 2' or Erzähler 4'.) Non-octave-sounding mixture ranks are tuned to the natural harmonics heard by any well-trained organ tuner in a Diapason 8' or Octave 4'. The octave-sounding ranks and their corresponding natural harmonics are always of the same frequencies. In pedal mixtures all deeper ranks are sometimes tuned to the scale's frequencies, which may not be noticeable below tenor C, especially since deep flues sound weak partials.

Organs up to about 1600 were composed mostly of mixture ranks which multiplied upward in pitch the Foundation (Principal-like) tones. Important harmonics of the series indicated the stop-pitches used. Perhaps a brassy Regal and a smooth stopped Flute offered some variation. To make the organ louder the organist added the higher-pitched ranks, such as the 2', 1 1/3', etc., knowing the listener would interpret, as he does today, a brilliant tone to be a loud tone. Today we can make the organ louder by multiplying unison 8' stops, such as the Tuba Magna or Stentorphone, or by following the early organist's method of building up a façade of mixture pitches. Other ways also exist on larger instruments, as, for example, drawing the Chorus Reeds of 16', 8', and 4', perhaps with intramanual couplers. The Reeds' partials and the mixture ranks clash very little when all are in tune.

In function all mixtures attempt to build up ensemble or solo tone into higher reaches of the series they belong to. Properly, all mixtures and Cornets belong to a particular series of pitches, such as the 8' (unison on the manuals), 16' (unison on the pedals), 32', 4', and even 2'. Theoretically, mixture pipes speak at all of the notes in the organ; in practice most of them are above C^2. The overtones can be as valuable as the fundamentals, and in some ranks the second and third harmonics are voiced to be louder than their fundamentals, making the tone much livelier. The higher harmonics, even when not clearly audible, constantly mutate the volumes (not the pitches) of *all* stops sounding. It is important, therefore, that a C^5 Principal pipe, for example, be in good voice and in tune to enable it to have proper effect on the lower tones. Playing the mixture stops *staccato*, either combined or drawn alone, provides the organist with one of the most useful agents of expression he has available, especially in the music of the Classical school. This exhibits to the fullest the initial harmonics of these small, intense pipes. No degree of tremolo is tolerable, of course, in such a device.

Basically, mixtures satisfy the craving of the ear and nervous system for the upper limits of audibility, somewhat like the pleasure received from seeing a brilliant violet (also a short wave-length). Functions duplicate one another in mixture stops, but generally one stands out: the simulation of natural harmonics by individual ranks of pipes. Organists have individual ways of using the mixtures they have at hand, and, indeed, builders give their specimens wholly different timbres, numbers of ranks, and powers. This is a desirable thing, because a mixture is a work of artistic taste, like the detail in any painting. More than one Fourniture sounds like a Cymbal, and a Sesquialtera can have the marks of a Cornet. A variety of functions follows, with suggested mixtures for carrying out these functions:

1) to clarify the tone by the corroboration of the basic harmonics (Fourniture);
2) to build up tones of the sub-unison and sub-sub-unison ranks on both manuals and pedal (Full Mixture);
3) to make luminous the inner pitches of chords so that harmony will be apparent (Fourniture, Sesquialtera, or Harmonics);
4) to extend the Diapason Chorus upward (Plein Jeu, Fourniture, or Acuta);
5) to fill the pitch gaps in combinations (Grand Chorus or Grand Mixture);
6) to emphasize the upper limit of audibility (Plein Jeu or Cymbal);
7) to strengthen the treble range (Cornet, Clarion Mixture, or Acuta);
8) to strengthen the bass range in the pedals (Fourniture or Pedal Cornet);
9) to give animation and intensity to the tone (Sesquialtera or Acuta);
10) to extend the brilliance of the Chorus Reeds (Stentor Mixture or Acuta);
11) to make the loud Reeds more brass-like (Clarion Mixture or Cymbal);
12) to make a brilliant solo tone (Cornet, Grand Cornet, Harmonic Cornet, or Stentor Sesquialtera);
13) to make more of a *whole* tone of the Diapason Chorus and Chorus Reeds (Grand Mixture);
14) to create a soft background tone (Harmonia Aetheria or Kleine Mixture);
15) to create a neutral-toned accompaniment (Dolce Cornet, Dulciana Cornet, Gemshorn Mixture, or Kleine Mixture);

16) to make the sound of soft bells (Carillon or Jeu de Clochette) ;
17) to make a better means of identifying each octave or part of the pitch range (Fourniture or Acuta or both of these) ;
18) to build up supporting power in the pedals (Compensating Mixture, Grand Chorus, or Grand Bourdon) ;
19) to intensify String quality in manuals or pedals (String Mixture or Pedal String Mixture) ;
20) to build up the Echo Organ ensemble (Echo Mixture or Dulciana Mixture) ;
21) to build up the Choir Organ ensemble (Grave Mixture, Acuta, Fourniture, Dulciana Mixture, or Cymbal) ;
22) to build up the Bombarde Organ ensemble (Stentor Mixture or Harmonic Cymbal or both) ;
23) to augment the Swell Organ Reeds (Plein Jeu, Cymbal, Grand Mixture, or Clarion Mixture).

The student of organ tone can doubtless work out other functions as well; in fact, each piece of music might be said to "require" its own special mixture. The pipes from which mixtures (and mutations) are made vary considerably. Certainly each builder should be permitted to use what appeals to him. The organist usually expects to hear Diapason or Echo Principal tone from most examples, and he usually does, but Geigens, Echo Geigens, Gemshorns, a wide variety of conical Principals, Dulciana-Diapason hybrids, and open metal Flutes are used. Wooden pipes are not unusual, even in manual types. Spotted metal is now customary in all manual ranks, and gives the expected clean, bright, but not overly windy timbre. Pure tin is sometimes used for bright effects. Pipe species and materials may be intermixed with each other in a compound stop, and a Wood Diapason at 4', a Viola at 2 2/3', a Gemshorn at 8', or a Sifflöte at 1/2' may appear. Musical function is the prime consideration, but addition of needed harmonic pitches is always to be considered. A skillful device to increase intensity without hardness, dissonance, or windiness is to use duplicate (in-tune) ranks at the same pitch, such as two, perhaps even four, 2' Principals in a powerful Hauptwerk *Major Mixtur*. But this is typically European and is not customary in America. Two very thorough books in German that will tell the reader what is actually included in organs are:

1. Mahrenholz, Christhard, *Die Orgelregister: ihre Geschichte und ihr Bau,* Kassel, 1930;
2. Supper, Walter, *Die Orgeldisposition,* Kassel, 1950.

Mixtures and other stops are well covered by these writers, and these two books have unusual illustrations in them. The publisher of both is Bärenreiter.

Mixtures should be mounted unenclosed if possible, since their high-pitched overtones are more easily absorbed than most pipes' tones. There are certain mixtures, as in an enclosed Swell or Echo, that are naturally an exception to this generalization. Since all mixtures are custom-designed for the division, organ, and building in which they are to perform, it is necessary to locate the mixture pipes in a great variety of places in relation to the rest of the organ. But the principle of getting to the ears of the listeners the tone quality put into the mixtures by the designer and builder is of prime importance. Various ways of doing this have been followed. A resonant acoustical environment is the most feasible to depend upon, since all sorts of special plasters and tiles designed to absorb noise will also quickly absorb the valuable higher overtones of the mixture pipes. Small pipes make weak sounds because of their smaller *masses* of air, and this is the basic reason why those very faint, but most needed, mixture overtones are sometimes erased completely from existence by one brush with a wall or ceiling right beside them. Other means of getting high tones to the listeners are seen in the large gallery organ in St. Bartholomew's, New York City, the large marble sanctuary floor in St. Matthew's Lutheran, Hanover, Pennsylvania, and the unenclosure of the mixture ranks so beautifully displayed in front of the main divisions in St. Thomas's Church, New York City. Small divisions have sometimes been built out on the front of a gallery. This places their pipes right out in the air-space where the sound is intended to travel.

Greater brilliance and strength of tone can be obtained by the following: higher wind pressures, greater quantity of wind, alloys rich in tin, harmonic length (i.e. double the unison), placing pipes farther apart, and putting enclosed mixtures near large tone openings. Even inverted-conical pipes and the multiplication of ranks up to fourteen or twenty-two in a manual example are devices used. Perhaps it would be well here to state that some mixtures are extremely soft; a most valuable and beautiful *Echo Dulciana Mixture* can sound much softer than an 8' Quintaton. The player must expect *variety* in mixtures, as he expects variety in all other art forms. Mixture pipes sound at bass pitches as well as treble. In larger organs there are specialized uses for the harmonics of the 64', 32', and 16' series. The back left end-paper chart shows these harmonic pitches in order. Mixtures create resultant tones, especially noticeable in the bass. A series like 16', 10 2/3', 8', 5 1/3', and 4' in the pedals makes a distinct resultant of 32'. The 8' and 5 1/3' create a 16' resultant on either pedals or manuals, and a 2' and 1 1/3' will create some 4' effect. However, above the note of GGG these effects seem to be simply *harmony* between notes. Flute mixtures do not coalesce enough to have a unity of tone, but they can be useful, as augmented stops or solo stops. String mixtures serve to make the String division more opaque in timbre. The pedals or Swell sometimes have such mixtures, but it should be said that, except in the case of a very large division, the obvious harmonics of a 32', 16', 8', or 4' Gamba are in better tune with each other and less likely to obscure notes played. The writer has played more than one 32' and 16' manual string that does not obscure the notes even in chords. Any builder can design a *conical* 32', 16', or 8' Gamba intended to serve as a source of these open-pipe components: a mixture in itself. The Principals of most compound stops have harmonics *in just enough quantity* to coalesce with a neighboring rank, but not to obscure the pitch.

Building up ranks in a mixture creates a new tone quality. Each rank comes to the combination with its own complete set of partials. Every one must be reckoned with. The 3 1/5′ pedal Tierce or the 4/5′ manual Twenty-fourth are useful or destructive of ensemble tone according to how they are designed and voiced. Timbre, loudness, and breaks in pitch must be worked out to produce unity of effect with all other stops in the division. The majority of mixtures and Cornets are formed from the *octave-sounding* and *fifth-sounding* ranks. In chords, perhaps with couplers or Reeds, these two kinds of pitch are quite safe in all sorts of music. The *third-sounding* Tierces are used extensively too, especially in the Cornet and Sesquialtera, but here the organist must consider the exact notes of the music to be played: will it be dissonant with certain chords? As a solo voice, the Cornet needs the Tierce. The *flatted-seventh-sounding* Septièmes give a complete and really full timbre, but their usage is indeed a specialization in detailed registration. Of course they are in only very large manual divisions and pedals. The *ninth-sounding* ranks are more useful as a cymbal-like device than is generally supposed. It is the proper function of some music to give that brilliant and dazzling climax of color, sweeping from one end of the tonal spectrum to the other. The None 8/9′ can do this to perfection. The *fourth-sounding* 8/11′ has few uses even in compounded effects. It might be assimilated with all of these others in a truly cymbal-like choir of *Harmonics*. Pedal equivalents of all these exist.

Since the ear is unable to detect exact pitch in the higher treble range, say between 6,000 and 16,000 vibrations per second, pedal mixtures, played as contrapuntal or solo devices, may attract the interest of some organists. A really true pedal ensemble, even though small, needs the 5 1/3′ (the *Twelfth* of the 16′ series), the 3 1/5′, and the 2 2/3′. The first pedal mixture included in an organ, and this is sometimes the only one, should sound the first two of these three pitches. Ranks should be individually available in order to cut off the 3 1/5′ at times, although its effect in the

---

Chart Explanation: Stop-pitches of the 8′ Natural Harmonic Series

The eight stop-pitches that appear on this chart down the center are all heard from any *open* 8′ stop in the organ; in fact, all are heard from any single pipe of the 8′ rank. They are not individually discernible, but as a composite effect called *timbre*. The timbre of a Diapason, Clarabella, or Violin of 8′ depends upon their relative loudness to each other, as also upon other things, like initial harmonics, quickness of speech, etc. Some of these components can be billions of times softer than others. The 8′ prime tone is not always the loudest of the group. In a Principal, Viol, or Major Flute the second or even third harmonic has the ascendancy in some specimens, but the prime tone (fundamental) speaks at the pitch indicated on the stop knob. Here is illustrated one of the most important lessons about organ stops: the stops' pitches are merely the pitches of the harmonics of an open rank of pipes. The non-octave harmonic pitches sound just a little off the pitches of the equal-tempered scale notes. Therefore in a chord of notes some slight undulation is heard, but this is merely another source of color in a well-tuned organ, making the timbre more interesting. Of course this is not the complete 8′ train of harmonics; there are others of higher pitch not on this chart. A Violin pipe can sound more than fifty! Many of these higher ones are completely off the notes of the scale, the eleventh and thirteenth being noteworthy among the lower ones. Some harmonics do not have equivalents among the organ's stop-pitches. See the back left end-paper for more series of pitches.

STOP PITCHES OF THE 8′ NATURAL HARMONIC SERIES

Number of Harmonic	Name of Stop whose Pitch Corresponds to Harmonic	Pitch on Stop Key	General Effect of Adding a Stop of this Pitch to the Ensemble	Present in Tones of Stopped Pipes**	Note that Speaks when Middle C is Depressed
8	SUPER SUPER OCTAVE (octave-sounding)	1′	bell-like brilliance	trace	C^4
7	SEPTIEME* (flatted-seventh-sounding)	1 1/7′	close, full brilliance	yes	$B\flat^3$
6	LARIGOT (NINETEENTH)* (fifth-sounding)	1 1/3′	pungent, "quinty" tone, sounding one octave above the Twelfth	trace	G^3
5	TIERCE (SEVENTEENTH)* (third-sounding)	1 3/5′	sharp, acute tone which cuts through the ensemble	yes	E^3
4	SUPER OCTAVE (FIFTEENTH) (octave-sounding)	2′	clear brilliance	trace	C^3
3	NASARD (TWELFTH)* (fifth-sounding)	2 2/3′	pungent, "quinty" tone (lowest non-octave-sounding harmonic)	yes	G^2
2	OCTAVE (octave-sounding)	4′	brightness, power; amplifies the effect of the unison tone quality	trace	C^2
1	UNISON (piano pitch) (octave-sounding)	8′	supports prime tone	yes	C^1

*Non-octave-sounding stops are referred to as Mutation Stops.
**Open pipes and Reeds sound all of this series of harmonics.

bass is different from that in the higher treble. Pedal mixtures, almost always unbroken in pitch, are likely to include more octave-sounding ranks than those in the manuals. Many organists feel that these might as well all be individual stop controls. A large pedal mixture can cost as much as a small organ. It consumes a vast space. Expedients to reduce both cost and pipe-space are much used in pedal stops.

The name *Mixture* on a stop key, unlike *Harmonics,* usually indicates a Fourniture of some type or just the needed harmonics for the ensemble. It does not have a clear meaning, like *Cymbal.* Four *manual* examples speaking from middle C:

Example No. 1		Example No. 2		Example No. 3		Example No. 4	
III		V		V		V	
C^2	4'	C^3	2'	D^4	8/9'	C^6	1/4'
G^1	5 1/3'	G^2	2 2/3'	C^4	1'	G^5	1/3'
C^1	8'	C^2	4'	G^3	1 1/3'	C^5	1/2'
		G^1	5 1/3'	E^3	1 3/5'	G^4	2/3'
		C^1	8'	C^3	2'	C^4	1'

Nos. 1 and 2 are based on 16' manual tone. No. 3 is brilliant but composed of harmonic pitches. No. 4 is about as high as the organ can reach into high pitch. The Aeolian Skinner organ in the Mother Church, Boston, contains this interesting series of mixtures: *Hauptwerk:* Sesquialtera II, Mixture IV-VI, Scharf IV-VII; *Great:* Full IV, Scharf IV, Cornet IV-VI; *Swell:* Sesquialtera III, Plein Jeu VI, Cymbale III, Fourniture III; *Choir:* Sesquialtera II, Carillon III; *Positiv:* Cornet V, Scharf IV-VII, Zimbel III; *Bombarde:* Grand Fourniture VI, Scharf III, Cornet V-VI, Harmonics VIII; *Solo:* Plein Jeu IV, Harmonia Aetheria III -V; *Pedal:* Grand Cornet V (based on 32'), Cornet IV, Fourniture IV, Mixture III, Scharf IV. See ACUTA, CORNET, CYMBAL, GRAND MIXTURE, SESQUIALTERA.

MONTRE. A French stop-name used to indicate that the pipes exposed in the architectural screen really play, and that they are Principals of some variety, at 32', 16', 8', or 4' on manuals or pedals. Most of the beautiful gold or painted pipes seen as part of the screen are silent, or without backs above their operating air columns! A famous example of screen pipes that make music is in the Mormon Tabernacle, Salt Lake City. The French *Montre,* easily heard on recordings if you have a really efficient high-fidelity set-up, is distinctly different from German, English, or American Diapasons. It sounds every note with a mild "explosion" of initial harmonics and some inharmonics. Since at least one-half of a listener's impression of timbre comes from initial effects, this sound is animated and strong in the ears. Its windy and assertive display of energy fills the mind with a sense of warmth, and perhaps what seems like a warning to listen to the exact notes being heard. The Montre, along with brilliant mixtures, is the trademark of the French organs. Notre Dame and St. Sulpice in Paris are good examples. Mutations are also a distinctive part of French organs. Montres blend well with Reeds in these organs, notably in the larger French cathedrals. See DIAPASON, PRESTANT.

MUSETTE. A moderately soft solo Reed of 8' or 4' on the manuals, making a very thin point of brilliant, piercing tone. This short-resonator

Reed is plaintive and somewhat nasal, and suggests to the listener's mind an idyllic or pastoral scene. This very pleasant tone is useful in combination with flue stops, particularly at its 4' pitch, and also with other light-toned Reeds. The resonators are extremely narrow in scale, one-eighth to one-quarter unison length. Certain types are pierced by small holes in certain harmonic positions. Caps of various types may dampen certain ranges of partials. Some ranks have narrow, miniature flared bells on the tops of their slender stalk-like pipes. A high content of tin helps all types to create a brighter tone. *Sackpfeife*, a very thin-timbred and brilliant but soft variety of the Musette tribe of stops, is heard in Europe, as is also the *Dudelsack* (at 32' or 16' usually). The resonators and shallot designs vary quite a bit from builder to builder. Unusual Reeds like these, if created by an artist in organ-pipe design, are effective for contrapuntal lines and also as light Reeds for ensembles. This stop is shown here in a variety of light-toned choruses for either manuals or pedals:

Musette	4'		Brass Regal	2'		Sifflöte (flue)	1'		Brass Regal	2'
Fagotto	8'	or	Musette	4'	or	Brass Regal	2'	or	Musette	4'
Shawm	16'		Oboe Schalmei	8'		Fagotto	4'		Oboe	8'
			Clarinet	16'		Musette	8'			
						Echo Fagotto	16'			

MUTED 'CELLO. A String of 8' on the manuals, sounding with a soft but harmonically full timbre intended to imitate the rich, warm tone colors of the muted violoncello. It is a solo or ensemble stop, being useful also as an accompaniment, perhaps to the Keraulophone, Major Open Flute, Trumpet, Philomela, or Doppelflöte. It may appear in a String Organ, where it can dilute the Viols' keen tones. Wooden examples of great beauty exist. Metal pipes that are slightly conical may make this tone, or have Koppelflöte tops. See VIOLONCELLO. Synonym: VIOLONCELLO SORDO.

MUTED GAMBA. A String of 8' on the manuals, with a timbre less keen and bright than that of the Gamba. This is not necessarily a soft stop. It may be conical or just the top halves may be conical. See GAMBA.

MUTED STRINGS. Two or more ranks of 8' manual Strings voiced softly, perhaps as a céleste. See CÉLESTE, MUTED VIOLIN CÉLESTE, VIOLE CONIQUE.

MUTED TRUMPET. A Reed stop of 8' on the manuals, voiced to imitate the "sassy," brilliant, subdued timbre of the orchestral prototype. This Trumpet stop is different from the Petite Trompette, which is a soft Reed that does not have its higher overtones subdued. Few examples have been made, because this particular overtone structure is extremely difficult for the voicer to imitate, but it has been heard in several of the moving picture organs, many of which tried to reproduce every instrument. See TRUMPET.

MUTED VIOLA. A soft form of the Viola at 8' on the manuals, having only a suggestion of the harmonic structure of a String in its tone. Imitation of the muted instrument is accomplished by making the moderate-scaled pipes only *very slightly conical*, this being already a mild voice in its regular form. Narrowing the mouths is also a useful device in muting this stop. The Muted Viola is one of the most usable accompaniment stops, because its tone is pointed sufficiently by its *String* harmonics to escape being dull, and always remains definitive enough to hold up a solo stop like the Melodia, Oboe, Clarinet, or Gamba. It forms a rather dull céleste, but one that is useful on any division if tuned to a slow beat. The Muted 'Cello is a more interesting solo stop than this. See Viola. Synonym: Viola Sorda.

MUTED VIOLIN. See Viole Conique.

MUTED VIOLIN CÉLESTE. An 8' undulating stop on the manuals, formed from two, preferably three, ranks of Muted Violin pipes. If two, they are *normal-sharp, normal-flat,* or *sharp-flat* in pitches, the last pattern denying the organist a single rank for combination. The *normal-sharp-very sharp* pattern reproduces the orchestral effect very realistically. These three ranks need not be more than one or two beats per second from the normal pitch, and will not therefore sound too sharp in combinations. An additional three-rank céleste made from this same stop and tuned to be *normal-flat-very flat,* if added to the three-rank sharp céleste above, would create the most realistic orchestral effect possible, and it is from these *muted* pipes that one of the most realistic String sounds comes, since the ear remembers the violins of the orchestra most ideally as soft. This soft céleste, whether two, three, or six ranks, is usually found only in the String Organ, since it gives out too much dissonance, even though quite pleasant to the ear, to combine well with other divisions. Many organs of all types, including the church organ, have a String division which can be coupled when desired to any manual or the pedals, by means of a stop key marked "String Organ." This stop key is duplicated among the stop keys of each division. When "on," it brings whatever ranks are drawn by the String Organ's regular controls. The muted violins of the organ appeal to some organists as the most usable of the stops of this family of tone. The intense Viole d'Orchestre, although it can be given any timbre, acuteness, loudness, or pitch desired, mixes best with other String stops. The String stops of the church organ must be able to blend with many other stops. This excludes the most small-scaled and incisive, but not necessarily the imitative, muted or otherwise. The Muted Violin Céleste is formed from an alloy high in tin content, of quite small scale, and very low mouth cut-up. See Céleste, Viole Conique.

NACHTHORN. A Foundation rank, at 8' or 4' on the manuals, and occasionally at 8' (the octave pitch) on the pedals. The pipes are of stoppered construction in many examples, which makes this the only Foundation rank of this form. However, some builders make the Nachthorn open, quite large in scale, and of spotted metal throughout. It may even appear as conical pipes of slight taper. The noticeable horn-like partials seem to justify calling it a member of the same family as the Diapason, Gemshorn, and Keraulophone. Classification can be very academic here. Its tone, stoppered or otherwise, is soft, warm, strong in the fundamental, and makes a tranquil and quiet effect on the ear. It can bind together a soft ensemble. Its purring, gentle sound can be a solo voice. It may be an accompaniment. *Pastorita* may indicate a soft specimen.

It is sometimes tuned a little off-normal to céleste *slowly* with other soft stops, and may even be called an *Unda Maris,* but this name is applied to many other soft stops as well. The Nachthorn is a frequent member of the Positiv's ensemble, at either 8' or 4'. It can also be heard from any other division of the organ, perhaps most often from the Choir. Its 2' and even 1' ranks are not unknown, but may be less useful than other stops at these pitches. Lessening its scale causes its low mouth cut-up to form more overtones, totaling even less volume, since smaller-scaled pipes make a somewhat softer sound than those of larger scale for the same pitches. Its thick cylindrical walls absorb very few of the overtones that they create. Since these overtones make a somewhat subtle sound, these pipes are better unenclosed. Most Nachthorns have more of the third harmonic than the Stopped Flute. They also have less than the Quintaten or the Nason Flute, in relation to their fundamentals. A few examples have rohrs in their stoppers to make their tones a little more "open." This may be a mixture or mutation rank. The 5 1/3', 2 2/3', and 4' are especially valuable in small but brilliant flue Choruses. See QUINTADE. Synonym: COR DE NUIT.

NASARD. See TWELFTH.

NASARD FLUTE. See QUINT FLUTE.

NASAT. See TWELFTH.

NASON FLUTE. A "wooden Quintaten" made from stoppered pipes, rarely with rohrs. It is in a variety of scales, but frequently moderately large. Its pitches are at 16', 8', or 4' on the manuals, and occasionally at 16' on the pedals. This is a soft Flute yielding a round, pervading, mysterious timbre that is valuable as a solo stop and as a component in softer flue combinations, as with the Gemshorns, softer Diapasons, and mutations. Its valuable *third harmonic* helps to bind other stops together. This third harmonic sounds at 2 2/3' from the 8' rank, 5 1/3' from the 16' rank, and 1 1/3' from the 4' rank, with a slight discrepancy in pitch between these *third harmonics* and other ranks tuned by hand to these 16', 8', and 4' pitches. This discrepancy is one of the most delightful sources of color in the organ.

The Positiv may have a 16' Nason Flute, its fundamental never blurring the tone because it is quite soft. This stop's third harmonic is a little softer than that of the Quintaten or Quintadena, and a little stronger than in the Nachthorn of stoppered form, in relation to the fundamental. *Quint Flute* is more likely to be a synonym of *Nasard Flute* than of *Nason Flute.* A Harmonic Flute 8' and a Gedeckt 2 2/3' have been circuited together under one stop-name — *Nason Flute,* the tone being powerful and pervasive as a solo voice as well as an ensemble tone. See QUINTADE, QUINT FLUTE.

NINETEENTH. A Foundation rank of Diapason tone at 1 1/3' on the manuals, and 2 2/3' on the pedals, speaking at the note two octaves and a fifth above the keys struck. In both mixtures and mutations it is tuned to the natural sixth harmonic of the 8' Principal. In actual practice an expert tuner might use the 4′ Principal to tune it, this stop's tone containing a 1 1/3′ ingredient. It therefore corroborates the natural sixth harmonic of the unisons, but clashes slightly with the *notes* of the tempered scale as sounded by the octave-sounding ranks, like 2′, 4′, etc. It adds a mild and high-pitched pungency to any combination. It speaks the octave above the Twelfth 2 2/3′. It is a "Twelfth" in those Baroque ensembles which are based on the 4′ series of stop-pitches (instead of the 8′). It really never should be called a *Twelfth*. It takes many timbres to itself: Geigen Principal, Dolce, Dulciana, Echo Dulciana, Echo Diapason, etc. From middle C it sounds at G³, and from the low pedal CCC at G (pitched just below middle C). See FIFTEENTH, SEVENTEENTH, TWELFTH. Synonym: LARIGOT.

NINTH. A rare stop-pitch which sounds at 3 5/9′ on the manuals, and 7 1/9′ on the pedals. This rank speaks at the note one octave and a second above the key depressed on manuals and pedals. This is at D² from middle C, and at DD from the low pedal CCC key. The manual pitch speaks between the 4′ and 3 1/5′ stops. It is quite inharmonic in combinations, but may aid the brass stops' effect. It may be seen in some Harmonic Choruses. The *None* of 8/9′ is a *Twenty-third* and is easier to assimilate into an ensemble, even of Diapasons, than might at first be thought. It complements the Septième of 1 1/7′ as a super-brilliance. It sounds at D⁴ from the middle C key. This component is in the tone of most open 8′ pipes, such as a 'Cello, etc. See CYMBAL, ELEVENTH, TWENTY-THIRD.

OBOE. A Reed stop of 8′ manual pitch, and 16′ or 8′ pedal pitch. The 4′ manual form is called an *Octave Oboe*. The 32′ pedal form is mostly unheard, since the Fagotto and Bassoon can take its place. This stop-name indicates a somewhat louder and more Cornopean-like Oboe than the *Orchestral Oboe*, which is nasal, thin, pungent, and quite brilliant. This organ type of Oboe is usually a hybrid stop, perhaps the only Reed in the Swell of a small church organ, and has Cornopean, Horn, and even Trumpet-like qualities, or any combination of these. It serves as the source of the reed's impact on the ear when it is the only Reed stop, and thus provides the organist with some variety in solo and ensemble effects. It is unfortunate that the Oboe in *labial* form lacks the same "spit" of initial harmonics heard from the lingual form, because the Reed stops go out of tune a different amount from the flue stops for each change in temperature. An organ with all labial stops would stay pretty much together in tune during all the seasonal changes. The Reed form is also to be preferred because it sounds a greater variety of proportions in

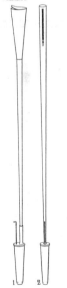

Oboe pipes in the two most common forms: 1 is an organ type of Oboe, and 2 is an Orchestral Oboe.

the loudness between its harmonics, thus making timbres that are more distinctive than most flue stops. Even neighboring harmonics can be extremely different in volume, thus making a more vivid timbre than a flue. These *peaked* harmonics account in theory for the popularity of the Reed stops, and also for their unusual variety.

The Oboe is a solo and an ensemble stop. It adds bright timbre to any combination, and it must be combined with the flues in a small organ. The Cornopean quality enhances this function. On some organs this is a 4' stop, frequently with a Krummhorn or Clarinet of 8' in a large Solo. *Echo Oboes* are not uncommon, even in the Choir. The solo *Oboe Horn* 8' sounds the nasal, pungent timbre of the Oboe along with the round, warm tone of a soft Horn. The Baroque Oboe is reedier and of better blend than the modern version. *Hautbois* is sometimes used to indicate a manual 4' Oboe of light tone.

The resonators of the Oboe are of unison or half length, most examples being unison, like the Trumpet's. The unison tubes resonate the *fundamentals* in their tones, along with most other, higher-pitched overtones. The half-length tubes resonate the *octave* component, letting the fundamental sound without amplification, making a brighter timbre than the pipes of unison length. Shorter resonators, such as quarter, sixth, and eighth length, are used in the Schalmei, Regals, and many "short" Reeds, and they amplify, therefore, only the very high-pitched components in the tone. It is said by physicists that the resonator tube cannot create any new harmonics, but must confine itself to simply amplifying those created by the thin brass reeds down in the boots. Thus resonator and reed are *coupled* in function, interacting on each other to create certain partials and then strengthen them to travel outward. The resonator can control the reed's motion to a limited extent by moving the wave in its tube in time with *most* of these partial vibrations, and also with the fundamental. Some motions it cannot make, and thus certain partials go unsupported.

The Oboe resonators are very slender, inverted-conical, and topped by a bell-shaped portion. Some capping, perhaps full capping, is employed, in which case slots are necessary near the pipes' tops. *Bajoncillo* is a thin-toned Oboe-like Reed stop. See ORCHESTRAL OBOE.

OBOE CLARION. See OCTAVE OBOE.

OBOE d'AMORE. A soft imitative Reed stop of 8' on the manuals, resembling the Oboe or Orchestral Oboe in tonality, although this stop has a delicate, piquant timbre not heard in other Oboe varieties. Its plaintive, thin tone is useful in solo playing and for soft ensembles of light Reed stops. It is often an Echo Organ stop. See OBOE. Synonym: HAUTBOIS D'AMOUR.

OBOE HORN. A Reed stop of solo tone quality, at 8' on the manuals, sounding with both the Oboe and Horn qualities. The thin, pungent, nasal timbre of the Oboe is in its tone, and so is the round, warm effect of the Horn stop. Carefully voiced examples make a pleasant sound and are heard from all types of organs, usually from the Solo. Organists remember this tone from the moving picture organs and sometimes request it in their new instruments. It may be in a small Swell, although this Reed is not as useful for solo and combination uses as the Orchestral Oboe or Oboe. This is not one of the Classical examples of Reed tone. This Reed can support a soft ensemble with firmness of pitch, and add some bright texture as well. It speaks with that percussive quickness noted in almost all Reeds, yet it does not obviate the flue's tonal effects. The resonators are made from inverted-conical sections. The lower one, of about half length, is tapered like the Oboe; the upper one is tapered at a greater angle. Capping to some degree is used. Slots emit the sound waves if the caps cover the tops completely. See FRENCH HORN, OBOE, ORCHESTRAL OBOE.

OBOE SCHALMEI. A Reed stop of 8′ manual pitch, and 8′ or 4′ pedal pitch. It has the thin, nasal, plaintive tone of the Oboe tribe and some of that peculiarly bright, acid sound that the Schalmei gives. This is a tonal unison of a unison-length and a very short resonator. This stop's resonators vary between one-quarter and one-half the unison length. The pedal tone makes a distinctive line of notes, with flues or uncombined. In counter-melody on the manuals this stop adds much individuality of effect and can emphasize any notes. This acid, whining voice may be a solo stop upon occasion. It is different from most short-resonator Reeds heard in this country, but a few have been made here. These slender, cylindrical pipes may have narrow brass bells on their tops. See OBOE, REGAL, SCHALMEI.

OCTAVE. A Foundation stop of Diapason tone, at 4′ on the manuals, and 8′ on the pedals. It is voiced to sound with the Diapason or Principal of unison pitch, mutating the unison to be a less dull tone, but never destroying pitch impression. The *Principal* 4′ may be of smaller scale, particularly if both are present in a division. There are Octaves for all families of tone: Foundation (Diapason), Flute, String, and Reed. Theoretically, at least, each unison stop should have its own Octave, on both manuals and pedals. The true Octave gives to the unison tone a surprising new personality, extending its color and showing a different variety of its timbre, without destroying its basic quality. Too often the Octaves do not do this, but merely add a few harmonics an octave higher than those in the unison stop. The Octave forms in the main flue Chorus a support for the Twelfth and Fifteenth and mixture ranks. The Octave also fulfills one of the most important functions of the treble in music: it makes a bright, ringing tone to carry aloft the melodies that every composer puts in the treble notes. The Octave may be a solo stop at "unison" if played an octave lower. The octave coupler makes it into a 2′ stop.

The Octave binds the high pitches to the unison pitches. It is the most important "Copula" in the vertical ensemble of pitches because it is in a cardinal position with the unison's pitch. Its harmonics mesh with those of both the unison and the higher mutations and mixtures. It is voiced downward as well as upward, so to speak, since it must blend with both 8′ and 4′, 2 2/3′, and 2′ pitches. The ear notices gaps in the façade of pitches of stops, as well as in harmonics, and, even in Strings, the absence of an Octave (or a Twelfth) component can be unbalancing. After the unison, the Octave is of greatest importance on manuals or pedals. The absence of the Twelfth or Fifteenth is noticed mostly by professional ears; the absence of the Octave may be noticed by the amateur musician. Since most unison 8′ stops sound in the middle reaches of the manuals at *pitches* that are somewhat hard for the ear to hear efficiently, the Octaves of 4′ really make listening easier and much more pleasant than just 8′ stops alone. The clear pitch impression they create in the mind is valuable to a vivid and complete enjoyment of most musical forms, especially the contrasting of two or more melodies at the same time.

Its notes are always twice the frequency of the unison's as 2:1 mathematically. The Twelfth and Fifteenth have a 3:1 and 4:1 relationship, respectively, with the unison. The importance of the Octave to the Chorus is seen most graphically in the following series: when all are sounding, the 8′, 4′, 2 2/3′, 2′, 1 3/5, 1 1/3′, 1 1/7′, and 1′ make a 1:2:3:4:5:6:7:8 frequency relationship. The Octave binds all pitches to the unison.

The 2:1 relationship between the Octave and the unison is necessary to balance the relationships between the other stop-pitches. The ear knows this. This whole series of pitches sounds with the greatest mathematical simplicity possible, and therefore with the greatest pleasure possible to the ear, which is constantly trying to analyze proportions between all pitches. The whole unity of sound within the Diapason Chorus is based on this series. The ear trained in the Classical tradition in music always attempts to reduce to a *unity of effect* the overtones as well as the notes heard. No series of musical sounds could have a greater simplicity within itself than the series of pitches given directly above. It is noteworthy also that the 32′, 16′, 4′, and 2′ series of stops also have within their own series of pitches this same simplicity of relationship. Listening to all of these series interweave is one of the joys of listening to an organ. Steadiness of pitch, in-tuneness, and good acoustical factors are necessary backgrounds to this enjoyment. The tremolo may destroy some important pitch relationships.

Four-part hymn tunes and other organ music are easier to hear if played on flue stops of the lowest four pitches of the 8′ series. Notes in the innermost chord positions have more transparency if played on the unison choirs of pitches, listed below:

Manual series		Pedal series	
Super Octave (Fifteenth)	2′	Super Octave (Fifteenth)	4′
Twelfth (Nasard)	2 2/3′	Twelfth (Nasard)	5 1/3′
Octave	4′	Octave	8′
Unison (piano's pitch)	8′	Unison	16′

Occasionally just a combination of the *manual* pitches above will sometimes prove useful in the music. It may be of interest to see a complete listing of all combinations of these pitches:

a) 8′	f) 8′ and 2 2/3′	k) 8′, 4′, and 2′
b) 4′	g) 8′ and 2′	l) 8′, 4′, and 2 2/3′
c) 2 2/3′	h) 4′ and 2 2/3′	m) 8′, 2 2/3′, and 2′
d) 2′	i) 4′ and 2′	n) 4′, 2 2/3′, and 2′
e) 8′ and 4′	j) 2 2/3′ and 2′	o) 8′, 4′, 2 2/3′, and 2′

Some of these combinations of pitches, which may blend Diapasons, Gems-horns, stopped or open Flutes, or Violas, have a solo tone; others are useful in the accompanying function; others are useful as devices in countermelody, so many of which the organist can make use of in all types of composition. With the 16′ and 5 1/3′ ranks also considered, and perhaps also the 1 1/3′, 1 3/5′, and 1′ ranks, many more pitch combinations can be made.

The overtones of the Octave continue those of the unison Diapason upward in pitch, not as exact duplicates, but in the same relative pitch positions and a proper degree of volume. The meshing together of these two trains of overtones adds to the interest in the melody and harmony heard, for there is *harmony* in overtones (harmonics) as well as in notes. A melody played on a different tonal combination brings out a different sequence of effects on the ear. Variety of tone-color shades is almost limitless in even a smaller organ. Millions of shades can be created on most of the two-manual church organs that are in use. Couplers, breaks in the mixtures' pitches, the tremolo, and the swell pedal, and also other devices, give organists a great gamut of effects for different types of music. The chief glory of the early organs, however, was to *combine* different stop-pitches, including many mutations. How far have we strayed from this glory of the old organ by making available over five hundred different 8′ tone colors?

The pedal's *Octave*, Twelfth, and Fifteenth are important to clean ensemble tone. They make the pedal more suitable for solo, melody, counter-melody, bass, contrast, and emphasis in certain phrases in the music. Frequently the addition of the pedal's 8′ or 5 1/3′ will remove all vague-ness of pitch. The Octave can do more than any other stop to keep the pitch clear. See DIAPASON, FIFTEENTH, TWELFTH, WOOD DIAPASON. Synonym: OCTAVE PRINCIPAL.

OCTAVE FLUTE. A 4′ manual and 8′ pedal Flute, usually of open wood construction, designed to augment the tones of the unison flues. The loudness of its fundamental and the prominence of its overtones are both voiced to sound well with other stops of the division. The pedal rank is larger, louder, and more prominent than the manual's. The form of this stop may be with beveled lip, like the Clarabella or Major Open Flute, or inverted lip, like the Melodia or Hohlflöte. See BASS FLUTE, WOODEN OPEN FLUTE.

OCTAVE HORN. A smooth-toned Reed stop of 4′ on the manuals, and 8′ on the pedals, voiced to blend with the light Reeds of any division. This stop may be taken from the same rank of pipes as the 8′ and 16′ Horn stops in a unit organ. See FRENCH HORN.

OCTAVE OBOE. An imitative Reed of 4′ on the manuals, and 8′ on the pedals, formed from either the organ type of *Oboe* or the *Orchestral Oboe*, depending upon which tonality is needed to supplement the light-toned Reeds. It is smaller in the scale of its resonators and less pronounced in volume than the unison Oboe types. It frequently appears in the Swell Organ as a member of a Reed chorus such as:

Octave Oboe	4'		Octave Oboe	4'		Octave Oboe	4'
Chalumeau	8'	or	Clarinet	8'	or	Orchestral Oboe	8'
Contra Fagotto	16'		Contra Dulcian	16'		Bassoon	16'

A moderately soft stop of this tone quality is valuable as a source of timbre even with some flue stops. Its plaintive, thin, bright timbre is too high in pitch over most of its range to be very pungent or to detract from other stops' tone qualities. Some examples are quite soft and delicate in tone. The narrow resonators are unison in length and topped by small bells, which frequently have caps over part of their surfaces. If wholly capped, the sound comes from a small hole in each pipe near the top. Spotted metal may be used in the whole pipe or just the bells. The more orchestral variety is simply a capped narrow flared pipe. See OBOE, ORCHESTRAL OBOE. Synonyms: ECHO CLARION, OBOE CLARION.

OCTAVE PRINCIPAL. See OCTAVE, PRINCIPAL.

OCTAVE QUINT. See TWELFTH.

OCTAVE VIOLIN. See VIOLETTA.

OCTAVIN. A Foundation rank of open metal pipes, at 2' on the manuals, sounding as a Fifteenth of prominent voicing and somewhat more than the usual volume of sound. See FIFTEENTH.

OFFENFLÖTE. An *open* wood or metal Flute of 8' or 4' manual pitch, and 16' or 8' pedal pitch, sounding any volume of sound and tone quality appropriate to the other stops in its division of the organ. The manual rank may be a Principal Flute or a Clarabella, and the pedal rank a Major Open Flute or a Flute-Diapason hybrid. See BASS FLUTE, FLÛTE OUVERTE.

OPEN DIAPASON. See DIAPASON, GEIGEN DIAPASON, PRINCIPAL.

OPEN TWELFTH. See TWELFTH.

OPHICLEIDE. A Chorus Reed of unusual brilliance and probably more power than any other stop in the organ. It is at 16' or 8' on the manuals, and 32', 16', or 8' on the pedals. Its fundamental is developed to the maximum extent, as is its long train of from fifty to seventy overtones. Some examples may approach even eighty overtones in number. It is louder than the Tuba Mirabilis, but may be without so much brassy clang-tone. Some examples have the free-toned vibration of the Trumpet tribe; others incline more towards the firm tone of the Tubas. In most examples the salient overtones of this stop pass far out of the realm of audibility even at the low manual CC pipe. Higher pipes are intensely brilliant and dominate the full ensemble, changing its color to conform to their particular type of voicing. The louder overtones of the essential (lower-pitched) complement of the train number from fifteen to twenty-five. Even from *one pipe* this magnificent chord of louder harmonics makes an ensemble of most of the stop-pitches of the organ. The sounding also of a series of spurious inharmonics makes this tone somewhat cymbal-like and interesting. These are much less noticeable, of course, than the on-pitch harmonics. Couplers should be avoided unless they make a pleasant tone. Each note in a chord proportionally brightens the tone of this stop. This is a solo Reed, a source of brassy but very pleasant ensemble power, and a fanfare of the greatest magnitude. It is a climax effect brought on *last* by the Crescendo Pedal (except for the 4' Ophicleide). Larger organs have a very loud variety of this Chorus Reed; smaller organs have a less loud version of this stop.

The Ophicleide pipes are made from very thick spotted metal, perhaps just in their top halves or quarters in the big pipes of the bass range. The inverted-conical flare is not pronounced, since the maximum number of partials is desired. Increasing the wind pressure can also increase the proportion of fundamental to the whole tonal complex. If the shallot, reed, boot, and other parts of each pipe are of sufficiently heavy construction, the high wind pressures usually associated with this tone will not force the harmonics too much out of pitch-relationship with the fundamental. These pipes may be on their own windchest, because the pressure may be from 25 to 50 inches. In the Convention Hall Organ, in Atlantic City, there are four 100-inch pressure Chorus Reeds: Ophicleide, Trumpet Mirabilis, Tuba Maxima, and Tuba Imperial. The Solo Tuba Magna is on 50 inches.

The Ophicleide is frequently a unison 8' member of a Bombarde Organ. It is shown here in two examples. A Bombarde is usually an ancillary organ:

Bombarde Organ No. 1		Bombarde Organ No. 2	
*Stentor Diapason	8'	*Grand Principal (II ranks)	8'
*Stentor Mixture	VI	*Octave	4'
Contra Bombarde	16'	*Fourniture	V
Ophicleide	8'	*Cymbal	VI
Harmonic Clarion	4'	*Cornet	III
		Contra Trumpet	16'
		Ophicleide	8'
		Brass Trumpet	8'
		Clarion	4'

*Flue ranks.

The large Bombarde Organ in the Aeolian Skinner instrument in the First Church of Christ, Scientist, Boston, contains 27 ranks (1637 pipes), and only the Bombarde 16', Trompette 8', and Clarion 4' are reed ranks. There are four mixtures and a two-rank 8' Principal as well. The magnificent effect of these many small mixture pipes sounding the natural harmonics of the scale greatly aids the tones of the Reeds. See TUBA.

ORCHESTRAL BASSOON. An imitative Reed of 16' or 8' on the manuals, 16' on the pedals, voiced with the delicate, pungent, reedy timbre of the instrument. It is brighter in most specimens than the stop named *Fagotto* (*Orchestral Fagotto* has been seen), and on modern organs this usually means that the resonators are slightly smaller-scaled in the Orchestral Bassoon. This is one of the better imitations on the organ, sounding with much of the characteristic lightness, but the soft clatter of the spurious inharmonics that come from the cane reed is lost to the organ pipe, and also to the Orchestral Oboe. The brass reed is actually less likely to give a quantity of inharmonics than the real instrument. This is a solo and ensemble stop, but frequently meets competition in the organ from the Fagotto, Oboe, Clarinet, and English Horn. It may appear as the bass octave of the Oboe or Orchestral Oboe stop. It is usually met with in its most ideal voicing on the Solo manual; here it is likely to have its own individuality in the highest form. Its extremely slender resonators are unison in length, and inverted-conical. They are capped, with a long, slender slot near the top of each pipe for the emission of the sound wave. Synonym: BASSOON.

ORCHESTRAL CLARINET. See CLARINET.

ORCHESTRAL CORNET. A Chorus Reed of 8′ on the manuals, rarely seen under this stop-name. The Cornopean is more typically organ-like in tone. This Cornet à piston is smaller in voice and less loud than the Trumpet stop. Solid brass resonators give the most realistic imitation. See CORNOPEAN, TRUMPET.

ORCHESTRAL FLUTE. An open 8′ or 4′ Flute on the manuals intended to simulate the full, fluid, sylvan tone of the orchestral instrument, even to the familiar "chiff" of the initial edge-tones that sound before the air column has had a chance to accelerate into full vibration. The variations of the player's breath control, holding position, and the inevitable wavering of the pitch on certain notes are not in the organ pipes, and this all detracts from the air of realism of the steady-pitched organ tones. As in the Orchestral Piccolo stop, the harmonic-length pipes are usually found in the organ chamber where the best imitations have been heard. This is primarily a solo Flute, and is frequently on the fourth manual. It can be a source of brilliance for certain flue combinations. Its limpid, pervading tones are at their best when heard against a background of very soft tone, such as a Viola Aetheria 8′.

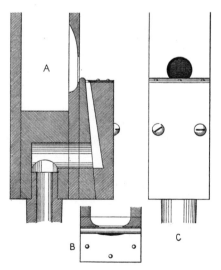

Orchestral Flute at middle C. An elaborate wind-way achieves some degree of realism in tone quality. A, interior view; B, cross-section at mouth; C, front view.

Many materials have been used in its construction, and some good examples have been made of unison length as well as harmonic length. Pure tin and spotted metal have produced excellent results. Rosewood, mahogany, teak, cherry, maple, walnut, and birch have produced beautiful formants of tone. Pipes of round, hexagonal, square, rectangular, triangular, and half-covered form have all been used with varying results. What is to be looked for in purchasing a good example is the skill of the voicer, not a certain material or shape. Some specimens are quite narrow in scale. The lips are inverted in many good examples; sometimes the harmonic wooden form is seen in the same stop. The flue that projects the wind over the upper lip may be built far out in front in some ranks.

The Orchestral Flute and a great many of its varieties are referred to as *imitative*. The *Flauto Traverso,* one of these, may be louder and more brilliant than a good imitation of the orchestral instrument. Other Flutes, like the Melodia and Waldflöte, may seem to be imitative in certain pieces of music or in certain organs. Synonyms: FLAUTO TRAVERSO, QUERFLÖTE, TRAVERSFLÖTE, VIENNA FLUTE, WIENERFLÖTE.

ORCHESTRAL HORN. See FRENCH HORN.

ORCHESTRAL OBOE. An imitative Reed of 8′ manual pitch, intended to simulate the tone of the orchestral prototype. The stop simply named *Oboe* is less imitative, and may share some of the Cornopean's or Trumpet's overtone structure. (Such a distinction does not exist between *Clarinet* and *Orchestral Clarinet.*) The Orchestral Oboe has a thin, pointed, nasal, direct tone that commands the attention, although not at all loud. It also seems flexible and unusually piquant when expressing gaiety. When played in slower passages it is plaintive, although not generally sylvan in effect. The very soft clatter of the inharmonics of the cane reed is not in this organ stop; brass has its own series of partials. This stop lacks the piercing quality of the Musette, the obvious fundamental of the Clarinet, the round tone of the English Horn, and the acidity of the Schalmei. It is never truly brilliant in tone, but sounds with a constantly varying set of peaked harmonics very high up in pitch above its soft fundamental. Standing close to a new rank of Orchestral Oboe pipes in the voicing room of a factory makes them sound with a very marked and unique brightness. Hearing them later within the confines of a swell box makes a different impression. Many of those most charming and light-toned overtones that so satisfied the ear have now been absorbed. Of course the organ voicers try to compensate for this type of loss, but they cannot achieve quite the same effect. However, this solo and ensemble stop performs better when enclosed, making it flexible in dynamic for solo melodies. Its pipes are unusually slender in scale, and inverted-conical in form. They are of all spotted metal, preferably clear down to the 16′ CCC pipe, if used. They are partly or fully capped in most examples. If fully, the sound comes out of a very long slender slot near the top of each. See OBOE. Synonym: HAUTBOIS.

ORCHESTRAL PICCOLO. See PICCOLO.

ORCHESTRAL SAXOPHONE. See SAXOPHONE.

ORCHESTRAL STRINGS. This stop-name is used to refer to a series of two, three, or more ranks of small-scaled Viole d'Orchestre pipes at 8′ on the manuals. It may be tuned as a complex céleste, or all pipes may be at the normal pitch. Each rank may have its own stop key, or they may all be controlled by a group key. This is a favorite residence organ stop as well as concert and theater organ stop. The more realistic specimens are not too loud and have a moderately slow undulation. See CÉLESTE, VIOLE D'ORCHESTRE.

ORCHESTRAL TRUMPET. See BRASS TRUMPET.

ORCHESTRAL VIOLIN. See VIOLE D'ORCHESTRE.

PEDAL STRING MIXTURE. A pedal mixture composed of either the incisive, small-scale Strings or the larger-scale pipes that sound more like Principals. This composite of tone supports the String ancillary or the Swell's Strings. Fortunate is the organist who has a separate stop key for each rank. Little approach to standardization of design is possible. The ranks usually do not break back in pitch as the scale is ascended, whereas manual ranks do. This permits the pedal scale to be ascended without changes in the weight or harmonic structure of the tone. Third-sounding ranks are less likely to be seen in pedal mixtures than they are in manual mixtures, since the pedal tone is more usable as a tone-builder than as a melody line. However, the 3 1/5′ (or 1 3/5′) can be included in this mixture if a more harmonically complete tone is desired. These pitches may all be taken from one rank of pipes (although this is not considered an orthodox procedure) if space or funds do not warrant individual, "straight" ranks. In this case special scaling of the pipes would have to be used by the builder to balance the loudness of the tone. Two examples, from the low pedal CCC key, follow:

Example No. 1
IV
C   4′
GG   5 1/3′
CC   8′
CCC   16′

Example No. 2
VII
G   2 2/3′
C   4′
GG   5 1/3′
CC   8′
GGG   10 2/3′
CCC   16′
CCCC   32′

See STRING MIXTURE.

PERCUSSIONS. Tonal effects that are obtained by striking rather than blowing the sounding device, and whose tones die away, unless damped like the Chimes, in their own natural period of time. Percussions fall into two classifications: *non-chromatic*, which do not make a different pitch for each of the organ's keys, and *chromatic*, which make a pitch to conform to each key in the scale, sometimes extending to the ends of the keyboards. The non-chromatic percussions of the organ are much the same as those of the orchestra, although a few have survived from the days of the motion picture organ. An incomplete listing includes: Cymbal, Persian Cymbal, Bird Whistle, Bass Drum, Snare Drum, Parade Drum, Chinese

Wood Block, Tom Tom, Tambourine, Castanets, Chinese Gong, Triangle, Rain, Wind, and Thunder. They are actuated by pistons (either manual or pedal) or sound on *every* key of a particular manual when drawn; Castanets, for example, would give a single vibration for each of the notes of the music played. The use of these percussions is limited to the pieces of music whose subject matter directly suggests their tones, as the Tambourine in a dance, or the Bird Whistle in a sylvan setting. The triangle is used in some orchestral music.

The chromatic percussions are much more versatile. Every organ factory has a percussion department where percussions are either made in their original forms, or adjusted to some particular organ's use. Residence organs, of which there are many hundreds in the country, require quite a few percussions. Chimes, Harp, Glockenspiel, and Cymbalstern have appeared in the most Classical of organs through the many centuries of organ building. The church organ may have use for these four percussions, particularly if it is used for recital purposes. Only since the comparatively recent invention of the electromagnet have the percussions become easy for the organist to use. Formerly he had to pull a lever or signal an attendant to do so. The simplest system merely actuates an electrical contact (like a door bell) in the piston or key, which in turn collapses a small bellows to which is attached the hammer. Swell shutters allow the organist to control volume in the percussions in accordance with the muscular pressure of the player.

Tubular Chimes, frequently heard in both large and small church organs, are, like the other organ imitations, most realistic when moderately soft. Manufacturers have had a difficult time inventing forms that do not sound too loudly the many inharmonics that are so prominent in a vibrating solid, but which are less noticeable in a vibrating air column (particularly a flue pipe). However, the characteristic timbre of Chimes comes from *a few inharmonics,* and the silvery effect comes from an almost equal loudness in a whole group of overtones of lower pitch. Sub-harmonics and partial tones between the first (fundamental) and second (octave) harmonics are heard in all of the following listing, and are also in the non-chromatic variety. Characteristic inharmonics are needed in all percussions to give color. Those that are unpleasant the builders try to exclude. Many of the following chromatic percussions sound from the pedal keys at the super-octave or octave pitches, since the pedal's keys sound only from CCC to G (16').

8'	CARILLON (which may consist of real bells in a tower)
8' 4'	CELESTA (metal bars, singe stroke)
8'	CHIMES (metal tubes, sometimes of large tower size, single stroke)
8' 4'	CHRYSOGLOTT (metal bars, single stroke)
8'	CLOCHES (small metal bars, single stroke)
8' 4'	CYMBALSTERN (single stroke on certain keys, like C, D, E, F, G, A, B♭)
8' 4' 2'	GLOCKENSPIEL (metal bars, single stroke)

8′		GONGS (metal gongs, single stroke)
8′ 4′		HARP (metal bars with resonators, single stroke)
8′ 4′		MARIMBA (wooden bars with resonators, single and repeat strokes)
8′ 4′		MARIMBA HARP (wooden bars, single stroke)
8′ 4′		ORCHESTRA BELLS (metal bars, single and repeat strokes)
8′ 4′		PIANO (concert grand in some examples, single stroke)
	2′	SLEIGH BELLS (metal spheres with slots, single stroke)
8′ 4′		VIBRAPHONE (metal bars, resonators, tremolo, single stroke)
8′ 4′ 2′		XYLOPHONE (wood bars, single and repeat strokes)

PETITE NAZARD. A soft, small-scale 2 2/3′ Diapason or Harfen-prinzipal on the manuals, voiced to sound well with the soft flue chorus, perhaps made up of Gemshorns, Octave Diapasons, or other diminutive Foundation ranks. Such a stop is of much use on the Choir or Great, since the regular Twelfth (Nasard) is frequently too loud to sound with the quieter ranks. See TWELFTH.

PETITE TROMPETTE. See ECHO TRUMPET.

PHILOMELA. An open wooden Flute of 8′ on the manuals, always voiced with a clear, penetrating, and particularly bright tone, but not necessarily a loud tone. It is never string-like in timbre. Occasionally this stop is formed as an open Doppelflöte. It can also be an inverted-pyramidal shape (square or rectangular in cross-section) with either inverted or beveled lips. It is distinctly a solo voice, and is seen on the fourth division of quite a few large organs. Metal Philomelas are also heard from the Solo Organ.

PHONEUMA. A soft Flute of 8′ manual pitch, having a timbre that is strengthened slightly in the third harmonic. The pipes are small-scaled, metal, fully capped, and designed in their mouth parts somewhat like a String stop. It sounds a soft type of Quintaton in some stops, but is not generally seen in organs. See QUINTATEN.

PICCOLO. A Flute stop of 2′ on the manuals, made from open pipes of either metal or wood. It is a harmonically full, liquid, smooth tone of great usefulness in many ensembles of flue stops, both loud and soft. This orchestral instrument is more realistically reproduced by harmonic pipes of either metal or wood, because this type of construction gives that round, "plump," pervading quality so difficult to make at high pitches. This pitch sounds the fourth harmonic of the unison series of stops on the manuals. It is often seen in the Swell or Solo Organs, not being in the Choir or Great usually, since these divisions sound better with a Diapason or Blockflöte or Hohlflöte at 2′ pitch. The regular Diapason Fifteenth is sometimes ten to twenty times as loud as the Piccolo, and it builds up a much more complete harmonic structure than most Flutes.

Compared to the Fife, the Piccolo is less loud and without shrillness of tone; compared to the Flageolet, it is a little louder but less round; compared to the Hohlflöte, it is somewhat softer in tone. The Blockflöte and

EFFECT OF SINGLE VARIABLES OF
FLUE PIPE STRUCTURE ON TONE

Variables in open and stopped *flue* pipes (wood or metal) of any pitch, loudness, or tone quality (disregarding Law of Diminishing Returns)	Effects of an INCREASE of the variables on opposite side of page (a decrease would have the opposite effect)
Body of Pipe:	
1. Length	Lowers pitch; more overtones
2. Diameter in relation to length (scale)	Fewer overtones; raises pitch
3. Proportion of depth to width (Bourdon)	Fewer overtones; slower speech
4. Proportion of width to depth (Hohlflöte)	More overtones; quicker speech
5. Thickness of walls (Tibia Clausa)	Fewer high overtones
6. Density of material (% of tin)	More overtones
7. Smallness of top diameter in proportion to mouth-line diameter (Erzähler)	Weakness in higher overtones; strength in lower overtones
8. Flare of inverted-conical taper (Dolce, Dolce Flute, Tibia Dura)	More overtones of all series
9. Smoothness of interior walls (Gedeckt)	Fewer overtones; raises pitch
10. Area of slot (Viole d'Orchestre)	More overtones
11. Narrowness of slot (Keraulophone)	More high overtones
12. Diameter of rohr (Rohrflöte)	More even-numbered harmonics
13. Length of rohr (Rohrbordun)	Fewer and lower-pitched harmonics
14. Angle of flare of bell (Bell Gamba)	More high overtones
15. Length of bell (Bell Flute)	More high overtones
16. Angle of truncated section (Koppelflöte)	Fewer high, more low overtones
17. Length of truncated section (Spillflöte)	More high, fewer low overtones
Mouth of Pipe:	
18. Height	Fewer overtones; raises pitch
19. Cross-sectional area	Fewer overtones; softer
20. Width of a low mouth	More overtones; louder
21. Width of a high mouth	Fewer overtones; softer
22. Thickness of upper lip	Fewer overtones
23. Smoothness of upper lip	Fewer overtones
24. Sharpness of upper lip	More overtones
25. Angle of bevel of upper lip	Fewer initial harmonics
26. Moving upper lip outward	Fewer overtones; quicker speech

EFFECT OF SINGLE VARIABLES OF
FLUE PIPE STRUCTURE ON TONE

Wind:	
27. Length of foot of pipe	Decreases windiness of tone
28. Wind pressure	More overtones; louder
29. Size of foot-hole (quantity of wind)	More overtones; louder
30. Windway cross-sectional area	Increases windiness of tone
31. Sloping back of languid (or block)	More overtones; slower speech
32. Number of nicks	Fewer overtones
33. Depth of nicks	Fewer overtones
34. Closeness of nicks	Fewer overtones
35. Wideness of nicks	Fewer overtones
36. Acuteness of bevel of languid (or block)	More overtones
37. Steadiness of wind (less tremolo)	Fewer initial harmonics; softer
External Structures:	
38. Size of ears	Lower pitch; quicker speech
39. Closeness of ears to ends of mouth	Lower pitch; quicker speech
40. Closeness of bridge to optimum position	Quicker speech of fundamental
41. Approach to optimum bridge diameter	Increases loudness of all harmonics

Chart Explanation: Effects of Single Variables of Flue Pipe Structure on Tone

The flue pipe sounds without the aid of the reed's vibrating motion. Compressed air enters the foot of the pipe and grazes the outside of the upper lip in such a way that a vacuum is formed in the bottom portion of the enclosed column of air, in accordance with Bernoulli's famous principle. This pocket of vacuum grows steadily until much of the air is exhausted to the outside. Finally the atmospheric pressure gains entrance and fills the vacuum. It enters a stopped pipe through the mouth, and an open pipe through both mouth and top. Naturally, like a swinging pendulum, the air passes the center of its equilibrium, and *too much* enters to merely fill the vacuum. This excess triggers the next cycle (vibration). The fluttering "reed" of air at the lip of the pipe frictions several whole series of whirling *vortices* in the air. The mass (weight) of the air column is in sympathy with a few of these, both as to fundamental and overtone resonance. It couples itself to them, and strengthens them, projecting them outward. All pipe structures also vibrate, especially in the lower frequencies, contributing some small parcel of their own inharmonics, and subtracting by absorption others from the tone. The edge-tones that escape this friction-trap add a *gaussian*, cymbal-like "top" to all tones. (In the Rankett's reed pipes this fringe of highs is exaggerated.)

Friction patterns presented to the moving pockets of air around the pipe by bridges, mouths, ears, and walls of the pipe create, therefore, a design of natural sounds that identifies the pipe organ as an individual instrument. The alternate pockets of compression and vacuum (rarefaction) in the air molecules that travel outward (spherically) finally impact everything in a church or room, and are reflected back on themselves, eventually dying by many inner collisions. Most of this tonal complex is inaudible except to the subconscious, but all waves affect that unity of sense we call *music*.

Noel A. Bonavia-Hunt gave permission to take some of the chart's facts from his writings.

Sifflöte are both louder than the Piccolo, and also of more harmonic structure. The Piccolo has rather improperly been made from stopped pipes. To make graphic the fact that there is not necessarily a correlation between loudness and brightness in timbre, the following chart is given:

1) a Piccolo stop that is soft and bright in tone;
2) a Piccolo stop that is loud and bright in tone;
3) a Piccolo stop that is soft and dull in tone;
4) a Piccolo stop that is loud and dull in tone.

Piccolos of all of these types can be found in organs. The tone will affect the use that this stop may have in combination with other stops. Synonym: ORCHESTRAL PICCOLO.

PICCOLO d'AMORE. A soft, half-covered Flute of 2′ manual pitch, which is sometimes given the structure of a Flûte d'Amour: small-scale rectangular wooden pipes with narrow brass rohrs in their stoppers. Its refined and gentle tone is useful in the Choir Organ, perhaps the Echo. It is suitable for the softest of combinations with flues. See PICCOLO.

PLEIN JEU. A manual mixture of octave-sounding and fifth-sounding ranks of Principals, open, metal, and made from usually the finest quality spotted metal stock. It either gives a complete chorus of Foundation tone or adds any design of high-pitched top to extend the Chorus upward. It is generally considered to be not merely a source of brilliance, as the Cymbal is, but an integral part of the flue Chorus. There may be more than one example on an organ, as there may be more than one important Chorus. Many examples are just three or four ranks, smaller organs having this stop, but its design may be extensive and include up to fourteen or even more ranks. The Pedal may have a Plein Jeu, extending its Diapasons. Pipes may be of large scale and heavy wind pressure, perhaps with unusual measurements in their scales, perhaps with the traditional scales, as in Dom Bedos. It may be found on any manual. Here are notes sounding from just the middle C pipes:

Example No. 1 V		Example No. 2 VII		Example No. 3 VII		Example No. 4 IX	
C^5	1/2′	C^5	1/2′	G^3	1 1/3′	C^5	1/2′
G^4	2/3′	G^4	2/3′	C^3	2′	G^4	2/3′
C^4	1′	C^4	1′	G^2	2 2/3′	C^4	1′
G^3	1 1/3′	G^3	1 1/3′	C^2	4′	G^3	1 1/3′
C^3	2′	C^3	2′	$*G^1$	5 1/3′	C^3	2′
		G^2	2 2/3′	C^1	8′	G^2	2 2/3′
		C^2	4′	C	16′	C^2	4′
						$*G^1$	5 1/3′
						C^1	8′

*Belongs to the 16′ series.

Breaks in the pitches must be custom-designed for such a specialized tone-producer as the Plein Jeu. The highest-pitched may break twice in an octave, the lower-pitched once. In the higher one or two octaves below-unison pitches sometimes appear to prevent the tendency to sound unnaturally brilliant. No third-sounding Tierces are included in the above examples, because this acute effect might hinder the effort of the organ builder to create Chorus unity. See CYMBAL.

PLEIN JEU HARMONIQUE. A manual mixture designed for the functions of the Plein Jeu, but with a more impressive, loud, and sweeping sound that carries every note played to the top threshold of audibility. This stop is almost cymbal-like in its brilliance and is suitable for addition to the louder flues and Chorus Reeds of any division. Harmonic-length, spotted metal pipes of unusually bold tone make up its ranks. These three examples would sound these notes from the middle C key:

Example No. 1		Example No. 2		Example No. 3	
IV		VIII		VIII	
C^4	1′	C^4	1′	C^5	1/2′
G^3	1 1/3′	G^3	1 1/3′	G^4	2/3′
C^3	2′	C^3	2′	C^4	1′
C^2	4′	G^2	2 2/3′	G^3	1 1/3′
		C^2	4′	C^3	2′
		*G^1	5 1/3′	G^2	2 2/3′
		C^1	8′	C^2	4′
		C	16′	C^1	8′

*Belongs to the 16′ series.

Notes below C^1 are not harmonic. See PLEIN JEU.

POMMER. See GEDECKTPOMMER.

PORTUNAFLÖTE. See BORDUNALFLÖTE.

POSAUNE. A Chorus Reed of loud and freely vibrating tone, quite like the Trombone in timbre, at 16′ or 8′ on the manuals, and 32′ or 16′ on the pedals. It is usually more brilliantly voiced than the Trombone stop, the names being not entirely synonymous in organ lore. In many instruments it is capable of supporting the full ensemble of the organ, even with the couplers drawn. In the largest of organs it is just another loud Reed stop. It should never be placed on the manuals or pedals of any organ with the idea that it can substitute for a flue stop of any sort. It properly belongs in the Reed Chorus. Its fundamental is less prominent than that of the Diaphone or Bombarde. It lacks the brilliance of the Tuba Magna, Tuba Mirabilis, or Ophicleide. The 8′ manual rank is heard from Solo Organs, although this is more likely to be a 16′ stop on the manuals. The manual examples may be somewhat horn-like in tone color. The inverted-conical pipes may be less wide in flare than some of the other Chorus Reed ranks of comparable pitch. The walls of the pipes (resonators) are of heavy construction, especially in the 32′ and 16′ octaves, and also in all pipes that withstand a heavy wind pressure, as, for example, between eight and twenty inches. Rolled zinc may be found in the CCCC octave. The CCC octave may have spotted metal in the pipes' top halves, perhaps for the full lengths. The CC (8′) octave and above are usually all spotted metal. Wood lends a useful formant in the deeper pipes. See TROMBA, TROMBONE, TUBA.

POST HORN. See ENGLISH POST HORN.

PRESTANT. A Diapason of 4′ sounding either from the organ's screen, as is common with this name, or from the regular windchests. The timbre is bright and lively, perhaps stringy. See DIAPASON, MONTRE, OCTAVE, PRINCIPAL.

PRINCIPAL. A stop-name used to indicate any of the following:

1) the chief Diapason 8′ on any manual;
2) the second, smaller-scale Diapason 8′ on any manual;
3) the chief Octave 4′ on any manual;
4) the second, smaller-scale Octave 4′ on any manual;
5) a Fifteenth 2′ on any manual;
6) a Double Diapason 32′ of wood or metal on the pedals;
7) a Diapason 16′ of wood or metal on the pedals;
8) the chief *unison flue* stop on any manual or the pedals;
9) any mutation of Foundation tone on any manual or the pedals.

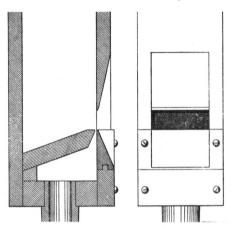

A form of wooden Principal useful in both
manual unison and manual bass pitches.
The upper lip is made sharp to generate
additional overtones.

Although this name is practically synonymous with *Diapason,* there is
some general tendency to reserve it for the lighter-toned Diapasons. See
DIAPASON OCTAVE.

PRINCIPAL FLUTE. A large-scale metal Flute of open form, at 8′ or
4′ on the manuals, and also at these same pitches on the pedals. Its tone is
loud or moderately loud, and the timbre is somewhere in the realm between
a metal Diapason and an open Flute with a mouth of high cut-up. Builders
can make a great variety of hybrid tones between these two families of
stops. Some examples may have a little string tone* in them as well.
Such a Flute can be added to the Diapason Chorus without subtracting
from the true Chorus tone. It may appear on the Great, Swell, or Solo
manual and sound alone or in combination with louder Reeds or flue stops.
It may be used for a single line of notes or in chord form. The Harmonic
Flute, Clarabella, Tibia Plena, or Major Open Flute may be preferred to
it on the Great. The *Prinzipalflöte,* as it is sometimes spelled, is never a
substitute for a Diapason, except in the very smallest organs, although
it is often used to accompany hymns. This name indicates both *Principal*
scale (i. e. like a Diapason), and importance as a Flute of big tone. The
pipes are usually of plain metal, but spotted may be preferred. Wood is
seldom used for this Flute. See MAJOR OPEN FLUTE.

*Reference to "string tone" in any flue pipe does not mean that the timbre is at all
stringy. It simply refers to stronger overtones in the train.

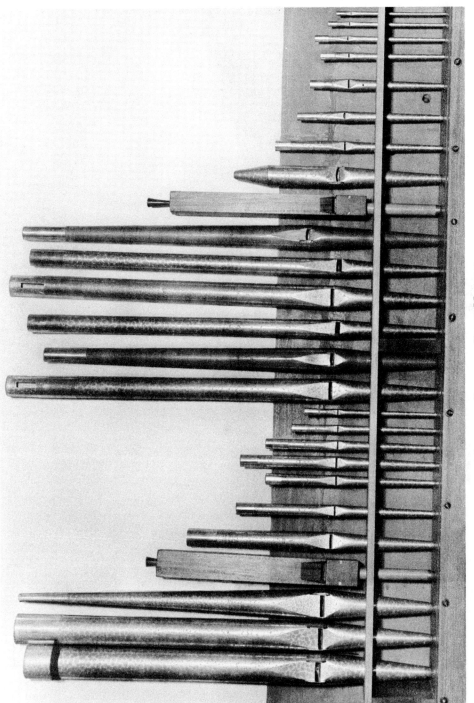

AEOLIAN SKINNER FLUE MODELS

AEOLIAN SKINNER FLUE MODELS

A rack of specimen flue (non-reed) pipes photographed in the flue voicing room of the Aeolian Skinner factory. This set of pipes is always in front of the voicer, and serves as a guide to him in adjusting the volume and timbre of new pipes that come from the pipe shop. All of those shown here sound from the middle C key. In three sections, from left:

GREAT: Quintaten 16' (capped), Principal 8', Gemshorn 8', Bourdon 8', Octave 4', Twelfth 2 2/3', Fifteenth 2', and a four-rank Fourniture of four pipes.

SWELL: Viola Pomposa 8', Flauto Dolce 8', Viole de Gambe 8', Viola Céleste 8', Viole Céleste 8', and Flute Céleste 8'.

POSITIV: Nason Flute 8' (stopped wood), Koppelflöte 4', Lieblichprinzipal 2', Tierce 1 3/5', Larigot 1 1/3', Sifflöte 1', and a three-rank Cymbal of three pipes.

Courtesy: Aeolian Skinner Organ Company.

PYRAMID FLUTE. An open wood Flute of 16′, 8′, or 4′ manual pitch, whose pipes are shaped like the lower sections of very slender pyramids. The Conical Flute, of similar form, is usually a little brighter than this Flute, especially in the treble notes. The partials of these two Flutes are not peaked in loudness as they are in many straight-walled metal and wooden Flutes. They are also dampened almost out of existence by the tapered walls, except down near the fundamental. Compared to the Major Open Flute and Principal Flute, this is a comparatively dull Flute. It is chiefly a combinational or ensemble Flute. It is a substantial and firm-toned aid to any solo stop, such as the Tuba Magna, Stentorphone, or Trumpet, and it can add body of tone and all of the lower-pitched harmonics of the train to any loud combination. Triangular Flutes of tapered form are also made, and are quite dull in tone, although sometimes loud. There is little appeal in the tone of this Flute as a solo stop to sound by itself. It has accompaniment functions of various kinds, as with the loud or brilliant solo stops. It is never unable to support a loud sound, and its tone blends well. See CONICAL FLUTE.

QUERFLÖTE. See ORCHESTRAL FLUTE.

QUINT. A Foundation stop that speaks at the fifth-sounding pitch between the unison and octave stops. This is at 5 1/3′ on the manuals, and 10 2/3′ on the pedals. The other fifth-sounding stops on the manuals, such as the 10 2/3′, 2 2/3′, 1 1/3′, and 2/3′, are sometimes referred to as "Quints," and the pedal's pitches of 21 1/3′, 5 1/3′, and 2 2/3′ may also be referred to by the same name. Properly speaking, however, only the 5 1/3′ on the manuals and the 10 2/3′ on the pedals map be called *Quints*. The Quint sounds at the interval of a fifth above the key depressed. This is at G¹ on the manuals, and at GGG on the pedals, assuming that middle C and the low pedal CCC have been depressed. The Quints on both manuals and pedals are the "Twelfths" of the sub-unison (sub-octave) series of stop-pitches, or, more properly speaking, they are the third harmonics of these series. They are usually not drawn by the organist unless with a 16′ flue on the manuals, and a 32′ stop on the pedals. Otherwise, they will set up a series of unbalanced effects with the unison's harmonics. The 10 2/3′ pedal Quint can be drawn with any flue of 16′ in order to create a Resultant of 32′. The special effects of the manual Resultants (as be tween the 8′ and 5 1/3′) may be used occasionally to deepen the tone.

These stops introduce into the composite of the harmonics heard *a whole series of harmonics from their own pipes,* and from each note played. The Quints on both manuals and pedals create a cleanness of tone when they are not too loud for the rest of the ensemble. If they are too loud, they create an opaqueness of sound that merely defeats the purpose of the music. They can help the listener to orient pitch and hear timbres more precisely, and they make a more unified tonal impression on the ear. They sound at three times the frequency of the sub-unison stops, and one and one-half the frequency of the unison stops. These are simple fractions for the ear to analyze, so their effects on the tones are clarifying rather than confusing. No simple proportion in frequencies escapes the surveillance of the ear, and this stop has one of the simplest relationships with other stops that exists. Metal or wooden Diapasons usually make up this stop. Synonyms: FIFTH, GROSS NASARD.

QUINTADE. A stopped metal Flute of cylindrical form and very large scale, at 32′, 16′, or 8′ on the manuals, and 32′ or 16′ on the pedals. The tone of this stop sounds with prominence in both the fundamental and the third harmonic, varying in proportion in the examples of the many organ builders. On both manuals and pedals, the 32′ rank, therefore, sounds the 32′ and 10 2/3′ components noticeably; the 16′ rank sounds the 16′ and 5 1/3′ components noticeably; the 8′ rank sounds the 8′ and 2 2/3′ components both in some prominence. The source of this strong third harmonic is the large cylindrical spotted metal cap on the top of each of the Quintade pipes. It suppresses the even-numbered harmonics, as in all stopped Flutes, and permits the energy of the pipe's air column to emphasize the third harmonic. It is interesting to listen for the fifth harmonic (a "Tierce") in stopped pipes; it can sometimes be heard in single notes, and uncombined, but mostly it is masked. This stop could hardly be described as loud, but it is pervading without being too noticeable in any combination. In adding this stop to any combination, the organist should be concerned as to whether the "Twelfth" component will produce an overly pungent effect, sometimes called the "rustle of the Quint." Some combinations cannot tolerate this strong source of the third harmonic. On the other hand, depriving a flue combination of the binding effect of this "perfectly tuned Twelfth" may lead to lack of cohesion in tone.

Comparisons between the whole series of "Quint Flutes" could not include the dynamic level of each stop because all are designed to sound appropriately in their own organs. Some are designed with rohrs, others with narrow mouths. The following list, which was arranged with the aid of one of the most practical authorities in the country, shows the progression of the Quint Flutes, and a few other stopped forms, as they attain more of the third harmonic *in proportion to their fundamentals*. At the top of the list the fundamental is practically the only component audible; at the bottom the third harmonic is as strong as or stronger than the fundamental:

  a. Tibia Clausa (a solo Flute of unusually large scale)
  b. Lieblichgedeckt
  c. Gedeckt
  d. Lieblichbordun
  e. Bourdon
  f. Stopped Flute (Stopped Diapason)
  g. Nachthorn
  h. Nason Flute
  i. Quintaten (Quintaton)
  j. Quintade
  k. Quintadena
  l. Gedecktpommer (Pommer)
  m. Quint Flute (Nasard Flute)

QUINTADENA. A stopped metal Flute of 16′, 8′, or 4′ on the manuals, and 16′ or 8′ on the pedals. This moderately loud *Quint Flute* produces a very strong third harmonic (properly referred to as a *Twelfth* in only the unison ranks at 8′ on the manuals, and 16′ on the pedals). In this particular species of tone this third component can be as loud as the fundamental (first harmonic), but it is usually just a little below the dynamic level of the fundamental. Therefore, both of these components are clearly audible to the listener when this Flute is played uncombined and in single notes. The third harmonic in this Flute is a little greater in proportion to the fundamental than in the Quintade, and considerably more so than in the Quintaten or Quintaton. The Quintadena is usually louder than either the Quintade or Quintaten, in spite of the Quintade's larger scale. The Quintaten and Quintade are about the same in dynamic level.

The function of this stop is to bind together the flue combinations on any division by means of its *naturally tuned* third harmonic. It is usable with louder combinations than the Quintaten or Quintaton. It also makes a mysterious and somewhat horn-like solo register. To other solo flues (not Reeds) it can lend new dimension and some real penetration without being noticed itself. Examples of such solo stops are: Melodia, Viola, Doppelflöte, Dolce, Gamba, Rohrflöte, Harmonic Flute, and Major Flute. If the 8′ Quintadena is drawn, the 2 2/3′ is strengthened; if the 16′ is used, the 5 1/3′ is strengthened, and may clash with the drawn 8′ stops; if the 4′ Quintadena is drawn, the 1 1/3′ is strengthened. The pipes of this 4′ rank, if subjected to the intramanual octave coupler, will sound at 4′, 2′, 1 1/3′, and 2/3′, giving the effect of a small compound stop of very light tone. These pipes are cylindrical, capped like the Quintade, and of high tin content, sometimes so high that the spots disappear and a silvery white color appears. The walls are thick, as in the Quintade and Quintaten, to discourage absorption of the overtones by the pipes themselves. Some have harmonic bridges and ears. The mouth is relatively low, compared to that of most stopped Flutes, and encourages the third (and even fifth) harmonic. Wood pipes are rare in the Quintade and Quintaten, but may be seen in this stop. Rohrs are usually not provided. See QUINTADE.

QUINTATEN. A stopped Flute on the manuals at 16′, 8′, or 4′, and on the pedals at 16′ or 8′, sounding with a wide variation in loudness in the many thousands of specimens throughout the country. There is also a wide variation in the proportion of strength between the third harmonic and first harmonic (prime tone) in this species of Flute, more so than in the Quintade and Quintadena. In this Flute, however, the third harmonic is quite likely to be considerably less noticeable than the prime tone. Little standardization is possible in this series of *Quint* names, because an organist will request his favorite name, and the builder will then try to balance the voicing to suit the other stops. Traditions also vary between factories in naming all stops. *Quintaton* refers in many cases to a soft form of the Quintaten with its same proportion between harmonics. The soft "singing" tone of this Flute is usable as a solo effect, perhaps accompanied by the Echo Dulciana or Dulciana. Its prime use, however, is to bind flue combinations, somewhat of the softer type. The dynamic level of this Flute is somewhat like that of the Quintade, or a little softer, but the degree of blend achieved is more dependent upon exact scale and mouth cut-up than just volume. The ear adjusts more to volume differences than to degrees of overtone development. The Quintade adjusts itself more to heavier, rather than brighter, combinations. The pitches of the Quintade are also lower than this stop in many examples. The Quintade is more likely to be a pedal rank, as are also the Gedecktpommer and Bourdon. The Quintaten (of weak third harmonic) may be a Choir stop and the Quintadena (of strong third harmonic) is usually also a manual stop. Choice between the 16′, 8′, or 4′ pitches depends upon the series of stops to which a third harmonic is to be added. The Quintaten at 16′ or 4′ may be more useful than the Quintadena at these pitches, the Quintadena's strong *mf* dynamic level fitting well the 8′ stops.

Which of the Quint Flutes, and the Gedeckt must be included, is used in any combination by the organist is a matter of taste after the dynamic level and pitch considerations have been settled. These Quint Flutes all carry differently to different parts of an auditorium; *they react very differently in different combinations;* they are variable in effect over their great range, from CCCC to C^5. Open pipes of quiet and unobtrusive tone are used by all builders to finish off the higher treble ranks, stopped pipes being impractical around G^3 to C^5. Holes in the centers of the caps, rohrs, and wooden pipes are not infrequently seen, and at any part of the range. The Quintaten's scale is less than that of the Quintade, although either one can be a manual or a pedal stop, but it doesn't vary much from the Quintadena's. Its mouth cut-up may be a little higher than the Quintadena's, so it will produce less of the third harmonic. This is a matter, however, to be correlated with its scale. A pipe can be given a stronger third component by either lowering its cut-up or reducing its scale, or both. This Flute has the cylindrical capped pipes seen in most of the *Quint Flute* series. Since it is a stopped rank, the low manual CC is about four feet long, and the middle C is about one foot long, speaking lengths considered (lip to cap). The C^4 pipe is 1 1/2′ inches if stopped and 3 inches if open, theoretically considered. See QUINTADE.

QUINTATON. A diminutive form of the Quintaten, at 16′, 8′, or 4′ on the manuals, and 16′ or 8′ on the pedals. It is very soft for a pedal rank, but may be combined with soft pedal flue stops, like the Bourdon or Gemshorn. Or this name may be used on the pedals and the sound correspond to that of the Quintaten, Quintade, or Quintadena. In some manual ranks this is a beautiful solo tone of tranquil, Nachthorn-like effect that may also have any of the ensemble functions of the other Quint Flutes. The pipes are of small scale and soft intonation. See QUINTADE, QUINTATEN.

QUINT BASS. A Foundation stop of Diapason tone, but occasionally a stopped or open Flute, at 10 2/3′ on the pedals. This stop makes a 32′ Resultant with any 16′ flue on the pedals. If this stop sounds with any independent 32′ *open* rank it will set up yet another 32′ Resultant, this one perhaps inaudible, with the second harmonic (at 16′) of the 32′. This Diapason is properly added to the 32′ series of pedal stops in order to form a full ensemble tone. It also aids the pedal line in sounding clean pitches and making better blend with other stops in that division. See DIAPASON, QUINT. Synonym: QUINTENBASS.

QUINT DIAPASON. A Diapason or Principal of 5 1/3′ on the manuals, and 10 2/3′ on the pedals. It belongs to the sub-unison series of pitches, and is necessary for a complete chorus of the sub-unison series of stops that is sometimes added to the unison series of stops in order to make the tone of the flue Chorus heavier and of greater depth. It is usually not drawn without a 16′ on the manuals. See DIAPASON, QUINT, QUINT BASS.

QUINTENBASS. See QUINT BASS.

QUINTE OUVERTE. A Diapason or Diapason-Flute hybrid of 5 1/3′ on the manuals, and 10 2/3′ on the pedals, belonging to the sub-unison series of stop-pitches. It is formed from open metal or wood pipes varying in loudness according to the 16′ manual and 32′ pedal stops it is meant to augment. It sounds the important *third harmonic* of this series on manuals and pedals, and speaks at the fifth above the key depressed. See DIAPASON, FLÛTE OUVERTE, QUINT, QUINT BASS, QUINT DIAPASON.

QUINT FLUTE. An 8′ manual or 16′ pedal Flute of stoppered construction, either metal or wood, designed to make a third harmonic, or "Twelfth," as prominent from the same pipes as its fundamental. These two components vary in proportion, but many examples have very noticeable third harmonics. The fundamental (the first harmonic) may even be inaudible in some specimens, but it is physically present to some extent in the tone. The prominent third component of the 16′ rank is the 5 1/3′, and of the 8′, the 2 2/3′ pitch. Since these third harmonics are slightly off the true pitches of the equal-tempered scale (as sounded by the octave ranks), they undulate very slightly to make a beautiful and serene effect not obtainable in any other way. This stop may not be drawn with a 4′ but it would nevertheless undulate with *any notes* played from any 4′ stop. It is thus an impressive solo Flute of pervading, subtle effect on the ear. It is, of course, a Copula in effect because of its third harmonic of strong sound.

This name has been used for 5 1/3′ and 2 2/3′ Flutes improperly; these should be referred to, respectively, as a *Flute Quint* and a *Flute Twelfth*. A truly compound *Quint Flute* may be heard in a few organs, made from two ranks such as an 8′ Harmonic Flute and an open metal 5 1/3′ of softer tone. This is a solo and an ensemble stop. The *Grand Quintaten* and the *Nasard Flute* can also be compound. See QUINTADE. Synonym: NASARD FLUTE.

QUINT MIXTURE. A manual or pedal mixture composed of Foundation ranks of open metal construction, designed to amplify the sub-unison series of pitches. Middle C and the low pedal CCC keys speak in these examples:

Manual Example		Pedal Example	
III		III	
G²	2 2/3'	GG	5 1/3'
C²	4'	CC	8'
G¹	5 1/3'	GGG	10 2/3'

QUINT TRUMPET. See TROMPETTE QUINTE.

RANKETT. A very old form of short-resonatored Reed stop, at 16' or 8' on both manuals and pedals. It makes a piping, sibilant vibration that is a little less off the basic pitches in its overtone series than the Kinura, yet less distinct in pitch than the Vox Humana or Dulcian. It lacks the metallic twang of the Regals and the nasal, acid timbre of the Schalmei. The myriad of soft *inharmonics* that sounds from its tone lends to the flue stops, like the Diapason, Gemshorn, Dolce, or open Flutes, a soft glittering sheen that is invaluable in making them stand out against the other stops in polyphonic music. This stop and the Regals have a sudden effect of surprise on the ear, yet remain in the realm of the conventional. The Rankett is a kind of Regal, and often classified as such. Although it is quite soft in dynamic value, it penetrates because it fills up a particular range of hearing in which the ear is sensitive. It can make dozens of overtones in the same range in which the average Reed or flue produces only a dozen. And these all vary constantly in pitch, some a great deal, others by just a slight undulation. These many overtone pitches revolve constantly around the fundamental, which is very weak in this stop. This brilliant daub of soft partials is equally useful in manual and pedal line. It is not so effective when chorded. It is not so much a tonal entity as an adjunct to other stops' tones. It is frequently heard uncombined from the pedal, a typical use being in a Hindemith Sonata. Some *pedal* and *manual* light Reed Choruses:

Messingregal	4'		Regal	2'		Rohrschalmei	4'	Schalmei	4'
Knopfregal	8'	or	Rohrschalmei	4'	or	Rankett	8'	or	Rankett	8'
Rankett	16'		Fagotto	8'		Dulcian	16'	Fagotto	16'
			Rankett	16'				*Dulcian	32'

*The 32' pedal (and manual) short-resonatored Reed forms are not unheard of in several European organs. The writer knows of none in America. Also useful would be the Kinura, Rankett, and the very short Fagotto.

These choruses are not always used combined with other stops, nor even all together themselves, but offer the organist a complete selection of pitches and a wide variation of tone colors for many uses. Couplers can obtain any of them at most pitches on any manual. Each is a distinctive solo stop, or usable with a soft flue. They are more typical of the Classical school than the Romantic, and the tone of each of these stops has survived for centuries. The Rankett pipes are short, cylindical, and capped. Small holes near the base of each pipe emit the smothered and windy sound. See HOLZRANKETT, REGAL.

RAUSCHQUINTE. A compound stop of II ranks of Diapasons, intended to supplement the tone of the flue Chorus, or any other combination with one of the oldest groups of pitches in the organ: the *Twelfth* and *Fifteenth*. The ranks are usually extended unbroken in pitch throughout the compass. Example No. 2 sounds an octave above No. 1, and No. 3 sounds an octave above No. 2. Notes from middle C key are:

Example No. 1   *Example No. 2   Example No. 3
    II   II   II
  C^3 2′ C^4 1′ C^5 1/2′
  G^2 2 2/3′ G^3 1 1/3′ G^4 2/3′

*Example No. 2 is sometimes called a *Quartain.*

REGAL. Probably the oldest Reed stop in the organ, with resonators of shorter than unison length, pitched at 16′, 8′, 4′, and 2′ on both manuals and pedals. There is a tremendous variety of Regals because there is a great variety of combinations of relative loudness possible among the higher-pitched overtones of the short-resonator Reeds. Regals are frequently named for the shapes and materials of their pipes rather than for their timbres. Also, many *hybrid* Regals with other stops, such as the Vox Humana, Krummhorn, and Oboe, have been invented. Even the *Harfenregal* is to be heard in some places. The very short resonators do not support the tones of the fundamentals and other lower-pitched harmonics of these Reeds. The resonance given the higher harmonics emphasizes their pitches, as is done in the buccal and nasal cavities of the human voice. This makes a tone of highly individual characteristics, and one quite different from the many unison-length ranks of flues and Reeds in the organ. There is always an element of surprise in the tone of a Regal because some higher harmonic — such as, to make an example, the nineteenth — is made much louder than surrounding harmonics. Perhaps it is a whole *group* of higher harmonics that is emphasized, rather than just one, but the cymbal-like motions of the edges of the brass reeds are not under so much control in one of these short-resonatored stops as in the Trumpet or Oboe. Such a novel and bright reedy tone also happens to have the happy characteristic of traversing a long nave without losing its ability to impart to the listener the exact sense of pitch.

Regals are accenting agents for any line of notes. Each makes the tone colorful, especially at a great distance; each makes the pitch more defined in the memory, and gives the ear the stimulus of reaching towards the threshold of audibility. Regals may sound too intense and their harmonics may be too close in pitch for ears attuned to the Romantic type of organ, but accepting the Regal is very much a matter of education. Its high-pitched harmonics are no further from the notes of the scale than those of the thin Viols. Regals give vitality to the organ's tones because they present a variety of timbre that is in startling contrast to the average timbres in the organ. Their functions include melody, either alone or combined with another stop, accent of the bass line in manuals or pedals, and contrasting countermelody. They have little use as tone builders. Regals and Ranketts can sometimes be identified after the organist has taken his hands from the keys; they continue to vibrate longer than most flues or Reeds, giving a delightful twangy sound that shows that the "dying away" transients can affect color too. Records of organs, particularly of Classical music, sound these effects. They are used mostly, of course, in contrapuntal music.

Regals present great variety: they can snarl, growl, sigh, or sound with an acid whine. A few glitter with metallic brilliance, and others give a percussive tinkle just as the key is depressed. The stop simply named *Regal* is usually a source of brilliant, metallic sound, not bell-like, but a sustained glitter, as it were, most useful at 2′ or 4′. The term *Schnarrwerk* is used to indicate the Regals and Ranketts, the thin-toned imitators of the human vowels, little shepherd's pipes, and the Barpfeife and Vox Humana. Pipes of brass, pure tin, lead and tin alloyed, and wood make the sounds from lengths between one-sixteenth to one-quarter unison. The Schalmei's pipes are spotted metal in narrow cylindrical forms; the Regal's are mostly topped by a damping shape with holes in it that rests on very narrow short cylinders of brass. The reeds and shallots must receive special treatment to make them emit the variety of tones that they do. The formant of the brass parts is also a source of the Regal's color. Manual and pedal choruses of light Reeds containing the Regal follow. All stops are suitable for the Classical organ:

Brass Regal	4′		Dulcian Regal	8′		Brass Regal	4′		Cymbelregal	2′
Rohrschalmei	8′	or	Euphone	16′	or	Musette	8′	or	Rohrschalmei	4′
Barpfeife	16′		Dulcian	32′		Euphone	16′		Holzregal	8′
									Euphone	16′

See APFELREGAL, BARPFEIFE, BASSOON REGAL, DULCIAN, EUPHONE, KNOPF-REGAL, RANKETT, VOX HUMANA.

RESULTANT. A deep and penetrating bass effect that is usable in only the lower range in the pedals. By making use of the principle of musical beats, a series of continuous pulsations that come at the same pitches (frequencies) as the notes of the 64′ and 32′ stops can be easily and inexpensively produced. Although these are usually below the normal loudness for pedal stops at these pitches, the space and expense of installing the long, heavy pipes is saved. The organist also gains an impressive tonal "bottom" for his combinations which he would not otherwise have. Each note of this stop is produced by sounding *together* any two pipes that are an interval of *a fifth apart*. Each pedal key is wired to sound these two pipes at the same time. For example, the pipes of CCCC and GGGG in a 32′ rank will beat at the pitch of the low CCCCC of a 64′ stop. The pipes of CCC and GGG in a 16′ rank will beat at the pitch of the CCCC of a 32′ stop. Also, DDDD and AAAA will simulate DDDDD, and GGGG and DDD will simulate GGGGG. Other notes, including flats and sharps, sound in the same relationship. Other types of Resultants also exist from other combinations of notes, but a note and its fifth (above) is the loudest type.

The two pipes needed for each note of this stop can be taken from the same or different ranks, but authorities agree that they should be from the same general location within the organ. Reed and diaphonic pipes do not make satisfactory Resultants. They must be either stoppered or open *flues*, or, perhaps, one of each. The louder their fundamentals, the more penetrating their bass effect. They can be metal or wood. Large-scale pipes are usually preferable. Those developed with brilliant String overtones are not so satisfactory as the Diapasons, Bourdons, and Violones.

Any organist can make his own Resultant of 32′ from a flue rank of 16′, or a Resultant 64′ from a heavy flue of 32′. The 16′ Bourdon present in most organs, large and small, produces a satisfactory 32′ in most cases. Thus the smallest church organ can usually have this weighty bass tone. Probably the best effect is achieved by the larger-scaled Diapasons, and they are sometimes scaled especially for this purpose by builders. The Gedeckt, Flûte Ouverte, Violone, and bass Tibias also make satisfactory results. The organist must use two feet, of course, to make his own Resultant. To obtain the low CCCC of the 32′ stop, draw the 16′ flue best suited for the purpose and depress both the low CCC and GGG keys at the same time. Listen for the surging of the 16.3 cycles per second. This is the pitch of the 32′ CCCC. All other notes of the scale can be made by moving the two feet up the keyboard, keeping them a fifth apart. The note heard is one octave below the left foot. This extends the bass range one octave below the lowest note of the pedalboard. On larger organs the 16′ and 10 2/3′ pedal flues can be combined to make the Resultant 32′, and the 32′ and 21 1/3′ to make the 64′. These combinations of pitches make the same Resultants referred to above. Probably the builder would wire this stop to only the lowest pedal octave.

Perhaps the 64′ tone is a little more satisfactory than the 32′ because it is farther from the efficient range of hearing. The 8.17 cycles per second of the low CCCCC of the 64′ can almost be sensed individually. The 16′ Resultant is not satisfactory because it is too near the efficient range of hearing. It is never constructed, although some organists purposely draw the 8′ and 5 1/3′ together on either manuals or pedals to make a simulated 16′ effect. The overtones of all pipes contribute to building up the timbre.

Since so little circuitry is needed for this stop, it is well worth the expense of its installation, although it may be agreed that no Resultant is a worthy substitute for the big, long bass pipes' ability to move the tons of atmosphere in any building. The deep bass is needed in both small and large installations, and this stop is the most practical way of obtaining it when space and funds are limited. Electronic basses at 64′ and 32′ have been available for some time, but the large-diameter speakers and the electronic apparatus needed cost a considerable amount if they are of high quality, and if there is a sufficient number of speaker-cones to penetrate the mass of air. It is also worthy of note that many well-known organists use a deep bass in both soft and loud combinations, because it has the ability to make the ear focus more precisely on exact pitch, and therefore harmony and tone quality as well. Mathematically, the organist can figure out the pitch of a Resultant's note by subtracting the frequency (cycles per second) of the lower pitch from that of the higher pitch (see CÉLESTE). Since the whole science of harmony is based on the relationships between the pitches represented in a chord and the *resultants* they make, this stop, whatever name it may be given on a stop knob, should not be considered unorthodox in tone. It blends a little better than its components and it is non-directional.

The actual value of this pedal stop varies widely with the structures of the buildings and the particular ranks of pipes used to create it. Some of its effects are unbelievably impressive, and it can support an ensemble with a massive bass tone; other examples are inaudible, and the organist soon forgets to make use of them. Buildings with light walls that can be easily shaken by the long wave-lengths have a tendency to absorb the sound before it reaches the ears. Acoustic tiles and plasters, however, do not absorb this stop so quickly as they do the higher treble notes. In many large cathedrals and auditoriums with heavy walls that cannot be shaken appreciably by this stop the effect is quite good, and the organist can look upon the Resultant as a valued extra bass stop. In the smaller buildings the success of the effect depends more upon reverberation, the longer the better. One reason Double Diapasons and Contra Bourdons fail to sound with a round, full *prime tone* is that their walls are sometimes made of wood or metal that is not sufficiently thick. This would also cause any Resultants made from them to fail to be effective. In all pipes the lower harmonics are more easily absorbed by the structures of the pipes themselves.

The larger-scaled pipes and those with the stronger fundamentals make better Resultants. Sometimes three, four, or more pipes are wired to one key to reach the volume of sound needed for audibility. Experimentation after the organ is installed is sometimes the only way to be sure of a Resultant's effect. Uncrowded positions help all bass pipes to extend their long sound waves outward without having them collide with other obstacles, such as other pipes. This effect can sound quite different in different parts of a building. Sometimes the organist cannot hear the Resultant at all, but it may be effective to the audience. There are also different aural cues and different educational levels in the minds of the listeners.

Both the 64′ and 32′ Resultants can sound together without canceling each other out, but both are rarely in the same organ. The overtones of the ranks used for this effect, whether stopped or open, are close enough to the pitch-positions on the equal-tempered scale not to be discordant with either the Resultant or other stops. The larger flues in the bass may have only one harmonic, and that the fundamental. There are also undulations between the overtones of any ranks used. A few examples follow; none is assured of sounding well in any building. Nos. 4 and 8 may be stronger or weaker than average, depending upon inner conflicts between their sound waves:

No. 1	32′		No. 5	64′	
*Bourdon		10 2/3′	*Bourdon		21 1/3′
*Bourdon		16′	*Bourdon		32′
No. 2	32′		No. 6	64′	
Diapason		10 2/3′	*Diapason		21 1/3′
Bourdon		16′	*Diapason		32′
No. 3	32′		No. 7	64′	
Diapason		10 2/3′	Bourdon		21 1/3′
Violone		16′	Violone		32′
No. 4	32′		No. 8	64′	
*Diapason		10 2/3′	Flûte Ouverte		21 1/3′
Bourdon		10 2/3′	Violone		32′
*Diapason		16′	Tibia Clausa		32′

*May be same rank.

Improvement in the tone may be effected by recombining ranks, turning pipes, moving pipes, and adjusting valve speeds. It is not possible to control completely the weakening of these long sound waves when they collide, but often a small adjustment of a minor physical factor will make the tone much stronger or more penetrating. Experimenting seems to be a necessity.* Synonyms: ACOUSTIC BASS, GRAVISSIMA, VOX GRAVISSIMA.

RIPIENO. This Italian word refers to a mixture stop. See FOURNITURE.

ROHRBORDUN. A half-covered wood (or metal) Flute of large scale and heavy construction, particularly in the pedal division. It speaks at 16', 8', or 4' on the manuals, and at the same pitches on the pedals. It has the Bourdon's volume of sound, but with less strength in its fundamental harmonic. All of the above six pitches are very useful in any organ except the very smallest on both manuals and pedals. A typical use of this Flute is to combine it with a flue stop (or two) on the Swell or Solo Organ in order to achieve a deeper and smoother tone quality. If it is of the *right volume* it can make the 'Cello or Gamba, not more string-like in tone quality, but more obvious in the mind of the listener as a well-defined and clearer *timbre* that is oriented with the other timbres of the organ.

This is the peculiar function of the half-covered (rohr) Flutes: they make any tone to which they are added stand out in clearer perspective to the other stops. To some degree they also point up the *true loudness* and the *true pitches* being heard, the former being probably the most difficult factor for musicians to comprehend. This stop is therefore very valuable on the pedals as well as the manuals, for it does help the listener to identify pitch. Below the C above middle C the ear's ability to catalogue true pitch falls off sharply. Below tenor C it is especially poor. In the bass notes, as below CC, the ear is also unable to identify true loudness to any great extent. It is for this reason that a pedal stop of 16' or 32', especially if it is a purer tone without much overtone development, can be used for either a loud or a soft combination. The Rohrbordun is just the right balance between fundamental and overtone development to cause it to emphasize low pitches and also degrees of dynamic value. It has a modicum of harmonics (even a few even-numbered) to help it to corroborate a note's pitch; it has a marked fundamental to support the prime tone in other stops. It cannot rectify the central nervous system's inability to classify true pitch and true loudness in the bass ranks of pipes, but it can aid in making the bass less vague as to impression. The Rohrflöte can also do the same thing, but it is more likely to be a treble stop. Both of these stops aid in identifying timbre, timbre being not a third essence in music, but simply the differential effect on the mind of hearing many harmonic-pitches, each at a different loudness, whether from one stop or several. See BOURDON, ROHRFLÖTE.

---

*All sound waves, even from the Diapasons, are in continuous collision. This actually takes the form of minute collisions between the atmosphere's molecules. If the collision takes place between particles going in the same direction, strengthening results; if in the opposite, weakening of tone follows.

ROHRFLÖTE. A half-covered solo and ensemble Flute of 16′, 8′, 4′, or 2′ on the manuals, yielding a liquid, light-toned, but not bright timbre with its own characteristic transparency. The rohrs of these capped metal (or wooden) pipes admit in the short time available between sound waves a soft interlamination of the even-numbered harmonics; the odd-numbered are already present in the tone of the body of the pipe. A wider-diametered rohr admits more even-numbered components (the 4′, 2′, 1 1/3′, and 1′ of the 8′ rank) ; a longer rohr will reinforce some particular lower-pitched harmonic, depending upon its exact length. Damping the third harmonic permits the tone to stay liquid, not quinty. The scale is moderately large and the dynamic is usually around *mp* or *mf*. This useful stop may be on the Solo, Swell, or Choir. The Solo's Rohrflöte 4′ is especially useful alone and in combination. A *Gemsrohrflöte* sounds a little on the dull side. See DOPPELROHRFLÖTE. Synonym: CHIMNEY FLUTE.

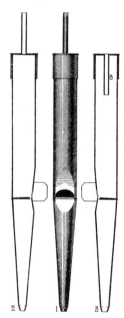

Rohrflöte middle C pipe. 1 and 2 show the same pipe with chimney A extended outside of pipe, as is customary. 3 shows an interior chimney at B, giving slightly less brightness. Large ears tune the pipe. The additional harmonics formed in the chimney are very obvious to the ear when heard within a church with extended reverberation time. Combined with other stops they are not easily heard.

ROHRFLÖTENQUINTE. A 5 1/3′ half-covered manual Flute belonging to the sub-unison series of stop-pitches. See QUINT, ROHRBORDUN, ROHR-GEDECKT.

ROHRGEDECKT. A half-covered metal or wood Flute of 16′, 8′, or 4′ on the manuals, and 16′ on the pedals. See GEDECKT, ROHRBORDUN, ROHR-FLÖTE.

ROHRNASAT. A half-covered manual Flute of 2 2/3′ forming a

Twelfth of soft tone and excellent blend. See ROHRBORDUN, ROHRFLÖTE, TWELFTH.

ROHRPOMMER. A half-covered *Gedecktpommer* of large scale, at 16' or 8' on both manuals and pedals. It resembles the Rohrflöte in structure. The third harmonic (the "Twelfth") this stop makes is perfectly tuned by natural forces, unlike the rank of *Twelfth* pipes, and therefore gives a degree of blend unheard elsewhere except from one of the *Quint Flutes*. Volume of the third harmonic in proportion to the fundamental varies quite a lot between examples of this stop, and some *Gedecktpommers* really have rohrs in their stoppers without the term *rohr* appearing on the stop knob. The third harmonic, which speaks at the "Twelfth's" pitch in unison ranks, can be as loud as the fundamental in this stop and in the Gedecktpommer. However, this stop is a little easier to blend with other flue stops, such as the Diapason, Gemshorn, and the Flutes, than the Gedecktpommer. This stop might be called *Rohrgedecktpommer*. Compared to a separate rank of 2 2/3' pipes, this source of the third harmonic has some advantages:

a) its third harmonic is in perfect tune with the unison;
b) it does not have a separate train of harmonics based on the 2 2/3';
c) its fundamental can be voiced almost out of existence;
d) its 1 3/5' harmonic (based on the 8' rank) is also a useful binder;
e) it lacks the hard tone in some of the open Twelfths.

See GEDECKTPOMMER, QUINTADE, ROHRFLÖTE, ROHRGEDECKT.

ROHRQUINTE. A half-covered Flute of 5 1/3' pitch on the manuals, with a tone quality similar to that of the Rohrgedeckt or Rohrflöte. It belongs to the sub-unison stops and sounds considerably softer than many open Quints. See QUINT, ROHRFLÖTE, ROHRGEDECKT.

ROHRSCHALMEI. A variety of the Schalmei, at 8' or 4' on manuals and pedals. This short-resonator Reed gives a *covered* variety of the nasal, somewhat acid, reedy tone quality heard in the Schalmei. Some of the Schalmei's higher overtones are dampened by this form of pipe. This is a very useful color Reed which can be added to either pedal or manual combinations. It lends a distinctive tone quality to any flue stops, but at the same time does not drown out their pitches. It can point up any line of notes in polyphonic music or add a bright nasal sound to the pedal's bass, making it stand in contrast to the manual's sound. Each pipe consists of a short brass tube inserted in the boot, with a cylindrical portion of larger diameter set over each brass tube, the top of the larger pipe being capped. The sound is thus forced from the bottom of the pipe, losing on the way some of the reed's brilliance, but not its pungent, nasal timbre. See SCHALMEI.

SACKBUT. A Chorus Reed of 16' manual pitch, and 32' or 16' pedal pitch. This early form of the Trombone stop has a brassy, loud, somewhat percussive voice. It lacks the smoothness heard from most of the modern Chorus Reeds. See POSAUNE, TROMBONE.

SALICET. A String stop of 4′ on the manuals, resembling the Salicional in tone quality, although of smaller scale and volume of sound. This soft Octave String may accompany the Salicional on any manual. See SALICIONAL.

SALICETINA. A String stop of 2′ manual pitch, resembling the Salicet in tone, but sounding so high in pitch over most of the keyboard that it is able to do little except point up the Salicional's and Salicet's tones with some additional brightness. See SALICET, SALICIONAL.

SALICIONAL. A bright, somewhat keen String stop of 16′ or 8′ on the manuals, and 16′ on the pedals. It is the most common String stop in the organ and usually appears in the Swell, mostly accompanied by another rank of similar tone, but perhaps milder voicing, that is tuned slightly off-pitch to form a Voix Céleste of 8′ with the on-pitch Salicional rank. This stop is less soft and not so glistening in timbre as the Aeoline. It is softer and less keen than the Gamba. The Ethereal Violin is brighter in tone and also softer than the Salicional. Although the traditional Salicional has a silvery shimmering effect on the ear, it also has "an additional something" these other Strings do not have. This is undoubtedly a noticeable unison-octave harmonic component, also heard in the Dulciana, Dolce, and Dolcan.

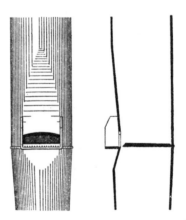

Salicional showing nicking and harmonic bridge (frein harmonique) at mouth.

The Salicional is primarily an ensemble stop. It blends well even with the Gedeckt tribe, but hardly the Bourdons of heavier tone. It is most useful with the Dulciana, Diapason, and the open Flutes. To the Gemshorn it adds just the right amount of stringiness to lift up this tone. It contrasts with the dull flues upon occasion, and it sounds by itself as the chief String-tone stop for episodal passages on the smaller organ. It makes about as much contrast with the stopped Flutes as the sensitive ear can tolerate.

Salicional pipes are small in scale, have mouths of very low cut-up, and a very high percentage of tin in their alloys. Each of these three factors ensures a great quantity of soft overtones, most of which come from high up in the train of partials that each pipe emits. Pure tin is not unknown in the Salicional, and gives a tone that, for want of better adjectives, must be called *more silvery* rather than more brilliant. Harmonic bridges on the fronts of the mouths hasten the steady tones of the pipes, making the initial period when the pipe is accelerating much shorter. The small ears that hold these bridges stablize the tone and keep the pitches of these narrow air columns steady. The short treble pipes have neither bridges nor ears. Slots at the tops of some ranks create additional overtones, and permit the tuner to sharpen the pitch by rolling the metal downward, or flatten it by rolling it upward. A few ranks have tuning collars without slots. *Salamine* indicates a Salicional-Principal hybrid of very soft intonation. See VIOL.

SALICIONAL DIAPASON. A Foundation stop of 8′ manual pitch, sounding like a bright, stringy Diapason, but without the strong fundamental heard in most Diapasons and Violin Diapasons. The scale of this hybrid between the Diapason and Salicional is smaller than that of most other varieties of Diapason pipes. Since the Salicional itself has a little of the diminutive Foundation timbre, this union between a String and a Diapason is quite effective. It is a refined and beautiful ensemble stop for the Swell or Echo. See DIAPASON, SALICIONAL.

SANFTBASS. A Flute of 16′ manual pitch similar to the Lieblichgedeckt or Echo Gedeckt in tone and volume. It is seen on the Choir or Swell of a few organs. See ECHO GEDECKT, LIEBLICHGEDECKT, SANFTFLÖTE.

SANFTFLÖTE. A Flute of 8′ or 4′ manual pitch, similar to the Lieblichgedeckt or Echo Gedeckt in tone and volume. It has ensemble as well as solo functions, and may add some ground tone to the very soft stops like the Dolcan or Vox Angelica. See ECHO GEDECKT, LIEBLICHGEDECKT.

SAXOPHONE. An imitative Reed stop of 8′ on the manuals. It is very difficult to imitate the harmonically rich, woody, free, fluty tone color of this instrument with even the thinnest of brass reeds. The cane reeds have partials that the brass reeds cannot simulate. There is always a possibility that the organ pipes can build up the Saxophone's tone by eliminating some partials and strengthening others, but the inverted-conical pipes with bells on their tops have infrequently done this so far. The variable pitch and the sensitivity of the instrument to the moods and positions of the player make it even harder to remind the listener that he is hearing a Saxophone and not just a big Clarinet with a different style of resonator. The initial "explosion" of harmonics from the organ's pipes bears some resemblance to the original. By playing more notes staccato, the organist can sometimes heighten the effect. The labial pipes of W. E. Haskell make a realistic tone, but these have not been seen in any quantity. *Solo Saxophone* and *Major*

Saxophone are sometimes seen on stop keys on the larger theater organs. Synonym: ORCHESTRAL SAXOPHONE.

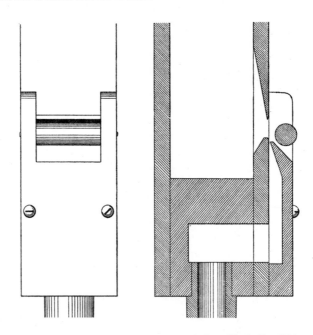

Labial Saxophone, as invented by Haskell. This middle C pipe shows an inverted upper lip, harmonic bridge, large ears, and small wind-way.

SCHALMEI. An imitative Reed stop of 16′, 8′, or 4′ on both manuals and pedals. The Schalmei speaks from extremely short, narrow, cylindrical resonators with a peculiarly bright, nasal, whining tone that is very acid and rich in harmonics. Most specimens are between *mf* and *f*. This is a pleasant tone, with a unique plaintive character that brings to mind scenes that are picturesque or pastoral. Unlike the other short-resonator Reeds, such as the Rankett, Regal, and Barpfeife, this is primarily a *solo* stop with a tone quality that is well adapted to following the melody line. It is not primarily a combination stop, although it can be used as a source of timbre in certain combinations. Other stops often spoil its tone and make it lose its best color. Contrasting with this is the Rankett, which is improved in combination.

The tone quality of the Schalmei makes it penetrate other tones, but, like other Baroque Reeds, it is light rather than weighty in tone. It is not so piercing as the Musette nor does it have that stop's quaint character. The peculiar charm of the Schalmei rests in its ability to multiply partials in the higher range much *closer together* than is normally heard from a short-resonatored stop. This closeness between the pitches of the partials creates an acid, cutting, stringent effect on the ear that tries to analyze them. It makes clear to the ear the moving lines of any type of melodic form, but is most suitable in the Classical literature. Here it can play against a Diapason, Gemshorn, or another colorful Reed. It can give

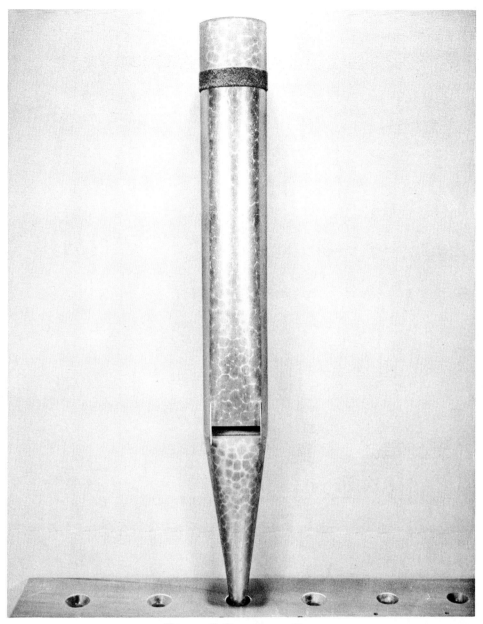

TENOR C QUINTATEN PIPE

Capped spotted metal pipe of the Quint Flute type. An open pipe for this note would be about four feet in length from its languid to its top. The cap stoppering this pipe enables it to make the same fundamental (130.8 vibrations per second) with about two feet speaking length. Since it is of wide scale, it can be a little shorter than normal. This particular pipe would speak from the middle C key of a 16′ stop, the tenor C key of an 8′ stop, or the bass CC key of a 4′ stop. If considered at 8′ and blown with sufficient wind, it would make obvious components at 8′, 2 2/3′, and 1 3/5′. The 4′, 2′, and 1 1/3′ components would be practically excluded by the cap and the low cut-up of the mouth. The 16′ stop could produce the 16′, 5 1/3′, and 3 1/5′ tones from only one pipe. Some organists use the 4′ Quintaten with the octave coupler for a very soft *Echo Harmonics* stop, containing 4′, 2′, 1 1/3′, 4/5′, 2/3′, and 2/5′ components.

Courtesy: Casavant Frères, Ltd.

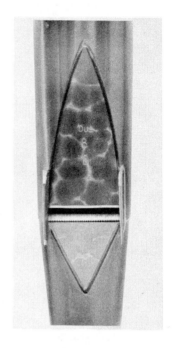

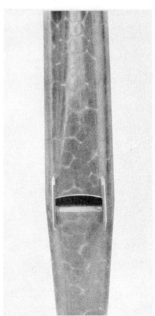

MOUTH DETAILS OF FOUR FLUE PIPES

Four flue pipes especially photographed to reveal their mouth structures.
Upper left, a Traverse Flute (wood) of inverted, low mouth-line. Upper right, a
Dulciana with ears at sides of mouth and low mouth-line to create a great number
of partials. This pipe is soft, since it receives very little wind. Lower left, a
spotted metal Diapason, showing nicking very clearly. Lower right, a Gemshorn
of conical shape.

Courtesy: Casavant Frères Ltd., Louis Martel, photographer.

clarity to the pedal line, or merely brighten a pedal Gemshorn's texture. The snarling, grave notes at the bottom of the 16' octave is one of its most useful effects. It adds a new tint of color to each flue with which it is combined. It may contrast with the Clarinet, Oboe, or a Regal. A well-voiced rank of Schalmei pipes is something to be treasured by the organist, and moved to a rebuilt organ when at all possible. Examples of *manual and pedal* Reed Choruses* with this stop follow. Every organist would naturally want to make changes in them to suit his particular taste:

Schalmei	4'	Rohrschalmei	4'	Oboe Schalmei	4'	Regal	2'
Fagotto	8'	or Schalmei	8'	or Musette	8'	or Schalmei	4'
Euphone	16'	Barpfeife	16'	Schalmei	16'	Oboe	8'
				Dulcian	32'	Fagotto	16'
						Dulcian	32'

The pipes of the Schalmei are sometimes made from 80% tin to improve the tone. Many shapes exist in the organs of the world, particularly in Europe, where most examples are to be found. They range from one-sixteenth to one-quarter of the unison length, perhaps changing fractional length within one rank. Usually they are very narrow to choke the partials out by friction against the pipes' walls. This, of course, is the function of all small resonators. See REGAL, ROHRSCHALMEI. Synonyms: CHALUMEAU, SHAWM.

SCHALMEI REGAL. A variety of Regal, at 8', 4', or 2' on the manuals, and 8' or 4' on the pedals, yielding an intensely brilliant tone that suggests the acid whine of the Schalmei as well as the windy, piping, thin tone of most Regals. It is a hybrid that joins in one stop two large tribes of short-resonatored Reeds: the Schalmeis and the Regals. The functions are the same as those of the Regals, except that this stop sounds more appropriately by itself in countermelody than most Regals. The resonators amplify just a certain range of partials, this range changing somewhat from higher to lower as the scale is ascended. The very short pipes usually break back to a greater length towards the top of the compass of the stop. Narrow brass tubes (sometimes of spotted metal) from one-eighth to one-quarter of the unison length sit on the tops of the boots. On the tops of these narrow cylinders may be brass bells of long slender form or short wide form, depending upon the type of tone desired. See REGAL, SCHALMEI.

SCHARF. See ACUTA.

SCHÖNGEDECKT. A stopped wooden Flute of 8' on the manuals, resembling a Gedeckt or one of the larger-scaled Lieblichgedeckts in structure and tone color. This particular name seems to be associated with the examples that have a resonant, "singing" tone, putting this Flute in the solo class. Some examples are moderate in scale, but all are quite smooth and pure even in the upper notes. The third harmonic is not so noticeable in this stopped Flute, nor does the fundamental (first harmonic) sound overly intense. The Schöngedeckt is most useful by itself in the solo line,

*The Reed Chorus is a most useful adjunct in every division, except the Positiv or a small Great. It permits great variety in combinations.

but it can add to any other flue in the Solo (or Swell) Organ some ground tone and a little stability in pitch. The cut-up is quite high and the upper lip is polished or leaded, the whole front of the pipe usually being made from a hardwood. The resulting smooth, round timbre is often reminiscent of the Tibia Clausa, but this stop has none of the intensity of the Tibia. It is rounder in tone and louder than the Gedeckt. See GEDECKT, LIEB-LICHGEDECKT.

SCHWEIZERFLÖTE. A Flute of 4′ or 2′ manual pitch, formed from open metal pipes of bright, harmonically full timbre. Some examples suggest a String-Flute hybrid tone because of the large number of overtones.

SEPTADECIMA. See SEVENTEENTH.

SEPTIÈME. A Foundation rank of soft open metal pipes, at 1 1/7′ on the manuals, and 2 2/7′ on the pedals. Each of these two ranks speaks at the notes two octaves and a flatted seventh above the keys depressed. The 4 4/7′ and 4/7′ are not properly called *Septièmes* unless the 32′ and 4′ series of stop-pitches, respectively, are referred to. This is both a mixture rank and a mutation rank, in both cases tuned to the natural seventh harmonics of the Principals. It is many times an independent stop knob, or it may sound in a bright Cymbal of unusual pattern. The 1 1/7′ is necessary to complete just the *eight* lowest harmonic-pitches of the Chorus on the manuals. The pedal pitch is not so important. From middle C the 1 1/7′ speaks at Bb³, between the 1 1/3′ and 1′ stops. The 2 2/7′ speaks at Bb from the low CCC key on the pedalboard. When middle C is depressed with this rank drawn the pitch is equivalent to a variation of about 33 vibrations per second — fewer in the lower octaves, more in the high — below the nearest Bb considered as a note in the scale. This produces a "gritty" effect in some examples. There is no inner conflict between the harmonics of the pipes of the Septième itself. This is the most controversial pitch among the stops.

This rank may seem to be necessary on the organ because of its closeness to the 1′ Twenty-second, and indeed it is to many organists. The great conductor, Toscanini, noticed its absence when he was one time being shown a new organ. It is a logical "top harmonic" in the large Diapason Chorus or unusually complete Positiv. Its effect can be brilliant and satisfying. Quite a few organs in this country and abroad have it among their stops. It is shown below as a member of the first twelve stop-pitches in the manual's unison series. Only the octave-sounding stops speak right on the notes of the scale. The others ("mutations") speak a little off-scale: 8′, 4′, 2 2/3′, 2′, 1 3/5′, 1 1/3′, 1 1/7′, 1′, 8/9′, 4/5′, 8/11′, 2/3′. It can be used with success if the organist is aware of its potential ability to cause dissonance. It may be in a bright solo mixture and certain Cymbals and Grand Choruses. Closely fingered chords, couplers, out-of-tuneness, and poorly selected combinations may impair the use of this unique source of brilliance. It is the seventh tier in the vertical structure of Diapasons, perhaps unenclosed.

In First Church, Scientist, Seattle, Washington, Eugene M. Nye, the organist, has developed a specification of stops that is unique in its balance between the *usual* and the *unusual* tones. Here in an organ of moderate size is found a most comprehensive instrument that is capable of all regular forms of music, as well as the Baroque. The manual 1 1/7' he has included is completely successful as a mutation and as an ensemble element. Its slender spotted metal pipes make a *soft* and beautiful effect on the most sensitive of ears. In the full ensembles its effect is broadening and brilliant. As a piquant mutation for the 4' or some other pitch, it sounds altogether in keeping with good taste. It is never unnatural in effect. The *"Sept-Terz"* (a 1 1/7' and 4/5' combined as a *double mutation* rather than a mixture) exists in the Positiv of the Salt Lake City Tabernacle Organ, Utah, and is most satisfactory for the extraordinary effect, reports Alexander Schreiner, organist. The pedal Diapason mixture of this same instrument contains a None 1 7/9' element. Synonym: TWENTY-FIRST, FLATTED.

SERAPHONFLÖTE. An open metal or wood Flute of 8' or 4' on the manuals, having two mouths per pipe, usually on opposite sides. Its loud and bright tone is inclined towards roundness rather than brilliance. It is both a solo and an ensemble stop. Synonym: JUBALFLÖTE.

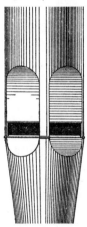

Double-mouthed Seraphonflöte. Two mouths give additional intensity of tone, a little more harmonic structure, and are sometimes seen in a dull solo Flute.

SERAPHONGEDECKT. A stopped wooden Flute of 8' or 4' on the manuals, having two mouths per pipe and on opposite sides. It is of large scale and yields a loud smooth tone of solo quality. See DOPPELFLÖTE.

SERPENT. A Reed stop of 16' manual pitch, and 16' or 8' pedal pitch, with a tone that is imitative of the ancient instrument with the curled tube and cup mouthpiece for the lips of the player. The organ's Serpent is just a little louder than the Fagotto, and has a tone quality that is *both* brasslike and distinctly reedy. It is percussive and vigorous in speech rather than smooth like the Trombone, and has a mild degree of penetration. It can sound as a solo stop, and is shown below as the bass rank of three manual or pedal choirs of light Reed tone. There are few examples

NAMES OF TONAL DIVISIONS

Names	General Description
Regular (each division on its own keyboard)	
Great	Diapason Chorus, mixtures, secondary flue chorus
Swell	Brilliant Reeds, mixtures, Strings, Flutes, all enclosed
Choir	Accompaniment stops, secondary Diapason Chorus, woodwinds
Solo	Prominently voiced Diapasons, Flutes, Strings, Reeds
Pedal	Large-scale bass pipes of all tonal families, mixtures
Extraordinary (may be regular or ancillary)	
Echo	Soft stops placed at distance from main organ
Orchestral	Reeds, Strings, Flutes of prominent harmonic development
Accompanimental	Diminutive Foundation stops, Diapasons, Flutes, dull Strings
Processional	Small division placed in part of church where choir marches
Antiphonal	Complete tonal division placed apart from main organ
Ethereal	Powerful Diapasons, Chorus Reeds, Flutes, mixtures
Celestial	Powerful division of any size placed high up in building
Dome	Powerful Diapason Chorus, Chorus Reeds high up in dome
Grand Choeur	Harmonically complete division, sometimes placed in gallery
Sanctuary	One or two complete divisions placed near altar
Altar	One or two complete divisions placed near altar
Gallery	One or more complete divisions placed in gallery
Ancillary (playable on any keyboard)	
String	Variety of String célestes, String mutations, soft mixtures
Bombarde	Powerful Chorus Reeds, Diapasons, mixtures
Stentor	Powerful Chorus Reeds, Diapasons, mixtures
Fanfare	Trumpets, Tubas of bright tone, occasionally mixtures
Brass Chorus	Trumpets, Tubas of bright tone, occasionally mixtures
Tromba Chorus	Trombas at several pitches, Trombones, smooth Tubas
Harmonic Chorus	Flue ranks at pitches of usual and unusual harmonics

Chart Explanation: Names of Tonal Divisions

Although the small instruments will have only a Great and a Swell Organ, with pedals, organ literature is full of the names of divisions other than these. The printed jacket-notes for high fidelity records of American and European organs describe the various divisions of the organ, as well as frequently giving a complete specification of stops. The Extraordinary and Ancillary groups are most likely to be seen in the larger organs, but not in every case. Ancillary ("floating") divisions permit the number of manuals on the console to remain low — two, three, or four — while at the same time providing the variety of contrasts so typical of organ tone.

	European
Brustwerk	Stops of refined, soft tone built in front of main organ
Clavier des Bombardes	Bombarde Organ
Echoklavier	Echo Organ
Fernwerk	Echo Organ
Grand Orgue	Great Organ, sometimes based on 16′ series of stops
Hauptwerk	Great Organ, sometimes based on 4′ series of stops
Hornwerk	Brass or Tuba Chorus, Solo Organ
Oberwerk	Bright, powerful stops of penetrating, sometimes sharp, tone
Pédale	Pedal Organ
Pedalklavier	Pedal Organ
Positiv	Choir Organ of light and brilliant flue stops, mutations
Récit	Contrasting division to Great Organ, all enclosed
Rückpositiv	Division of flue stops built in front of main organ
Schwellwerk	Swell Organ
Soloklavier	Solo Organ
Unterwerk	Choir Organ or Accompanimental Organ

anywhere. Full-length or half-length inverted-conical pipes of gentle taper, preferably of full-length spotted metal, make its tone.

Schalmei	4′		Fagotto	4′		Orchestral Oboe	4′
Krummhorn	8′	or	Fagotto	8′	or	Cornopean	8′
Serpent	16′		Serpent	16′		Serpent	16′

SESQUIALTERA. A manual mixture consisting basically of a 2 2/3′ and a 1 3/5′ rank, with the 2′ rank, which is between these two pitches, sometimes added, as well as other pitches, the 2 2/3′ and 1 3/5′ being the same in pitch as the second and third components of an 8′ (unison) Quintadena or Bourdon. There are examples for all series of stops from 32′ to 4′. The pipes are usually Diapasons, and the ranks may not break in pitch from the bottom to the top of the manuals. This is not true, however, in many examples. The specimens of higher pitch will break more often than those of lower pitch. This mixture adds a pronounced bright timbre to combinations, but it is not for this function that it is mostly valued. Its Diapason tones lend a rich timbre and a distinctive organ-like quality to all music. It is penetrating, reed-like, pungent, and telling without heaviness or masking effect in the music. It is heard from the Choir, Swell, or, perhaps, the Solo manuals. It is not so much of a Great Organ device. Although a few examples have a solo function, like a Cornet, this stop is not usually looked upon as a "solo" device. The *Stentor Sesquialtera* can be quite powerful, but most Sesquialteras are mild enough for good combination when tested with other stops, such as the Diapason 8′, Trumpet 8′, etc. This stop can be an ideal polyphonic Baroque stop and is heard from some (modern) Baroque tracker organs. Some examples follow with the notes heard from the middle C key:

Example No. 1	Example No. 2	Example No. 3
II	III	V
E³ 1 3/5′	E³ 1 3/5′	C⁴ 1′
G² 2 2/3′	C³ 2′	G³ 1 1/3′
	G² 2 2/3′	E³ 1 3/5′
		C³ 2′
		G² 2 2/3′

The 10 2/3′ and 6 2/5′ sound in the 32′ series. The 5 1/3′ and 3 1/5′ sound in the 16′ series. The 1 1/3′ and 4/5′ are in the 4′ series. The 8′ series is in the examples. Pedal examples exist in a few organs.

SEVENTEENTH. A rank of Foundation pipes that speaks at 1 3/5′ on the manuals, and 3 1/5′ on the pedals. With reference to the unison pitches, these are the fifth harmonics of the 8′ and 16′ stops, respectively. Authorities on organ design continually advocate this stop's being placed on a *separate* stop control, therefore removable from any mixture. It sounds two octaves and a third above the key depressed. From middle C this would be at E³, from the pedal CCC key at E. Although a little Principal rank upon inspection, and probably spotted metal, this stop imparts an "acute," sharp (not pungent), *third-sounding*, pointed, and Cornet-like timbre to all other stops. It is sometimes used as a mutation rank for color. It is naturally the fifth harmonic of an 8′ manual stopped rank, and may be heard even in a large-scale Gedeckt. Nevertheless, it deserves some attention as the companion to the Twelfth (third) harmonic of *any* unison stopped rank. It can be quite conspicuous in a small-scaled stopped rank. It is in the tones of the Quintadena and Nachthorn. Overblowing the pipes to obtain a strong Twelfth (third harmonic) naturally brings out a little more of this fifth harmonic. (See TIERCINA).

The source of the harmonics (or overtones) in an organ pipe is illustrated graphically by the visible motions of a violin string. As it vibrates in just *one* loop to form its fundamental, because of its flexibility it also *at the same time* vibrates into *two, three, four, five,* and more loops to form respectively its Octave, Twelfth, Fifteenth, and Seventeenth (to use organ terms). The flexible air column, which is a fluid, does the same thing. It has, especially in narrow-scale pipes, much the same long, slender shape as the string. Of course certain of these natural harmonics are louder than others because certain pipe-shapes build up certain pockets of friction in the air column. Looping of the air column in the pipe is naturally less strenuous in the upper part of the train of harmonics, making them, as a rule, much softer than a fundamental. Five loops of the air column make the Seventeenth's sound. The Aeolian Skinner Organ Company usually makes this 1 3/5′ rank unbroken in pitch, and of small-scale spotted metal pipes. It may have wide mouths and a slender form to make it speak with greater articulation. The organist should remember the octave coupler makes it a 4/5′ component. In a combination played staccato it sounds with a chiff-like and accented timbre. The pipes may be carried down only to the tenor G or C key to avoid possibility of sharp undulations, but this practice might limit the usefulness of this mutation. Synonyms: SEPTADECIMA, TIERCE.

SHAWM. See SCHALMEI.

SIFFLÖTE. An open metal Flute of 2′, 1′, or 1/2′ on the manuals, rarely on the pedals. Its tone is brilliant without being shrill. Its clean, pointed statement of pitch is of much usefulness alone or with combinations of flues. Alone it seems to have a satin-like sheen that no other high-pitched stop possesses, especially since it manages to be intensely brilliant but not in the least hard, sharp, or string-like. It is versatile, sounding well with Diapasons, mixtures, light Reeds, or Strings. It is heard in Baroque ensembles and in more modern combinations as well. It manages to combine with soft flues without masking them, and yet serves as a brilliant "top" for louder ensembles. Various specimens differ quite a lot in loudness; a few are soft. The pipes are medium to quite large in scale, but some are actually small. They are of pure tin or spotted metal, but never brass or aluminum, because the formants of these metals do not suit the Sifflöte's tone. Many specimens of this much-used Flute are cylindrical but with conical tops, as in the Koppelflöte, this top being half, a third or even less of the whole pipe's length. This type of top wipes out most dissonance, and even some of the higher harmonic partials, but does not taper the harmonic series back so far as the Erzähler shape. Stoppered metal pipes are seen in a few examples, with wide mouth and very low-cut-up.

SILVER FLUTE. A *conical harmonic* metal Flute of 8′ or 4′ manual pitch. The tone of this unusual combination of pipe-structures is unusually transparent and luminous, owing to the fact that it comes from a small chord of on-pitch partials down near the fundamental's pitch. It is bright without being stringy, delicate without being hard to hear clearly, and distinct in pitch alone as a solo voice or in combination with other flue stops. The conical shape (of the Gemshorn) gives it partials near the range of its fundamental, and the harmonic structure gives it a roundness and smoothness of tone that conical ranks generally do not have. It lacks the conspicuous effect on the ear of the Doppelflöte; its beauty must be carefully listened for. Some organists consider it a superior kind of Harmonic Flute, but it lacks that Flute's penetration and power in combination. A high percentage of tin enhances its bright quality. It may be smaller in scale than the Gemshorn. Its dynamic range varies with its scale, the bigger scales naturally being somewhat louder. See CONICAL FLUTE, GERMAN FLUTE, HARMONIC FLUTE.

SINGENGEDECKT. A stoppered wooden Flute of 16′, 8′, or 4′ manual pitch. This variety of the Gedeckt tribe sounds with a warm, fluty, round effect on the ear that is suitable for solo playing as well as a source of fundamental to be added to other stops. The better examples of this beautiful Flute have a "singing" quality that is really just a superior *inner resonance* within the structures of the pipes. Dimensions of the pipes' parts (and there are at least fifty measurements for each organ pipe) must permit the pipes to vibrate with the greatest amount of ease, i. e. with the fewest collisions between the sound waves of all partials within the pipes' structures. Making use of the principle of resonance to the full degree in the design of organ pipes is one of the most difficult of arts, but occasionally a rank of pipes is heard that does sound with this beautiful "bloom" of tone, perhaps through only a part of the compass. See GEDECKT, SCHÖN-GEDECKT.

SIXTEENTH. A rank of Foundation pipes that speaks at 1 7/9' on the manuals, and 3 5/9' on the pedals. This is at the note two octaves and one note above the key struck. This pitch is not a common harmonic of any series of stops on the organ, but may be seen in the ancillary Harmonic division of a very large instrument. It can add an unusual variety of brassiness to a loud chorus of Reeds, but it must be remembered that it brings with it a whole train of partials from its own pipes, at least twelve, if the pipes are open metal Diapasons or Geigen Diapasons. Sometimes pipes as soft as Dulciana pipes are used for ranks of these unusual pitches to keep the tone from being too assertive. From the middle C key this rank sounds at D^3, and from the low pedal CCC key, at D (below middle C). The manual pitch is between the 2' and 1 3/5' pitches.

SOFT FLUTE. A stop-name that indicates a stopped Flute in most cases, although it is vague in regard to the tone quality. It may be at 8' or 4' on the manuals; this name usually does not appear among the pedal stops.

SOFT MIXTURE. A manual mixture stop of soft intonation, with a variety of pitches and tone qualities among its examples. It may be a Kleine Mixture, Dolce Cornet, or Dulciana mixture. It may contain Gemshorn, Dolce, Dulciana, Echo Diapason, or Echo Viola ranks, or any mixture of these tone qualities. The soft Diapasons make ideal accompaniment sound and form the higher pitches in this mixture better than some other ranks. This mixture can serve as a source of the basic pitches by which to build up tone in the Choir, Echo, or Accompanimental Organ. If all of the following ranks are separately available on stop controls, any of these examples could serve to make more flexible the tone of a small division, and at the same time offer accompaniment and ensemble effects of much usefulness. Even No. 4 could be used on a small organ of two manuals. Middle C would sound these notes:

Example No. 1		Example No. 2		Example No. 3		Example No. 4	
III		IV		V		VI	
C^3	2'	G^3	1 1/3'	C^4	1'	C^4	1'
G^2	2 2/3'	C^3	2'	G^3	1 1/3'	G^3	1 1/3'
C^2	4'	G^2	2 2/3'	C^3	2'	E^3	1 3/5'
		C^2	4'	G^2	2 2/3'	C^3	2'
				C^2	4'	G^2	2 2/3'
						C^2	4'

It is assumed that a soft 8' rank of diminutive Foundation pipes, such as the Dulciana, Dolce, Erzähler, Gemshorn, or an Echo Diapason, perhaps a Viola or 'Cello, will be added to any of these mixtures. If not, they will all form the 8' acoustically anyway by action of the 2 2/3' and 4' ranks, although quite softly. The fifth-sounding ranks are tuned softer than the octave-sounding ranks, and the third-sounding rank is tuned softer than the fifth-sounding ranks, so that in single notes or chords these mixtures will sound like a *single unit of tone*. There is one drawback in using the above series of stops for accompaniments: they must be in tune to be as satisfactory as a single rank of accompaniment pipes. However, the organ will have a more vital tone and be much more interesting for the ear to follow if more *pitches* are used in combinations and fewer unison stops.

SOLO 'CELLO. A String stop of 8' on the manuals formed from Violoncello pipes of large scale and prominent voicing. The term *Solo* indicates that a rank of pipes is somewhat more conspicuous in tone color than the average rank of the same name. In some cases it may have the same scale and the same wind pressure, but certain salient dimensions which give to the tone a different harmonic structure from that of the average rank. In a few cases the solo form of the stop may even be softer than average, as in a *Solo Muted 'Cello* or *Solo Muted Violin*. The *distinct* tonality of a solo stop sets it apart from other ranks of the same name. The term *Solo* need not be included in the name, but frequently has been in the theater organs, since two Clarinets or two Tibia Clausas may be included in the same organ on the same or different manuals. Then *Solo Clarinet* and just *Clarinet* are used on the stop keys. *Major Clarinet* and *Minor Clarinet* have somewhat different meanings, not always implying the solo tonality. See VIOLONCELLO.

SOLO FLUTE. A name used to indicate that a certain 8' or 4' manual Flute stop is of prominent and probably loud voicing and suitable for following the solo line of notes. In the theater organs this may be a bigger-scale Tibia Clausa or Doppelflöte. The term is not used on other than theater organs. See DOPPELFLÖTE, SOLO 'CELLO, TIBIA CLAUSA.

SOLO TIBIA CLAUSA. A very liquid, penetrating form of the 8' Tibia Clausa, made from stopped wooden pipes of even larger scale and thicker and smoother walls than the *Tibia Clausa*, which itself is a solo stop. *Solo Flute* 4' is sometimes given to pipes of the same rank, and *Solo Piccolo* 2' may also be used for the same rank if these stops are unified, and they usually are in a theater organ. The Solo Tibia Clausa may be heard from the fourth manuals of many of the big theater organs and the many recordings made from them. See SOLO 'CELLO, TIBIA CLAUSA.

SOLO TUBA. A name that indicates the loudest and sometimes the brassiest Tuba stop in a theater organ, for names that are not explicit are commonly seen on the theater organ consoles, being devised to simplify the great variety of stop-names for the organist. This manual stop-name (8') usually indicates either a round-toned and intense Tuba Sonora or a very brass-like and commanding Tuba Mirabilis. There are always other Tuba stops present on the same organ when such a name as this is used. See SOLO 'CELLO, TUBA, TUBA MAGNA, TUBA MIRABILIS, TUBA SONORA.

SOLO VIOLIN. A String of 8′ on the manuals formed from slender, small-scaled, overblown pipes of the Viole d'Orchestre. This String has a tone that is cutting and keen, with some dissonance from its upper partials, not always louder than the other Viols of the same organ, but more conspicuous in tone. It does not necessarily have the same timbre as the *Grand Viol* stop, but it is probably more orchestral in coloring. Like the Grand Viol, it is probably most suitable in a special division of only Strings, where it cannot unbalance the harmonic structure of the ensemble. Solo Viols are more usable with a noticeable amount of fundamental. See GRAND VIOL, SOLO 'CELLO, VIOLE D'ORCHESTRE.

SOLO VOX HUMANA. A Reed of 8′ on the manuals, louder and perhaps more guttural than other Vox Humanas in the same organ. Some examples of this name have some of the Krumet or Krummhorn or Clarinet quality in their tones to enable them to carry better and sound the pitches more obviously, since many examples of the "Vox" lack ground tone. In a whole chorus of Vox Humanas it would be the chief unison rank, perhaps being called a *Major Vox Humana*. See SOLO 'CELLO, VOX HUMANA.

SORDUN. A soft-voiced Flute, stoppered in many examples, at 16′ or 8′ on the manuals. Occasionally this name indicates a muffled, soft Regal.

SOUBASSE. See MAJOR BASS.

SPILLFLÖTE. An open metal Flute of 8′, 4′, 2′, or 1′ on the manuals.

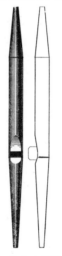

The form is cylindrical except that each pipe is topped by a truncated cannister from one-fourth to one-half the full speaking length of the pipe. The bottom portion is cylindrical. Since the foot of each pipe is tapered, this form appears to be a spindle. It is smaller in scale than the Koppelflöte, another rank of the same shape, and lacks that Flute's liquid, pervading quality. It is unimitative of any other Flute stop. It is only moderately bright, its conical top stimulating the first overtone. The dynamic level is soft. It can build up brightness in other flues without destroying the chorus's unity of effect. It hardly has a distinctive color, but any Flute may play episodic passages or serve as a solo stop. The *Schweigel* is of similar construction, but bigger in scale, and with a more delicate but mildly percussive voice. Synonym: SPINDELFLÖTE.

Spillflöte (or Spindelflöte) showing conical top and large ears used for tuning.

SPINDELFLÖTE. See SPILLFLÖTE.

SPIREFLÖTE. See SPITZFLÖTE.

SPITZ DIAPASON. See CONE DIAPASON.

SPITZFLÖTE. An open metal Flute of 16', 8', 4'. or 2' on the manuals, with a moderately soft or soft tonality suggestive of the Strings. This Flute is made in
a great variety of scales and degrees of
Flute-String proportions, but the form of the
pipes remains the same: conical, with the
top diameter roughly two-thirds of the
mouth-line diameter. It differs from the
Gemshorn and Erzähler by having a much
less pointed form, and therefore a less covered tone. Compared to a cylindrical Flute
of the same general dimensions, the Spitzflöte is stronger in those partials down in
the pitches near the fundamental. This stop
therefore has a less bright tone in the upper
partials, the object being to exclude even
mild dissonance that may come from soft
upper partials, and at the same time to increase the blend in this stop by stimulating
the lower partials. The mouth is cut-up fairly
high and the upper lip arched, both devices
being intended to make the tone a little tenuous and just suggestive of the *dull* quality.

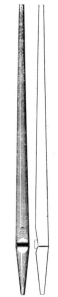

Spitzflöte at tenor C. The conical form removes some of the
higher-pitched harmonics, placing more energy in the lower-
pitched.

Although this is distinctly a soft Flute, the String partials do appear in
most specimens, and give the tone some added color. This is one of the
many hybrid stops in the organ, making a very beautiful céleste of quiet,
background tone. It can be a soft solo Flute, and also a tone to bind together the Strings and the Diapasons or Flutes. Synonym: SPIREFLÖTE.

SPITZFLÖTE CÉLESTE. A very gentle undulating stop of quiet tone,
at 8' on the manuals, sometimes called a *Flute Céleste*, although this term
may also refer to a *Dolce Flute Céleste* or a *Viola Flute Céleste*. This
céleste, even though it is not a String céleste, is one of the few cases among
the organ's stops where a céleste is as useful as the single rank. It is either
normal-sharp or *normal-flat* in pitch design, a few stops being *sharp-flat*,
but this last design denies the organist the use of a normally tuned rank
of Spitzflöte pipes, although it contrasts better with an on-pitch solo stop.
The mysterious, tranquil sound that comes from this soft céleste is heard in
many church services during the prayer, or when filling in the short periods
between parts of the service. Added to the 'Cello, it gives more warmth of
tone. When combined with the Dulciana, Dolce, or Melodia, it makes a
broad accompaniment tone for solo stops like the Keraulophone, Viola
Pomposa, Harmonic Flute, or any orchestral Reed stop. To the Vox
Humana it gives a new species of tone color, furnishing a mild undulation
and a little ground tone. With the softer Strings, like the Viola, Aeoline,
Muted Violin, or Salicional, it binds the tones together as well as furnishes
a slow-beating dilutant to their brightness, for any céleste added to another

stop, except a loud stop, creates a *different* céleste coloring.* This stop may be on any division. See CÉLESTE, SPITZFLÖTE.

SPITZGAMBA. See CONE GAMBA.

SPITZGEDECKT. An 8′ or 4′ stopped manual wood Flute of pyramidal shape and very dull tone. It sounds fewer harmonics than even the regular straight-walled Gedeckt. The conical metal form also exists. See GEDECKT.

SPITZPRINZIPAL. See CONE DIAPASON.

SPITZQUINTE. A Spitzflöte or conical Principal of 2 2/3′, rarely at 5 1/3′, on the manuals. This is a soft stop that is not at all dull in tone. It has the same functions as the Twelfth of soft quality. Not only does this stop serve as a true Copula, it also is a Copula at the *Twelfth's pitch,* making it of even more value in binding other flues, like the Flutes with the Diapasons, the Diapasons with the Strings, and also the Strings with the Flutes. It is free from the brilliant fringe of harmonics heard in the straight-walled Twelfths, even of softer tone. It is a very valuable mutation also at 1 1/3′. See QUINT, SPITZFLÖTE, TWELFTH.

STARKGEDECKT. A loud and pervasive form of the Gedeckt, at 16′ or 8′ on the manuals, made from large-scale wooden pipes. It gives a strong ground tone to any combination but lacks the distinctively beautiful smoothness of the Schöngedeckt and Singengedeckt. It is less heavy than the Bourdon tribe and does not approach the round-toned Tibia Clausa in intensity. In case anyone should believe that there is no available space on the dynamic range between the Gedeckt and the Tibia Clausa where this "loud" Flute can be defined, it should be remembered that a Tibia Clausa is at least twenty times as loud as the average Gedeckt. Dynamic levels in the ear cover a tremendous range, not only between stops, but between *one pipe's* harmonics as well. If this were not so the ear (and mind) could not be trained to hear the differences between the *tone qualities* of one hundred different Gedeckts of the same loudness! See GEDECKT.

STATE TRUMPET. A brilliant and unusually loud Chorus Reed of 8′ on the manuals, sometimes referred to as a *Festival Trumpet, Pontifical Trumpet,* or *Silver Trumpet,* and designed to imitate the state trumpeters in the European cathedrals who announce by fanfares the entrance of a king or bishop. The tone is commanding, harmonically full, and usually of such volume of sound that it can overwhelm the full organ, or at least sound in contrast to it. Such Reeds are merely loud Tubas or Trumpets, perhaps Ophicleides, that are voiced to sound their fundamentals as well as their extensive trains of overtones to practically the maximum degree of development for a Reed. The unison or harmonic-length resonators are usually installed horizontally in the front of the main organ or at some point distant from the main organ. This position enables the pipes more

---

*The basic reason for combining stops is to create a new *tone color* (timbre), a new *dynamic value,* and a new *use* for the stops. Although all stops lose their individualities in combination, they also gain new effects not otherwise possible. Combinations vary in color in different pitch ranges.

easily to move the air-volume in the whole church or cathedral than if they were installed vertically up against the ceiling of an organ chamber. The many dissonant harmonics that give these loud Reeds such a cymbal-like and stately sound are thus able to reach the listener's ear without being absorbed by the walls and other structures on the way. These harmonics that spell the difference between this type of Trumpet and the average Trumpet of the organ are mostly high-pitched and also quite perishable because of their softness. Also, twenty or so of the lower-pitched overtones are needed to make this brass-like sound. A sound is *brass-like* when it has all of its lower components developed to be about as loud as its fundamental. The overtones diminish quickly in power after, approximately, the twentieth in a Reed as loud as this. The beating between the higher ones causes many transient harmonics. Fanfares, contrasts with the full organ, solo playing, and processional marches are some of the many uses of the State Trumpet.

Specifically, the *State Trumpet* built by the Aeolian Skinner Organ Company at the west end of the long nave, high up under the large rose window, in the Cathedral of St. John the Divine, New York City. This company, which also rebuilt the 140-rank organ at the east end above the choir, experimented extensively to find a Trumpet tone worthy of this huge Gothic edifice. The State Trumpet is stunningly brilliant and possesses all of the clang and brass formant necessary to make it realistic.

The horizontal, unenclosed position of this Chorus Reed permits the whole gamut of its overtones to expand throughout the long nave without undue absorption by walls or organ chambers. It is playable from the Solo manual, and its 50-inch wind pressure, from a special blower, is controlled by a special switch at the console. Several excellent high fidelity recordings of it and the magnificent Tuba Major of the main organ are available for home playing, but they require an unusual speaker system to do them justice. In this organ the many pipes are ideally spaced far apart to allow the sound waves to expand freely. See TROMPETTE EN CHAMADE.

STENTHORN. A solo labial stop of loud 8′ manual tone, made from metal pipes of large scale, inverted-conical in form, and with wide, low mouths. Its train of harmonics is unusually complete, owing to this pipe-shape, and its tone, although mostly Foundation, resembles that of a heavy Reed. Slots further increase the number of loud overtones. It is quite penetrating, but not truly brilliant.

STENTOR BOMBARDE. An extremely powerful and penetrating Chorus Reed of 16′ or 8′ manual pitch, and 32′, 16′, or 8′ pedal pitch, with the Bombarde's quality of tone. Its thick inverted-conical pipes send out the maximum of fundamental and overtones, making a sound at any of these manual and pedal pitches that is capable of supporting a large ensemble of both Reed and flue stops. The pedal rank at 32′ is appropriate in only the largest organs, and then in an acoustical environment that is capable of assimilating it. Loud pedal stops must support other *pedal* stops as well as manual divisions. Wooden pipes can make this tone. See BOMBARDE.

STENTOR DIAPASON. A very loud and assertive Diapason of 8′ on the manuals, resembling the chorus type of Diapason rather than the brilliant solo flues. A few examples might rightfully be called *Stentorphones.* This stop may have considerable development in its complex of overtones, but generally conforms to the definition of a Diapason: a loud fundamental and limited development of the lower-pitched overtones. It rarely justifies use of the word *brilliant.* It is less inclined to be bright in timbre than the Diapason Sonora, but it may be louder than that stop. It is in the Solo, Stentor, or Bombarde Organ in many cases, and can be joined with Chorus Reeds, like the Trumpets and Tubas, for ensemble tone, or sound alone or with another loud stop in solo line. The Octave, Twelfth, and Fifteenth may be voiced to sound with it. See DIAPASON, DIAPASON MAGNA.

STENTOR DIAPHONE. An extremely penetrating and loud Diaphone of 32′ or 16′ on the pedals, making the weightiest roll of bass sound in the organ. Its functions are the same as the Diaphone's. It is not designed in many specimens to have erected on it a façade of other stops, but may have added to the 32′ rank a 16′, 10 2/3′, and 8′, and to the 16′ rank an 8′, 5 1/3′, and 4′ Diapason of loud tone. The function of most Diaphones is to provide sufficient fundamental ground tone to balance the louder ensembles. The blend resulting from the meshing of the harmonics is not so apparent in the range from CCCC to CCC, which is the most useful range for this thunderous and stentorian bass. See CONTRA DIAPHONE.

STENTORFLÖTE. An open metal or wooden Flute of 8′ manual pitch, yielding a loud and brilliant tone suitable for loud ensembles of flues or Reeds, and also solo playing. This Flute is less loud than the Stentorphone or Tibia Plena. It is a little louder and more brilliant than the Major Open Flute. It may be heard from the Great or Solo division. Varieties of the stop can include smooth tones, similar to the Clarabella, or hard, hollow tones, similar to a large-scale Hohlflöte. A few examples have two mouths per pipe. See MAJOR OPEN FLUTE, STENTORPHONE.

STENTOR GAMBA. A String stop of solo quality, at 8′ on the manuals, possessing a brilliant and keen Gamba tone that is also quite loud for a String rank. It is a String Organ or Solo Organ stop. See GAMBA.

STENTOR HORN. A solo lingual stop of 8′ manual pitch, made from large-scale inverted-conical pipes of loud tone. It is brass-like without the freedom of vibration that can be sensed in the Trumpets. Some examples are smooth, big-toned, mellow Reeds that are useful in combination as well as for following the melody lines of the music. See BALLAD HORN.

STENTOR MIXTURE. A loud and very brilliant manual mixture of open metal pipes designed as Diapasons. This stop aids both loud flue and Chorus Reed ensembles by being *quick-speaking,* filled up with a complete complement of harmonics, and of good blend with Chorus Reeds because of its freedom from the louder *dissonant* partials. Devices to increase its loudness, as well as its cleanness of tone, are harmonic-length pipes, big scales, and inverted-conical form. It lifts up all other stops to a high level of brilliance and sounds itself like a Reed when played staccato. It may be in the same division as the Reeds. Middle C sounds these notes in these four examples:

Example No. 1	Example No. 2	Example No. 3	Example No. 4
III	III	VI	VII
C^3 2'	G^3 1 1/3'	C^4 1'	C^4 1'
G^2 2 2/3'	C^3 2'	G^3 1 1/3'	G^3 1 1/3'
C^2 4'	G^2 2 2/3'	C^3 2'	E^3 1 3/5'
		G^2 2 2/3'	C^3 2'
		C^2 4'	G^2 2 2/3'
		*C^1 8'	C^2 4'
			*C^1 8'

*Unison ranks may be omitted.

A Stentor Mixture designed for addition to a loud Bombarde or Fanfare division follows. In each octave, from bass to treble, there is an additional rank of pipes to build power, since smaller pipes usually lack enough impact to support Reeds' overtones properly. Only G's and C's sound; E's are not included, as from *any* C key depressed. The figure "1" represents the 8' pitch, and the "8" the 4', etc. Refer to Appendix D on MIXTURES.

	Ranks								
	I	II	III	IV	V	VI	VII	VIII	IX
CC to BB	19	22	26	29	33				
C to B	15	15	19	22	26	29			
C^1 to B^1	12	12	15	15	19	22	26		
C^2 to B^2	8	8	12	12	15	15	19	22	
C^3 to C^4	1	1	8	8	12	12	15	15	19

At middle C (that is C^1) the ranks in this large mixture are easily named, from left to right, the Twelfth at 2 2/3', the Fifteenth at 2', the Nineteenth at 1 1/3', the Twenty-second at 1', and the Twenty-sixth at 2/3'. As the player runs the scale towards the treble each higher octave has an additional duplicated pitch in it. This gives volume but keeps the highest pitch reasonably low. Repeating below the pitches heard from C^1 to B^1:

2 2/3'   2 2/3'   2'   2'   1 1/3'   1'   2/3'   (in order)

It is typical of German books on the organ to lay out the entire mixture in terms of stop-pitch, as immediately above. English and American books prefer the system shown in the whole presentation above. This example is indicated as V-IX.

STENTOR OCTAVE. A Foundation stop of octave 4' pitch on the manuals, and sometimes at 8' on the pedals. It is voiced to extend upward all of the louder Diapasons, such as the Diapason Magna, Stentor Diapason, and Grand Diapason, whether of chorus or solo voicing. Its voice is also a source of brilliance to the Chorus Reeds, like the Tuba Magna and Trumpet, giving them a natural train of harmonics, starting at the octave pitch. See DIAPASON, OCTAVE.

STENTORPHONE. An open metal or wood Flute of unusual loudness as well as the maximum harmonic development that can be given to a labial stop. It speaks at 8' on the manuals, but can be coupled to the pedals by the Solo to Pedal coupler on almost all organs. It adds great volume to any ensemble of Chorus Reeds or flue stops of loud tone, such as the Diapasons, louder Flutes, and Strings. Alone or in combination, it is a solo stop of commanding presence. It supplies all other stops with a complete complement of the harmonic components up to about the fortieth or fiftieth, filling out their tones, but not usually lending a distinctive character of its own. To the Tuba Magna or Trumpet it gives additional brilliance and a firmer pitch. This stop, although of Flute classification, is really a Diapason-Flute hybrid. Many varieties can be voiced, and the horn-like or string-like sound can be injected at will. All Stentorphones are not overwhelming; smaller organs sometimes have specimens of moderate power useful in building up any tonal ensemble except the soft type, and also in accompanying hymns and playing marches. See TIBIA PLENA.

STENTOR SESQUIALTERA. A manual and pedal mixture of prominent Twelfth and Tierce ranks. There are examples at 32′, 16′, and 8′. This louder than normal form is found on the pedals at 32′ and 16′ and on the manuals at 8′, rarely 16′. Its open metal Diapasons do not break in pitch in many examples. It builds up a colorful, well-timbred sound of use in solo as well as countermelody playing. Pedal examples can be heard in only the larger organs, where they are valuable in creating a tone that brings up the harmonic structure to a point where it can balance the manuals. In many types of music the tone of the pedals must be capable of carrying a prominent melody line that has strength as well as uniqueness of timbre. This mixture on the pedals, particularly in the 16′ series, has many uses in the larger church and concert organs. In the following four examples these notes speak from middle C and the low pedal CCC key:

Manual 16′ series III		Manual 8′ series IV		Pedal 32′ series III		Pedal 16′ series III	
E^2	3 1/5′	E^3	1 3/5′	EE	6 2/5′	E	3 1/5′
C^2	4′	C^3	2′	CC	8′	C	4′
G^1	5 1/3′	G^2	2 2/3′	GGG	10 2/3′	GG	5 1/3′
		C^2	4′				

See SESQUIALTERA.

STILLGEDECKT. A stopped Flute of wood (occasionally metal) belonging to the Gedeckt tribe. It is usually either at 8′ or 4′ on the manuals. This Gedeckt is very soft and not at all colorful and velvety in tone, like the Schöngedeckt and Singengedeckt. It lacks the smoothness of the Lieblichgedeckt. It is able to furnish any soft flue stop with an additional amount of fundamental, and to dilute the string-like effects of some of the softer Strings, such as the Viola, Echo 'Cello, and Aeoline. It may be combined with the Dulciana, Dolcan, Erzähler, or Dulciana in order to make a variety of accompaniment tones. It increases roundness of tone when added to such stops as the Harmonica or Suabe Flute. It has some ability to place the soft flues in clearer dimension by making the exact proportions in loudness between the harmonics more apparent. See GEDECKT. Synonym: LOCHGEDECKT.

STOPPED DIAPASON. See STOPPED FLUTE.

STOPPED FLUTE. A wooden Flute of stoppered form, at 8', sometimes 16' or 4', on the manuals. This tone quality, at the unison pitch, is made up primarily of fundamental, Twelfth, and a little Tierce. The even-numbered harmonics are excluded by the stoppers. This is a lighter Flute than the Bourdon, frequently on the same organ, and less dull than the Gedeckt. The Nachthorn usually has a more obvious third harmonic than this stop. This Flute has a somewhat lower mouth cut-up than either the Bourdon or the Gedeckt, and consequently blends a little better, although not so well as the Quintaten or Quintadena. Nevertheless, it can serve as a *Quint Flute* in certain combinations. It is on many Swell Organs, and is frequently the only stopped rank available on a smaller church organ. Its solo voice can be well accompanied by the Dulciana, Dolce,

Stopped Flute

or Dolcan. It may accompany a solo on the Great Organ's Melodia. It adds body of tone to the Vox Humana, Spitzflöte Céleste, Salicional, or Vox Céleste and never stands away from the stops found on a smaller organ. It is too dull in timbre for a vocal accompaniment. The CC pipe ranges from 3.75 x 3.5 to 4.25 x 3.25 inches in measurement. *Tapadillo* is a name for stopped Flutes of various types. See QUINTADE. Synonym: STOPPED DIAPASON.

STOPPED TWELFTH. A 2 2/3' manual Flute of stopped metal or wooden construction. It adds a soft Twelfth to the manual flue combinations. *This* stop's *Twelfth* sounds about D^4 when middle C is depressed, and may make an obvious impression in the tone. This is a beautiful mutation effect to add to the Clarinet or Melodia or 8' Gedeckt. See GEDECKT, TWELFTH.

STRING CÉLESTE. See CÉLESTE, VIOLE CÉLESTE, VOIX CÉLESTE.

STRING MIXTURE. A manual mixture composed of either keen or dull String stops, perhaps in various combinations in order to build up a particular tone, as on an Accompanimental or String Organ. A few of the great numbers of examples possible follow, with the notes from Middle C:

Viola Ranks III	Viole d'Orchestre Ranks IV	Salicional Ranks V	Aeoline Ranks V
		C^4 1'	C^4 1'
C^3 2'	C^3 2'	C^3 2'	C^3 2'
C^2 4'	G^2 2 2/3'	G^2 2 2/3'	G^2 2 2/3'
*C^1 8'	C^2 4'	C^2 4'	C^2 4'
	*C^1 8'	*C^1 8'	*C^1 8'

*Unison ranks.

See PEDAL STRING MIXTURE. Synonym: VIOL MIXTURE.

STRING TWELFTH. A 2 2/3′ manual rank of open metal pipes, composed of mild String tone, perhaps of Viola or soft Salicional quality. It is a Swell, String, or Echo Organ stop. Its train of thirty or so harmonics must not have the peaking in loudness sometimes heard in Strings, in order to be assimilated by the tonal complex. Since each one of these harmonics is not a duplicate of any octave-sounding stop's harmonics, this stop may thicken the tone instead of clarify it, giving mass rather than tonal transparency. A Spitzflöte or conical rank may be more useful than even a mild String. Some examples are String-Flute hybrids. See TWELFTH, VIOL.

SUABE FLUTE. An open wooden Flute of 8′ or 4′ on the manuals, of small to medium scale, and soft to moderate in volume. It resembles a Waldflöte in timbre, and may be made as a small-scale rank of that species, but with somewhat higher mouth cut-up. It may also be a small-scale Melodia and perhaps called *Echo Melodia*.

SUAVE FLUTE. An open wooden Flute of 8′ or 4′ on the manuals, of moderate scale and a soft volume, and a tone color that may be described as *smooth* (without peaks of loudness in the harmonics), *dulcet* (with a pleasing balance between the lowest four harmonics), and *comparatively dull* (of about twelve to sixteen partials). The high upper lips are rounded and very thick to discourage formation of the higher partials. This Flute has solo, ensemble, and accompaniment functions. It is more useful at 4′ than at 8′, and does not overbrighten or mark other stops with which it is combined. It is usable in any division of the organ.

SUB BASS. See MAJOR BASS.

SUB BOURDON. See MAJOR BASS.

SUB OCTAVE. A Foundation stop, usually of Diapason tone, but occasionally a stopped or open Flute, at 16′ manual pitch, and 32′ pedal pitch. It is not a common stop-name. See DOUBLE DIAPASON.

SUB PRINCIPAL. See DOUBLE DIAPASON.

SUB QUINT. A Foundation stop, usually of Diapason tone, at 10 2/3′ on the manuals, and 21 1/3′ on the pedals. Flutes, both open and stopped, may be substituted for this Diapason, and are sometimes borrowed or extended from some other rank of pipes of different name. On the organs

---

Chart Explanation: Families of Organ Stops

There are four families of organ stops: Foundation (including Diapasons of all sorts), Flute, String, and Reed. The lines of separation between these families are clearly drawn, although there are several open Flutes that may be said to have a Foundation tone, and a few Foundation stops, like the Keraulophone and Nachthorn, that may be said to have a Flute tone. A combination of harmonic analysis and pipe-form seems to be the only way to make a classification. These sub-divisions are merely suggested and do not have a traditional basis. The only type of tone missing here is the Percussion stop.

FAMILIES OF ORGAN STOPS

Name of Subdivision	General Tone Quality	Examples
FOUNDATION		
1. DIAPASON	Strong fundamental, firm, little overtone development	Diapason, Wood Diapason, Geigen, Viola Diapason
2. DIMINUTIVE	Diapason-like, soft but with moderate brightness, silvery	Gemshorn, Dolce, Dolcan, Erzähler, Dulciana
3. VALVULAR	Intense fundamental, loud, percussive, smooth, penetrating	Diaphone, Magnaton, Stentor Diaphone
FLUTE		
1. OPEN	Fundamental strong, odd and even-numbered harmonics strong	Major Flute, Clarabella, Hohlflöte, Philomela
2. HALF-COVERED	Odd-numbered harmonics strong, Octave harmonic usually soft	Rohrflöte, Koppelflöte, Cone Flute
3. STOPPED	Odd-numbered harmonics strong, dull, pervading, smooth	Gedeckt, Tibia Clausa, Bourdon, Quintade
STRING		
1. ORGAN-TYPE (unimitative)	Bright but not pungent, light in tone, usually soft	Salicional, Gamba, Aeoline, Sylvestrina
2. ORCHESTRAL (imitative)	Keen, pungent, thin-toned, weak fundamental, many partials	Viole d'Orchestre, Viola, Violoncello
REED		
1. CHORUS REEDS	Intense fundamental, brilliant train of harmonics, brass-like	Tuba Magna, Trumpet Bombarde, Posaune
2. SOFT ORCHESTRAL BRASS	Brass-like timbres that are soft in volume	French Horn, Waldhorn, Echo Trumpet
3. ORCHESTRAL WOODWINDS	Highly individualized timbres, bright, piquant, reedy	Clarinet, Orchestral Oboe, English Horn
4. ANCIENT INSTRUMENTS	Fundamental weak, thin, nasal, sibilant, bright	Schalmei, Kinura, Regal, Rankett, Barpfeife
5. ORGAN-TYPE	Varied	Krummhorn, Krumet, Corno d'Amore, Zink

in which every stop-control has its own set of pipes, commonly known as *straight* organs, these stops, manual and pedal, would have their own pipes somewhere back in the dark chambers. These stop-pitches represent the third harmonics ("Twelfths") of the sub-sub-unison series. They both speak at the notes two octaves below the true Twelfths of the unison series. They are necessary if the organist is to have available a complete choir of stop-pitches for his pedal 64' series and the manual's 32' series. The pedal's 21 1/3' Sub Quint will make a Resultant of 64' with any flue of 32'. The manual's 10 2/3' Sub Quint will make a manual Resultant with any flue of 16', but this latter effect is usable in only a few large organs, perhaps in large, high-ceilinged cathedrals, as a device occasionally to deepen the 32' manual tone. This stop speaks at the fourth note below the key depressed, as at GGGG from the low pedal CCC key. Synonyms: GROSS QUINT, GROSSQUINTENBASS.

SUPER OCTAVE. See FIFTEENTH.

SUPER SUPER OCTAVE. See TWENTY-SECOND.

SYLVESTRINA. A String stop of 8' or 4' on the manuals, formed from conical open metal pipes of slender scale and soft intonation. The timbre is that of a dull String, but there are many luminous and silvery effects possible with these two pitches that other String stops cannot duplicate. Some of the Erzähler's tone is present, and also a considerable amount of the octave harmonic, making this stop one of many beautiful combinational soft stops among the Strings and diminutive Foundation ranks. It is brighter than the Dulciana, but less bright than the Aeoline or Salicional. It creates a quiet and dulcet céleste, suitable for accompaniments if of slow beat.

TENTH. A rank of Foundation pipes that speaks at 3 1/5' manual pitch, and 6 2/5' pedal pitch, one octave and a third above the key depressed on manuals and pedals. It is not a harmonic of the unison series, but is about the same pitch as the fifth harmonic of the sub-unison series. The 3 1/5' should not be drawn without a 16' stop, and the 6 2/5' should not be drawn without a 32' stop, otherwise the Tenths will beat too much to be pleasant. The base-pitch of any series of stop-pitches is drawn with its own harmonics (i. e. pitches higher than it and from its own series), with very few exceptions. The Tenth is a stop found mostly in large organs; it is in mixtures as well. If middle C were depressed with this rank drawn, E^2 would sound. The low pedal CCC key would sound the Tenth at the note of EE. The following chart shows the juxtaposition of the Tenth on both manuals and pedals. The manual Tenth belongs to the 16' series, and the pedal Tenth to the 32' series. The chart also shows the six most important *series of stop-pitches* along with the eight *pitches* that make up most of the combinations in each case. These pitches should be memorized by every organist so that all may be immediately identified at the console. No other device can give so much confidence and freedom from confusion in this complex subject. All are important, except perhaps the Septièmes, as *separate stops* or as *mixture* or *mutation* ranks. The *base-pitch* is shown at the head of each column, and it also is the "fundamental" of each of these series of harmonics. Most of these pitches are on both manuals and pedals.

64' series	32' series	16' series	8' series	4' series	2' series
8'	4'	2'	1'	1/2'	1/4'
9 1/7'	4 4/7'	2 2/7'	1 1/7'	4/7'	2/7'
10 2/3'	5 1/3'	2 2/3'	1 1/3'	2/3'	1/3'
12 4/5'	*6 2/5'	*3 1/5'	1 3/5'	4/5'	2/5'
16'	8'	4'	2'	1'	1/2'
21 1/3'	10 2/3'	5 1/3'	2 2/3'	1 1/3'	2/3'
32'	16'	8'	4'	2'	1'
64'	32'	16'	8'	4'	2'

Asterisks mark the position of the Tenths among the other pitches. In mixtures the lower pitches appear in the higher octaves, and the higher pitches appear in the lower octaves. This chart is also an excellent place to study the pitches that belong to the pedal mixtures. The 64' octave is present in only two organs in the whole world, but the other pitches of this same series are present in thousands of organs. Synonym: GROSS TIERCE.

TERPODION. A rarely seen String stop of keen Gamba tone, at 8' on the manuals. It is formed from narrow-scale pipes of low but wide mouth construction in order to make a marked "spit" of initial harmonics meant to simulate the sound of the rare keyboard-percussion instrument of the same name. It is not likely that the partials in a percussion instrument can be simulated by any type of air column however narrow or overblown, because percussive partials lie *between* the partials of the air column on the scale of pitches.

TERTIAN. A compound manual and pedal stop composed in most examples of two or three ranks of pipes. Two of these ranks are pitched a third apart, but other ranks may accompany them to aid in the assimilation of the tone. The ranks are Foundation stops of various species, frequently Diapason. Breaks in the pitches do not occur in many examples. The following manual examples speak from the middle C key, and the pedal example speaks from the low CCC key:

Manual Example No. 1	Manual Example No. 2	Pedal Example No. 1
II	III	II
G^3 1 1/3'	G^3 1 1/3'	G 2 2/3'
E^3 1 3/5'	E^3 1 3/5'	E 3 1/5'
	C^3 2'	

TERZ. See THIRD.

THIRD. A rank of Foundation pipes that speaks at 6 2/5' on the manuals (32' series), and 12 4/5' on the pedals (64' series). The function of these unusual pitches is to corroborate the fifth harmonic of the sub-sub-unison series of pitches on both manuals and pedals. These pitches are one octave below those of the Tenth. When drawn with other pitches without their own series, they create resultant tones that are unusually grave and sometimes unpleasant. Their use is limited to a few combinations in even the very large organs. They are necessary to provide the organist with *a complete set of pitches* in these low series. Middle C would sound at E^1 (three notes above the key depressed), and the low pedal CCC at EEE. See TENTH. Synonym: TERZ.

THIRTY-FIFTH, FLATTED. A rank of Foundation pipes that is pitched at 2/7′ on the manuals, and 4/7′ on the pedals. This is at the note four octaves and a flatted seventh above the key depressed. Since this rank sounds only in the vicinity of the twenty-eighth harmonic, it will only partly corroborate its pitch, assuming combination with a unison stop. It speaks two octaves above the 1 1/7′ Septième on the manuals, and two octaves above the 2 2/7′ Septième on the pedalboard. It is of use in some mixtures, but much too high for a mutation stop. From middle C it would speak at $B\flat^5$; from the pedal's low CCC key it speaks at $B\flat^2$.

THIRTY-FIRST. A rank of open Foundation pipes speaking at 2/5′ on the manuals, and 4/5′ on the pedals, sounding the note of E^5 from the middle C key, and the note of E^2 from the low pedal CCC key. These notes are four octaves and a third above the keys depressed. This is at the approximate pitch of the *twentieth* harmonic. This rank will support this harmonic to some extent. The source of this harmonic (in either the pedals or manuals) is in the tone of a unison stop, and being an even-numbered harmonic, it would be assumed that it is not in the series of a stopped rank of any kind. It may be heard in the lower octaves of a few mixtures, since most mixture ranks break back (lower) in pitch as they rise.

THIRTY-SIXTH. An extremely high-pitched rank of open metal Foundation pipes, at 1/4′ on the manuals, and 1/2′ on the pedals. Both ranks are in considerable use, in spite of their altitude of pitch, because they are both octave-sounding. The timbre of *Flute* or *Diapason* cannot, of course, be well identified at this pitch, except, perhaps, in the lower octave of the rank. Not only do most of the overtones meet complete absorption by the pipes' walls, the atmosphere, etc.; the fundamentals also are in much danger of absorption from walls, clothing, etc. From middle C this rank sounds at C^6, in the pedals at C^3 from the lowest CCC key. It corroborates precisely the *thirty-second* harmonic. (Notice that the number of the stop-name and the harmonic are different.) It is three octaves above the manual's 2′ pitch. It is called the *Thirty-sixth* because it speaks at the thirty-sixth *note* above the key struck. It is necessary to break back the frequency of the pitch of this rank in order to keep the pipes from becoming too small to keep in tune, too high to hear, and extremely soft as well. The builder may break the pitch at every octave or at fewer points than this. These very small pipes are especially worthless to the organist if they are out of tune, and even an opened window can set them out of tune. Beats between them and the lower ranks, with which they are always combined, are likely to mask the tone qualities of all stops. But if they are in tune their effect can be amazingly beautiful, extending the brilliance of the other stops upward to the threshold of audibility. The tuner may go over them just before a recital or recording session to ensure this effect, since they are probably on the Crescendo Pedal and pistons. The 1/8′ rank, an octave higher than this rank, occurs in a few organs; it is called the *Forty-third*.

THIRTY-THIRD. A rank of Foundation pipes, speaking at 1/3′ on the manuals, and 2/3′ on the pedals. Both of these pitches speak at the notes four octaves and a fifth above the keys depressed. This rank sounds at G^5 from middle C, and G^2 from low pedal CCC. The twenty-fourth harmonic is fairly well corroborated by this rank, assuming that this harmonic belongs to the unison series of pitches. Such a rank of pipes as this has more use than might be imagined. It is in the lowest one or two octaves of several mixtures, like the Cymbal or Carillon. The 1/3′ speaks three octaves above the 2 2/3′ Twelfth.

TIBIA. This stop-name by itself on a stop control indicates an open wood (occasionally metal) Flute of 8′ manual pitch, frequently on the Great. It may be a Tibia Plena, which is a stop characteristic of fairly large instruments, or a less loud open Flute of unusually full choir of harmonics, intended to build up the Diapason Chorus, or perhaps a choir of loud Chorus Reeds. The loud *open* Flutes can melt into the tones of other loud stops unobtrusively. The Diapasons may not need this Flute, but in many cases the ideal voicing has not been arrived at, or the higher-pitched stops may be out of tune, or not included in the organ. This stop sounds at least fifteen to twenty harmonics that are strong enough to be telling in the ensemble, and many at common stop-pitches. (See TIBIA PLENA.)

In the nomenclature of the theater organ the term *Tibia* refers in most cases to a stopped Flute of huge scale and little harmonic development, although a few open Tibias are heard in the theater organ. The Tibia Dura, frequently at 4′, is a hard-toned, brilliant open Flute in concert or theater organ. There are also several other references to the term *Tibia*, practically all given here, among organ stops. Most are of wooden pipes, but a few are metal. A listing of the Tibia tribe's stop-names under *open* and *stopped* may aid the organist trying to learn the meanings:

Open ranks	Stopped ranks
Tibia Dura	Tibia Clausa
Tibia Flute (4′)	Tibia Flute (4′)
Tibia Major (Tibia Plena)	Tibia Major (Tibia Clausa)
Tibia Minor (Tibia Plena)	Tibia Minor (Tibia Clausa)
Tibia Mollis	Tibia Profunda (16′ on manuals)
Tibia Plena	Tibia Profundissima (32′ on manuals)
Tibia Rex	
Tibia Sylvestris (Waldflöte)	

TIBIA CLAUSA. A stopped Flute of wood (rarely metal) pipes, at 16′, 8′, 4′, 2′, or 1′ on the manuals, and 32′ or 16′ on the pedals. The 8′ manual pitch is the most used, but *Tibia Flute* (4′), *Flautino* (2′), and *Tibia Profunda* (16′) refer to unified stops of this Flute. (Stopped ranks of 8′ on the manuals sound the unison's notes, but really have a CC pipe about four feet long.) Open metal pipes of large scale are used in the high trebles of this stop; no builder makes the smallest pipes stopped. The break in tone between the two is usually not noticeable. The almost complete absence of overtones in this stop makes it sound in contrast to even the stoppered Bourdon and Gedeckt. The unusually large scales adopted by builders absorb almost every trace of the odd-numbered harmonics (except the first, or fundamental) that the smooth lips of this stop can make, and also the faint traces of the even-numbered harmonics that creep into the far-apart (wide-scaled) areas at the square corners of the unusually high mouths. Arching the upper lip also tends to eliminate some traces of even-numbered harmonics. Tuning-fork purity is practically achieved in the larger scales of this stop. However, the third harmonic is never completely absent, particularly in the upper stoppered octaves. The tonal effect depends mostly upon the imposing fundamental (which is right on the piano's notes when from the manual's unison 8' rank). The formant of the wood pipes contributes an extremely soft added parcel of overtones, since no pipe emits just the overtones of its *air column*. Although not apparent, these soft overtones do mutate the tones of all pipes somewhat into a different proportion. The effect on the ear of the Tibia is pliant. It surprises by being powerful although gentle. It is very easy to hear because its tones come from air columns two or three times as big as those from Gedeckt pipes of the same pitch. It accelerates relatively slowly into the steady tone, not giving the ear the impression of vitality. Its pitch is always somewhat vague, owing to the absence of confirming overtones.

It has done more to endear the pipe organ to the unmusical man than any other stop except the Diapason of the church organ. Its deep, smooth notes make the sound remembered from the theater organ, with the aid of the tremulant, of course, and it still gives pleasure to many from the big Wurlitzers and Kimballs still played, or the many high fidelity recordings made of it. Harmonically speaking, it could not be more different than it is from the stop with which it is usually allied — the Vox Humana. Contrasting with the massive fundamental of the Tibia, which is strictly on pitch, is the Vox Humana's tenuous and soft off-pitch daub of overtones that are so high up the scale that the ear can never identify them. Sounding together with the off-pitch characteristics of a rapid, intense valve tremulant, they make an appeal that is the exact opposite from that of the mathematically proportioned components of the Diapasons and mixtures.

The notes of the Tibia when chorded sound like just *one note*, as they do from the Diapason Phonon also. This one-note impression is fatal to any except the melodious music of popular songs. This fact places the Tibia Clausa strictly in the Solo Organ's domain. It is not so usable as a source of fundamental, like the Gedeckt or Grossflöte, because it is too intense for most other stops. It is in contrast to the Quint Flutes because its third harmonic is extremely soft. The 32' pedal octave can be very usable because at this profound pitch meshing of overtones with higher stops is not so apparent, and here it is right on the lower threshold of audibility, making but 16.35 oscillations in the air per second at low CCCC. Since this rank has been unified to almost every pitch between 32′ and 1/2′, it might be added that the top manual C key of this same *rank,* from open metal pipes, would sound at 8,372.02 oscillations per second as C^6.

This Flute's stopped pipes are of heavy construction, with thick walls, and the insides of the pipes are as smooth as possible. Absolutely air-tight stoppers exclude the atmospheric pressure except at the mouth. The thick upper lip is parabolically rounded in some cases to reduce friction between it and the air-reed to the absolute minimum. Leathered lips are effective, but not a permanent device. Most lips are beveled to reduce the "chiff" of initial partials. Cut-up varies according to musical function, and may be but one-half the mouth's height; in some ranks it is higher than the width. The CC pipe varies from 7 x 5 to 12 x 8 inches (inside). The CCCC pipe in the Atlantic City Convention Hall organ measures 30 x 24 inches, belongs to an 85-pipe rank, and is on 20 inches of wind pressure.

TIBIA DURA. An inverted-pyramidal open wood Flute, invented by Robert Hope-Jones, sounding at 4′, occasionally 8′, on the manuals. Its tone is brilliant, somewhat *hard,* as indicated by the name, and very loud. It has an unusual degree of penetration* through loud flue and sometimes Chorus Reed stops. It is a solo and combinational Flute for a large Solo.

TIBIA FLUTE. A stop-name to indicate either the 4′ manual Tibia Clausa or Tibia Plena, both species being equally represented. The stoppered Tibia Flute is likely to be on a unit organ, and the open Tibia Flute is likely to be on a straight organ, perhaps accompanying the Tibia Plena on the great. See TIBIA CLAUSA, TIBIA PLENA.

TIBIA MAJOR. A stoppered Flute of 16′ or 8′ on the manuals, fashioned after the Tibia Clausa, or a large-scale Gedeckt. Its tone is smooth and pure, and shows the penetration of an intense fundamental ground tone. This name can also refer to the larger of two Tibia Clausas in the same organ, this one having the solo type of voicing. Or it may refer to the larger of two open Tibias (perhaps with Tibia Plena tone) on a Great Organ. See GEDECKT, TIBIA CLAUSA, TIBIA PLENA.

TIBIA MINOR. A stoppered Flute of 16′ or 8′ on the manuals, fashioned after the Tibia Clausa, or a small-scaled Gedeckt. Its tone is smooth and pure, and lacks the intense fundamental heard in many other Flutes. This name may also refer to the smaller of two Tibia Clausas in the same organ, this one not being on the Solo manual. Or it may refer to the smaller of two open Tibias (perhaps with Tibia Plena tone) on a Great Organ. See GEDECKT, TIBIA CLAUSA, TIBIA PLENA.

TIBIA MOLLIS. A name that variously refers to almost any type of soft or small-scaled 8′ manual Flute of open construction.

TIBIA PLENA. A large-scaled open wood Flute of 8′ on the manuals, yielding a timbre of greater weight and somewhat less brilliance than the

Penetration in organ stops comes from two sources: sharpness of tone, as in the Tierce or a brilliant stop, and an intense fundamental.

Stentorphone. It is a loud Flute-Diapason hybrid of stentorian proportions. Not all of the modern examples have the fluty, cloying tone of the earlier ones; many are more brilliant and less intense. Two-mouth examples are given other names. The Tibia Plena is usually of wood and the Stentorphone is usually of metal. These different materials have distinctly different formants that fashion the tones accordingly. This stop is less loud than the Stentorphone, and the average dynamic level of the Stentorflöte is still lower. There is more variation in the loudness of the Tibia Plena than in most other loud Flutes. It appears in organs of moderate size, usually on the Great or Solo. It is a loud and dominating solo voice by itself and sounds with great clarity and emotional appeal. It can build up an ensemble of stops of Reed or flue classification, or both, extending the brilliant top of the ensemble as well as supplying all of the lower chord of harmonics for the keys depressed. It can smooth the Diapasons, if this needs to be done, extend the brilliance of the Tubas, and make the big Trumpets of better blend. In many ensembles it blends so well that its tone disappears into the ensemble at the same time that it is building it up. Large scale, beveled wide mouths, thick walls, and high wind pressure aid in delivering the tremendous volume of tone that is expected from this loud Flute. One very large cathedral has two specimens in its Great Organ. See STENTORPHONE.

TIBIA PROFUNDA. A 16′ Flute on the manuals, and a 32′ Flute on the pedals, varying in pipe form, but usually a Tibia Clausa under this name. Occasionally this name refers to an open rank of large scale. *Profunda*, like *Contra, Gross,* and *Double,* usually has the meaning of *suboctave pitch* on either manuals or pedals. This is not a useful manual stop at 16′, because it blends poorly with all other stops, including other Flutes. The Bourdon or Rohrgedeckt of 16′ is more useful for all types of music. The 32′ pedal octave is quite useful, since at this profound pitch the deep roll of fundamental tone is not easily associable with the higher pitches, owing to the inability of the ear to identify low pitches accurately, especially from pipes of dull tone. It can balance the moderately loud or soft combinations of the manuals quite well, but may be penetrating. See TIBIA CLAUSA.

TIBIA PROFUNDISSIMA. A 32′ manual pitch, and, if correct terminology is used, a 64′ pedal pitch of the stoppered Tibia Clausa. There is no theoretical or practical reason why this low pedal flue should not prove useful, except, perhaps, slowness of speech. See TIBIA CLAUSA.

TIBIA REX. A Flute of open construction, at 8′ on the manuals, yielding an unusually powerful and heavy tone from either metal or wood pipes. It is a rare stop-name, and indicates a louder form of the Tibia Plena. It may be used in contrast with a Tibia Plena of less volume. See TIBIA PLENA.

TIBIA SYLVESTRIS. See WALDFLÖTE.

TIERCE. See SEVENTEENTH.

TIERCINA. A stoppered metal Flute of moderate scale, speaking at the 8′ pitch on the manuals. The effect of the Tierce, or fifth harmonic, is obtained by overblowing the pipes to just the right amount to create both the 8′ and the 1 3/5′ components. The 2 2/3′ component is also present in the tone in varying amounts in different examples. The 4′ and 2′ components are absent from the tone. This stop may be used as a source of the soft Tierce, as the *Quint Flutes* are used as sources of the 2 2/3′. It is automatically tuned by the pipe's air column, rather than by the hand, so it is more desirable in some ways in soft combinations for this reason. It is in perfect tune with its fundamental. See ROHRPOMMER.

TRAVERSFLÖTE. See ORCHESTRAL FLUTE.

TROMBA. A Chorus Reed of 16′ or 8′ on the manuals, and 16′ on the pedals. It has the tonality of the Trombone, with a bigger, rounder sound, and considerably less of the brass quality. It is not horn-like in most specimens, and is quite free from clang. Its harmonically full, smooth, rich fabric of tone is useful in solo and ensemble passages alike. It is such an excellent balance between lightness and gravity that a few large organs have a whole chorus of Tromba stops, even at 5 1/3′ on the manuals. Some organists prefer this stop to the Trumpet on the Great, but this is a matter of taste, not correctness. It does combine well with the big stops there and does not overbalance the ensemble with brass-like effects. Its pipes are usually of metal, but wooden pipes do exist, especially in the lower octaves. The pipes are larger in scale than many Chorus Reeds, and are inverted-conical in form.

TROMBA CLARION. An octave Tromba, at 4′ on the manuals, and 8′ on the pedals, sounding with less prominence than the unison Trombas. This stop is usually not present without the unison Trombas. Manual examples of the Tromba Chorus may be made of the following ranks:

Tromba Clarion	4′		Tromba Clarion	4′
Tromba Real	8′	or	*Tromba Quint	5 1/3′
Contra Tromba	16′		Tromba Magna	8′
			Contra Tromba	16′

*Belongs to sub-unison series.

See TROMBA.

TROMBA MAGNA. See TROMBA REAL.

TROMBA QUINT. A powerful and assertive Quint of brass tone, at 5 1/3′ on the manuals, and rarely in the pedals. It belongs to the sub-unison series of stops, and should always be drawn with a loud Reed of 16′ pitch. It is less assertive and prominent in tone than the Trompette Quinte or Bombarde Quinte, also of this pitch. Since it speaks but five notes above the unison 8′ pitch, it should be drawn with caution. Its whole train of brassy overtones must be assimilated by the 16′, and perhaps 8′ and 4′ stops, to make it sound in balance. It is only on large organs. See QUINT, TROMBA.

TROMBA REAL. An unusually loud and assertive Tromba rank, at 8′ on the manuals. Without sounding horn-like, or as firm in tone as the Tubas, this solo and ensemble Chorus Reed furnishes the organ with a magnificent broad-toned, harmonically full brass sound that is at least as loud as the Tuba Magna. See TROMBA. Synonym: TROMBA MAGNA.

TROMBONE. A Chorus Reed of 16′ or 8′ on the manuals, and 32′ or 16′ on the pedals. This Reed has the sound of the orchestral instrument, although, like most orchestral imitations, it is louder and bigger in tone, because of the vibrations of a bigger air column. There is some tendency towards the horn sound not heard in the Trombas. The tone is less firm than the Tubas and less brilliant than the Trumpets. It lacks the heavy roll of sound heard from the Bombardes. Quite soft Trombones can be heard in the smaller organs, sometimes with just two manuals. This is a stop-name applied by builders to a great variety of Chorus Reeds, some more deserving of the name *Tuba*. The average Trombone stop is a smooth, brassy tone without much clang in it, and just loud enough to sound well in the ensembles without dominating them. It is a little more likely to be a pedal stop, but the 8′ Solo Organ rank is of great usefulness, although it may become blatant and fiery between tenor C and C³. Inverted-conical spotted metal pipes of slender taper are used. Deep octaves may be made of wood.

TROMPETTE. An unusually brilliant and loud Chorus Reed of 16′, 8′, or 4′ on the manuals, and sometimes at 16′ on the pedals. The name spelled as *Trompette* represents the more freely vibrating and brassy variety of Trumpet. It has very little fundamental in most specimens, but the Trumpet, a more typical chorus stop, has a great deal of fundamental. The Trompette, although it may be quite light in tone, dominates the ensemble by sounding with a maximum of éclat, a blaze of partials that come from as high up as *six octaves* above the note sounded, and the maximum of clang-like dissonance that can be voiced into a Reed stop and still have it usable as a musical sound. Some Trompettes are almost soft in effect, and their blending characteristics resemble those of the keen Strings in many cases. The 16′, 8′, and 4′ Trompettes (with intramanual couplers) make a broad and majestic brass tone that is equalled by few other stops. The organist should realize that there is an emotional let-down after hearing the climactic effect of such a stop, alone or in combination.

The 8′ Solo or Fanfare Organ Trompette may be used to carry melody line, like any other stop, or as a fanfare, chorded and uncombined. The Swell Organ's Trompette is usually voiced for ensemble playing as well as solo work. The 16′ manual rank always supports a chorus of Reeds, perhaps all Trompettes, and will give the unison pitch when played an octave higher.

The Trompette pipes are inverted-conical spotted metal tubes, whose narrow forms are white with a high content of tin to insure that many overtones are formed. Treble pipes are double-length to create volume in the higher notes of the scale. The shallots are fully "open" to encourage formation of partial tones. The reeds are tuned by wire springs that stick down into the boots of the pipes, and the resonators are tuned by rolling the metal in their slots. See TRUMPET. Synonym: FRENCH TRUMPET.

TROMPETTE en CHAMADE. A manual Chorus Reed of 8′, occasionally 16′ or 4′, mounted in an exposed position on the front of the screen of the main organ or in some other part of the building, as on the Echo Organ's screen, and in the *horizontal* position. This position of the pipes, unlike the normal vertical position, allows the fundamental and overtones alike to expand throughout the building without so much absorption by other pipes, swell shutters, organ chamber walls and ceiling, and peculiar angles of reflection. Sometimes as high as sixty per cent of a loud Trumpet's sound can be saved by this type of installation. The higher-pitched overtones, particularly, because they are sometimes millions of times softer than the louder components in *the same pipe's note*, are preserved for the listener's ears. Since sound spreads spherically throughout any building's air-space, except for reflections, any sound is one-quarter the intensity at 100 feet of what it is at 50 feet from the source. This stop may have the pipes of the exponentially curved solid Brass Trumpet, the Ophicleide, Tuba Magna, or an especially voiced Reed for a certain location. Short-resonator Reeds and even flue pipes are also occasionally mounted in this manner.

Processional marches, antiphonal contrasts with the full main organ, fanfares, solo effects, and other uses exist for this Reed. The tonal advantages that accrue from high fidelity hearing of *all* organ pipes help the organ to seem more vital and animated, and the extensive literature of this instrument more interesting. The Trompette en Chamade in the new Aeolian Skinner organ in St. Thomas's Church, New York City, is one of the finest examples of this stop to be heard anywhere. Its broad, brassy, brilliant tone is fiery and fully developed harmonically, yet remains stately and dignified. Many examples exist in Portugal and Spain. See STATE TRUMPET, TROMPETTE. Synonyms: CHAMADE, FAN TRUMPET.

TROMPETTE HARMONIQUE. An 8′ manual Chorus Reed similar to the Trompette in tone but of much greater power, but not more brilliance in the higher-pitched overtones. The double- or triple-length resonators increase the total volume of sound output considerably, adding much loudness in all of the overtones down near the fundamental, and also damping practically all of the blatancy and dissonance common to many unison-length Reeds of loud tone. This stop has a louder fundamental than the Trompette. It may be preferred to the Trompette in an ensemble of Chorus Reeds, like those below, because it has more penetration and is of better blend with the loud Diapasons and Flutes. It is frequently accompanied by a Clarion and sub-unison Reed, perhaps on the Stentor or Fanfare Organ. Alone it makes a solo voice of loud, assertive tone. Its functions are the same as those of the Trompette or Trumpet. The *flue* stops in these examples firm the pitch and increase the degree of blend with the rest of the organ. They may be omitted if desired:

Stentor Diapason (flue)	8′		Trompette Clarion	4′
Stentor Mixture (flue)	VI		Trompette Harmonique	8′
Harmonic Tuba Clarion	4′	or	Contra Bombarde	16′
Trompette Harmonique	8′			
Brass Trumpet	8′			
Contra Bombarde	16′			

See TROMPETTE.

TROMPETTE MILITAIRE. An extremely loud and assertive Trumpet (or Trompette) of either unison or harmonic length, at 8′ on the manuals. It may be on a large Solo Organ or a special division, like the Bombarde. Its tone is not so unusual as its name, since it is difficult to find orthodox names in sufficient quantity for a very large organ which may have six to ten loud Trumpet stops in it. It has all of the functions of all of the other loud Chorus Reeds. See TROMPETTE. Synonyms: FIELD TRUMPET, MILITARY TRUMPET.

TROMPETTE QUINTE. A 5 1/3′ manual Chorus Reed belonging to the 16′ series of stops, which speaks at the interval of a fifth above the keys struck. It should be drawn with a heavy 16′ Chorus Reed to keep from unbalancing the tone. In practical application it is not often used without the big 8′ and 4′ Reeds in combination. This is the third harmonic of the 16′ sub-octave series, and is typical of only larger organs. It may be heard from a Stentor, Bombarde, or Fanfare Organ, perhaps in a dome. Its absence from the 16′ Reed choir would probably be noticed by the trained ear, since the *third* harmonic of any series of stop-pitches is important, and always a source of a full and satisfying sound. Certainly, if once heard under ideal conditions, the ear would crave for it again, particularly in certain forms of music. It can be designed to be Cornopean-like or extremely assertive, but is usually under the 16′ Reed it serves in loudness. In trying to assimilate it into the ensemble the organist should realize that it creates from thirty to fifty harmonics from each pipe, and is based on a fifth-sounding note. It would not be easy to assimilate when based on an octave-sounding note, but the *Quinte* Trumpet is much more close-toned. With the 8′ (and 4′), but without the 16′ Reed, this stop may sound too penetrating and brilliant. Such chords as middle C, D, F♯, and A, and even middle C, D, E, and G, exhibit this stop at its fieriest. It is livelier than the Bombarde Quinte, and may or may not be of the same timbre as the Trumpet Quint. An octave coupler and a mixture can intensify its effects. Practically speaking, a reverberant auditorium, wise use by the organist, the in-tuneness of the organ, and a staccato touch can help it to be a success in the music. These are not manual divisions but just Reed choirs:

Tuba Clarion	4′		Harmonics	IV
Trompette Quinte	5 1/3′	or	Acuta	II
Ophicleide	8′		Grand Fourniture	IV
Contra Trumpet	16′		Clarion	4′
			Trompette Quinte	5 1/3′
			Tuba Magna	8′
			Contre Trompette	16′

Trompettes of 16′, 8′, 5 1/3′, and 4′ also make a useful choir of Reeds. See QUINT, TROMPETTE. Synonym: QUINT TRUMPET.

TRUMPET. A Chorus Reed of 16′ or 8′ on the manuals, and 32′, 16′, or
8′ on the pedals. The 4′ or 2′ pedal pitches
may be called *Kornett*. This stop is made by
builders in a great variety of dynamics and
qualities of brightness. It might be called a
standard Great Organ Reed, but may not be
wanted with the flues on this division by
some organists. Small church instruments
can be found with a Trumpet-Oboe hybrid
instead of the Trumpet on the Great and the
Oboe on the Swell. Its percussive and mildly
assertive timbre offers an interesting contrast with the flues, and can be combined
successfully with the Great or Swell flues
when a bigger tone is wanted. It can thus
be useful in accompanying hymns, especially
when a louder tone is desired. It is probably
the most useful of Reed stops, because its
animated and mild brass tones do not present any grave problems to the organist. It
fits into all but the softer combinations quite
well. It has none of the spectacular effects of
the louder Reeds. Its dissonance component
is too small to distract the attention from
the vertical line of pitches in the big flue
ensembles. However, it does not belong in

The Chorus Reed form of pipe.
In this case it was styled a
Trumpet by G. A. Audsley, who
drew all of the line-drawings
used in this book.

a small Choir or Positiv, or any other division that speaks from a carefully wrought combination of delicate flues.

The Cornopean can be the "Trumpet" of a larger Choir Organ, and the
fiery Trompette is a favorite on the Swell. The Great may have this stop
or a Tromba, and the Solo a special form of this stop or perhaps a Tuba.
Bigger and louder Trumpets can be heard in Bombarde or unusually large
Solo Organs. The pedal Trumpets are not so popular with organists because of their strong dissonance. The Bombarde or Trombone is mostly
preferred. In very large organs there are always several Trumpets of different timbres to sound in contrast to each other. Fagottos can be designed
to share the Trumpet's overtones at any pedal pitch. The 32′ pedal rank
is less useful than a Bombarde.

The most typical Trumpet quality is heard from GG to F^2. Below and
above these pitches this Reed stop sounds more like the average Chorus
Reed. Since this stop often sounds with the Diapason, let us compare the
harmonics of the *reed* and *flue* structures through these two stops, both at
8′. The Diapason's tone is generated by the flexible compacting and vac-
uuming of the (widely separated) air molecules at the upper lip of the
pipe. This motion is taken up in some of its modes by the body of air in
the pipe itself, which acts as a "resonating" column to the edge-tones of
the lip. The Trumpet sounds by means of a thin brass reed that swings

like a pendulum against a hollow shallot, which, in turn, is connected to the body of air in its "pipe." Since each of these devices has some sort of resonating air column that greatly extends the strength of its original tone, the lower *harmonics*, at least, of each will sound on quite similar pitches, as from middle C, for example. Scale, wind pressure, and many other factors affect the number and relative loudness of these harmonics. Each one has a prominent fundamental. The Trumpet's train of harmonics is at least twice as long as the Diapason's, and extends about five and one-half octaves above the note played; the Diapason's extends four and one-half octaves above its fundamental note. The Trumpet's train contains *neighboring* components which are very different in dynamic; the Diapason's components taper off quite smoothly in loudness, and quite suddenly after the third or fourth, perhaps even after the first. The loudest harmonic of the Trumpet can be any one of the first eight; the loudest of the Diapason is usually the first, but may be the second or third.

The Trumpet's lowest six to eight harmonics are of almost equal loudness, which, with a rapid speech, is the essence of *brass* tone. There are many dissonant harmonics in the Trumpet's tone, but only two or three, perhaps five, dissonants in the Diapason's. The reed speaks much more quickly than the flue, and its initial period is likely to be shorter but more inharmonic in the content of its transients. Practically no celesting between the two's trains of harmonics will be apparent if in perfect tune, since both series of harmonics are quite the same in pitch. The milder forms of celesting between stops just seem to be part of the timbre of the combination. Either one of these two stops can be the louder, of bigger tone, or stronger prime tone, but it is hard to imagine the Trumpet without some degree of brightness. Here are choirs of Reeds with the Trumpet, as on a Solo Organ:

Clarion	4'		Harmonic Trumpet	4'		Oboe Schalmei	4'
Trumpet	8'	or	Field Trumpet	8'	or	Trumpet	8'
Contra Posaune	16'		Contra Trumpet	16'		Dulzian	8'
						Contra Fagotto	16'

Many unusual examples of Trumpets and other Chorus Reeds, some *en chamade,* of many builders, may now be heard around the country. In order that the organist may understand more fully the *Reed* pipes that he uses with so much pleasure for himself and the listener, let us finish this Trumpet article with a few basic technical points. What really comes out of a Reed pipe is determined chiefly by three dimensional ratios:

1. the ratio of the large-end to the small-end *diameter* of the resonator; this determines which harmonics created by the reed will be emphasized in the timbre, and therefore the tone quality heard;
2. the ratio of the resonator length to the large-end *diameter;* this determines the support by resonance that the "pipe" will give to the deeper harmonics, and therefore the impression of pitch;
3. the ratio of the small-end (bottom) cross-sectional *area* of the resonator bottom to the minute opening between the reed *lamina* and the shallot (*échalote*) ; this, the first resonance cavity the sound wave enters, determines which components from the reed's creation shall enter the resonator.

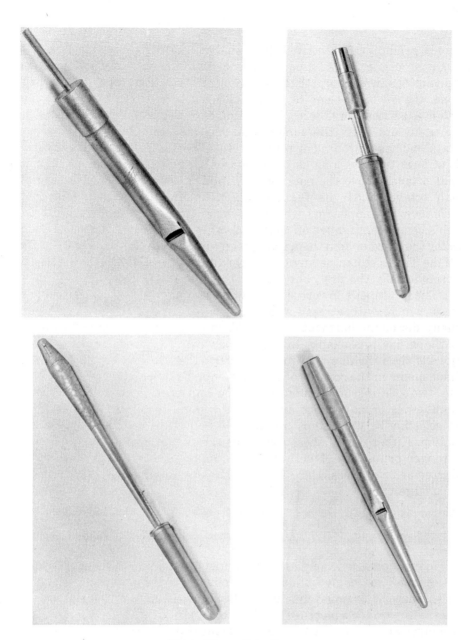

FOUR BASIC PIPE-SHAPES

Four middle C pipes especially photographed to show their structures. Top left, a *Rohrflöte* (Chimney Flute) of shiny spotted metal showing rohr in metal cap and ears at mouth. Top right is a *Chalumeau* of short length revealing its tuning wire extending from the pipe's boot. It tunes the brass reed in the boot, and the steel collar at the top tunes the small air column. Lower left picture is of an *English Horn,* shaped somewhat like the instrument. It is capped in some examples and not in others. When capped, sound waves must emerge from tiny opening above the roll of spotted pipe metal. Lower right reveals a *Koppelflöte* of conical form in just the top section. This specimen is less pointed than the average Koppelflöte, and would have a more "open" tone, subduing fewer of the higher partials. The Koppelflöte and Rohrflöte are *flue* (reedless) pipes; the Chalumeau and English Horn are reed pipes.

Courtesy: Wicks Organ Company.

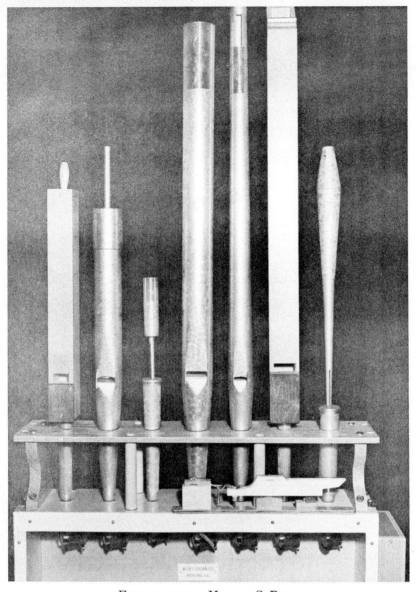

EXPERIMENTAL MIDDLE C PIPES

A rack of pipes photographed in the Research Room of the Wicks Organ Company. These pipes show a wide variety of construction features. On the left is a wooden Stopped Flute with stopper handle sticking out of the pipe's top, a high mouth cut-up, and a beveled upper lip. A Rohrflöte with metal stopper, chimney (rohr), and ears is next. The short pipe is a one-quarter length Chalumeau with a slender scale at its bottom. The fourth pipe is a Principal of full unison length, low cut-up, and steel tuning collar at its top. A conical Dolce Flute with a narrow mouth and a wide slot at its top is fifth. The sixth pipe is a Flauto Traverso with an inverted upper lip and metal shade rolled up on its top. The pipe on the right is an English Horn with a shape like that of the orchestral instrument. The two wooden pipes have hard-wood caps on their fronts below the mouths. The Chalumeau and English Horn are Reed pipes, the reeds and shallots hidden in the boots. A model of the Direct Electric Action of this company is seen at the bottom right of the picture. Magnets that open the pipes' valves against the wind pressure can be seen below the pipes' feet. Between the key contacts and these magnets there is nothing but the electrical circuit.

Courtesy: Wicks Organ Company.

There are resonant factors from the pipe-boot, other pipes' air columns, air-spaces in the chests, and the air-mass of the auditorium. The dimensions and pattern of flexibility of the reed itself determine the original elements in the sound; the above three factors determine which waves will be allowed to escape the pipe. These three have a natural authority over the timbre, pitch stability, loudness, and attack partials.

The wider the resonator is, considered as a whole, the weaker the overtones will be in relation to their fundamental; the narrower the resonator is in relation to its length, the less fundamental it will emit compared to its overtones. In a cylindrical, straight-walled pipe, like the Clarinet or Vox Humana, the even-numbered components are very weak and the odd-numbered strong. This makes the color easy to hear in pitch, pungent, penetrating, and sometimes quinty. Now if we can imagine the straight-walled resonator pipe *growing wider* ever so slightly at its top, which makes it a little tapered in form, we will hear the *even-numbered* components grow in the tone very fast, and all pungency quickly disappear, and the full bloom of the Chorus Reed's sound will appear. Another minute increase in the taper of the resonator will aid *all* higher harmonics to grow. Finally, after tapering has changed the form of the pipe from almost straight to funnel-shaped, as in the dullest of Horns, there is little left to hear except a poorly disciplined fundamental and a dim snarl of partials. In summary: *tapering* has moved the tone quality through the areas of the very bright Clarinet, Sackpfeife, Orchestral Oboe, organ-type Oboe, Trompette, Trumpet, Tuba, Tromba, and Horn, *in order*. Merely making the diameter of the resonator thinner, but keeping its sides straight (cylindrical), moves it through the color zones of the Basset Horn, Clarinet, Solo Vox Humana, Vox Humana, Krummhorn, Musette, Schalmei, and Regal, *in order*. Making the flue pipe or Reed resonator extremely narrow can choke out some of the partials, but *this* law of diminishing returns operates sparingly. Capping also muffles bright effects, but in a different way. These orders apply to unison and short Reeds.

It can be seen that one duty of the resonator is to marshal the complex of the reed's many harmonic (occasionally inharmonic) components into a musically acceptable tone. (The half-length resonator simply erases strength in the lowest harmonic: the fundamental; the quarter-length resonator erases strength in the lowest three harmonics [the 8', 4', and 2 2/3' in an 8' Reed].) The tubeless reed of the American reed organ (melodian) and the very few, typically European, tubeless reed stops of the pipe organ give the ear an interesting contrast with so many well resonated sounds. Perhaps the use of the *Aeoline Reed* and *Physharmonika* could add vitality to some kinds of music.

The large-scaled Reed pipes emit fewer harmonics because they can't support by their structural resonances many natural harmonics of the reeds. This is because these structural resonances are mostly inharmonic in frequency. The smaller-scale resonators can emit more harmonics, and therefore seem brighter, because their structural resonances are more nearly likely to be harmonic, i. e. like the true harmonics that come from the reeds. True *inharmonics* that sound between the natural frequencies are practically non-existent in low-pressure steady tones. High-pressure reed tongues assume a few of the plate-like vibrations that resemble the shaking in percussion devices, since they are solid metal and sometimes relatively thick. The reader is reminded here that the human ear can interpret overtones that vary in loudness, even in the same sound wave, over a trillion times in strength; it can hear, therefore, unbelievably "soft" frequencies. It can also accept unusually subtle variations in the timing of all sounds, including the initial transients. Formant frequencies from both flue and Reed pipes can contain inharmonic whisperings. True inharmonics are most easily detected in initial and dying-away transients. Their effect adds to the percussive impact of all pipes on the ear. Their ever-changing character is of great usefulness to all organists, and particularly those who specialize in the staccato sounds of the Classical compositions. For example, a Trumpet pipe can turn out a frequency of 2.875 x the fundamental's. Such a component in the initial period of a 16' or 32' stop, or even at 8' or 4', can greatly increase the listener's interest in the timbre, as well as pitch. Inharmonics can linger because of reverberation (like the four seconds in St. Patrick's Cathedral, New York City) in the ear, and also linger in the memory.

In a clean-toned Tuba pipe of, say, fifty natural harmonics, in perfect tune, at least three-quarters of these harmonics are dissonant with the notes of the scale, *especially those higher up in the train.* These dissonant harmonics are perfectly normal, and must be distinguished from true *inharmonics,* which are less common. All of these harmonics that are not octave-sounding with their own fundamental will beat, perhaps imperceptibly, with practically all the harmonics of the other notes in the same chord. It can thus be seen that one of the distinguishing elements of Trumpet or Tuba timbre consists of great masses of harmonic components which, although much louder than in Strings, extend upward to five or six and one-half octaves above the notes struck. This does not take into account octave couplers or complex chord-forms.

A general conclusion is that the more harmonics sound from a pipe the greater will be the ascent into the realm of the dissonant, as well as that of the brilliant. Since the highest harmonics are relatively soft, Reed tone is not usually unpleasant.

A Trumpet pipe at CCC is from 9 to 5 inches in diameter at its top; the CC pipe is from 6 to 3.5 inches. Spotted metal tubes give a better timbre. Basses may have it in their tops. Unison length is used. See TROMPETTE.

TRUMPET CLARION. See CLARION.

TRUMPET ROYAL. An 8' manual Chorus Reed of the Trumpet species, sounding with some degree of blatancy, a free-toned vibration, and great loudness. It is a Solo or Fanfare Organ stop. See TRUMPET, TRUMPET SONORA.

TRUMPET SONORA. An 8' manual Chorus Reed of the Trumpet

species, sounding with less blatancy than the Trumpet Royal, but relatively smooth for a Trumpet. Both stops are used as solo or ensemble Reeds of great penetration and assertiveness. These names indicate highly academic differences, since the builders interchange names and timbres. See TRUMPET, TRUMPET ROYAL.

TUBA. A general stop-name used to indicate the Chorus Reeds of louder and *firmer* quality than the Trompettes or Trumpets, and mostly made from thicker *reed* stock (a soft brass alloy) than these. Manual Tubas are in great variety, even within one stop-name, and at 16′ or 8′ on the manuals, and 32′ or 16′ on the pedals. The *Tuba Clarion* (not a Trumpet timbre) is at 4′ on the manuals and 8′ on the pedals. The listener is equally aware of a Tuba stop's firm fundamental and elaborate extension of loud overtones, which tower upward from a 16′ fundamental, for instance, as frequencies equivalent to 8′, 5 1/3′, 4′, 3 1/5′, 2 2/3′, 2 2/7′, 2′, 1 7/9′, 1 3/5′, 1 5/11′, and 1 1/3′ ranks ("stops"). Since *all* of the lower twelve Chorus Reed harmonics can be almost equally loud, one can "hear" all of these pitches *in any one note*, as from middle C. They are not individually discernible because natural law does tune each accurately, making an unusual degree of unity among them.

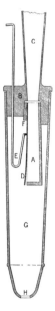

Mechanism of a reed pipe: A, shallot; B, block; C, resonator of the reed's vibrations, sometimes referred to as the "pipe"; D, the reed; E, tuning spring; F, wedge to hold reed in place in the block; G, the boot that encloses the reed and shallot away from the atmosphere, and also supports the whole mechanism and the resonator. Reed boots are needed also for resonance of tone. H is the foothole for the entrance of the wind.

In the Trumpets the fundamental may be weakened to give energy to the overtones. The free-vibrating sound of the Trumpets is not in most Tuba tones. Either stop can climb to the seventieth or eightieth harmonic in any middle-range note. Almost any manual Tuba pipe sounds its overtones to past the threshold of audibility, and some far beyond, as G^1, for instance. For this reason the octave Clarion 4′ on the manuals need not be made too bright. Weighted reeds in the Tuba basses make a better blend and finer articulation, since they create strength in the lower part of the train and also eliminate some higher partials, as well as steady the pitch of the longer reeds. The Tuba Sonora is developed in the lower overtone range, and the Tuba Magna throughout the whole overtone range, for example.

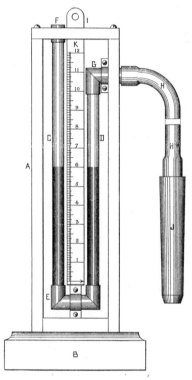

Water gauge for measuring wind pressure. J is placed in pipe-hole of windchest, and difference in heights of water in C and D indicates pressure in inches. A is frame, B is base, E is metal elbow tube, F is funnel, G is an elbow, H is flexible hose, I is ring, and K is scale in inches.

The *harmonic structure* of the Tubas is a little more on-pitch than that of the Trumpets, but not so much on-pitch as that of the big flues like the Stentorphone and Diapason. As the train of harmonics is ascended *all stops* are likely to have more and more individual harmonics stray from their accepted positions as even multiples of the fundamental's frequency. This makes the tone color interesting up to a certain point, depending upon the pitch. Beyond that point it ceases to give pleasure, and the listener dislikes the tone as too dissonant. Chords, couplers, tremulants, and re-reflections from walls all complicate the matter unbelievably for the ear. Truly spurious partials (not to be called *harmonics*, but *inharmonics*) also occur, especially at higher wind pressures. These roughen the tone and must be masked by other well-chosen stops. The thin edges of all brass reeds also have their own pattern of cymbal-like motion, giving a pleasant variation to all tones. The formant of the brass and the resonator, as well as the air column's resonant action, all contribute to the Tuba's tone, either by addition of certain partials or subtraction of other partials.

Tuba resonators are inverted-conical in shape, and sit on the tops of the boots of the reeds, where they can pick up the reeds' sound waves and relay them to the auditorium. They amplify the fundamental and most of the lower-pitched overtones, as well as some of the higher-pitched. The weaker ones and those that are not mathematically related to the majority may be lost by actual collision with the stronger waves. Pipe metal, wood, rolled zinc, laminated metals, and spotted metal are used in resonators. The last named gives the best tone in the brilliant Tubas. Up to a point of diminishing returns, a greater flare gives more support to the fundamental, and a more slender shape support to the overtones. Resonators of greater flare must be longer to be effective; resonators of less flare are shorter. Wooden resonators, quite frequently seen, are less likely to absorb the lower fundamental tones, but may absorb the higher overtones in their cells. This makes them quite usable in the 32' octave, sometimes in the 16' octave.

A simple classification of the Tubas and Trumpets follows. It should be remembered that these stop-names are assumed to have their *average* voicing. Builders frequently interchange the tone qualities and names. There are also differences between the European and American traditions:

1. Typical Tuba tone of loud fundamental and brilliant overtone structure:
   > Tuba Harmonic
   > Tuba Imperial
   > Tuba Magna
   > Tuba Major
   > Tuba Mirabilis

2. Loud fundamental tone emphasized at the expense of the brilliance of the overtones:
   > Bombarde
   > Bombardon
   > Stentor Bombarde
   > Trumpet (chorus type)
   > Tuba Sonora

3. Free and "open" brass tone emphasized at the expense of the fundamental:
   > Brass Trumpet
   > Posaune
   > Trombone
   > Trompette
   > Trompette en Chamade
   > Trompette Harmonique
   > Trompette Militaire

4. Free and "open" brass tone less noticeable than the fundamental:
       Tromba
5. Extremely powerful in both fundamental and overtones:
       Ophicleide
6. Less powerful Chorus Reeds:
       Cornopean
       Tuba d'Amour
       Tuba Minor

See TRUMPET.

TUBA CLARION. An octave Tuba (not a Trumpet) at 4′ manual pitch, and 8′ pedal pitch. This Reed forms the treble of the Tuba choruses, as the *Clarion* (not a Tuba) forms the treble of the Trumpet choruses. This is a typical selection of stop-names found in each manual chorus:

Trumpet Chorus		Tuba Chorus	
Clarion	4′	Tuba Clarion	4′
Trumpet	8′	Tuba Magna	8′
Contra Trumpet	16′	Contra Tuba	16′

The pedal choruses have much the same names, except that they are an octave lower — 16′ instead of 8′, etc. The Tuba Clarion, like the Clarion, should not take the listener's attention from the unison pitches. The Clarion is more free in tone than the Tuba Clarion, and also more likely to contain clang. See TUBA.

TUBA d'AMOUR. A smooth-toned Chorus Reed of 8′ manual pitch, with a tone color that is comparatively free from many of the brilliant upper partials that are in all other Tuba stops. The tone is harmonically full up to approximately the twentieth or twenty-fifth harmonic position, and definitely brass-like, since it has many of the lower harmonics in almost equal loudness. The Tuba Sonora's forceful and big tone is, however, never achieved by this Tuba. This is both a solo and ensemble stop. It is sometimes warm in tone, but never mellow like the Waldhorn. It has none of the horn quality of the French Horn. It has practically no clang-tone. It is free from dissonance and that assertive manner of speaking heard in most of the Tuba tribe. It has none of the *Tuba Horn* quality of the theater organ. Its partly capped tubes are small compared to average Tuba scale. It is found in any division of the organ except the Choir or Positiv. See TUBA.

TUBA HARMONIC. See HARMONIC TUBA.

TUBA IMPERIAL. An 8′ manual Tuba of loud, brilliant tone, in most examples louder than even the Tuba Magna. It usually does not assume the brassy and dominating quality heard from the Tuba Mirabilis, however. It is a solo and ensemble Tuba typical of the brass-wind quality heard from all but the few soft Tuba stops. This particular Tuba is voiced, not to agree with its name, necessarily, but as another in the variety to be heard in a large organ. Some large organs have five to ten loud solo Tubas of different degrees of *volume, brilliance, strength of fundamental,* and *clang-tone*. The Imperial Tuba is usually strong in all of these four tone qualities, and is usually in the Solo, Fanfare, or Bombarde division. There are several different kinds of loudness in a loud organ stop of any sort. Each loud stop, whether flue or reed, bass or treble, has some variety of the following *elements of loudness*:

a) amplitude of the fundamental;
b) total number of overtones;
c) amplitude in any particular range in the train of overtones;
d) brilliance of initial overtones;
e) percussive generation of *each* individual sound wave;
f) degree of clang (beating between loud, high-pitched overtones);
g) many repeated reflections from hard walls (reverberation);
h) multiplication of overtones by many notes in a chord;
i) multiplication of notes by couplers;
j) in-tuneness of the organ;
k) total number of dissonant partials (usually the higher-pitched);
l) number of spurious partials not in any relation to pitch;
m) closeness of pitch of notes in a chord (C-D-E-G being "loud").

See TUBA, TUBA MAGNA.

TUBA MAGNA. A typical *loud* and *brilliant* Tuba tone, at 8′ on the manuals, and 16′ on the pedals. The fundamental as well as the train of overtones are both developed to close to the maximum extent possible for any particular wind pressure, but not to the extreme extent as heard from the Ophicleide or Tuba Mirabilis. Many large church organs have this stop, sometimes just as "Tuba" on the stop knob. It blends well with itself when intramanual couplers are drawn, and it also joins the stops of the Swell, Great, or Pedal Organs with excellent blend when the intermanual couplers are drawn. It is the supreme solo voice of many organs of moderate size, and can be heard from many others on the Swell or even Great when only two manuals are present. It should not overwhelm the ensemble, however, because the full organ will become in effect nothing but a Tuba if it is voiced to be too loud. The flue stops, including mixtures, must be heard to make a desirable ensemble. The flue chorus of the organ, not the Reed Chorus, is still the *basic tone* of the organ. The Reed Chorus is the basic tone of the Bombarde or Fanfare division.

The pedal's Tubas are in a great variety of loudness and timbre, always being designed to match the manual's Tubas, the building where the organ is installed, and the type of music to be played. The average rank is quite firm in tone, having none of the 32′ and 16′ trumpets' looseness of vibration. The brilliance and transient partials of most deep Ophicleides and Posaunes are kept out of the Tubas. A common problem of builders is to design a pedal Reed to balance the tone of a whole ensemble as well as that of only a particular chorus of stops. Space and funds are not always available with which to supply the organist with the variety of pedal stops that he needs. (See CONTRA BOMBARDE, CONTRA TUBA.)

The inverted-conical pipes of the Tuba Magna are of spotted metal, at least in the top halves or thirds, of wider flare in those ranks intended to be less brilliant, and thick-walled to keep them from absorbing the lower harmonics they themselves resonate. Tubas and Trumpets have the unison length, except the treble octaves, where they are double-lengthed to both build up power and eliminate the unneeded higher partials. The bass reeds may have weights screwed on the bottoms of their tongues. These increase the fundamental harmonic, a desirable factor at this pitch, and make it possible to voice the reed more efficiently, as well as quickening the speech. If of very high pressure, the brass reeds will have to be especially curved to make a tone quality to conform to the name on their stop key. Enclosure, although better for most solo stops, wipes out much of the timbre of any stop, including a loud Reed such as this. See TUBA.

TUBA MAJOR. See TUBA MAGNA.

TUBA MINOR. A Chorus Reed of 8′ manual pitch, having a true Tuba quality of tone in both strength of fundamental and harmonic development, but not of the same loudness. (This Tuba would be referred to as "close-toned" if of limited harmonic train.) This Tuba in a large organ may appear in the Echo, Swell, or even the Choir. It adds that energy of tone and percussive impact heard in all Tubas, but at less intensity than normally. This Tuba may have any type of voicing (the name merely indicates reduced volume), either brassy, comparatively dull, like the Tuba Sonora, or of the average type heard in the Tuba Magna. It is a solo and ensemble stop alike. It has none of the horn quality heard in the *Tuba Horn* stop. It usually has no clang-tone or blatancy. It is a most versatile Reed, firmer in voice and louder than the Cornopean. See TUBA.

TUBA MIRABILIS. An unusually brass-like and intensely loud Tuba, of 8′ manual pitch, voiced to give the maximum amount of clang-tone and higher upper partials possible from a brass reed with resonator. It is a brilliant fanfare stop and a solo voice of great magnificence. It can build up any ensemble of flue or Reed stops to an impressive tone, particularly with 4′ and 16′ intramanual couplers, although it is usually inferior to the Ophicleide in volume of sound. Several styles of voicing exist. Probably the most useful is the "silvery" type, because it blends more easily. The rough, strident form, much admired by a small clique of organists, has unusual penetration, but blends poorly. The 40 to 80 harmonics of *each pipe* of this rank make a stately and splendid peal of sound; chorded, the notes build up a cymbal-like effect that is of much usefulness in processional marches and in contrast to the full flue Chorus. The magnificent mid-range usually given this Reed is its most typical sound. The pipes vary from other Tubas mostly by having reeds of unusual curvature and shallots of more open construction. See TUBA, TUBA MAGNA.

TUBA PROFUNDA. See CONTRA TUBA, TUBA, TUBA MAGNA.

TUBA QUINT. A Chorus Reed of 5 1/3′ on the manuals, and 10 2/3′ on the pedals. These pitches are the third harmonics of the sub-unison series of stops. They should be drawn with powerful Chorus Reeds of 32′ on the pedals, and 16′ on the manuals. Such pitches as these, speaking from loud Reed pipes, are useful in filling up the tone of a large Reed Chorus with unusual brilliance. They are proper in only the acoustical environments that can absorb them, needing at least the 1.8 seconds of reverberation that are considered by experts to be the ideal for music. They are heard only in the largest organs that have the other stops to sound well with them, such as the 32′, 16′, 8′ and 4′ Tubas or Bombardes, and perhaps also a large mixture. Typical choruses that include this stop are as follows:

Bombarde Organ		Pedal Organ	
Stentor Mixture	VI	Contra Tuba	32′
Tuba Profunda	16′	Bombarde	16′
Tuba Magna	8′	Tuba Magna	16′
Tuba Mirabilis	8′	Tuba Quint	10 2/3′
Tuba Quint	5 1/3′	Octave Tuba	8′
Tuba Clarion	4′		

See BOMBARDE QUINTE, CONTRA TUBA, TROMPETTE, QUINTE, TUBA, TUBA MAGNA.

TUBA SONORA. A solo and ensemble Chorus Reed of 8′ manual pitch, not usually represented on the pedals. This species of Tuba is distinctly different from the other Tubas. It has an unusually intense ground tone (fundamental), and its complement of harmonics is mostly down in the range near the fundamental. The source of clang and dissonance—the higher harmonics of the train — is not very audible in it. Frequently it appears in the same Solo of large organs as the Tuba Mirabilis or Brass Trumpet, because these together can give an unusually majestic tone, both in chords and as single solo notes; each singly also has its uses. This is not a dull Reed, however. If chorded, it assumes more brightness; if played in a melody, it can penetrate almost all other stops. The player should remember that adding notes to a chord, either with couplers or more fingers, makes all stops brighter, perhaps increasing the harmonics heard several hundred per cent. The twenty to thirty-five harmonics in each note taper quite evenly in loudness as they ascend in pitch from the ground tone, and there are many really sounding at approximately the same loudness, but none that "peak" in volume, as in the Tuba Mirabilis and Trompette. This tone is therefore *smooth, firm, very loud,* and dominating. Contests between theater organ and orchestra mostly gave the victory in loudness to the big keyboard instrument, no doubt because of this Tuba and a few couplers. See TUBA.

TWELFTH. A Foundation rank of 2 2/3′ on the manuals, and 5 1/3′* on the pedals. This is an individual rank of pipes, usually open metal under this name alone, and sounding the *third harmonic* of the unison series of stops on both manuals and pedals. It speaks at the notes one octave and a fifth above the keys struck, as at G^2 from middle C, and GG from the pedal's low CCC key. Its frequency relationship with the unison stops is as 3:1. That is, the number of vibrations per second at any key on any keyboard is three times as high when heard from a Twelfth as when heard from a unison. The Twenty-second, Fifteenth, Octave, and 8′ stops bear, respec-

*If the pedal's Twelfth is taken from an 8′ or 16′ rank it will not be in perfect tune because these ranks are tuned to the "tempered" scale. A separate rank would be tuned to the natural harmonics.

tively, pitch relationships with the unisons as 8:1, 4:1, 2:1, and 1:1. The
3:1 relationship exists between the third harmonic in a *Quint Flute*, like
the Quintaten, and its own fundamental, at any note on the keyboard. This
3:1 relationship is one of the true glories of the organ, and it is one of the
points of highest interest in the Baroque organ to some listeners, although
this organ has many other specialties of tone as well.

All series of stop-pitches have their own "Twelfths" as follows: 21 1/3'
(64' series), 10 2/3' (32' series), 5 1/3' (16' series), 2 2/3' (8' series),
1 1/3' (4' series), and 2/3' (2' series). Every organ, however small, should
have a Twelfth of 2 2/3' on at least one manual. A large variety of 8', 4',
and 2' stops does not give the thrilling effect of the unison's Twelfth in
many combinations. There is a hiatus in the complex of harmonics as
heard from any flue chorus when only 8', 4', and 2' stops are sounding.
The 8' and 4' need no other pitch to complete their ensemble, and the 8', 4',
and 2 2/3' ensemble is of use in some phrases of music. The Twelfth is
important for vitality of sound and, most of all, *unity of sound*. Without
it the ear is quickly cloyed; when it is too strong, the ear is satiated for
further listening. It binds the high-pitched stops to the unison-octave component. It sets the ear in readiness to hear other high ranks that are not
octave-sounding. *At the right volume* it gives transparency, not thickness,
to the tone. By itself, it furnishes no element of stringiness or horn-like
timbre to any combination. It is actually craved by those trained to listen
for it. It is a substantial element in the 8', 4', 2 2/3', 2' choir of pitches that
is at least the *theoretical pattern* for all stop combinations. As the lowest-
pitched non-octave-sounding stop it is the most important *unison* mutation.
Its octave, the 1 1/3' on the manuals, is also of importance. Both take part
equally well in solo as well as ensemble combinations. A piquant solo combination is the soft 2 2/3' and 4'.

There is no practical limit to the varieties of effect that the Twelfths
can give to the organ's tone. As an Echo Geigen Diapason, Diapason,
Gemshorn, open Flute, stopped Flute, half-covered Flute (Rohrgedeckt),
harmonic stopped Flute, or Viola, the 2 2/3' of the manuals offers many
new dimensions not appreciated until actually heard. More than one
Twelfth should be in each division if possible. There is no difficulty in
blend if the partials of the Twelfth are subdued to just the right extent.
Noticing the strength of the Twelfth in combinations is as necessary as
noticing the loudness of the 16', 8', or 4'. The obviousness of the Twelfth
often determines the usefulness of a combination of stops.

The normal Twelfth on manuals and pedals is an open metal Diapason
of less volume of sound and fewer overtones than the 4' and 2' Diapasons
that sound at either side of it. Its overtones must mesh and cohere with
those of the 4' and 2' alike. On it rest the mixtures and the Fifteenth. As
a stopped Flute the Twelfth is useful with softer ranks, often making them
"plump" with tone but not pungent or too stimulating. From middle C
every stopped Twelfth rank sounds approximately a D^4 as the third harmonic of *its own rank*. The Silver Flute, Harfenprinzipal, Dolce, and Dulciana all make valuable Twelfths for softer combinations. The recent

tendency of builders to emphasize the *vertical structure* of pitches, rather than additional 8' unison stops, could not be shown better than in the following examples of "straight" ranks. Couplers are fully effective with these ranks:

Example No. 1		Example No. 2		Example No. 3		Example No. 4	
Diapason	2'	Dulciana	2'	Erzähler	2'	Viola	2'
Diapason	2 2/3'	Dulciana	2 2/3'	Erzähler	2 2/3'	Viola	2 2/3'
Diapason	4'	Dulciana	4'	Erzähler	4'	Viola	4'
Diapason	8'	Dulciana	8'	Erzähler	8'	Viola	8'

Above these pitches, the 1 3/5', 1 1/3', and 1' may also be useful, perhaps as just soft open Flutes or Echo Geigens, higher pitches becoming softer. The smaller flue pipes of the higher stop-pitches make a great deal less volume of sound merely because their columns of air are of less weight.

The pedal's Twelfth is necessary in a complete choir of pitches, and especially for that clarity and pointedness of tone desired in much of the literature of the Classical school. Soft Twelfths are useful too, as well as the 10 2/3', which is the "Twelfth" of the 32' series of stops.

Since all Twelfths bring out a whole series of harmonics not duplicated by any other pitch, they must be relatively dull in some choruses of stops. This is especially true because the Twelfth is almost as low in pitch as the Octave. Spotted metal Twelfths are usually seen in the main flue Chorus. Plain pipe metal is also used, because it gives fewer overtones than spotted metal. Stopped metal Twelfths exist, but furnish only softer tones. Conical pipes and chimnied pipes are frequently seen at 2 2/3'; the first shape obviates any hardness of tone, while the second makes an *Echo Twelfth*. The *Major Twelfth* is a very loud form heard in the biggest Diapason Choruses. See Diapason, Fifteenth, Geigen Diapason, Octave, Wood Diapason. Synonyms: Nasard, Nasat, Octave Quint, Open Twelfth.

TWENTY-EIGHTH, FLATTED. A rank of Foundation pipes that speaks at 4/7' on the manuals, and 1 1/7' on the pedals. These pitches sound at the notes three octaves and a flatted seventh above the keys struck, which is at Bb^4 from middle C, and Bb^1 from low pedal CCC. It is best identified as the octave of the well-known Septième. It is a mixture rank in a few cases, speaking in the lower octaves where the Septième might be too low in pitch. It is never a separate stop knob.

TWENTY-FIFTH. A rank of open metal Foundation pipes that speaks at the unusual pitch of 8/11' on the manuals, and 1 5/11' on the pedals — that is, three octaves and a fourth above the keys depressed. It sounds from middle C at F^4, and from the pedal low CCC key at F^1. The 8/11' is between the 4/5' and 2/3' pitches, but, unlike these, it is not an orthodox mixture constituent. It has been heard in a few unusual Cymbals. It very roughly corroborates the eleventh harmonic of the unisons. It lends a very brassy brilliance and unusual timbre to any loud combination.

TWENTY-FIRST, FLATTED. See Septième.

TWENTY-FOURTH. A rank of open metal Foundation pipes at 4/5' on the manuals, and 1 3/5' on the pedals. It speaks at three octaves and a third above the keys depressed. It approximates the tenth natural harmonic of the unison stops, and sounds the E⁴ from middle C, and the E¹ from the pedalboard's low CCC key. It is included in the lower octaves of some Cymbals, Carillons, and Grand Fournitures. It is never a separate stop knob. It is brilliant and sharp in effect, sounding the octave of the Tierce 1 3/5'.

TWENTY-NINTH. A rank of open metal Foundation pipes at 1/2' on the manuals, and 1' on the pedals. On both manuals and pedals these pitches are represented in mixture ranks and also separate stop controls. This rank speaks precisely on the *natural* sixteenth *harmonic* of the unison stops. For example, its tone is in the composite of harmonics that make up the Viols, Oboes, and open Flutes. The manual's 1/2' is two octaves above the 2' pitch. It sounds at C⁵ from middle C, and at C² from the bottom pedal CCC. It may be labeled *Campana* or simply *Twenty-ninth*. The pipes may be large-scaled to emphasize the fundamental, almost the only valuable constituent in this rank. The pipes may be conical as an additional effort to strengthen the fundamental. This stop appears in almost every mixture, probably near the bottom. It adds brilliance to any ensemble or stop. It has none of the pungency of the fifth-sounding 2/3', 1 1/3', or 2 2/3'. It has none of the acuteness of the third-sounding 4/5' or 1 3/5'. It is a soft stop, breaking back in pitch two or more times as the scale is ascended. This keeps the rank in better tune as well as keeping the fundamental and a few overtones within the realm of hearing. In this high range there is not much point in designating pipes as Diapasons or Flutes or hybrids because many of their overtones are inaudible, as are also, for some persons, their fundamentals when approaching the note C⁷. If these small pipes are not made conical by the designer, the voicer may assume the privilege of coning their tops inward to prevent any fringe of shrill partials, and also to strengthen the lower harmonics (which include the fundamentals). Pure tin or spotted metal imparts a silvery, clean tone to these high sounds rather than just the daub of brilliance sometimes heard.

TWENTY-SECOND. A rank of open metal pipes of Foundation tone, fashioned after small Diapasons, speaking at 1' on the manuals, and 2' on the pedals. That is at C⁴ from the middle C key and at C¹ (middle C) from the pedal's low CCC key. The manual's 1' sounds three octaves above the unison 8' pitch. It is well known both as an independent stop knob and as a mixture rank. It may be a Hohlflöte, Spillflöte, Geigen, Sifflöte, Blockflöte, or a small-scaled Diapason in form but with the name *Twenty-second*, but it is most likely to be a soft Geigen whose short, narrow pipes are spotted white with tin crystals. Tin can impart brightness without hardness or shrillness.

Its small pipes duplicate many of the harmonics of the 8', 4', and 2' ranks of open form, but at a higher pitch on the eleven-octave range of the organ. Many of the harmonics are lost to the listener because there is only one reflection against the organ chamber walls; some are *too weak to escape even the walls of the narrow pipes*. Small pipes like these speak very quickly and thereby give the listener the idea of an animated tone and build up interest in the notes of the music; they are perhaps interpreted as a "new" timbre.

This stop's relationship to the other ranks of the 8′ *manual* series is shown in the following chart. It brings together the stop's (or rank's) *name, note* from the middle C key, *pitch* indication, and *harmonic* number:

Twenty-third	D^4	8/9′	(ninth harmonic)*
Twenty-second	C^4	1′	(eighth harmonic)
Twenty-first, flatted	Bb^3	1 1/7′	(seventh harmonic)*
Nineteenth	G^3	1 1/3′	(sixth harmonic)*
Seventeenth	E^3	1 3/5′	(fifth harmonic)*
Fifteenth	C^3	2′	(fourth harmonic)
Twelfth	G^2	2 2/3′	(third harmonic)*
Eighth (Octave)	C^2	4′	(second harmonic)
Unison (piano's pitch)	C^1	8′	(first harmonic; fundamental)

*These harmonics sound varying amounts off the notes of the equal-tempered scale when made by a rank of unison 8′ pipes. When made by individual ranks at these pitches, either as mixtures or mutations, the pitches of the ranks are pulled to conform to the natural harmonics' pitches. Each of the above ranks of pipes also has a complete set of harmonics *of its own* with its *fundamental* pitched on 1 1/3′, 1 3/5′, etc.
Synonym: SUPER SUPER OCTAVE.

TWENTY-SIXTH. A rank of open metal Foundation pipes resembling Principals of smaller scale. It speaks at 2/3′ on the manuals, and 1 1/3′ on the pedals, and sounds on both manuals and pedals three octaves and a fifth above the keys depressed. It is at G^4 from the middle C key, and G^1 from the pedal's low CCC key (the foregoing *names* of the keys, such as CCC, etc., are based on the assumption that a unison stop's notes are used to name the *keys*). It is heard in many mixtures.

TWENTY-THIRD. A rank of open metal Foundation pipes at 8/9′ on the manuals, and 1 7/9′ on the pedals. It sounds the notes three octaves and one note above the keys struck, at D^4 from middle C key, and D^1 from the pedal low CCC key. It is roughly in the position of the *ninth* harmonic of the unison series (on both manuals and pedals). It is a somewhat undiscovered source of brilliant, cymbal-like brassiness on organs. Although it must be used with caution, there are many possibilities for unusual beauty in this rank, particularly in the larger, higher-pitched mixtures, like the unusual Cymbals, Grand Mixtures. In actual practice it is seen as a small-scale, soft Diapason or Geigen Diapason. It could be a Dulciana as well. It is heard in ancillary Harmonic Choruses. It is usable as a separate *mutation* as well, since it is usable in a very few mixtures. If sufficiently subdued, it can add a new variety of timbre to some of the louder combinations.

UNDA MARIS. An undulating 8′ manual stop of very delicate tone, made from either one or two ranks of pipes. Its quiet and sedate tone frequently comes from a rank of Echo Dulciana or Viola Aetheria pipes tuned slightly *sharp* or *flat* to the normal pitch, perhaps as little as one-half to two beats in a second of time. It is assumed that it will be drawn with a soft rank of normal pitch, like an Aeoline, Echo 'Cello, Echo Open Flute, Nachthorn, or Spitzflöte. If of two ranks, it is *normal-flat* or *sharp-flat* in design. Sometimes two different qualities of tone are used, the less bright sounding the off-pitch effect. Some additional timbres that are used for this stop are: Echo Viola, Quintaton, Echo Violin, Muted Violin, Echo Dolce, Flauto Dolcissimo, and Dolcan. Specially voiced ranks are also sometimes used. The very soft Quint Flutes make an interesting Unda Maris, because their third harmonics make a very mysterious and placid tone in undulation with another rank. This is a soft background stop, hardly loud enough for accompaniments in many examples. See CÉLESTE, DULCIANA CÉLESTE, ECHO DULCIANA CÉLESTE.

UNTERSATZ. See MAJOR BASS.

VIENNA FLUTE. See ORCHESTRAL FLUTE.

VIOL. A general name for a String stop, whether imitative or unimitative. The Viole d'Orchestre, 'Cello, Viola, and Viole Conique (muted) are imitative, and the Salicional, Aeoline, and Gamba are unimitative. If this name, as just *Viol*, occurs on a stop key, it is usually an imitative String of keen, incisive tone, and mostly at 8′ on the manuals, and 16′ on the pedals. All String stops have come more recently to the organ than Foundation and Flute stops. Their harmonic structures are less easily blended with the flues and Reeds than those of other stops. Their inclusion in the main divisions of the organ (Great, Swell, Choir, Solo, and Pedal) is on a limited basis, even in organs of the orchestral design. The String stops sound a great mass of overtones, especially higher up, *not in pitch* necessarily, but in the range that is approximately between the fifteenth and sixtieth harmonics above each note's fundamental. (Each String pipe sounds from twenty-five to sixty harmonics, the keener stops sounding many more harmonics.) This is in the realm where the harmonics are dissonant with the notes of the scale, rather than consonant. This dissonance, of course, is the chief asset of any String stop, and is the source of the incisive, brilliant, cutting effect noted to some extent in even the mild Echo Viola. It must be kept in a certain proportion to total loudness in the stop in order to live up to the definition of its name, as *Keen* Strings, *Muted* 'Cello, etc.

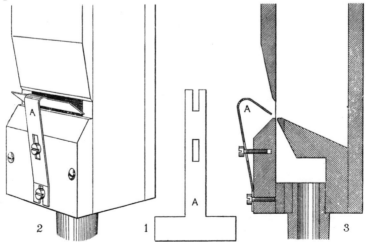

Wooden form of Violin at tenor C. 1 is detail of harmonic bridge (frein harmonique), 2 is front view, and 3 is interior, all of same pine.

THE NATURAL HARMONIC SERIES

Number of Harmonic (First Harmonic is the Fundamental)	Based on an 8' rank of open pipes sounded from middle C*		Pitch on Manual Stop Control	Present in Stopped Pipes**	Amount of Dissonance with Equal-tempered Scale Notes	Contribution to Tone Quality (Depending upon Pitch of Note Heard and Strength of Harmonic)
	Note Nearest Harmonic	Frequency of Harmonic				
32	C⁶	8372.02	1/4'	no	none	Most of these harmonics are not on the pitches of the equal-tempered scale, but speak between the notes. Frequently they are soft or inaudible. Many are octaves of lower harmonics. They form a mass of complex, beating tone among themselves. If this beating is loud, it sounds as clang.
31	B⁵	8110.39	none	yes	extensive	
30	B⁵	7848.76	none	no	extensive	
29	A♯⁵	7587.14	none	yes	extensive	
28	A♯⁵	7325.51	2/7'	no	extensive	
27	A⁵	7063.89	none	yes	considerable	
26	G♯⁵	6802.26	none	no	considerable	
25	G♯⁵	6540.64	none	yes	extensive	
24	G⁵	6279.01	1/3'	no	moderate	
23	F♯⁵	6017.39	none	yes	extensive	
22	F♯⁵	5755.76	none	no	extensive	
21	F⁵	5494.14	none	yes	extensive	
20	E⁵	5232.51	2/5'	no	considerable	
19	D♯⁵	4970.88	none	yes	moderate	
18	D⁵	4709.26	none	no	moderate	
17	C♯⁵	4447.63	none	yes	moderate	
16	C⁵	4186.01	1/2'	no	none	great brilliance
15	B⁴	3924.38	8/15'	yes	considerable	strong undulation
14	A♯⁴	3662.76	4/7'	no	extensive	coarseness
13	A⁴	3401.13	8/13'	yes	extensive	coarseness
12	G⁴	3139.51	2/3'	no	little	brilliant pungency
11	F⁴	2877.88	8/11'	yes	extensive	strong undulation
10	E⁴	2616.25	4/5'	no	moderate	thickness, density
9	D⁴	2354.63	8/9'	yes	moderate	moderate undulation
8	C⁴	2093.00	1'	no***	none	brilliance
7	B♭³	1831.38	1 1/7'	yes	considerable	fullness, closeness
6	G³	1569.75	1 1/3'	no***	little	pungency
5	E³	1308.13	1 3/5'	yes	little	thickness, density
4	C³	1046.50	2'	no***	none	brilliance
3	G²	784.88	2 2/3'	yes	very little	slight pungency
2	C²	523.25	4'	no***	none	brightness
1	C¹	261.62	8'	yes	none	unison support

*Middle C is taken as a typical note on the scale. Other notes would have the same harmonics relative to the pitches of their fundamentals. (Middle C has 261.6254954 vibrations per second; the equal-tempered interval is 1.059463.)

**Stopped pipes do not necessarily sound every one of the odd-numbered series. Half-covered pipes sound the odd-numbered series and selected even-numbered harmonics. All pipes have a spatter of inharmonic, high partials.

***Present in traceable amounts in stopped pipes because of "leakage" around the areas of the square corners of the mouths, especially in lower-winded pipes.

Chart Explanation: The Natural Harmonic Series

The open and Reed pipes sound all of this series of harmonics, providing the pipes are developed in brightness (number of harmonics) up to the top of this chart, or the thirty-second harmonic. The Reed's harmonics are slightly off the positions of the flue pipes', and this accounts for some of the "orchestral" effect they make. The stopped pipes sound only the odd-numbered, except for traces of the lower-pitched even-numbered. Small-scaled and high-pressured pipes are also likely to sound their harmonics off the accepted positions. Unlike notes of the scale, the pitches of harmonics are simply multiples of the frequencies of the fundamental.

The Strings in most organs are not permitted to upset the vertical façade of pitches that is the most distinguishing thing about the organ's tone. Main divisions have one or perhaps two String stops apiece, and the truly orchestral Strings are usually segregated in a division of their own. Even the mild Viola can disturb a very clean line of *vertical pitches,* such as 8', 4', 2 2/3', 2', 1 3/5', 1 1/3', etc., because it injects noticeable harmonics that are off the pitches of this basic series. The effects of the massed, bright tone of the Strings are more useful in the *horizontal* line, as is heard in the combining of several 8' unison Strings. Some Strings, like the Viola, can serve as accompaniments to solo stops. Others can form a background tone of any dynamic. Strings are solo stops, even when quite dissonant in timbre. A few serve as a source of bright timbre to the other flues, such as the Salicional, Aeoline, and Viola. They relieve the ear from too much hearing of the on-pitch harmonics, as in the Diapasons and Flutes. Except for the Reeds, Strings are the most colorful and vivid stops in the organ. The pedal notes are well served by Strings, especially the Violone 16', which could profitably be used in even smaller organs than it is usually found in.

The *Viols* of the organ are listed below according to their imitative, unimitative, and diminutive tones, so that a quick estimate can be made of those available. Some names are duplicative. Many of the Diapason-Strings and Flute-Strings of hybrid tone are omitted:

Imitative Strings

Double Bass	Viola
*Echo 'Cello	Viola da Gamba
*Echo Viola	Viola Major
*Echo Violin	*Viola Minor
*Ethereal Violin	Viola Phonon
Grand Viol	Viola Pomposa
Keen Strings	*Viola Sorda
Muted 'Cello	Viole
Muted Strings	Viole à Pavillon
*Muted Viola	Viole Conique
*Muted Violin	Viole d'Orchestre
Orchestral Strings	*Viole Sourdine
Orchestral Violin	Violin
Solo 'Cello	Violoncello ('Cello)
Solo Violin	Violoncello Pomposa
Viol	Violoncello Sordo
	Violoncello Vibrato

Unimitative Strings

*Aeoline	Muted Gamba
Bell Gamba	Salicional
Cone Gamba	*Sylvestrina
*Echo Gamba	*Viola d'Amore
Gamba	Violone

*Diminutive Strings

The String Organ is almost always a separate division of the organ, with its own stop controls, tremolo, swell box, swell pedal, couplers, pistons, and, most of all, its own tonal entity. Its separation from the main divisions provides it with additional pitches, variety of scales, mixtures that it could not otherwise have. Any of the String Organ's stops drawn sound on any manual when the *String Organ* stop control with the regular stops is drawn, and each manual has such a control among its stops.

There is a tremendous variety among the Strings. There is almost twice the number of harmonics in a String stop as in the average flue. It is true many of these are transients to the tone, but they serve to create that brilliant and undulating fringe of timbre that the ear recognizes as *String* timbre.

The Dulciana, Erzähler, Dolce, Gemshorn, and the open Flutes are dilutants to the keenness in String tone. If this ancillary is large enough, some should be included. Three examples of String Organs follow. The second needs a Violone 16' in the pedals, and the third needs a Contra Violone 32', Double Bass 16' (slender scale), 'Cello 8', and perhaps 5 1/3' and 10 2/3' String ranks of mild, soft tone. Some extensions down into the pedal's range are possible:

String Organ No. 1 (small)		String Organ No. 3 (large)	
Viole d'Orchestre (normal)	8'	Contrabass (normal)	16'
Viole d'Orchestre (sharp)	8'	Contra Dulciana (normal)	16'
Muted Violin (normal)	8'	Grand Viol (normal)	8'
Muted Violin (slightly flat)	8'	Viole d'Orchestre (normal)	8'
		Viole d'Orchestre (sharp)	8'
		Viole d'Orchestre (very sharp)	8'
String Organ No. 2 (medium)		'Cello (normal)	8'
		'Cello (very flat)	8'
Contrabass (normal)	16'	Viola (normal)	8'
Viole d'Orchestre (normal)	8'	Viola (flat)	8'
Viole d'Orchestre (very sharp)	8'	Ethereal Violin (normal)	8'
'Cello (normal)	8'	Ethereal Violin (sharp)	8'
'Cello (sharp)	8'	Muted Violin (normal)	8'
Viola d'Amore (normal)	8'	Muted Violin (slightly sharp)	8'
Muted Violin (normal)	8'	Sylvestrina (normal)	8'
Muted Violin (flat)	8'	Echo Aeoline (normal)	8'
Dulciana (normal)	8'	Dulciana (normal)	8'
Erzähler (normal)	8'	Fagotto (normal; reed)	8'
Violetta (normal)	4'	Violetta (normal)	4'
Sifflöte (normal)	2'	Dulciana (normal)	4'
		Viola (normal)	2 2/3'
		Sifflöte (normal)	2'
*5 1/3', 4', 2 2/3', 2'		*Dulciana Cornet	IV
**1 3/5', 1 1/3', 1'		**Carillon (tin)	III

All ranks, including mixtures, should be available on separate stop controls. *Very sharp* and *very flat* do not necessarily mean greatly off-pitched, but slightly more off-pitch than *sharp* and *flat*. See VIOLE D'ORCHESTRE. Synonym: VIOLE.

VIOLA. An imitative String stop of mild tone, at 16′ or 8′ on the manuals and pedals alike. This orchestral imitation has a somewhat round timbre for a String. The tone quality of most Viola stops can remind the listener of a soft Principal because of its firm ground-tone. It sounds harmonically rich and resonant. It just suggests keenness and incisiveness rather than displaying them openly. It is definitely a String, however, even in the *Muted Viola* and *Echo Viola*. It supplies a touch of pungency and just a little fundamental. The pipes are less small in scale than the Viole d'Orchestre. The 16′ manual rank is frequently found in the Choir Organ, where it provides a clean-toned and definitely pitched bass line to reinforce the accompaniment unisons. The Viola is one of the organ's four basic orchestral imitations among the Strings:

         1.   Viole d'Orchestre (Violin)
         2.   Viola
         3.   Violoncello
         4.   Contrabass (Double Bass)

The Viola forms a useful chorus, especially for the Accompanimental or Choir Organ:

Viola	2′	(Fifteenth)
Viola	2 2/3′	(Twelfth)
Viola	4′	(Octave)
Viola	5 1/3′	(Quint; to be drawn with a 16′ flue stop)
Viola	8′	(Unison)
Viola	16′	(Sub-unison)

The Viola is an ideal accompaniment tone, being midway between bright and dull, but with definite pitch-line that the ear can hear even far back in a building. A whole choir of Violas is used on several organs for this purpose. The *Echo Viola* is a truly beautiful soft String, and it makes a pleasing céleste. The solo Violas, *Viola Pomposa* and *Viola Phonon*, are louder than most Violas, and the Phonon is less bright in tone than the Viola Pomposa. The stop's metal pipes have tuning collars in some cases, since the slots reinforce the wrong harmonics in mild open metal Strings.

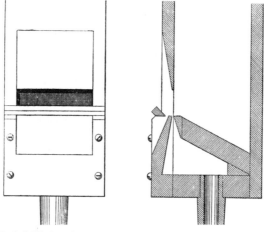

Pedal Viola pipe designed by Schulze as a 16′ stop.

Harmonic bridges and ears also are on the pipes, except in the treble ranks. Wooden specimens of great beauty exist, the wood cell's absorption of the higher partials being not unwelcome in this stop

VIOLA AETHERIA. A very soft String stop of Viola tone, at 8′ on the manuals. This is somewhat more like String tone than what is heard in the Dolcan and Echo Dolce, since those stops are inverted-conical in form, and the Viola Aetheria is cylindrical or even a little conical in shape. It has a soft purring of the String's overtones along with a fundamental that is obvious to the ear, but it is not on the dull side in most examples, although it is very soft, and makes an ideal accompaniment stop and background stop for all types of music. It would be desirable in the Great of a small church organ, since too few accompaniment stops are usually found there, and it will be suitable for the Choir's ensemble, giving the Gedeckt or Dolce a little pick-up in brightness. See VIOLA.

VIOLA CÈLESTE. An undulating stop of mild String tone, at 8′ on the manuals, and made from two ranks of Viola pipes, perhaps of different scale for a variety of effect. The off-pitch rank may be smaller and brighter to make the céleste beat a little more in the higher overtones. Or one rank may be of wood and one of metal, or one of tin and one of spotted metal. This is a milder céleste than most String célestes and is very suitable for accompaniment and background playing. It is not suitable for the Choir division, in most organs, because it forms too many undulations with the in-tune ranks. Such stops as this should be played by themselves at times, since the emphasis on the organ's *variety* of timbres always contributes to its effect of animation and to interest among those listeners who are not musical. See CÉLESTE, VIOLA.

VIOLA da GAMBA. A String stop of 8′ on the manuals, and occasionally 16′ on the pedals, which bears the name of the old instrument that it is intended to imitate. The modern *Gamba* stop does not imitate this instrument, but it derived its name from it. Compared to the Gamba, the Viola da Gamba sounds lighter, more shimmering and delicate, and of somewhat less volume. It always lacks the big-scaled depth of tone that is in most Gamba stops. It is inclined to be delicate, gentle in effect on the ear, and sometimes even soft, rather than keen and strong, and it thus lives up to the *Viola* classification. It has the usual functions of the String: massed tones in chords, solo parts, and contrasts with the less bright stops. Its slight degree of orchestral pungency comes from pure tin pipes in some organs. But it is at least of spotted metal. Its scale is a little larger than the Salicional's and its cut-up is very low, as in most Strings, to create a multitude of the higher partials. *String Gamba* indicates this stop. See GAMBA.

VIOLA d'AMORE. A variety of the Viola species, at 8′ or 4′ on the manuals, having a round, resonant, quiet sound, yet still being definitely a String timbre. This is a refined and soft tone. It may be heard from the Swell of a small church organ. It has quite a variety of tone qualities and degrees of brightness. Some examples are near-Flutes, while others are as stringy as the Viola. This is not an Echo Viola or Muted Viola in tone, because of the peculiar "singing" quality that characterizes it. This effect comes from only an unusual degree of *inner resonance* within the

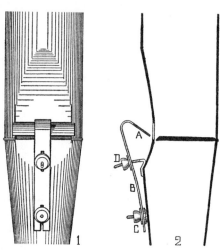

Viola d'Amore pipe at tenor C showing an unusually elaborate bridge: 1 is a front view, 2 is an inside view of the same pipe. A and B represent structure of bridge, C bottom attachment, and D adjustable attachment.

pipes themselves, at least in most cases, but sometimes from two ranks of 8′ pipes. Some examples are slightly flared, like the Dolcan, and most have harmonic bridges to stabilize the tone and encourage prompt speech. It is not properly a céleste of any sort. The functions include solo, accompaniment, and background playing. It can become richer and more pervading if added to a Dolce or Dolcan of the same pitch. See VIOLA.

VIOLA FLUTE. A Flute stop of 8′ or 4′ on the manuals, compounding in one rank the mild String tone of the Viola and the sympathetic round overtones of an open Flute of soft intonation. The *Viol Flute* is brighter in tone. This stop may resemble a very round-toned Viola d'Amore, and may in some examples even become quite string-like. See VIOLE FLUTE.

VIOLA MAJOR. A String of 8′ on the manuals, with a broad, prominent Viola tone that is not usually bright as well. Nor is it inclined towards the Diapason tone. It is a solo and ensemble stop. Most examples are larger than normal in scale and also somewhat louder. This name may refer to the louder of two Violas in the same division. See VIOLA.

VIOLA MINOR. A String of 8′ on the manuals, with a soft and sympathetic tone of less brightness than the Viola itself. It may be synonymous with the *Echo Viola* in some cases. This name may stand in contrast to a louder Viola in the same division, as in the String Organ. The name *Viola* may be used for a rank of soft Viola pipes in some cases. It combines with Strings and diminutive Foundation stops like the Dolce, Dulciana, Erzähler, etc. It can form any number of usable accompaniment tones with these and other soft stops. See VIOLA.

VIOLA PHONON. A solo String stop of 8′ manual pitch, with a tone quality that is typical of the Viola tribe of stops, except that this stop sounds broader and a little richer in harmonics than most Violas. Compared to the Viola Pomposa, this stop has more fundamental and fewer overtones. Although it is loud for a String, it can combine with Flute, Foundation, and other String stops. If on the Solo manual, it can be brought down to the other manuals by the *Solo to Great, Solo to Swell,* or *Solo to Choir* couplers. It is never cutting or keen in tone. A Viola may be given this tone without the use of this name. See Viola, Viola Pomposa.

VIOLA POMPOSA. The loudest Viola in the organ, at 8′ manual pitch, perhaps on the Solo or String division. This variety of Viola has the greatest harmonic development of any of this tribe, and is intended to be a solo stop, but is quite usable with all classes of tone. It has just a little keenness and orchestral pungency, but even as a loud stop it never approaches the Viols in keenness. See Viola, Viola Phonon.

VIOLA SORDA. See Muted Viola.

VIOLE. See Viol, Viole d'Orchestre.

VIOLE à PAVILLON. A small-scale String of 8′ or 4′ on the manuals, with an unusually bright but delicate tonality, inclining towards the Viols in timbre. Its pipe-form imparts to it a somewhat compound train of harmonics that is developed in the extreme heights and also in the range down near the fundamental. The pipe-form that accomplishes this feat is conical and very slender, and each pipe is topped by a narrow bell that is from one-half to one-eighth of its speaking length. The conical portion of the pipe dampens the middle range of harmonics and slightly increases the fundamental, usually weak in a String. The bell strengthens a fringe of brilliantly high harmonics that generally do not escape the walls of a cylindrical pipe of the same general dimensions. This is a solo and ensemble String, suitable for the Swell, Echo, or String Organ, and, if of louder voicing, the Solo. It forms a refined and very beautiful céleste. This stop is not assertive, as a Viole d'Orchestre may be, but easy for other stops of the same pitch to absorb. The Bell Gamba is of bigger scale and louder tone. Tuning these narrow pipes is accomplished by bending inward their large ears to flatten, or outward to sharpen, the pitch. This rank deserves the front position on the windchest because its myriad of high partials is easy to lose by absorption. See Viol.

VIOLE à PAVILLON CÉLESTE. A String stop of undulating tone, at 8′ pitch on the manuals, formed from two or three ranks of Viole à Pavillon pipes. Compared to the Viole Céleste, made from cylindrical pipes of about the same scale, this is a slightly softer céleste, and one of more fragile tone quality. It is not so generally useful as the Viole Céleste, or Voix Céleste made from Salicional pipes. It lacks the warm quality of timbre noted in many célestes of Strings. It is solely on the brilliant side, and not even pungent nor particularly orchestral in tone. It can be tuned to any of the pitch-patterns of a céleste but *normal-sharp* gives a normal rank for other combinations. It may appear in an Echo or String Organ, both of these locations offering other stops suitable for combinations with it. Chorded and with couplers it makes an opaque mass of tone which surprises the listener by being bright but not very loud. See CÉLESTE, VIOLE À PAVILLON, VIOLE CÉLESTE, VIOLE D'ORCHESTRE.

VIOLE CÉLESTE. A String stop of undulating tone, composed of *Viole d'Orchestre*, Viole Conique, or Muted Violin ranks. It is at 8' on the manuals. String Organs may also have it at the 4' or even 2 2/3' pitches, sometimes extremely soft at these pitches. The brilliant, keen, cutting tone of the Viols is heard in most examples. The Salicional is heard in most Voix Célestes. The names may be interchanged, but an orchestral, thin tone is usually heard under this name. This stop gives that realistic String tone that only pipes of extremely small scale can give. In fact, the pipes of this stop practically wipe out by friction (between the sound wave and the narrow diameter) any vestige of a fundamental, making the timbre a glittering mass of both on-pitch harmonics and dissonant partials that defies any analysis by the ear. The pitches of all partials, even in the lower part of the train, are somewhat distorted by the narrow scale and high pressure usually given this String. Chording this stop's notes, especially with couplers, creates a tonal mask best drawn by itself, or with other keen stops. Flutes of stoppered tone, even the Gedeckt, should be drawn with it with caution, since they stand apart. Open Flutes can bind themselves with it.

Because it undulates from three to seven times in a second, it wipes out of existence many of its own partials, changing the *Viole d'Orchestre* tone to a somewhat warm, neutral-colored, tenuous, and bright texture that is almost useless unless played in chords. Therefore it is not a solo stop, as a single-rank String of any species can be. This céleste is pleasant on the ear, even having some emotional appeal, but it makes problems for the organist who must use it without diluting the effect of the other registers. It is best used as a *contrast-tone with other stops,* and played just a short time by itself, perhaps with tremulant. It even contrasts with other célestes. It is usually too keen for the Swell Organ. See CÉLESTE, VIOLE D'ORCHESTRE, VOIX CÉLESTE. Synonym: STRING CÉLESTE.

VIOLE CONIQUE. A String of 8' on the manuals, having the tone of a soft Violin, more or less imitative according to the need of the other stops. *Violino Sordo, Muted Violin, Viole Sourdine,* or even *Muted 'Cello* may indicate the same tone quality. In the orchestra the mute absorbs many of the very high overtones; in the flue organ pipe the conical form of the pipe (and air column) do somewhat the same thing. The higher-pitched, and therefore weaker, overtones are the first to disappear in any pipe, even in a Reed, when a source of friction is met by the sound wave. Since muting involves the *number* of partials rather than loudness of the stop, lower wind pressure, lower wind quantity, a rounder edge on the lip, more nicking, a higher mouth, less tin content, and an increase in scale will also mute a flue pipe. A very slight taper serves to mute this rank in most cases, but a more pronounced taper will further reduce the overtones. Their strength will be given to the fundamental, octave, and a few other lower-pitched harmonics. The very slender Viole d'Orchestre as well as the large-scale Solo 'Cello are muted in this way, although either stop could be made cylindrical in form. Many pipes are tapered inward without that fact being recorded on the stop key by the builder.

The Viole Conique is a solo, ensemble, or accompaniment stop of the greatest usefulness, depending somewhat upon its volume. Better specimens may have a silvery, clean-toned, luminous timbre that comes from the reduction of the very high overtones. A muted céleste in any String tone is made by this form of pipe. See MUTED CÉLESTE, VIOLE D'ORCHESTRE. Synonyms: MUTED VIOLIN, VIOLE SOURDINE, VIOLINO SORDO.

VIOLE d'ORCHESTRE. An imitative String of 8' manual pitch, and 16' pedal pitch. Other pitches have different names, like *Violetta* 4' and *Contrabass* 32'. This name is associated with the thin, brilliant, cutting tones of the very small-scale Strings used by Robert Hope-Jones and other builders. Such small scales are not needed to fulfill the definition of this name, but the biting, pungent, rubbing quality of the orchestral sound is best simulated by the narrow scales, since nothing else but a reed can really turn out myriads of higher partials. In smaller organs, in the Swell, this stop may not have such a keen and brilliant timbre. It is less useful in a small church organ than the Salicional's *Voix Céleste*. The smaller church organs also have lower wind pressures than concert organs, and this automatically eliminates many of the most brilliant examples. Even in its milder (larger-scaled) forms this Viol is unsuitable, even in com-

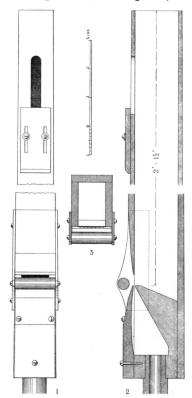

Imitative Viol pipe of wood, showing 1 as front view, 2 as inside cross-sectional view, and 3 as transverse section at mouth-line.

bination, to accompany the choir or congregation, because it lacks a definite pitch-characteristic. It functions as a solo stop, especially usable when combined with an 8' or 4' open Flute of soft tone, and forms a marked contrast with Foundation or Flute stops. The milder ranks of this stop may be usable as sources of bright timbre with other stops. Reeds and mixtures undulate severely, however, with some Viols. This Viol thickens the tone of any combination by injecting noticeable partials that are between the pitch-positions of the equal-tempered scale, thereby making a whole series of célesting tones, even when all ranks are on-pitch.

This masks the true timbre in other stops, a common objection to *all* Strings, and keeps them from lending their best to combinations. Dissonant partials are not in themselves unpleasant, but when they destroy tone quality and pitch and proper volume in other ranks, they are being improperly injected into the tone.

This beautiful and brilliant tone is sometimes placed in the Solo, perhaps not as a céleste. Its fundamental must be made louder than normal, however, in this division to make the melody notes that it plays clear in pitch. The Echo also has softer and milder forms, perhaps as the delicate *Ethereal Violin*. The Choir and Great are generally not considered suitable locations for it. The Pedal Organ's forms are needed when a String Organ is included in the specification. However, this Viol is most useful in a division of its own where it can have its own tremolo, swell shades, and pistons. It can make célestes of any degree of complexity there, and have a tremolo of even five or six beats per second without disturbing other stops. It is sometimes in the Swell with the bright Reeds and louder Flutes.

This stop has almost as many overtones* as the Trumpets and Tubas, but many of them are *transients* which come and go from the tone several times in a second. Fully 10,000 different tonal components are sounded by a chord on this stop in a second of time. Most are beats and beats within beats, etc. that are far too complex for any practical analysis, yet they contribute to the tone of this stop. This is not a convincing imitation of an orchestral instrument by the organ's pipes. It is only natural that the patterns of flexibility and vibration in the violin's gut and steel will not be the same as those from the "little tin throats," nor is the tonal formant of the soundboard available to the organ. The most realistic imitation of the violins is from six or more ranks of small-scale spotted metal pipes, some conical, some cylindrical, and all tuned to undulate very slowly as a tonal composite. If the undulation pattern is based on so slow a beat as one-quarter to two per second, the unrealistic fluttering of most Viole Célestes is avoided.

The low manual CC pipe (two octaves below middle C) is but 1.1 to 1.2 inches in diameter in the very thin and biting forms of this String. But realistic tones can be obtained from a scale of from 1.3 to 2.5 inches. The larger the scale the less keen and brilliant the tone. The Diapason's CC pipe, comparatively, is from 5.0 to 6.5 inches in diameter. The slender scale of the Viol may seem very small indeed when it is realized that the vibration formed at the lip must travel fully eight feet from mouth to slot at the top. It is no wonder that a higher wind pressure is needed by many Viols, because the intense friction between this wind and the pipe's wall breaks up the sound wave into many partials before it reaches the end. This rubbing, tortured tone comes from a twisting mass of air not unlike the violin's string in form.

*A profitable exercise for the organ student would be to make a complete list, arranged in numerical order, of the *frequencies* (i. e. pitches) of the lowest forty harmonics from *all* pipes of the 8' Viol sounding E^1, G^1, Bb^1, C^2 as a chord. Harmonics are even multiples, such as 1x, 2x, 3x, etc., of the frequencies of the fundamentals.

Standard procedure in the small-scaled open metal pipes is to fix the harmonic bridge on each pipe by hand in the optimum position to bring back into the tone some fundamental after the pipe has been purposely overblown. Steel collars over the slots at the pipes' tops are moved upward to flatten the pitch, and downward to sharpen it. The long slots amplify a few of the partials that would otherwise remain soft. The larger organs sometimes have their String divisions on from 10 to 25 inches of wind pressure. Organs of lesser magnitude in small churches and school auditoriums may have their Strings on from 3 to 7 inches of wind. Average pressure is around 3 to 5 inches. Tin in high proportion is needed by all String ranks, and all smaller pipes as well. Special solo Viols are sometimes made from *pure* tin. Tin, more so than any other metal, has the peculiar attribute of a special friction between its crystals and the moving wind, resulting in musically beautiful trains of overtones not heard from brass, steel, aluminum, lead, or other metallic pipes. Its formant is also not cold or hard in tone, as is aluminum's, for example. Very thick swell shades (with a large tone opening) enhance the tone and usefulness of the Viols. Of course, swell shades absorb the brilliant top part of any train of overtones, making the tone seem more like the milder Viola, and less like the Violin. See VIOLE À PAVILLON, VIOLE CÉLESTE, VIOLE CONIQUE. Synonyms: ORCHESTRAL VIOLIN, VIOLIN.

VIOLE SOURDINE. See VIOLE CONIQUE.

VIOLETTA. A String of octave pitch, on the manuals at 4', and on the pedal at 8'. The loudness, brilliance, pungency, and penetrating ability of this Octave are designed to supplement the unison ranks, but should not take the listener's attention from the harmony or melody being played. The Diapason-String hybrid tone may be heard from this stop, or it may be even more intense and keen than the unisons. All very slender flue pipes, especially those of short length (high pitch), make *weak* tones because they have only a small air mass to vibrate. Synonyms: OCTAVE VIOLIN, VIOLINA.

VIOL FIFTEENTH. A String of 2' on the manuals, and perhaps 4' on the pedals, conforming in loudness and timbre to the 4' and 8' manual Strings, with which it is usually combined, probably in a large String division. See FIFTEENTH, VIOLETTA.

VIOL FLUTE. A Flute of small scale and bright timbre, at 8' or 4' on the manuals. This is another in the great number of soft open metal or wooden hybrid tones in the organ that are made up of both the Flute and the bright String quality of tone. Under such a name any number of gradations of brightness or dull quality is possible. The String proportion in overtones appears in *any* flue pipe that is reduced sufficiently in scale. The relatively strong fundamental ground tone of all Flutes may be brought into a flue rank by manipulating the mouth's *cut-up* with the *scale* and *wind*. Hybrids between Diapasons and Flutes, Diapasons and Strings, and even the horn-like and woodwind-like timbres are possible to an experienced voicer. This is a brighter Flute than the Viola Flute. See VIOLA FLUTE.

VIOLIN. See VIOLE D'ORCHESTRE.

VIOLINA. See VIOLETTA.

VIOLIN BASS. See CONTRABASS, CONTRA VIOLONE.

VIOLIN DIAPASON. A Foundation rather than a String stop, at 8′ on the manuals, and 16′ on the pedals. It sounds at any of the many positions between Diapason and String tone that the designer of the organ believes appropriate to the rest of the stops of the division. The *Viola Diapason* is less bright than this stop, and has about the same amount of fundamental in its tone. The *Salicional Diapason, 'Cello Diapason,* and *Violone* are also hybrids. This is frequently the second Diapason on the Great or the first Diapason on the Swell of a smaller church organ. This is not a Geigen Diapason in spite of the name; the Geigen merely extends the normal Diapason's harmonic structure in volume, generally not also in number of harmonics. The *String Diapasons* are definitely stringy and quite incisive in their tones. They may accompany hymns or solo stops, or build up the timbre of any division. They are not usually so loud as the big Great Diapason. See DIAPASON, GEIGEN DIAPASON, WOOD DIAPASON.

VIOL MIXTURE. See STRING MIXTURE.

VIOLONCELLO. An imitative String of 16′ or 8′ on the manuals, and 16′ or 8′ on the pedals, the 32′ octave bearing the name *Contra Violone.*

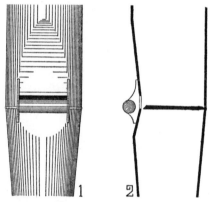

Violoncello pipe showing: 1, front of low mouth; 2, inside view with harmonic bridge in front of mouth and languid as a horizontal line.

It has the characteristic color of the orchestral counterpart, even to the extent of the "fuzzing" of the initial partials, the rich, broad timbre, and the well-known mellowness of the upper bass range. It has the mild pungency of the better String imitations, and it suggests some keenness and that big, warm tone that is very useful as a solo voice. Individuality is not lost by the organ's pipes because they make a tone that is several times louder than the actual instrument. This factor is characteristic of most of the organ's orchestral imitations. The 'Cello is often a céleste on the Solo manual, its on-pitch rank being usable with other on-pitch ranks, but it meets with some competition from the Gamba Céleste. It is frequently on the String Organ, and dilutes the thinness of the Viole d'Orchestre ranks there. It provides a wealth of overtones with which to brighten up the 16′ manual pitch, but this tone is better placed in the String Organ to avoid damaging the regular divisions' ensembles.

The pipes are of larger diameter than most Strings, and the 'Cello gives a fundamental, accordingly, of considerable weight. The Diapason's scale is always greater, however. At CC the cylindrical spotted open metal pipes are around 3.7 to 5 inches. Harmonic bridges on all but the high treble stabilize the pitches in the whole train of harmonics and make the pipes speak more quickly. The ears that hold these bridges stabilize the air-reed at the mouth, making the complement of partials more consistent. Wooden specimens are much more resonant than the metal, and some unusually beautiful ones exist, even in célestes, which may have only the off-pitch rank of wood. *Two on-pitch ranks of 8′* produce a magnificent solo timbre with célesting (but not beating!) between partials. Synonym: 'CELLO.

VIOLONCELLO POMPOSA. A solo form of the Violoncello, at 8′ on the manuals. This rich, resonant, big-toned, stringy timbre has a few more overtones in it than the average 'Cello stop. It is one of the loudest Strings in the organ. It may be on the Solo or String windchest, and may make the loudest céleste in the organ. It is usually made from metal pipes but wood provides an equally loud, deep, bright-toned effect if the rank is so designed. See VIOLONCELLO.

VIOLONCELLO SORDO. See MUTED 'CELLO.

VIOLONCELLO VIBRATO. A single rank of 8′ manual 'Cello pipes, of less than average loudness and harmonic development (brightness). Like the one-rank Aeolina and Unda Maris, this stop may be used to make a céleste with such ranks as the Nachthorn, Dolce, Salicional, Dulciana, Gemshorn, Viola, Erzähler, or a normally tuned 'Cello. It is more usable if of slower undulation, because the other rank with which it will be combined will probably be somewhat dull. See CÉLESTE, VIOLONCELLO.

VIOLONE. A 16′ or 8′ manual stop, and a 32′ or 16′ pedal stop, voiced as a Diapason-String hybrid, usually on the stringy side. It is most often seen as a bass stop, and on the pedals, but the manual forms, even at 8′,

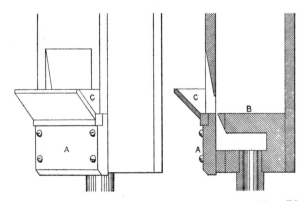

Wood Violone at CCC with a novel harmonic bridge. Pipe is 6 5/8 inches square inside. A is cap, B block, and C mouth.

are most useful as a tone builder in combination. It lacks the pungent orchestral type of timbre, and is likely to be louder than most Violin Diapasons and stringier. See CONTRABASS, CONTRA VIOLONE.

VIOLONO SORDO. See VIOLE CONIQUE.

VIOL QUINT. A String stop of mild tone, at 5 1/3′ on the manuals, and 10 2/3′ on the pedals, either voiced with the orchestral timbre of the small-scale pipes or as a sort of Violone. This is the "Twelfth" of the sub-unison series of stop-pitches. It should be combined with a heavy-toned 16′ on the manuals, or a 32′ stop on the pedals, to keep from unbalancing the tone. The organist should remember that all of its extensive series of overtones duplicate none of those heard from a 32′, 16′, or 8′ rank. If of the proper loudness with the other stops, it makes the tone cleaner and the pitches more obvious; if too loud, it will make the tone too "quinty," and the listener will lose all sense of balance between harmony and melody. It is usually heard from a large String Organ. See QUINT, VIOL.

VIOL TIERCE. A mild String stop of 1 3/5′ on the manuals, and 3 1/5′ on the pedals, intended to furnish the fifth harmonic of the unison series in String tone. Its effect is sharp, even from a Diapason of this pitch, therefore it should be drawn with caution in those few organs in which this is an independent stop. It adds closeness of pitch to the complex of harmonics that would be heard from the whole combination in which this stop would occur. It is seen in the larger String Organs, where it is necessary for a complete complement of harmonics. It is less valuable than the String Twelfth or String Octave. It may sound from a String mixture. Soft Viola pipes may be used for it. See SEVENTEENTH, VIOL.

VIOL TWELFTH. A mild String stop of 2 2/3′ on the manuals, and 5 1/3′ on the pedals, intended to furnish the third harmonic to the unison series in String tone. Both of these pitches in String tone are valuable. They add clarity and point to any *louder* flue combination, but it must be remembered their harmonics duplicate none of those of the octave-sounding stops. They are timbre creators and sources of brightness in combination, but they will slightly thicken the tone instead of making it luminous if added to any softer stops. They are String Organ Twelfths in String tone. The average Swell Organ could not tolerate such a stop, but an unusually large one could if the tone were mild, like that of an Echo Viol. The scale is determined by the brightness and loudness desired. Although narrowing the scale makes a generally softer tone, it also makes it on the brighter side, so a compromise must be reached in these two factors. It should never take the listener's attention from the unison tone. This is a stop that should not be overused, because it tires the ear and induces indifference to the music being played. The hybrid String-Diapasons are more useful than this stop, but are not so suitable in a String division. See TWELFTH, VIOL.

VOIX CÉLESTE. A String stop of undulating tone, at 8′ on the manuals, and composed in many examples of only two ranks of Salicional pipes, tuned *normal-sharp* or *normal-flat*. The off-pitch rank may be given a very mild voicing in order to keep at a minimum the beating effect of this stop, since each harmonic (and a Salicional has approximately forty harmonics) will beat with all other harmonics sounding anywhere near it in pitch. This is true even between different divisions of an organ, and even at some distance apart. It the off-pitch rank were brighter than the on-pitch rank, the minimum of beating would still be maintained, but this would leave the on-pitch rank duller in tone for other combinations. This is the most common céleste in a large or small Swell Organ. It is easier to combine with other stops than a Viole Céleste of keen and incisive timbre, although this is certainly not true of all Viole Célestes. The Voix Céleste has a mildly bright tone quality, and considerable warmth of effect on the ear, because it emits great numbers of soft but *high-pitched* partials that constantly vary in loudness; the Tremolo varies them in frequency.

Organists use it a great deal in accompaniments, but it is hardly suitable for this function, with either solo stops or voices, since it leaves a poor pitch-impression and creates a mask in front of all other tones. The single-rank Viola or Muted 'Cello is an ideal String accompaniment. However, a Melodia, Hohlflöte, Krummhorn, Harmonic Flute, or Cornopean may be well accompanied by the Voix Céleste, but this accompaniment takes on more of a *background* function than an accompaniment that gives good pitch-contrast.

Closing the swell shutters dulls the timbre of this stop as well as makes it sound with less of the célesting effect. The tremulant increases the célesting effect because it creates a myriad of initial partials every time it beats, and all of these beat with all other partials in the tonal complex. With or without other stops this one sounds well with intramanual couplers, if in tune, especially when chorded. It adds little to other stops in the way of brightness, since the beating wipes out many higher partials. Added to an 8' 'Cello this stop would make a full and broad-toned big 'Cello effect, well accompanied by a Gemshorn or Erzähler. It must be remembered that all in-tune String stops when added to other stops, especially at the same pitch, will céleste to some extent, for example a *Salicional* with a Gemshorn or Dulciana. Therefore the organist without a céleste may be able to obtain one by combining soft ranks, perhaps from distant divisions that are under different temperature conditions. This is not a successful expedient, however, between Flutes. See CÉLESTE, VIOLE CÉLESTE. Synonyms: CÉLESTE, VOX CÉLESTE.

VOX ACUTA. See ACUTA.

VOX ANGELICA. The name given to the softest single rank in the organ. It is at 8' manual pitch, and the pipes are either a special form made for this stop or those of an Echo Dulciana, Echo Dolcan, Flauto Dolcissimo, or Viola Aetheria. The Echo Aeoline may be used if a Stringy tone is desired. It can thus be seen that this stop may be Foundation, Flute, or String in timbre. It makes little difference, since its coloring is hardly discernible even to the organist. It should have sufficient overtones to confirm its own pitch, and this would seem to eliminate the soft stoppered Flutes, but perhaps not a Nachthorn of noticeable third harmonic.

It is one of the best of background stops and can make a soft accompanimental tone. Many beautiful examples exist, some in the Echo, others in the Swell or Choir. A *céleste* of two soft ranks may be heard for this stopname, perhaps between two different ranks of the above stops. This is a good stop to use when the organist wants to begin inaudibly, gradually making the congregation aware that there is sound coming from the organ. This very soft stop is frequently on the threshold of audibility, and may be enclosed in a swell box within a swell box, the inner shades being worked by a set of pistons. See DULCIANA, DULCIANA CÉLESTE, ECHO DULCIANA, ECHO DULCIANA CÉLESTE.

VOX CÉLESTE. See VOIX CÉLESTE.

VOX GRAVISSIMA. See RESULTANT.

VOX HUMANA. A Reed stop of manual and pedal pitches at 16', 8', or 4'. This well-known short-resonator stop in one of the oldest Reeds in the organ. It is classified as a *Regal* because of its covered, bright, intense series of overtones, made from shorter than unison resonators. It is in most of the world's organs: religious, entertainment, and residence. It attempts to simulate the human voice singing quietly in the distance. If it is accepted as an impressionistic interpretation, it is successful. This stop is useful in two ways:

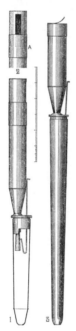

Vox Humana tenor C pipes. 1 shows capped and slotted form, 2 top of the same, and 3 open form with shade on top. Long resonance cavity in the form of a boot enhances tone in 3.

1. It is a tenuous, whispering, softly sounding mass of *high-pitched* overtones, *with tremulant,* and played in close-fingered chords near the middle of the keyboard. In thousands of church services throughout the country this sound effect may be used to uplift the sentiments of the congregation in such hymn tunes as *Rock of Ages* or *Abide With Me.* Perhaps a Gedeckt, Dolce, Dulciana, or 'Cello at 8' will enhance this tone.

2. It is a short-resonatored member of the *Schnarrwerk* class of Reeds, without tremulant, and played alternately with the Trumpet and Hohlflöte in such a piece as Bach's *O Lamm Gottes, unschuldig.*

Perhaps the very same pipes of the Vox Humana are used for these two types of music. Since this stop is usually at the 8' manual pitch, it may be desirable to use a 4' or 16' intramanual or intermanual coupler to obtain it where the organist wants it.

The *Vox Humana,* which was only a fan tremulant in the old parlor reed organs, may be found in any division but the Positiv or Great. It is found in the Swell of most smaller organs of two manuals, and in the Echo and Swell of larger organs. Many stops combine well with it to make ensemble tones, namely the Nachthorn, 'Cello, all soft Flutes, Dulciana, Clarinet, Dolce, Melodia, and Erzähler. It is not particularly useful as a source of high-pitched timbre; rather it adds a mysterious, somewhat inexplicable tone that at once demands attention, and therefore automatically accents any lines of music played on it. It is a stop that cannot be used in neutral effects; it always stands out. Some specimens are useful in the same way that the Rankett is, the Vox also having some of this stop's windy, sibilant, piping effect on the ear, but it is not always apparent. The Vox may be combined or alone as a device to accent the pedal's notes. It stands out in contrast to the Diapason, Gemshorn, and many of the commoner stops of the Great and Choir. It is usable in single notes or in chords. As a solo stop of guttural tone, perhaps on the fourth manual of a large theater organ, it is not conspicuously useful, since it lacks the ground tone needed to make the melody line obvious. If it is combined with the Clarinet, Krumet, Schalmei, or Krummhorn, it always assumes more value as a solo voice. In the larger theater organs of from forty to eighty ranks, there may be as many as three Vox Humanas, typically called *Minor Vox Humana* (Accompanimental Organ), *Major Vox Humana* (Orchestral Organ), and *Solo Vox Humana* (Solo Organ). Such a choir of lingual beauty, it must be remembered, can all be *coupled* down to *one* manual, where, from both sides of the proscenium arch at once, all can intensify any emotion that the audience may be feeling!

The resonators are of medium to large Clarinet scale, and vary in length even in the same rank from one-half to one-sixth unison length. The boots also vary in length to give a variety of resonances to this tone. The open, funnel-shaped, and English Horn-type resonators do not give the covered, muffled tone usually heard. The fully capped cylinders, with a hole in one side of the cap to match another near the pipe's top, are the type most frequently seen. A separate swell box to seclude this stop apart from the others is not unusual. This box may be inside another swell box, in which case it is opened by a special manual piston or along with another swell pedal. Or it may stand by itself in one of the higher tiers of the organ, having its shades coupled to another swell pedal. Closing both swell shades would reduce it to a mere whisper; opening them would provide the organist with a new variety of Regal at the normal dynamic level. Oddly shaped pipes can produce all of the vowel sounds of *a, e, i, o, u,* but the most commonly heard Vox sounds a continuous *ee* timbre. See REGAL. Synonym: MENSCHENSTIMME.

VOX HUMANA KRUMMHORN. A short-resonator Reed at 8' manual pitch. This stop sounds with the fundamental and horn-like overtones of the Krummhorn and the high-pitched, thin, covered timbre of the Vox Humana. It is a solo voice as well as a timbre creator, since its fundamental can make the notes of the melody audible. See KRUMMHORN, VOX HUMANA.

NOTES THAT SOUND IN MANUAL AND PEDAL MIXTURES

Notes heard from the middle C key		Pitch of Rank	Notes heard from the low pedal CCC key	
Name of *MANUAL* Rank	Name of Note		Name of Note	Name of *PEDAL* Rank
Thirty-sixth	C^6	1/4′	C^4	Forty-third
Thirty-fifth, flatted	$B\flat^5$	2/7′	$B\flat^3$	Forty-second, flatted
Thirty-third	G^5	1/3′	G^3	Fortieth
Thirty-first	E^5	2/5′	E^3	Thirty-eighth
Twenty-ninth	C^5	1/2′	C^3	Thirty-sixth
Twenty-eighth, flatted	$B\flat^4$	4/7′	$B\flat^2$	Thirty-fifth, flatted
Twenty-sixth	G^4	2/3′	G^2	Thirty-third
Twenty-fourth	E^4	4/5′	E^2	Thirty-first
Twenty-second	C^4	1′	C^2	Twenty-ninth
Twenty-first, flatted	$B\flat^3$	1 1/7′	$B\flat^1$	Twenty-eighth, flatted
Nineteenth (Larigot)	G^3	1 1/3′	G^1	Twenty-sixth
Seventeenth (Tierce)	E^3	1 3/5′	E^1	Twenty-fourth
Fifteenth (Super Octave)	C^3	2′	C^1	Twenty-second
Fourteenth, flatted	$B\flat^2$	2 2/7′	$B\flat$	Twenty-first, flatted
Twelfth (Nasard)	G^2	2 2/3′	G	Nineteenth (Larigot)
Tenth (Gross Tierce)	E^2	3 1/5′	E	Seventeenth (Tierce)
Octave	C^2	4′	C	Fifteenth (Super Octave)
Seventh, flatted	$B\flat^1$	4 4/7′	$BB\flat$	Fourteenth, flatted
Fifth (Quint)	G^1	5 1/3′	GG	Twelfth (Nasard)
Third (Terz)	E^1	6 2/5′	EE	Tenth (Gross Tierce)
UNISON	C^1	8′	CC	Octave
Sub Septième	$B\flat$	9 1/7′	$BBB\flat$	Seventh, flatted
Sub Quint	G	10 2/3′	GGG	Fifth (Quint)
Sub Tierce	E	12 4/5′	EEE	Third (Terz)
Sub Octave	C	16′	CCC	UNISON
Sub Sub Quint	GG	21 1/3′	GGGG	Sub Quint
Sub Sub Octave	CC	32′	CCCC	Sub Octave

Chart Explanation: Notes that Sound in Manual and Pedal Mixtures

Most of the ranks of pipes that speak in mixtures and cornets are familiar to organists as separate pitches, such as the 2 2/3′, 8′, 1′, etc. The higher-pitched ranks, probably less familiar, are quickly identified if it is remembered that a stop-pitch that is one octave above another stop-pitch is equal to one-half its numerical indication. Thus, the 1/4′ could easily be seen to be *one octave* above the 1/2′ because it is one-half its numerical quantity. The 2/5′ is one octave above the 4/5′, and the 16′ is one octave above the 32′, all examples being true on both manuals and pedals alike. All notes on the scale can be worked out from the middle C and low pedal CCC notes given here. There are mixtures and cornets based on other series of stop-pitches than those of the unison (8′ manual and 16′ pedal) given here, in which case neither rank *names* nor names of notes are relative to unison pitches.

VOX HUMANA REGAL. A short-resonator Reed at 8' or 4' on both manuals and pedals. It is intensely brilliant, although moderately soft. It combines the reedy, windy effect of the Regals and the guttural tones of the Vox Humana. Its functions include those of most Regals, but especially the contrasting effect needed by manual and pedal line of notes against the smoother flue stops, like the Diapason and Flutes. See REGAL, VOX HUMANA.

VOX HUMANA SCHALMEI. A short-resonator Reed at 8' or 4' on both manuals and pedals. Its tone quality is a hybrid between the bright, nasal, acid timbre of the Schalmei, and the thin, indistinctly pitched Vox Humana. It is less brilliant than the Schalmei, and more substantial in tone than the Vox Humana. Its harmonically rich, piping, intense tone can be used in combination for contrasts in countermelodies or combined with flue stops for the same function, or even as a solo stop. See SCHALMEI, VOX HUMANA.

VOX MYSTICA. The softest Reed stop in the organ. It resembles the 8' Vox Humana in echo form, and makes a mere whisper of high-pitched overtones that do little for the soft flue stops except add a fringe of tenuously pitched and mysterious harmonics to them. This effect is possible from a distant Echo Organ or by enclosing these short Reed pipes in a swell box within another swell box, the inner being worked by a piston, the outer by a regular swell pedal. See VOX HUMANA.

WALDFLÖTE. An open wooden Flute of 8', 4', or 2' on the manuals, and not usually represented on the pedals. It yields a hollow, horn-like, smooth timbre that is of moderate loudness. Good specimens are resonant in tone as well. It is a solo voice of peculiar penetration and great beauty,

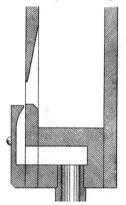

Mouth of a Waldflöte

especially in the middle and lower treble ranges. It has a bright effect in combination and adds a sympathetic quality of tone to other flue stops, like the Nachthorn, 'Cello, Diapason, Gemshorn, Major Open Flute, or a soft Principal. It is as valuable at 4' as at 8'. Some of the better features of the Melodia are in its tone, and the Hohlflöte's pleasant searching quality

can also be sensed, although the scale of this Flute is smaller than that
of the Hohlflöte, while larger than the Melodia. It is square or rectangular
in cross-section, the mouth being on either the longer side for a bright,
searching tone, or the short side for a tone that is harmonically filled out
but deep. The mouths are inverted and the shape may be somewhat flared
outward towards the top. See MELODIA, MELOPHONE. Synonyms: FELD-
FLÖTE, TIBIA SYLVESTRIS.

WALDHORN. A Reed stop of 16′ or 8′ manual pitch, intended to sound
like the hunting horn of the forest. Without having the Tromba's brass-
like timbre, this horn suggests the tone of a loud and full-timbred French
Horn stop. It has no clang or blatancy, but neither is it one of the smooth,
pungent Reeds of the organ. It is not a mellow horn but may be very
pleasing and even of stirring emotional effect on the listener, especially if
played by itself in chords. It has none of the Trumpet's timbre. It is of
excellent blend with all Reeds and flues, and makes a solo stop of much
usefulness. It is a Swell or Great Organ stop on many types of organs.
Synonyms: COR DE CHASSE, CORNO DI CACCIA, HUNTING HORN.

WHISTLE. A manual stop of Flute classification, at 2′, and derived
from a Hohlflöte, Tibia Clausa, Flautino, or Clarabella rank. See FLAUTINO.

WIENERFLöTE. See ORCHESTRAL FLUTE.

WOOD DIAPASON. An open Foundation stop of wooden pipes, at 16′
or 8′ manual pitch, and 32′, 16′, or 8′ pedal pitch, the pedal forms being
of heavier construction and louder tones than the manual forms. This tone
is a Diapason, but, since it lacks the peculiar formant of the metal pipes of
lead-tin alloy and the cylindrical shape, it is not adaptable to the Chorus
of Diapasons in its purest form. However, it has a round, resonant, warm
tone that is somewhat "plump" in its effect on the ear. It is a stop that at
8′ is "undiscovered" by organists as a whole at the present time. It may be
the second Diapason on the Swell or Choir, or an adjunct to the Great
stops. It is rectangular in cross-section, the mouths being on one of the
shorter sides. Shades of pipe metal partly cover the tops. A loud rank
would automatically become a solo Flute of bright tone, because the Diapason timbre is essentially quite dull. See DIAPASON, DOUBLE DIAPASON. Synonym: HOLZPRINCIPAL.

WOODEN OPEN FLUTE. An open rank of Flute pipes of wood, at 16′,
8′, or 4′ on the manuals, and 16′ or 8′ pedal pitch. This stop is of less
volume and brightness than the Major Open Flute of wooden form. This
versatile Flute is somewhat neutral in timbre, rather than being distinctively colored like the Hohlflöte or smooth in tone like the Clarabella. It is
useful in any division. It is a solo voice of bright, clean tone. It is a tone
builder, as are all open Flutes. It is not obvious in combination, giving its
natural overtones to any stop, even a String, inconspicuously, because they
taper from the fundamental evenly and quickly. See MAJOR OPEN FLUTE.

ZARTFLÖTE. A small-scaled open wood Flute of 8′ or 4′ manual pitch, of subdued but moderately bright tone, suggestive of the String's overtones. This is a solo or ensemble stop of less brightness than the Viola Flute. It may occasionally be made from conical metal pipes of spotted white alloy and small scale. The pipes are sometimes furnished with harmonic bridges.

ZARTGEDECKT. A stopped wood Flute of 8′ or 4′ on the manuals, resembling a very small-scale Gedeckt in structure and making a tone that is even softer than the Echo Gedeckt. See ECHO GEDECKT, GEDECKT.

ZAUBERFLÖTE. A *stopped* metal or wood Flute of *harmonic* construction, at 8′ or 4′ manual pitch. It is moderately soft but has a timbre that is round, clean, and full-toned. For a stop of its dynamic value it has

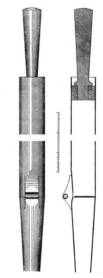

Zartflöte pipe at tenor **C**

an unusual amount of penetration. It is a very clean tone without shrillness or edge. It is a solo as well as an ensemble Flute. Its 2 2/3′ pitch is much valued by organists as a superior Twelfth of soft tone. Its 8′ rank is able to make more vivid and of clearer dimensions another solo stop, such as the Viola, Lieblichgedeckt, Principal, or Basset Horn. This it does by furnishing a gentle but firm second tone at the same pitch as the solo voice, but without any intrusive overtones to mutate the tone color. The 4′ rank has this same function except that it adds the octave in gentle but noticeable form to any unison. The 2′ rank is not unknown. This harmonic stopped Flute gives the impression of being a little on the "bright" side in spite of its meagre overtone structure. This effect comes from the listener's contrasting its strong *intensity* with its moderately soft dynamic level.

This Flute's upper portion absorbs many of the upper partials that would tend to destroy its clarity and roundness of voice. It is overblown to sound its third harmonic noticeably. Since this is fundamentally a stopped rank, the pipes must be three times the normal length needed by a stopped pipe to make the same tone; stopped pipes do not sound the second harmonic except in trace amounts. Very large ears are used to stabilize the tone and to tune the rank, bending inward to flatten and outward to sharpen the tone. See HARMONIC GEDECKT, HARMONIC STOPPED TWELFTH.

ZAUBERGEDECKT. A softer form of the Zauberflöte, at 8′ or 4′ on the manuals. The mouths of this Flute have a higher cut-up and the pipes are of somewhat smaller scale than the Zauberflöte, making the timbre less well-rounded, pervading, and clear. See GEDECKT, ZAUBERFLÖTE.

ZAUBERPICCOLO. A soft 2′ Flute on the manuals, in construction quite similar to the Zauberflöte. It is bright but not at all string-like and is a round tone, considering its pitch at two octaves above the unison. It is useful as a diminutive Flute tone to extend the other Flutes of 4' and 8' upward. It can blend well with the Zauberflöte, Dolce Flute, Spitzflöte, Nachthorn, or Dulciana. In fact, the stopped harmonic series of Flutes is well known for this quality of blend. It is not so versatile as the Piccolo or Harmonic Piccolo 2' in most uses, however, because it is quite soft, frequently around *mpp* or *pp*, as an average. See PICCOLO, ZAUBERFLÖTE.

ZIMBEL. See CYMBAL.

ZIMBELFLÖTE. See CAMPANA.

ZINK. A Reed stop on the pedals, at 4', 2', or 1', sounding with a bright, penetrating timbre, sometimes even brass-like. Its function is to make the pedal line of notes stand out loudly and more clearly in pitch. Some Zinks are pungent, nasal, Trumpet-like, or sharp in timbre, although this is not a loud stop in all specimens. The pedal's *Cornett* at 2' has allied uses, and is likely to sound quite acute in tone. Notes from C^1 (middle C) to G^3 are sounded by a 2' ("Twenty-second") on the pedals. These two Reeds aid in the playing of polyphonic music, a distinct pedal tone being necessary to make the pedal notes stand out clearly against the manual notes. Usually the high-pitched pedal stops are heard from only a medium or large-size instrument. Manual to Pedal couplers at the unison, fifth, and octave pitches are found on a very few organs. This name is sometimes spelled *Zinken.*

Summary of Dictionary of Pipe Organ Stops

Name of Stop	Average Dynamic Value	Pedal Pitches*	Manual Pitches*	Classification
ACOUSTIC BASS	*f*	64, 32		Foundation
ACUTA	*mf*		III, IV	Compound
AEOLINA	*mpp*		8	String
AEOLINE	*mpp*	16	8	String
AEOLINE CÉLESTE	*mpp*		8	String
AEQUALPRINZIPAL	*f*		8	Foundation
AMOROSA	*mpp*		8	Flute
APFELREGAL	*f*	8	8	Reed
BALLAD HORN	*mf*		8	Reed
BARPFEIFE	*mf*	16, 8	8, 4	Reed
BARYTON	*mp*	8	8	Reed
BASSET HORN	*mp*		8	Reed
BASS FLUTE	*mf*	16, 8		Flute
BASS HORN	*f*	16		Reed
BASSOON	*mp*	16	16, 8	Reed
BASSOON REGAL	*mf*	16	16	Reed
BASS VIOLIN	*mf*	32	16	String
BAUERFLÖTE	*mf*		4, 2, 1	Flute
BEARDED GAMBA	*mf*	16	8	String
BELL CLARINET	*mp*		8	Reed
BELL DIAPASON	*f*		8	Flute
BELL FLUTE	*mf*		8, 4	Flute
BELL GAMBA	*mf*	16	8	String
BLOCKFLÖTE	*f*	4, 2	4, 2, 1	Flute
BOMBARDE	*ff*	32, 16, 8	16, 8	Reed
BOMBARDE QUINTE	*mff*	10 2/3	5 1/3	Reed
BOMBARDON	*mff*	32, 16	16, 8	Reed
BORDUNALFLÖTE	*mp*		8, 4	Flute
BOURDON	*mp*	32, 16, 8	16, 8	Flute
BOURDON DOUX	*pp*		16	Flute
BOURDONECHO	*mppp*	16	16, 8	Flute
BRASS TRUMPET	*mff*		8	Reed
BUCCINA	*mff*	32, 16	16, 8	Reed
BUZAIN	*mfff*	32, 16	16, 8	Reed
CAMPANA	*p*		1, 1/2	Flute
CARILLON	*mpp*		II, III, VI	Compound
CÉLESTE	*mp*		8	String
CELESTINA	*pp*		8, 4	Flute
'CELLO	*mf*	16, 8	16, 8	String

*The pitches given here are those that are found on a wide variety of consoles. They are not exhaustive — there is no good reason not to make a 32′ Barpfeife or a 2′ Campana, for example, if taste so dictates.

Name of Stop	Average Dynamic Value	Pedal Pitches	Manual Pitches	Classification
'CELLO CÉLESTE	mf		8	String
'CELLO VIOLIN	mf	16	8	String
CHALUMEAU	f	16, 8, 4	16, 8, 4	Reed
CHAMADE	fff		16, 8, 4	Reed
CHIMNEY FLUTE	mp		16, 8, 4, 2	Flute
CHORALBASSET	f	4, 2		Foundation
CLAIRON	f	8	4	Reed
CLAIRON HARMONIQUE	ff	8	4	Reed
CLARABELLA	mf		8, 4	Flute
CLARIBEL FLUTE	mp		4	Flute
CLARINET	mp	16	16, 8	Reed
CLARINET FLUTE	p		8, 4	Flute
CLARION	f	8	4	Reed
CLARION HARMONIC	ff	8	4	Reed
CLARION MIXTURE	f		III, IV, V	Compound
CLEAR FLUTE	mf		4	Flute
COMPENSATING MIXTURE	mf	III, V, VI		Compound
CONCERT FLUTE	mp		8, 4	Flute
CONE DIAPASON	mf	16, 8	16, 8, 4	Foundation
CONE GAMBA	mf	16	16, 8, 4	String
CONE GAMBA CÉLESTE	mf		8	String
CONE GEDECKT	p		8	Flute
CONICAL FLUTE	mp	16, 8	16, 8, 4	Flute
CONTRABASS	mf	32	16	String
CONTRA BASSOON	mp	32	32, 16	Reed
CONTRA BOMBARDE	ff	32	16	Reed
CONTRA BOMBARDON	mff	32	16	Reed
CONTRA BOURDON	mp	32	16	Flute
CONTRA DIAPHONE	ff	64, 32	16	Foundation
CONTRA DULCIANA	p	32	16	Foundation
CONTRA FAGOTTO	mp	32	16	Reed
CONTRA GAMBA	mf	32	16	String
CONTRA OBOE	mp	32	16	Reed
CONTRA POSAUNE	mfff	32	16	Reed
CONTRA PRINCIPAL	f	32	16	Foundation
CONTRA SAXOPHONE	mf	32	16	Reed
CONTRA TROMBONE	ff	64, 32	16	Reed
CONTRA TRUMPET	mff	32	16	Reed
CONTRA TUBA	mfff	32	16	Reed
CONTRA VIOLA	p		16	String
CONTRA VIOLONE	mf	32	16	String
CONTRE VIOLE	mf	32	16	String
COPULA	mp	16, 8	8, 4	Flute
COR ANGLAIS	mp		8	Reed
COR D'AMOUR	mp		8	Reed
COR DE BASSET	mp		8	Reed
COR DE CHASSE	mff		16, 8	Reed
COR DE NUIT	mp	8	8, 4	Foundation
CORNET	f	III, VI	II, III, IV, V	Compound
CORNET DE RÉCIT	mff		VIII	Compound

Name of Stop	Average Dynamic Value	Pedal Pitches	Manual Pitches	Classification
CORNET DES BOMBARDES	ff		III	Compound
CORNET DES VIOLES	mp		III, V	Compound
CORNO CLARION	mp		4	Reed
CORNO D'AMORE	mp		8	Reed
CORNO DI BASSETTO	mp		8	Reed
CORNO DI CACCIA	mff		16, 8	Reed
CORNO DOLCE	mp		16, 8	Foundation
CORNO FLUTE	mp		8	Flute
CORNOPEAN	f		8, 4	Reed
CREMONA	mp		8	Reed
CROMORNE	mp		8	Reed
CYMBAL	mf	V	III, V, VI	Compound
DIAPASON	f	32, 16, 8, 4, 2, 1	16, 8, 4, 2, 1	Foundation
DIAPASON MAGNA	mff		8	Foundation
DIAPASON PHONON	mff	16	8, 4	Foundation
DIAPASON SONORA	ff		8	Foundation
DIAPHONE	ff	64, 32, 16	16, 8	Foundation
DIAPHONIC DIAPASON	ff	64, 32, 16	16, 8	Foundation
DIAPHONIC HORN	mff	16	8	Foundation
DOLCAN	mppp		16, 8, 4	Foundation
DOLCAN CÉLESTE	mppp		8	Foundation
DOLCE	mp		16, 8, 4	Foundation
DOLCE CORNET	p		III, IV	Compound
DOLCE FLUTE	mpp		8, 4	Flute
DOLCETTE	p		4	Foundation
DOLCETTE FLUTE	p		4	Flute
DOLCISSIMO	ppp		8	Foundation
DOPPELFLÖTE	f		16, 8, 4	Flute
DOPPELGEDECKT	mp		16, 8	Flute
DOPPELROHRBORDUN	mp	16, 8, 4	16, 8, 4	Flute
DOPPELROHRFLÖTE	mf		8, 4	Flute
DOPPELROHRGEDECKT	mf	16, 8	8, 4	Flute
DOPPELSPITZFLÖTE	mp		16, 8, 4	Flute
DOUBLE BASS	mf	32	16	String
DOUBLE DIAPASON	f	32	16	Foundation
DOUBLE FLUTE	p	32	16	Flute
DOUBLE GEMSHORN	f	32	32, 16	Foundation
DOUBLE MELODIA	mp		16	Flute
DOUBLE OBOE	mp	32	16	Reed
DOUBLE OPEN DIAPASON	f	32	16	Foundation
DOUBLE SALICIONAL	mp	32	16	String
DOUBLE STRING	mp		16	String
DOUBLE TRUMPET	mff	32	16	Reed
DOUBLETTE	mf		II	Compound
DOUBLE TUBA	mfff	32	16	Reed
DOUBLE VOX HUMANA	p		16	Reed
DULCET	p		4	Foundation
DULCIAN	p	32, 16	16, 8, 4	Reed
DULCIANA	p	32, 16, 8	16, 8, 4	Foundation
DULCIANA CÉLESTE	p		8	Foundation

Name of Stop	Average Dynamic Value	Pedal Pitches	Manual Pitches	Classification
DULCIANA CORNET	*p*		IV, VI	Compound
DULCIANA FLUTE	*mpp*		8, 4	Flute
DULZIAN	*p*	32, 16	16, 8, 4	Reed
DULZIANREGAL	*mp*	16, 8, 4	16, 8, 4	Reed
ECHO	*mppp*		8, 4	Flute
ECHO BOURDON	*mppp*	16	16, 8	Flute
ECHO 'CELLO	*p*		8	String
ECHO CLARABELLA	*mpp*		8, 4	Flute
ECHO CLARION	*mpp*	8	4	Reed
ECHO CORNET	*mp*		III, IV, V	Compound
ECHO DIAPASON	*mp*		16, 8, 4	Foundation
ECHO DULCIANA	*pp*		16, 8, 4	Foundation
ECHO DULCIANA CÉLESTE	*pp*		8	Foundation
ECHO FLUTE	*mppp*		8, 4	Flute
ECHO GAMBA	*mpp*		8	String
ECHO GEDECKT	*pp*		16, 8, 4	Flute
ECHO GEMSHORN	*mpp*		8, 4	Foundation
ECHO HORN	*mpp*		8	Reed
ECHO MIXTURE	*mp*		III, IV, V, VI	Compound
ECHO NACHTHORN	*mpp*		8, 4	Foundation
ECHO OBOE	*mpp*		8	Reed
ECHO OPEN FLUTE	*mppp*		16, 8, 4	Flute
ECHO STOPPED FLUTE	*ppp*		8, 4	Flute
ECHO TIBIA CLAUSA	*mp*		16, 8, 4, 2	Flute
ECHO TRUMPET	*mf*		8	Reed
ECHO VIOLA	*mpp*		8	String
ECHO VIOLIN	*pp*		8	String
ECHO VOX HUMANA	*ppp*		8	Reed
EGYPTIAN HORN	*mff*		8	Reed
EIGHTEENTH	*mppp*	2 10/11	1 5/11	Foundation
ELEVENTH	*mppp*	5 9/11	2 10/11	Foundation
ENGLISH HORN	*mp*		8	Reed
ENGLISH POST HORN	*ff*		8	Reed
ERZÄHLER	*mp*		8, 4	Foundation
ERZÄHLER CÉLESTE	*mp*		8	Foundation
ETHEREAL VIOLIN	*p*		8	String
ETHEREAL VIOLIN CÉLESTE	*p*		8	String
EUPHONE	*p*	16	16, 8	Reed
EUPHONIUM	*mf*	16	16	Reed
FAGOTTO	*mp*	32, 16, 8	16, 8, 4	Reed
FAGOTTONE	*mp*	32	32	Reed
FANFARE	*mff*		8	Reed
FAN TRUMPET	*fff*		16, 8, 4	Reed
FELDFLÖTE	*mf*		8, 4, 2	Flute
FERNFLÖTE	*mppp*		8, 4	Flute
FERNHORN	*mpp*		8, 4	Foundation
FIELD TRUMPET	*fff*		8	Reed
FIFE	*f*		2, 1	Flute
FIFTEENTH	*p*	4	2	Foundation
FIFTH	*mp*	10 2/3	5 1/3	Foundation

Name of Stop	Average Dynamic Value	Pedal Pitches	Manual Pitches	Classification
FLACHFLÖTE	f		8, 4, 2, 1	Flute
FLAGEOLET	mp		2, 1	Flute
FLAGEOLET HARMONIQUE	mf		2, 1	Flute
FLAUTADA	mf	32, 16, 8	32, 16, 8	Foundation
FLAUTINO	p		2	Flute
FLAUTO AMABILE	mpp		8	Flute
FLAUTO D'AMORE	p		8, 4	Flute
FLAUTO DOLCE	mpp		8, 4	Flute
FLAUTO DOLCISSIMO	ppp		8, 4	Flute
FLAUTO MAJOR	mff	16, 8	8, 4	Flute
FLAUTO MIRABILIS	ff		8, 4	Flute
FLAUTO TRAVERSO	mp		8, 4	Flute
FLÖTENBASS	mf	16, 8		Flute
FLUGELHORN	f		8	Reed
FLÛTE À BEC	mp		8, 4	Flute
FLÛTE À FUSEAU	p		8, 4, 2	Flute
FLÛTE À PAVILLON	f		8	Flute
FLUTE BASS	mf	16, 8		Flute
FLUTE CÉLESTE	p		8	Flute
FLUTE CONIQUE	mp	16, 8	16, 8, 4	Flute
FLÛTE D'AMOUR	p		8, 4	Flute
FLÛTE DOUCE	mpp		8, 4	Flute
FLÛTE HARMONIQUE	mp		8, 4, 2	Flute
FLUTE NASARD	p	5 1/3	2 2/3	Flute
FLÛTE OUVERTE	mf	32, 16, 8	8, 4	Flute
FLÛTE QUINT	mp	10 2/3	5 1/3	Flute
FLÛTE TRIANGULAIRE	mf		16, 8	Flute
FOREST FLUTE	p		8, 4	Flute
FOURNITURE	f	III, IV	III, IV, VI	Compound
FOURTEENTH, FLATTED	mppp	4 4/7	2 2/7	Foundation
FRENCH HORN	mf		8	Reed
FRENCH TRUMPET	mfff	16	16, 8, 4	Reed
FUGARA	mf		4	String
FULL FLUTE	mff		4	Flute
FULL MIXTURE	ff	VI	VI	Compound
GAMBA	mf	32, 16, 8	16, 8	String
GAMBA CELESTE	mf		8	String
GAMBETTE	mf		4	String
GEDECKT	p	32, 16, 8, 4	32, 16, 8, 4	Flute
GEDECKTFLÖTE	p		4	Flute
GEDECKTPOMMER	mf	16, 8	16, 8	Flute
GEDECKTQUINTE	mpp	10 2/3	5 1/3	Flute
GEDECKT TIERCE	mppp	3 1/5	1 3/5	Flute
GEDECKT TWELFTH	mpp	5 1/3	2 2/3	Flute
GEIGENBASS	mf	32	32, 16	Foundation
GEIGEN DIAPASON	mf	32, 16, 8	32, 16, 8, 4	Foundation
GEIGEN FIFTEENTH	mpp	4	2	Foundation
GEIGEN OCTAVE	mp	8	4	Foundation
GEIGEN PRINCIPAL	mf	32, 16, 8	32, 16, 8, 4	Foundation
GEIGENREGAL	mf	8, 4	8, 4	Reed
GEIGEN SUPER OCTAVE	mpp	4	2	Foundation
GEIGEN TWELTH	p	5 1/3	2 2/3	Foundation

Name of Stop	Average Dynamic Value	Pedal Pitches	Manual Pitches	Classification
GELINDGEDECKT	*mppp*		16, 8, 4	Flute
GEMSHORN	*mf*	32, 16, 8, 4	16, 8, 4	Foundation
GEMSHORNBASS	*f*	32	32, 16	Foundation
GEMSHORN CÉLESTE	*mf*		8	Foundation
GEMSHORN FIFTEENTH	*pp*	4	2	Foundation
GEMSHORN MIXTURE	*mf*		VI	Compound
GEMSHORN OCTAVE	*mpp*	8	4	Foundation
GEMSHORNQUINTE	*pp*	10 2/3	5 1/3	Foundation
GEMSHORN SUPER OCTAVE	*pp*	4	2	Foundation
GEMSHORN TWELFTH	*mpp*	5 1/3	2 2/3	Foundation
GEMSHORN VIOLIN	*mp*		8	String
GERMAN FLUTE	*mp*		8, 4	Flute
GERMAN GAMBA	*mf*		8	String
GLOCKENFLÖTE	*mf*		8, 4	Flute
GLOCKENGAMBA	*mf*	16	8	String
GLOCKENSPIEL	*mpp*		II, III, VI	Compound
GRAND BOURDON	*ff*	VIII, X		Compound
GRAND CHORUS	*mff*	XVIII	XIII	Compound
GRAND CORNET	*mff*		V	Compound
GRAND DIAPASON	*mff*	16	8	Foundation
GRAND FOURNITURE	*mff*		VI	Compound
GRAND MIXTURE	*ff*	VIII	VIII	Compound
GRAND PRINCIPAL	*mff*	16	8	Foundation
GRAND QUINT	*f*	10 2/3	5 1/3	Foundation
GRAND VIOL	*mff*		8	String
GRAVISSIMA	*f*	64, 32		Foundation
GROSSDOPPELGEDECKT	*mp*	16	16	Flute
GROSSFLÖTE	*mf*	8	8	Flute
GROSSGAMBA	*mf*	32	16	String
GROSSGEDECKT	*mp*		16, 8	Flute
GROSSGEMSHORN	*f*	32	32, 16	Foundation
GROSS NASARD	*mp*	10 2/3	5 1/3	Foundation
GROSS QUINT	*mp*	21 1/3	10 2/3	Foundation
GROSSQUINTENBASS	*mp*	21 1/3	10 2/3	Foundation
GROSSRAUSCHQUINTE	*f*		II	Compound
GROSS TIERCE	*mpp*	6 2/5	3 1/5	Foundation
HARFENPRINZIPAL	*p*		8, 4	Foundation
HARMONIA AETHERIA	*mpp*		V	Compound
HARMONICA	*pp*		8	Flute
HARMONIC CLARIBEL	*mf*		8	Flute
HARMONIC CLARION	*ff*	8	4	Reed
HARMONIC CORNET	*mff*		III	Compound
HARMONIC CYMBAL	*ff*		VI	Compound
HARMONIC DIAPASON	*mff*		8	Foundation
HARMONIC FLUTE	*mp*		8, 4, 2	Flute
HARMONIC GEDECKT	*mp*		8, 4	Flute
HARMONIC OCTAVE	*mff*		4	Foundation
HARMONIC PICCOLO	*f*		2	Flute
HARMONICS	*p*	IV	III	Compound
HARMONIC STOPPED TWELFTH	*p*		2 2/3	Flute
HARMONIC TRUMPET	*ff*		8	Reed

Name of Stop	Average Dynamic Value	Pedal Pitches	Manual Pitches	Classification
HARMONIC TUBA	*fff*		8	Reed
HARMONIC TWELFTH	*p*		2 2/3	Flute
HAUTBOIS	*mp*		8	Reed
HAUTBOIS D'AMOUR	*p*		8	Reed
HECKELPHONE	*mf*		8	Reed
HELLFLÖTE	*f*		8, 4	Flute
HOHLFLÖTE	*mp*		8, 4	Flute
HOHLPFEIFE	*mp*		·8, 4	Flute
HOLZFLÖTE	*mp*	16, 8	8, 4	Flute
HOLZGEDECKT	*p*	16	8, 4	Flute
HOLZPRINZIPAL	*mf*	32, 16, 8	16, 8	Foundation
HOLZRANKETT	*mp*	8, 4	8, 4	Reed
HOLZREGAL	*mf*	16, 8, 4	16, 8, 4	Reed
HORN	*mf*		8	Reed
HORN DIAPASON	*f*		8	Foundation
HUNTING HORN	*mff*		16, 8	Reed
JEU DE CLOCHETTE	*mpp*		II	Compound
JUBALFLÖTE	*ff*		8, 4	Flute
KEEN STRINGS	*p*		8	String
KERAULOPHONE	*mf*		8	Foundation
KINURA	*mp*		8, 4	Reed
KLEINE MIXTURE	*pp*		IV, V	Compound
KLEINERZÄHLER	*p*		4	Foundation
KLEINFLÖTE	*p*		4	Flute
KLEINGEDECKT	*mpp*		8, 4	Flute
KLEINPRINZIPAL	*mf*		4	Foundation
KNOPFREGAL	*f*	8, 4	8, 4	Reed
KOPPELFLÖTE	*p*		8, 4	Flute
KRUMET	*mf*		8	Reed
KRUMMHORN	*mp*		8	Reed
LARIGOT	*mpp*	2 2/3	1 1/3	Foundation
LIEBLICHBORDUN	*p*		16, 8	Flute
LIEBLICHFLÖTE	*mpp*		4	Flute
LIEBLICHGEDECKT	*mpp*	32, 16, 8, 4	16, 8, 4	Flute
LIEBLICHNASAT	*pp*		2 2/3	Flute
LITURGICAL TRUMPET	*mff*		8	Reed
LLENO				Compound
LOCHGEDECKT	*mpp*		8, 4	Flute
LUDWIGTONE	*mp*		8, 4	Foundation
MAGNATON	*mff*	32		Foundation
MAJOR BASS	*mp*	32	16	Flute
MAJOR DIAPASON	*mff*	16, 8	16, 8	Foundation
MAJOR FLUTE	*mff*	16, 8	8, 4	Flute
MAJOR OCTAVE	*f*	8	4	Foundation
MAJOR OPEN FLUTE	*mff*	16, 8	8, 4	Flute
MAJOR PRINCIPAL	*mff*	16	8, 4	Foundation
MELODIA	*mp*		8	Flute
MELOPHONE	*f*		8	Flute
MENCHENSTIMME	*mpp*	16, 8, 4	16, 8, 4	Reed
MILITARY TRUMPET	*fff*		8	Reed
MINOR DIAPASON	*mf*	16, 8	16, 8, 4	Foundation
MINOR OCTAVE	*mp*	8	4	Foundation
MINOR OPEN FLUTE	*mppp*	16, 8	8, 4	Flute

Name of Stop	Average Dynamic Value	Pedal Pitches	Manual Pitches	Classification
MINOR PRINCIPAL	*mf*	16	8, 4	Foundation
MIXTURE	*mf*		III, V	Compound
MONTRE	*f*	32, 16, 8, 4	32, 16, 8, 4	Foundation
MUSETTE	*mp*		8, 4	Reed
MUTED 'CELLO	*p*		8	String
MUTED GAMBA	*p*		8	String
MUTED STRINGS	*pp*		8	String
MUTED TRUMPET	*mp*		8	Reed
MUTED VIOLA	*pp*		8	String
MUTED VIOLIN	*p*		8	String
MUTED VIOLIN CÉLESTE	*p*		8	String
NACHTHORN	*mp*	8	8, 4	Foundation
NASARD	*mp*	5 1/3	2 2/3	Foundation
NASARD FLUTE	*mf*	16	8	Flute
NASAT	*mp*	5 1/3	2 2/3	Foundation
NASON FLUTE	*mf*	16	16, 8, 4	Flute
NINETEENTH	*mpp*	2 2/3	1 1/3	Foundation
NINTH	*mppp*	7 1/9	3 5/9	Foundation
OBOE	*mp*	16, 8	8	Reed
OBOE CLARION	*mpp*	8	4	Reed
OBOE D'AMORE	*p*		8	Reed
OBOE HORN	*mf*		8	Reed
OBOE SCHALMEI	*mf*	8, 4	8	Reed
OCTAVE	*mf*	8	4	Foundation
OCTAVE FLUTE	*mp*	8	4	Flute
OCTAVE HORN	*mp*	8	4	Reed
OCTAVE OBOE	*mpp*	8	4	Reed
OCTAVE PRINCIPAL	*mf*	8	4	Foundation
OCTAVE QUINT	*mp*	5 1/3	2 2/3	Foundation
OCTAVE VIOLIN	*p*	8	4	String
OCTAVIN	*mp*		2	Foundation
OFFENFLÖTE	*mp*	16, 8	8, 4	Flute
OPEN DIAPASON	*f*	32, 16, 8, 4, 2, 1	16, 8, 4, 2, 1	Foundation
OPEN TWELFTH	*mp*	5 1/3	2 2/3	Foundation
OPHICLEIDE	*ffff*	32, 16, 8	16, 8	Reed
ORCHESTRAL BASSOON	*mp*	16	16, 8	Reed
ORCHESTRAL CLARINET	*mp*	16	16, 8	Reed
ORCHESTRAL CORNET	*f*		8	Reed
ORCHESTRAL FLUTE	*mp*		8, 4	Flute
ORCHESTRAL HORN	*mf*		8	Reed
ORCHESTRAL OBOE	*mp*		8	Reed
ORCHESTRAL PICCOLO	*mf*		2	Flute
ORCHESTRAL SAXOPHONE	*mf*		8	Reed
ORCHESTRAL STRINGS	*f*		8	String
ORCHESTRAL TRUMPET	*mff*		8	Reed
ORCHESTRAL VIOLIN	*mp*	16	8	String
PEDAL STRING MIXTURE	*f*	IV, VII		Compound
PERCUSSIONS		8, 4	8, 4, 2	Percussion
PETITE NASARD	*p*		2 2/3	Foundation

Name of Stop	Average Dynamic Value	Pedal Pitches	Manual Pitches	Classification
PETITE TROMPETTE	*mf*		8	Reed
PHILOMELA	*f*		8	Flute
PHONEUMA	*p*		8	Flute
PICCOLO	*mf*		2	Flute
PICCOLO D'AMORE	*p*		2	Flute
PLEIN JEU	*mff*		V, VII, IX	Compound
PLEIN JEU HARMONIQUE	*ff*		IV, VIII	Compound
POMMER	*mf*	16, 8	16, 8	Flute
PORTUNALFLÖTE	*mp*		8, 4	Flute
POSAUNE	*mfff*	32, 16	16, 8	Reed
POST HORN	*ff*		8	Reed
PRESTANT	*f*		4	Foundation
PRINCIPAL	*f*	32, 16	8, 4, 2	Foundation
PRINCIPAL FLUTE	*f*	8, 4	8, 4	Flute
PYRAMID FLUTE	*mp*		16, 8, 4	Flute
QUERFLÖTE	*mp*		8, 4	Flute
QUINT	*mp*	10 2/3	5 1/3	Foundation
QUINTADE	*mp*	32, 16	32, 16, 8	Flute
QUINTADENA	*mf*	16, 8	16, 8, 4	Flute
QUINTATEN	*mp*	16, 8	16, 8, 4	Flute
QUINTATON	*p*	16, 8	16, 8, 4	Flute
QUINT BASS	*mp*	10 2/3		Foundation
QUINT DIAPASON	*mp*	10 2/3	5 1/3	Foundation
QUINTENBASS	*mp*	10 2/3		Foundation
QUINTE OUVERTE	*mp*	10 2/3	5 1/3	Foundation
QUINT FLUTE	*mf*	16	8	Flute
QUINT MIXTURE	*f*	III	III	Compound
QUINT TRUMPET	*mf*		5 1/3	Reed
RANKETT	*mp*	16, 8	16, 8	Reed
RAUSCHQUINTE	*f*		II	Compound
REGAL	*f*	16, 8, 4, 2	16, 8, 4, 2	Reed
RESULTANT	*f*	64, 32		Foundation
RIPIENO				Compound
ROHRBORDUN	*mp*	16, 8, 4	16, 8, 4	Flute
ROHRFLÖTE	*mp*		16, 8, 4, 2	Flute
ROHRFLÖTENQUINTE	*p*		5 1/3	Flute
ROHRGEDECKT	*p*	16	16, 8, 4	Flute
ROHRNASAT	*p*		2 2/3	Flute
ROHRPOMMER	*mf*	16, 8	16, 8	Flute
ROHRQUINTE	*p*		5 1/3	Flute
ROHRSCHALMEI	*mf*	8, 4	8, 4	Reed
SACKBUT	*mff*	32, 16	16	Reed
SALICET	*p*		4	String
SALICETINA	*mpp*		2	String
SALICIONAL	*mp*	16	16, 8	String
SALICIONAL DIAPASON	*mf*		8	Foundation
SANFTBASS	*mpp*		16	Flute
SANFTFLÖTE	*mpp*		8, 4	Flute
SAXOPHONE	*mf*		8	Reed
SCHALMEI	*f*	16, 8, 4	16, 8, 4	Reed
SCHALMEI REGAL	*mf*	8, 4	8, 4, 2	Reed
SCHARF	*mf*		III, IV	Compound

Name of Stop	Average Dynamic Value	Pedal Pitches	Manual Pitches	Classification
SCHÖNGEDECKT	*mf*		8	Flute
SCHWEIZERFLÖTE	*f*		4, 2	Flute
SEPTADECIMA	*mpp*	3 1/5	1 3/5	Foundation
SEPTIÈME	*pp*	2 2/7	1 1/7	Foundation
SERAPHONFLÖTE	*ff*		8, 4	Flute
SERAPHONGEDECKT	*mff*		8, 4	Flute
SERPENT	*f*	16, 8	16	Reed
SESQUIALTERA	*mf*		II, III, V	Compound
SEVENTEENTH	*mpp*	3 1/5	1 3/5	Foundation
SHAWM	*f*	16, 8, 4	16, 8, 4	Reed
SIFFLÖTE	*mp*		2, 1, 1/2	Flute
SILVER FLUTE	*mp*		8, 4	Flute
SINGENGEDECKT	*p*		16, 8, 4	Flute
SIXTEENTH	*mppp*	3 5/9	1 7/9	Foundation
SOFT FLUTE	*pp*		8, 4	Flute
SOFT MIXTURE	*mpp*		III, IV, V, VI	Compound
SOLO 'CELLO	*f*		8	String
SOLO FLUTE	*f*		8, 4	Flute
SOLO TIBIA CLAUSA	*mff*		8	Flute
SOLO TUBA	*fff*		8	Reed
SOLO VIOLIN	*f*		8	String
SOLO VOX HUMANA	*mf*		8	Reed
SORDUN	*mpp*		16, 8	Flute
SOUBASSE	*mp*	32	16	Flute
SPILLFLÖTE	*p*		8, 4, 2, 1	Flute
SPINDELFLÖTE	*p*		8, 4, 2, 1	Flute
SPIREFLÖTE	*mp*		16, 8, 4, 2	Flute
SPITZDIAPASON	*mf*	16, 8	16, 8, 4	Foundation
SPITZFLÖTE	*mp*		16, 8, 4, 2	Flute
SPITZFLÖTE CÉLESTE	*mp*		8	Flute
SPITZGAMBA	*mf*	16	16, 8, 4	String
SPITZGEDECKT	*p*		8, 4	Flute
SPITZPRINZIPAL	*mf*	16, 8	16, 8, 4	Foundation
SPITZQUINTE	*p*		5 1/3, 2 2/3	Flute
STARKGEDECKT	*f*		16, 8	Flute
STATE TRUMPET	*ffff*		8	Reed
STENTHORN	*mff*		8	Foundation
STENTOR BOMBARDE	*ffff*	32, 16, 8	16, 8	Reed
STENTOR DIAPASON	*mfff*		8	Foundation
STENTOR DIAPHONE	*fff*	32, 16		Foundation
STENTORFLÖTE	*ff*		8	Flute
STENTOR GAMBA	*ff*		8	Reed
STENTOR HORN	*mfff*		8	Compound
STENTOR MIXTURE	*mfff*		III, VI, VII	String
STENTOR OCTAVE	*ff*	8	4	Foundation
STENTORPHONE	*fff*		8	Flute
STENTOR SESQUIALTERA	*mff*	III	III, IV	Compound
STILLGEDECKT	*mpp*		8, 4	Flute
STOPPED DIAPASON	*mp*		16, 8, 4	Flute
STOPPED FLUTE	*mp*		16, 8, 4	Flute
STOPPED TWELFTH	*mpp*		2 2/3	Flute

Name of Stop	Average Dynamic Value	Pedal Pitches	Manual Pitches	Classification
STRING CÉLESTE	*mp*		8	String
STRING MIXTURE	*mf*		III, IV, V	Compound
STRING TWELFTH	*mp*		2 2/3	String
SUABE FLUTE	*mp*		8, 4	Flute
SUAVE FLUTE	*mp*		8, 4	Flute
SUB BASS	*mp*	32	16	Flute
SUB BOURDON	*mp*	32	16	Flute
SUB OCTAVE	*f*	32	16	Foundation
SUB PRINCIPAL	*f*	32	16	Foundation
SUB QUINT	*mp*	21 1/3	10 2/3	Foundation
SUPER OCTAVE	*p*	4	2	Foundation
SUPER SUPER OCTAVE	*p*	2	1	Foundation
SYLVESTRINA	*mpp*		8, 4	String
TENTH	*mpp*	6 2/5	3 1/5	Foundation
TERPODION	*mf*		8	String
TERTZIAN	*f*	II	II, III	Compound
TERZ	*mpppp*	12 4/5	6 2/5	Foundation
THIRD	*mpppp*	12 4/5	6 2/5	Foundation
THIRTY-FIFTH, FLATTED	*mpppp*	4/7	2/7	Foundation
THIRTY-FIRST	*mpppp*	4/5	2/5	Foundation
THIRTY-SIXTH	*mpppp*	1/2	1/4	Foundation
THIRTY-THIRD	*mpppp*	2/3	1/3	Foundation
TIBIA	*mf*		8	Flute
TIBIA CLAUSA	*f*	32, 16	16, 8, 4, 2, 1	Flute
TIBIA DURA	*ff*		8, 4	Flute
TIBIA FLUTE	*mp*		4	Flute
TIBIA MAJOR	*mff*		16, 8	Flute
TIBIA MINOR	*mp*		16, 8	Flute
TIBIA MOLLIS	*mp*		8	Flute
TIBIA PLENA	*ff*		8	Flute
TIBIA PROFUNDA	*mf*	32	16	Flute
TIBIA PROFUNDISSIMA	*mf*	64	32	Flute
TIBIA REX	*mfff*		8	Flute
TIBIA SYLVESTRIS	*mf*		8, 4, 2	Flute
TIERCE	*mpp*	3 1/5	1 3/5	Foundation
TIERCINA	*mp*		8	Flute
TRAVERSFLÖTE	*mp*		8, 4	Flute
TROMBA	*mff*	16	16, 8	Reed
TROMBA CLARION	*f*	8	4	Reed
TROMBA MAGNA	*fff*		8	Reed
TROMBA QUINT	*mf*		5 1/3	Reed
TROMBA REAL	*fff*		8	Reed
TROMBONE	*ff*	32, 16	16, 8	Reed
TROMPETTE	*mfff*	16	16, 8, 4	Reed
TROMPETTE EN CHAMADE	*fff*		16, 8, 4	Reed
TROMPETTE HARMONIQUE	*fff*		8	Reed
TROMPETTE MILITAIRE	*fff*		8	Reed
TROMPETTE QUINTE	*mf*		5 1/3	Reed
TRUMPET	*mff*	32, 16, 8	16, 8	Reed
TRUMPET CLARION	*f*	8	4	Reed

Name of Stop	Average Dynamic Value	Pedal Pitches	Manual Pitches	Classification
TRUMPET ROYAL	*fff*		8	Reed
TRUMPET SONORA	*fff*		8	Reed
TUBA	*mfff*	32, 16	16, 8	Reed
TUBA CLARION	*ff*	8	4	Reed
TUBA D'AMOUR	*f*		8	Reed
TUBA HARMONIC	*fff*		8	Reed
TUBA IMPERIAL	*fff*		8	Reed
TUBA MAGNA	*mfff*	16	8	Reed
TUBA MAJOR	*mfff*	16	8	Reed
TUBA MINOR	*mff*		8	Reed
TUBA MIRABILIS	*fff*		8	Reed
TUBA PROFUNDA	*mfff*	32	16	Reed
TUBA QUINT	*f*	10 2/3	5 1/3	Reed
TUBA SONORA	*mfff*		8	Reed
TWELFTH	*mp*	5 1/3	2 2/3	Foundation
TWENTY-EIGHTH, FLATTED	*mppp*	1 1/7	4/7	Foundation
TWENTY-FIFTH	*mppp*	1 5/11	8/11	Foundation
TWENTY-FIRST, FLATTED	*pp*	2 2/7	1 1/7	Foundation
TWENTY-FOURTH	*mppp*	1 3/5	4/5	Foundation
TWENTY-NINTH	*mppp*	1	1/2	Foundation
TWENTY-SECOND	*p*	2	1	Foundation
TWENTY-SIXTH	*mppp*	1 1/3	2/3	Foundation
TWENTY-THIRD	*mppp*	1 7/9	8/9	Foundation
UNDA MARIS	*pp*		8	Foundation
UNTERSATZ	*mp*	32	16	Flute
VIENNA FLUTE	*mp*		8, 4	Flute
VIOL	*mp*	16	8	String
VIOLA	*p*	16, 8	16, 8	String
VIOLA AETHERIA	*pp*		8	String
VIOLA CÉLESTE	*p*		8	String
VIOLA DA GAMBA	*mp*	16	8	String
VIOLA D'AMORE	*mpp*		8, 4	String
VIOLA FLUTE	*p*		8, 4	Flute
VIOLA MAJOR	*f*		8	String
VIOLA MINOR	*mpp*		8	String
VIOLA PHONON	*f*		8	String
VIOLA POMPOSA	*mff*		8	String
VIOLA SORDA	*pp*		8	String
VIOLE	*mp*	16	8	String
VIOLE À PAVILLON	*mp*		8, 4	String
VIOLA À PAVILLON CÉLESTE	*mp*		8	String
VIOLE CÉLESTE	*mp*		8, 4, 2 2/3	String
VIOLE CONIQUE	*p*		8	String
VIOLE D'ORCHESTRE	*mp*	16	8	String
VIOLE SOURDINE	*p*		8	String
VIOLETTA	*p*	8	4	String
VIOL FIFTEENTH	*mpp*	4	2	String
VIOL FLUTE	*p*		8, 4	Flute
VIOLIN	*mp*	16	8	String
VIOLINA	*p*	8	4	String

Name of Stop	Average Dynamic Value	Pedal Pitches	Manual Pitches	Classification
VIOLIN BASS	*mf*	32	16	String
VIOLIN DIAPASON	*mf*	16	8	Foundation
VIOLINO SORDO	*pp*		8	String
VIOL MIXTURE	*mf*		III, IV, V	Compound
VIOLONCELLO	*mf*	16, 8	16, 8	String
VIOLONCELLO POMPOSA	*mff*		8	String
VIOLONCELLO SORDO	*p*		8	String
VIOLONCELLO VIBRATO	*mp*		8	String
VIOLONE	*mf*	32, 16	16, 8	String
VIOL QUINT	*p*	10 2/3	5 1/3	String
VIOL TIERCE	*pp*	3 1/5	1 3/5	String
VIOL TWELFTH	*p*	5 1/3	2 2/3	String
VOIX CÉLESTE	*mp*		8	String
VOX ACUTA	*mf*		III, IV	Compound
VOX ANGELICA	*ppp*		8	Foundation
VOX CÉLESTE	*mp*		8	String
VOX GRAVISSIMA	*f*	64, 32		Foundation
VOX HUMANA	*mpp*	16, 8, 4	16, 8, 4	Reed
VOX HUMANA KRUMMHORN	*mp*		8	Reed
VOX HUMANA REGAL	*mp*	8, 4	8, 4	Reed
VOX HUMANA SCHALMEI	*mp*	8, 4	8, 4	Reed
VOX MYSTICA	*ppp*		8	Reed
WALDFLÖTE	*mf*		8, 4, 2	Flute
WALDHORN	*mff*		16, 8	Reed
WHISTLE	*mf*		2	Flute
WIENERFLÖTE	*mp*		8, 4	Flute
WOOD DIAPASON	*mf*	32, 16, 8	16, 8	Foundation
WOODEN OPEN FLUTE	*mp*	16, 8	16, 8, 4	Flute
ZARTFLÖTE	*p*		8, 4	Flute
ZARTGEDECKT	*ppp*		8, 4	Flute
ZAUBERFLÖTE	*mp*		8, 4	Flute
ZAUBERGEDECKT	*mp*		8, 4	Flute
ZAUBERPICCOLO	*pp*		2	Flute
ZIMBEL	*mf*	V	III, V, VI	Compound
ZIMBELFLÖTE	*p*		1, 1/2	Flute
ZINK	*f*	4, 2, 1		Reed

Appendix A

Harmonic Factors Affecting Tone Quality

The tonal complex that goes out from the pipes of an organ is created mostly by the structures of the pipes themselves. The organ chamber, windchest, auditorium, and listener also affect the tone. The limitless variation that can exist in sound waves from organ pipes and instruments is suggested by the factors listed below. Although incomplete, this list helps to explain why a Salicional sounds different from an Oboe of a different pitch, or even of the same pitch. Any one factor can assume prime importance; any one, or group, can be negligible in effect:

1. total number of overtones present in a sound;
2. aggregate loudness of all overtones;
3. general pattern of *presence* of overtones;
4. general pattern of loudness of overtones;
5. range of pitch covered by overtones;
6. areas of absence of overtones;
7. steadiness of pitch of overtones;
8. duration pattern of overtones;
9. number, pitch, and loudness of steady tone transients;
10. presence of each overtone as apart from the train;
11. loudness of each overtone as apart from the train;
12. sequence of growth of overtones;
13. rate of growth of overtones;
14. loudness of fundamental as compared to overtones;
15. pitch of fundamental;
16. disparity of overtones' pitches from that of fundamental;
17. duration pattern of fundamental;
18. rate of growth of fundamental;
19. steadiness of pitch of fundamental;
20. sequence of growth of initial partials;
21. sequence of decay of initial partials;
22. pitch of most prominent initial partial;
23. loudness of most prominent initial partial;
24. pattern of pitches of initial partials;
25. pattern of loudness of initial partials;
26. length of duration of initial partials before steady tone;
27. effect of tremolo on presence and pitch of initial partials;
28. effect of tremolo on presence and pitch of steady tone overtones;

252

29. pattern of dissonance with equal-tempered scale notes;
30. loudness of dissonance in relation to tonal complex;
31. sequence of decay of harmonics (fundamental and overtones) ;
32. subtraction or addition of partials owing to undulation;
33. pitch and loudness of summation tones;
34. pitch and loudness of gaussian edge-tones not coupled to air column;
35. presence of a sub-harmonic;
36. pitch, loudness, and number of spurious overtones (inharmonics) ;
37. addition to sound by formant of vibrating pipe-structure;
38. subtraction from sound by formant of vibrating pipe-structure;
39. total effect of formant of soundboard;
40. total effect of acoustics of building;
41. total effect of acoustics of organ chamber;
*42. subjective tones caused by non-linear motion of eardrum;
*43. physiological state of listener (fatigue, etc.) ;
*44. musical education of listener.

Appendix B

Miscellaneous Mechanical Controls

Since many organists preside at small two-manual organs that have very few mechanical controls, the following list of *pistons*, both manual and pedal, may prove to be interesting. It reveals some of the complexity that must sometimes be reached in designing organs, which, for efficiency's sake, must have master controls by which to control their regular controls. These mechanical matters can never be so important as the music to be performed, but the organ, unlike most other musical instruments, has a whole following of persons who are fascinated by the instrument itself. Perhaps this list of pistons can reveal more quickly and better than in any other way the kind of instrument the other fellow plays:

SFORZANDO F
SFORZANDO FF
SFORZANDO FFF
16' COUPLERS OFF SFORZANDO
8' COUPLERS ON SFORZANDO
SFORZANDO ON GREAT ONLY
SFORZANDO ON GREAT DOUBLE TOUCH
32' STOPS OFF SFORZANDO
CRESCENDO PEDAL F
CRESCENDO PEDAL FF
CRESCENDO PEDAL FFF
DIAPHONE 32' OFF CRESCENDO
CÉLESTES OFF CRESCENDO
ALL COUPLERS OFF CRESCENDO
SANCTUARY ORGAN OFF CRESCENDO
TUBA MIRABILIS OFF CRESCENDO
FANFARE ORGAN OFF CRESCENDO
STRING ORGAN OFF CRESCENDO
8' COUPLERS ON CRESCENDO
CRESCENDO ON GREAT AND SWELL
    ONLY
ALL PERCUSSIONS OFF
ALL 32' STOPS OFF
ALL 16' STOPS OFF MANUALS
INTERMANUAL COUPLERS OFF
ALL STRING STOPS ON SWELL
ALL CHORUS REEDS ON FANFARE
ALL DIAPASONS ON GREAT
FANFARE ON SOLO

FANFARE ONLY ON SOLO
PROCESSIONAL ORGAN ON CHOIR
ECHO ONLY ON SOLO
STRING ORGAN ON SWELL
BOMBARDE TO SOLO 8'
BOMBARDE TO SOLO 16'
BOMBARDE TO SOLO 4'
CHOIR AND GREAT INTERCHANGEABLE
SWELL UNISON OFF
PEDAL TO GREAT 8'
PEDAL TO PEDAL 8' AND 4'
ALL 16' AND 4' COUPLERS OFF
GREAT TO SOLO 8'
PEDAL 6
PEDAL 7
PEDAL 8
GREAT CANCEL
GENERAL CANCEL
COUPLER CANCEL
TREMOLO CANCEL
SUSTAINER ON GREAT
INTRAMANUAL COUPLERS ON
    INTERMANUAL COUPLERS
CHOIR CIPHER CUT OFF
ALL PERCUSSIONS OFF
    DOUBLE TOUCHES
TOWER CHIMES ON SOLO
    DOUBLE TOUCH
CARILLON ON PEDAL DOUBLE TOUCH

Carillon on Pedal
Resultant 64' on Pedal
    Double Touch
Tuba Sonora on Solo Double Touch
Solo Organ on Great Double Touch
Solo 4' on Swell Double Touch
Full Great on Double Touch
Full Great on Solo Double Touch
Melody Octave Coupler on Solo
Melody Octave Coupler on Solo
    Double Touch
All Double Touch Stops Silent
Pizzicato Touch on Orchestral
Chancel Swell Shades Closed
Nave Swell Shades Closed

All Shades on Choir Pedal
Choir Shades on Great Pedal
Ancillary Shades on Swell Pedal
All Shades Open
String Shades on Solo Pedal
Pedal Keyboard Divided
Damper on Chinese Gong
Snares on Street Drum
No. 2 Console on
Signal to Orchestra Leader
Signal to Choir Room
Signal to Maintenance
Signal to Radio Broadcast
Signal to Altar
Signal to Blower Room

Appendix C

Forms of Flute Pipes

The Flutes of the organ are in greater variety than the stops in other families of tone because a greater diversity of *shapes* of Flute pipes is possible. Open Flute tone is defined as a noticeable fundamental and a well-developed train of both odd-numbered and even-numbered harmonics; stopped Flute tone is defined as a strong fundamental and a poorly developed train of odd-numbered harmonics. The following listing of Flute pipe-shapes is not complete, but it will give the student some idea of the great variety of tones to expect from this ancient family of the organ's stops. Not considered here are the effects of scale, mouth cut-up, wind pressure, loudness, pitch, or the tonal effect of other pipes sounding at the same time. An example is added to each shape, with some names applied to more than one shape.

1. Open wood with beveled mouth on long side (Major Open Flute)
2. Open wood with beveled mouth on short side (Clarabella)
3. Open wood with inverted mouth on long side (Clear Flute)
4. Open wood with inverted mouth on short side (Melodia)
5. Open metal (Principal Flute)
6. Open metal with bell (Glockenflöte)
7. Stopped wood with beveled mouth on long side (Solo Gedeckt)
8. Stopped wood with beveled mouth on short side (Tibia Clausa)
9. Stopped wood with inverted mouth on long side (Starkgedeckt)
10. Stopped wood with inverted mouth on short side (Gedeckt)
11. Stopped metal (Quintaten)
12. Open harmonic wood with beveled mouth (Flauto Traverso)
13. Open harmonic wood with inverted mouth (Orchestral Flute)
14. Open harmonic metal (Harmonic Flute)
15. Stopped harmonic wood with beveled mouth (Harmonic Gedeckt)
16. Stopped harmonic wood with inverted mouth (Harmonic Gedeckt)
17. Stopped harmonic metal (Harmonic Stopped Twelfth)
18. Open pyramidal wood (Pyramid Flute)
19. Open conical metal (Spitzflöte)
20. Open harmonic pyramidal wood (Orchestral Flute)
21. Open harmonic conical metal (German Flute)
22. Stopped pyramidal wood (Pyramid Gedeckt)
23. Stopped conical metal (Spitzgedeckt)

24. Open inverted-pyramidal wood with mouth on long side (Tiba Dura)
25. Open inverted-pyramidal wood with mouth on short side (Dolce Flute)
26. Open inverted conical metal (Dolce Flute)
27. Half-covered wood with cylindrical rohr (Flûte d'Amour)
28. Half-covered wood with conical rohr (Gemsrohrflöte)
29. Half-covered wood with inverted-conical rohr (Cone Gedeckt)
30. Half-covered metal with cylindrical rohr (Rohrgedeckt)
31. Half-covered metal with conical rohr (Gemsrohrflöte)
32. Half-covered metal with inverted-conical rohr (Cone Gedeckt)
33. Open truncated top on wood (Koppelflöte)
34. Open truncated top on metal (Spillflöte)
35. Open triangular wood with beveled mouth (Flûte Triangulaire)
36. Open triangular wood with inverted mouth (Hohlflöte)
37. Open harmonic triangular wood (Orchestral Flute)
38. Open double-mouthed wood (Seraphonflöte)
39. Open double-mouthed metal (Seraphonflöte)
40. Stopped double-mouthed wood with opposite mouths (Doppelgedeckt)
41. Stopped double-mouthed wood with adjacent mouths (Seraphongedeckt)
42. Stopped double-mouthed metal (Seraphongedeckt)

Appendix D

Mixtures

The compound stops (mixtures and cornets) have been given in this book from only the keys of middle C and the low pedal CCC because it was felt most organists think of the tonal effects of timbre and pitch in these parts of the keyboards. However, practically every mixture rank breaks back to a lower pitch as the scale is ascended towards the treble. This keeps the pipes from becoming impractically small and the pitches too high to hear. In the III-rank *Cymbal* shown below the pitches are designed to break, as usual, between each B and C, except at the top. The ranges between the breaks are shown at the left, and the numbers at the right are indicative of the names of the ranks, such as *Thirty-third*, or 33, for example. Alternate octaves speak C-G-C or G-C-G. Another system merely shows this example as: Cymbal 29-33-36, which are the pitches at low manual CC.

	Ranks						Example No. 1	
	I	II	III				III	
CC to BB -	29 -	33 -	36		29 - 33 - 36		C⁵	1/2′
C to B -	26 -	29 -	33	or	26 - 29 - 33	or as	G⁴	2/3′
C¹ to B¹ -	22 -	26 -	29	simply	22 - 26 - 29	in this	C⁴	1′
C² to B² -	19 -	22 -	26	as	19 - 22 - 26	book		
C³ to C⁴ -	15 -	19 -	22		15 - 19 - 22			

Such specifications do not tell much about a mixture stop. Its actual tone is determined by the pipes' scales, cut-up, material, wind pressure, and method of tuning. Most ranks are tuned by tapping the small steel collars that grasp their tops like springs. Many unusual mixture stops exist. In fact, every mixture is custom-designed to suit a particular organ. Some have fewer than the above four breaks. Certain ranks may not break at all. Many mixtures sound in that high range where precise pitch identification is not possible by the human ear. Therefore, slight out-of-tuneness may not be noticed. A few specimens go up to the Forty-third (1/8′), but many are limited in pitch to the Twenty-ninth (1/2′). The pedal mixtures frequently carry their pitches clear through to the top note of the pedalboard without pitch breaks, although only certain ranks may break.

True-False Questions for the Student

1. All Flute stops in the organ are dull in tone.
2. A 4' stop speaks two octaves above a 16' stop.
3. No. 2 is true or false alike for pedals as well as manuals.
4. The average Diapason note sounds approximately fifty partials.
5. A division of ten stops is limited to about 100 combinations.
6. The Philomela is an open rank.
7. The 16' Bourdon sounds the 6 2/5' component.
8. All harmonics are exactly on the pitches of the equal-tempered scale.
9. The 64' pedal stops are too low in pitch to have true harmonics.
10. The fourth harmonic has the same pitch as the third overtone.
11. The fundamentals of the Diapasons are considered to be true harmonics.
12. A 1/2' mixture rank speaks three octaves above a 4' stop.
13. The Singendregal is a Reed stop.
14. The Sylvestrina is a hybrid tone.
15. The design of the Diapason Chorus does not determine reverberation time.
16. The Solo to Swell 4' Coupler is an intermanual coupler.
17. The Clarabella is an open rank.
18. All examples of the Acuta mixture have three ranks of pipes.
19. Overtones of céleste pipes also build up a célesting action.
20. The Harmonika is a Flute.
21. A reed resonator of one-quarter length would support the eighth harmonic.
22. Other factors being equal, a narrower scale makes more overtones.
23. The top threshold of hearing varies between 12,000 and 24,000 cycles.
24. All célestes have only one rank tuned off the normal pitch.
25. The pedal Twenty-ninth speaks at 1'.
26. C5 speaks four octaves above middle C.
27. The note CCC on the pedals has the same pitch as CC on the manuals.
28. The 4/5' is a fifth-sounding rank.
29. The Krummhorn is considered a stop of good blend.
30. An 8' Gamba would sound at least a little of the fourteenth harmonic.
31. Transient harmonics generally are in the top portions of the train.
32. An 8' Diapason has a prominent sub-harmonic to support its overtones.
33. The Sub Sub Octave on the manuals sounds at 32'.

259

34. For the same note, the Bourdon of bigger scale speaks more slowly.
35. Reed stops generally speak more quickly than flue stops.
36. Melodias have both beveled and inverted lips.
37. Display pipes in an organ's screen are more likely not to play than play.
38. A harmonic bridge can be used to both hasten and slow a pipe's speech.
39. The 1 1/7' is not a member of the 4' series of stops.
40. The 1/3' is the twelfth harmonic in a 4' ensemble.
41. The Percussion stops' harmonics sound at the same positions as the Reeds'.
42. Nicking a flue pipe reduces its content of overtones.
43. The stopped ranks are completely free from the even-numbered harmonics.
44. The 3 1/5' is two octaves below the 2/5' pitch.
45. A single Viole d'Orchestre pipe can sound as many as fifty overtones.
46. The third harmonic of a 32' Quintade sounds close to the 10 2/3' pitch.
47. Stop-pitches in pedal mixtures cover as wide a range as in manual mixtures.
48. Listeners generally interpret a brilliant tone as being a loud tone.
49. Short Reed pipes never resonate the fundamental harmonic.
50. Lengthening a pipe makes it speak with more overtones.

(Answers are at the bottom of page 219.)

Bibliography

Since this book does not enter into the subject of console accessories, windchests, actions, and expression devices, it may be of interest to the reader to obtain any of the following three books on the subject of the organ. Each book discusses mechanism, tonalities, families of stops, and the divisions of the organ. Specifications, diagrams, and many illustrations are also to be found in each. The three writers represented are all eminent authorities on matters pertaining to the pipe organ:

Barnes, William H., *The Contemporary American Organ*, New York, 1956.
Bonavia-Hunt, Noel A., *The Modern British Organ*, London, 1948.
Whitworth, Reginald, *The Electric Organ*, London, 1948.

Two new books on the subject of the organ have recently appeared in the United States. They are listed below. The first is an unusually scholarly and well-systematized study of registration. The second is a compilation of the writer's thoughts after a lifetime of organ building:

Geer, Harold E., *Organ Registration*, Glen Rock, N. J., 1957.
Jamison, James Blaine, *Organ Design and Appraisal*, New York, 1959.

Four dictionaries of organ stops that have been helpful to organists for many years are in the following list. Each is filled with an unusual amount of information about all phases of the organ's pipes and tonalities:

Audsley, George A., *Organ Stops*, New York, 1921.
Bonavia-Hunt, Noel A., *Modern Organ Stops*, London, 1923.
Locher, Carl, *An Explanation of the Organ Stops*, London, 1888.
Wedgwood, James I., *Dictionary of Organ Stops*, London, 1905.

For the reader who can understand German, the following new dictionary of the pipe organ is unusually comprehensive and broad in its approach:

Smets, Paul, *Die Orgelregister, ihr Klang und Gebrauch*, Mainz, 1958.

The following works on the stops and mechanism of the pipe organ are all of proved merit. As with all of the books in these lists, some are unfortunately out of print, but all can be found in libraries in large cities:

Audsley, George A., *The Art of Organ Building*, I and II, New York, 1905.
Audsley, George A., *The Organ of the Twentieth Century*, New York, 1919.
Audsley, George A., *The Temple of Tone*, New York, 1925.
Bonavia-Hunt, Noel A., *Modern Studies in Organ Tone*, London, 1933.
Bonavia-Hunt, Noel A., *The Organ Reed*, London, 1950.
Clutton, C. & Dixon, G., *The Organ*, London, 1950.
Goodrich, Wallace, *The Organ in France*, London, 1917.
Lewis, W. & T., *Modern Organ Building*, London, 1939.

Miller, George L., *The Recent Revolution in Organ Building*, New York, 1913.

Nevin, Gordon B., *A Primer of Organ Registration*, Philadelphia, 1920.

Skinner, Ernest M., *The Modern Organ*, New York, 1917.

Smith, Herman, *The Making of Sound in the Organ*, London, 1911.

Truette, E., *Organ Registration*, Boston, 1919.

Whitworth, Reginald, *The Cinema and Theatre Organ*, London, 1934.

Wicks, Mark, *Organ Building for Amateurs*, London, 1887.

The history of the organ through each century is thoroughly traced by:
Sumner, William Leslie, *The Organ*, London, 1955.

Acoustics as a science is well presented in the following very readable books. The technical facts, so difficult for many readers without a scientific background, are simplified and explained here:

Jeans, Sir James, *Science and Music*, London, 1953.

Lloyd, L. S., *Music and Sound*, London, 1951.

Olson, Harry F., *Musical Engineering*, New York, 1952.

Redfield, John, *Music, a Science and an Art*, New York, 1949.

Five periodicals that are devoted to the pipe organ and its music:

> *The American Organist*, New York
> *The Diapason*, Chicago
> *The Organ*, London
> *L'Orgue*, Paris
> *De Schalmei*, Amsterdam

Credits

The Journal of the Acoustical Society of America, New York, Dr. Floyd A. Firestone, Editor, presents articles each year of interest to organists. Some of the facts used in this book were taken by permission from the article entitled *Voicing of Flue Organ Pipes*, by Derwent A. Mercer, University College, London. Several facts on the flue and Reed pipes were taken by permission from Noel A. Bonavia-Hunt's *The Modern British Organ*, published by A. Weeks & Co., London.

Many organists gave permission to play their organs and to enter into the organ chambers for the purpose of inspecting pipework. A few of them are mentioned here: John A. Davis, Jr., West Point Cadet Chapel, N. Y.; J. Herbert Springer, St. Matthew's Lutheran Church, Hanover, Pa.; Alec Wyton, The Cathedral Church of St. John the Divine, New York; George Markey, Old First Church, Newark, N. J.; and Alastair Cassels-Brown, Grace Church, Utica, N. Y.

Organ factories are sources of both practical and theoretical information. Voicers and officials who granted certain permissions and who gave information are as follows: William Bunch and John Tyrrel of Aeolian Skinner Organ Co., Boston, Mass.; R. J. Piper and F. W. Kutschera of Austin Organs, Inc., Hartford, Conn.; M. P. Moller III of the Moller Organ Co., Hagerstown, Md.; Charles Perrault of Casavant Frères Limitée, St.

Hyacinthe, Que.; Walter Holtkamp of the Holtkamp Organ Co., Cleveland, Ohio; Alfred H. Thalman of the Wicks Organ Co., Highland, Ill.; Homer A. Frank of the Reuter Organ Co., Lawrence, Kansas; R. L. Hillgreen of Hillgreen, Lane & Co., Alliance, Ohio; and John Schantz of the Schantz Organ Co., Orrville, Ohio.

William R. Rosser of the Convention Hall, Atlantic City, N.J., and William Ruff of the John Wanamaker Store, Philadelphia, Pa., were generous with inspection privileges and information on the world's two largest organs under their care. William H. Barnes of Skokie, Ill., Senator Emerson Richards of Atlantic City, N.J., Eugene M. Nye of Seattle, Wash., and Oakley M. Parker of Lakewood, N.J. were generous with information of various kinds on the stops of the organ.

Dr. C. P. Boner of the University of Texas, and Dr. A. H. Benade of the Case School of Applied Science, Cleveland, were both generous in contributing facts on the subject of reed and flue tone.

Adolph Zajic and Ernest White of the Moller Organ Co., Hagerstown, Md. deserve credit for the arrangement of the pipes in the Frontispiece. Many of these pipes were designed by Mr. Zajic, who is one of the most noted of Reed voicers in America.

The line drawings in this book were reprinted from *The Art of Organ Building* by George Ashdown Audsley, adapted from *The Organ of the Twentieth Century* by George Ashdown Audsley, by permission of Dodd, Mead and Company, New York, New York.

Descriptions of Endpaper Charts

Front Left: Pitches of Stops

Stop-names that are only *pitch indications*, such as Twelfth, Quint, Tierce, etc., are applied to both manuals and pedals. However, the pitches that refer to the pedal stops are one octave lower (i.e., the pitch-number is twice as large) than those that refer to the manual stops. For example, the Octave of the manuals is at 4', and that of the pedals is at 8'; the pedal's Tierce is at 3 1/5', and the manual's at 1 3/5'.

The octave-sounding stop-pitches on both manuals and pedals are: 64', 32', 16', 8', 4', 2', 1', 1/2', and 1/4'.

The fifth-sounding stop-pitches on both manuals and pedals are: 21 1/3', 10 2/3', 5 1/3', 2 2/3', 1 1/3', 2/3', and 1/3'.

The third-sounding stop-pitches on both manuals and pedals are: 12 4/5', 6 2/5', 3 1/5', 1 3/5', 4/5', and 2/5'.

The flatted seventh-sounding stop-pitches on both manuals and pedals are: 4 4/7', 2 2/7', 1 1/7', 4/7', and 2/7'.

When a stop-name suggests a tone quality, like *Trumpet* or *Flute*, there is always a pitch-indication along with the name on the stop control. When no tone quality is suggested, the Diapason or Principal is usually implied.

Front Right: Relationship of Manual and Pedal Pitches

This chart will give the beginner at the organ a way to approach the stop-pitches directly from the piano. The 8' *manual* stops sound the same notes as they do on the piano. Those at 4′ sound an octave higher than the piano, and those at 16′ an octave lower. The pedal's unison pitch (like the manual's 8′ pitch) is set arbitrarily at 16′, just for the convenience of applying certain names to the pedal's stops according to a regular system. See FIFTEENTH.

Back Left: Natural Harmonics as Stop Pitches

The organist must know the groups of pitch-indications for each series of manual and pedal stops if he is to make well-balanced combinations. It is not only necessary to combine timbres well, it is also necessary to combine stop pitches well. Generally, the pitches of one series are combined, such as 8′, 4′, 2 2/3′, and 2′, or, perhaps, just 8′ and 4′. Gaps in the series may be permitted for a special purpose, as in the novelty solo combination of 8′ and 2′. The 5 1/3′ is intended to be drawn with the 16′, not alone with the 8′, nor the 2 2/3′ alone with the 4′. The base-pitch is usually needed to establish balance in the combination. However, many organs do not have complete series of pitches, so it is not always possible to make ideal combinations. Loud combinations may include two or more *series*.

Back Right: Classification of Orchestral Instruments as Organ Stops

Three of the four families of organ tone include most of the orchestral imitations in the organ: Flute, String, and Reed. Some are realistic; others are poor because of the impossibility of imitating the human breath control, which, for example, gives the Saxophone its characteristic wavering pitch. Orchestral names may be used without the intention of making a really good imitation. The Diapason is not imitated by the orchestral tone.

NATURAL HARMONICS AS STOP PITCHES

Number of Harmonic	Pitches of Stops and Mixture Components					
	2' Series	4' Series	8' Series Manual Unison	16' Series Pedal Unison	32' Series	64' Series
256						1/4'
224						2/7'
192						1/3'
160						2/5'
128					1/4'	1/2'
112					2/7'	4/7'
96					1/3'	2/3'
80					2/5'	4/5'
64				1/4'	1/2'	1'
56				2/7'	4/7'	1 1/7'
48				1/3'	2/3'	1 1/3'
40				2/5'	4/5'	1 3/5'
32			1/4'	1/2'	1'	2'
28			2/7'	4/7'	1 1/7'	2 2/7'
24			1/3'	2/3'	1 1/3'	2 2/3'
20			2/5'	4/5'	1 3/5'	3 1/5'
16		1/4'	1/2'	1'	2'	4'
14		2/7'	4/7'	1 1/7'	2 2/7'	4 4/7'
12		1/3'	2/3'	1 1/3'	2 2/3'	5 1/3'
10		2/5'	4/5'	1 3/5'	3 1/5'	6 2/5'
8	1/4'	1/2'	1'	2'	4'	8'
7	2/7'	4/7'	1 1/7'	2 2/7'	4 4/7'	9 1/7'
6	1/3'	2/3'	1 1/3'	2 2/3'	5 1/3'	10 2/3'
5	2/5'	4/5'	1 3/5'	3 1/5'	6 2/5'	12 4/5'
4	1/2'	1'	2'	4'	8'	16'
3	2/3'	1 1/3'	2 2/3'	5 1/3'	10 2/3'	21 1/3'
2	1'	2'	4'	8'	16'	32'
1	2'	4'	8'	16'	32'	64'